Psychoanalysis in the Barrios

GW00673214

Psychoanalysis in the Barrios: Race, Class, and the Unconscious demonstrates that psychoanalytic principles can be applied successfully in disenfranchised Latino populations, refuting the misguided idea that psychoanalysis is an expensive luxury only for the wealthy.

As opposed to most Latin American countries, where psychoanalysis is seen as a practice tied to the promotion of social justice, in the United States psychoanalysis has been viewed as reserved for the well-to-do, assuming that poor people lack the sophistication that psychoanalysis requires, thus heeding invisible but no less rigid class boundaries. Challenging such discrimination, the authors testify to the efficacy of psychoanalysis in the barrios, upending the unfounded widespread belief that poor people are so consumed with the pressures of everyday survival that they only benefit from symptom-focused interventions. Sharing vivid vignettes of psychoanalytic treatments, this collection sheds light on the psychological complexities of life in the barrio that is often marked by poverty, migration, marginalization, and barriers of language, class, and race.

This interdisciplinary collection features essays by distinguished international scholars and clinicians. It represents a unique crossover that will appeal to readers in clinical practice, social work, counseling, anthropology, psychology, cultural and Latino studies, queer studies, urban studies, and sociology.

Patricia Gherovici is a psychoanalyst and analytic supervisor in private practice in Philadelphia and New York City. The author or editor of six books, she received the Gradiva Award and the Boyer Prize for her book *The Puerto Rican Syndrome*. She is co-founder and director of the Philadelphia Lacan Group and Associate Faculty, Psychoanalytic Studies Minor, University of Pennsylvania, Honorary Member at the Institute for Psychoanalytic Training and Research (IPTAR), and Founding Member of Das Unbehagen, New York City.

Christopher Christian is Editor-in-Chief of *Psychoanalytic Psychology*; Dean of the Institute for Psychoanalytic Training and Research (IPTAR); and co-editor with Morris Eagle and David Wolitzky of *Psychoanalytic Perspectives on Conflict* and with Michael J. Diamond of *The Second Century of Psychoanalysis: Evolving Perspectives on Therapeutic Action*. He is co-executive producer of the documentary *Psychoanalysis in El Barrio*, winner of the Psychoanalytic Electronic Publishing (PEP) Video Grant award. He has a psychoanalytic private practice in New York City.

Psychoanalysis in the Barrios

Race, Class, and the Unconscious

Edited by Patricia Gherovici and Christopher Christian

Routledge
Taylor & Francis Group

LONDON AND NEW YORK

First published 2019
by Routledge
2 Park Square, Milton Park, Abingdon, Oxon OX14 4RN

and by Routledge
52 Vanderbilt Avenue, New York, NY 10017

Routledge is an imprint of the Taylor & Francis Group, an informa business

British Library Cataloguing-in-Publication Data
A catalogue record for this book is available from the British Library

Library of Congress Cataloging-in-Publication Data
A catalog record for this book has been requested

ISBN: 978-1-138-34638-3 (hbk)
ISBN: 978-1-138-34640-6 (pbk)
ISBN: 978-0-429-43729-8 (ebk)

Typeset in Times New Roman
by Apex CoVantage, LLC
Printed and bound by CPI Group (UK) Ltd, Croydon, CR0 4YY

For June

For the Socorros, Consuelos, Dolores, Antonios, Felixes,
Marías, Juanes, and Josés of the barrio that help us reinvent
psychoanalysis.

PG

Contents

Acknowledgements

The editors wish to thank Kerri Danskin for her discerning and invaluable attention in the editing of each chapter. To just say thank you to Kerri feels completely inadequate – if only she could edit this acknowledgement too. Special thanks to Leonell Torres-Pagán and the staff from the archives of the Center for Puerto Rican Studies at Hunter College, and to Jorge Matos from Hostos Community College for their assistance in tracking down material cited in the manuscript. We also extend our heartfelt thanks to Kate Hawes at Routledge for making this book possible.

Every effort has been made to contact the copyright holders for their permission to reprint selections of this book. The publishers would be grateful to hear from any copyright holder who is not here acknowledged and will undertake to rectify any errors or omissions in future editions of this book.

A passage from the book *Candle in the Sun* in Chapter 4 appears courtesy of Lilly Library, Indiana University, Bloomington, Indiana. Figure 4.1 "arc de cercle" by Paul Richer appears courtesy of the Musée d'Histoire de la Médecine – Paris.

Brief parts of Chapter 6 appeared in a short piece called "Latinx and the Neurologization of Self" in *Cultural Dynamics*, Volume 29, Issue 3, August 2017, pp. 160–176. Copyright 2017 by SAGE Publications, Inc. Reprinted by permission.

Excerpts in Chapter 8 are taken from *The House on Mango Street*. Copyright © 1984 by Sandra Cisneros. Published by Vintage Books, an imprint of Random House, Inc., and in hardcover by Alfred A. Knopf in 1994. Reprinted by permission of Susan Bergholz Literary Services, New York, NY, and Lamy, NM. All rights reserved.

Chapter 9 is a revised version of "Chencha's Gait," first published in *Women & Performance: A Journal of Feminist Theory*, Volume 18, Issue 3, November 1, 2008, pp. 287–301. Reprinted by permission of Taylor & Francis, LLC.

Excerpts in Chapter 10 are reprinted with permission of the publisher of *Arturo Islas: The Uncollected Works* by Arturo Islas (© 2003 Arte Publico Press – University of Houston).

Some sections included in part 2 of Chapter 13 "The Puerto Rican Syndrome and the Korean War" are revised versions of material published in Gherovici, P. (2018) "The Puerto Rican Syndrome and the Eye of Maria/El syndrome puertorriqueño y ojo de María" in UNA PROPOSICIÓN MODESTA: PUERTO RICO A PRUEBA/A MODEST PROPOSAL: PUERTO RICO'S CRUCIBLE, exhibition catalog: Spanish/English. An initiative of Allora & Calzadilla edited by Sara Nadal-Melsió, Barcelona. Reprinted here with kind permission.

Contributors

Ricardo Ainslie is a psychoanalyst in private practice and he holds the M.K. Hage Centennial Professorship in Education at the University of Texas at Austin, USA, teaching in the Department of Educational Psychology. He is also the director of the LLILAS-Benson Mexico Center and has affiliations with other institutes and departments across the university. He uses books, documentary films, and photographic exhibits to capture and depict subjects of social and cultural interest. He is a Guggenheim Fellow and has also been the recipient of numerous other honors and awards, including the Rockefeller's Bellagio Residency and the American Psychological Association's Division of Psychoanalysis Science Award. He is a member of the Texas Institute of Letters and the Texas Philosophical Society.

Alfredo Carrasquillo is a practicing psychoanalyst, organizational development consultant, and executive leadership coach based in San Juan, Puerto Rico. Educated in Spain, Puerto Rico, Mexico, the United States, and Québec, he serves as Full Professor of Graduate Studies at the Universidad del Sagrado Corazón (University of the Sacred Heart) and contributes to the formation of new analysts and the transmission of psychoanalysis at the Sociedad Psicoanalítica de Puerto Rico (Puerto Rico Psychoanalytic Society). He has co-authored seven books published in Puerto Rico, Venezuela, Spain, and Québec. He was the founder and first responsible for the Circle of Puerto Rico of the Freudian School of Québec (École Freudienne du Québec).

Christopher Christian is a training and supervising analyst, and Dean of the Institute for Psychoanalytic Training and Research (IPTAR), a component member of the IPA. He is Editor-in-Chief of *Psychoanalytic Psychology* and co-editor of the books *Psychoanalytic Perspectives on Conflict* with Morris Eagle and David Wolitzky (Routledge, 2017) and *The Second Century of Psychoanalysis: Evolving Perspectives on Therapeutic Action* with Michael J. Diamond (Karnac, 2011). He is a member of the Editorial Board of the *Journal of the American Psychoanalytic Association* and faculty and member of the Institute for Psychoanalytic Education, affiliated with NYU, School of Medicine. He is the executive producer of the documentary *Psychoanalysis in El*

Barrio, winner of the Psychoanalytic Electronic Publishing (PEP) Video Grant award in 2015. He has a psychoanalytic private practice in Manhattan.

Licia Fiol-Matta is Professor of Spanish and Portuguese at New York University, USA. She received an AB from Princeton University, with a major in Comparative Literature, and a Ph.D. in Comparative Literature from Yale University. She is the author of *A Queer Mother for the Nation: The State and Gabriela Mistral* (Minnesota, 2002) and *The Great Woman Singer: Gender and Voice in Puerto Rican Music* (Duke, 2017). She is the recipient of grants from the Ford Foundation, the American Association of University Women, and the National Endowment for the Humanities. She is co-editor of the series New Directions in Latino American Cultures (Palgrave) and *The Puerto Rico Reader: History, Culture, Politics* (under contract, Duke University Press). She writes on Latin American cultural studies, women's and gender studies, and music.

Daniel José Gaztambide is Assistant Professor of Psychiatry at the Icahn School of Medicine at Mt. Sinai, USA, and a Supervising Psychologist at the Mt. Sinai-St. Luke's Adult Outpatient Psychiatry Clinic and Psychology Internship. He is the recipient of the inaugural Multiculturalism & Psychoanalysis award of the NYU Post-Doctoral Program in Psychotherapy & Psychoanalysis, and a former fellow of the Minority Fellowship Program of the American Psychological Association (APA). He has served as liaison of Division 39 (Psychoanalysis) to the Committee on Ethnic Minority Affairs of the Board for the Advancement of Psychology in the Public Interest (APA). His scholarship focuses on race, cultural competency, liberation and community psychology, and psychoanalysis.

Patricia Gherovici is a psychoanalyst and analytic supervisor. She is Co-founder and Director of the Philadelphia Lacan Group; Associate Faculty, Psychoanalytic Studies Minor, University of Pennsylvania; Honorary Member at IPTAR; and Founding Member of Das Unbehagen. Her books include *The Puerto Rican Syndrome* (Other Press, 2003), winner of the Gradiva Award and the Boyer Prize; *Please Select Your Gender: From the Invention of Hysteria to the Democratizing of Transgenderism* (Routledge, 2010); and *Transgender Psychoanalysis: A Lacanian Perspective on Sexual Difference* (Routledge, 2017). She has edited (with Manya Steinkoler) *Lacan on Madness: Madness Yes You Can't* (Routledge, 2015), *Lacan, Psychoanalysis and Comedy* (Cambridge University Press, 2016), and *Psychoanalysis, Gender and Sexualities: From Feminism to Trans** (Cambridge University Press, forthcoming).

Crystal Guevara is a Ph.D. student in the Counseling Psychology program at the University of Texas at Austin, USA. Her research and clinical interests are the phenomena of migration, acculturation, and globalization. In particular, she seeks to understand an individual's immigration experience and its impact on identity formation as well as challenges presented during acculturation. Specific populations of interest are immigrant youth, also known as the

1.5 generation, and immigrant women who experience trauma and violence in their country of origin, immigration journey, and further unique challenges in the host country due to gender. Her clinical work has involved group counseling for immigrant women held at a Texas detention center, Spanish therapy in community mental health centers, and a primary care clinic. Her aim is to perform field research and explore how policy and social attitudes toward immigration affect an individual's development. In addition, she is interested in using qualitative data to explore common experiences among this population to better serve them in therapy.

Joshua Javier Guzmán is Assistant Professor in the Department of Gender Studies at UCLA, USA. Before arriving at UCLA, he was Assistant Professor of English at the University of Colorado, Boulder. He received his Ph.D. in Performance Studies at New York University, and is a former University of California President's Postdoctoral Fellow from UC Berkeley's Department of Gender and Women's Studies. In 2015, he co-edited a special issue of *Women and Performance: A Journal of Feminist Theory* entitled "Lingering in Latinidad: Aesthetics, Theory and Performance in Latina/o Studies." He is currently working on a book-length project tentatively titled *Suspending Satisfactions: Queer Latino Performance and the Politics of Style*, which examines stylized modes of Latina/o dissatisfaction with not only the U.S. nation-state, but also the activism that emerges in response to systemic state violence in a very contentious post-1968 Los Angeles. His work appears in *Women and Performance*, *Social Text*, and *English Language Notes*, among others.

Nancy Caro Hollander is a research psychoanalyst in private practice in Oakland, California, USA, and a member and instructor of the Psychoanalytic Institute of Northern California. She is Professor Emerita of Latin America History, California State University. Hollander has been a documentary filmmaker and for 13 years has produced and hosted a radio program for Pacifica Radio exploring themes related to psychoanalysis, feminism, and Latin American revolutionary and counter-revolutionary movements and ideology in popular film. Recent publications include "Trauma as Ideology: Accountability in 'The Intractable Struggle,'" *Psychoanalysis, Culture and Society* (2016), Special Issue on Israel, 21:1, 59–80; "The Freedom to Speak: Psychopolitical Meanings in Argentine History" (2016), *International Journal of Psychoanalytic Studies*, 13: 224–232; and *Uprooted Minds: Surviving the Politics of Terror in the Americas* (Routledge, 2010).

Jennifer Lambe is Assistant Professor of Latin American and Caribbean History at Brown University, USA. Her first book, *Madhouse: Psychiatry and Politics in Cuban History*, was published in 2017 by the University of North Carolina Press. She has published and has forthcoming articles in *Cuban Studies*, *Bulletin of the History of Medicine*, *Journal of Latin American Studies*, *Asclepio*, and *History of Psychology*. Together with Michael Bustamante, she is the editor of a collection of essays on the history of the Cuban Revolution, forthcoming with Duke University Press.

Hannah McDermott is a Ph.D. student in Counseling Psychology at the University of Texas at Austin, USA. Her research focuses on the experiences of women undertaking the overland migration journey from Central America through Mexico to the United States and on the journey's psychological impact. Other research interests include the psychology of immigration more broadly and the impact of incarceration/immigration detention on individuals and communities.

Carlos Padrón studied philosophy in his home country of Venezuela. He earned his M.A. in Philosophy with a concentration in Psychoanalysis at the New School for Social Research. He is currently a doctoral candidate in Latin American Literature at New York University USA. He has written and presented on the continuities and discontinuities between philosophy, literature, and psychoanalysis. He is a Licensed Psychoanalyst and has advanced training in psychoanalysis at the Institute for Psychoanalytic Training and Research (IPTAR). He has given talks on working psychoanalytically with underprivileged Latino patients in the U.S. He has been working both in outpatient mental health clinics and in a private setting and is currently a clinical associate of the New School Psychotherapy Program, supervising psychology Ph.D. students.

Mariano Plotkin is Principal Researcher at the Center for Social Research (National Council for Scientific and Technological Research, Argentina) and Professor of History at the Universidad Nacional de Tres de Febrero, Argentina. He has taught at Harvard University, Colby College, and Boston University. He received fellowships and grants from the National Endowment for the Humanities, the SSRC, and the John Simon Guggenheim Foundations, among others. His books include *Mañana es San Perón* (Ariel Historia Argentina, 1993; Scholarly Resources, 2002); *Freud in the Pampas* (Standford University Press, 2001; Sudamericana, 2003); *Histoire de la psychanalyse en Argentine* (Campagne Premiere, 2010); and in collaboration with Mariano Ruperthuz, *Estimado Dr. Freud. Una historia cultural del psicoanálisis en América Latina* (Edhasa, 2017).

Ben Sifuentes-Jáuregui is Professor of American Studies and Comparative Literature at Rutgers University, USA. His research focuses on Latino/a and Latin American literature and culture, gender theory and sexuality studies, and psychoanalysis. He is author of *Transvestism, Masculinity, and Latin American Literature* (Palgrave, 2002) and *The Avowal of Difference: Queer Latino American Narratives* (SUNY Press, 2014). He has published numerous articles on sexuality, queer identities in Latino/a America, and melodrama. He is currently working on a book on melodrama and masochism in a series of Latino American novels, performances, films, and essays.

Antonio Viego is Associate Professor at Duke University, USA, in the Program in Literature. He is the author of *Dead Subjects: Toward a Politics of Loss in Latino Studies* (Duke University Press, 2007) and several essays including "The Nightgown," "The Life of the Undead: Biopower, Latino Anxiety, and the Epidemiological Paradox," and "The Madness of Curing." He teaches seminars in Latinx Studies, Sexuality Studies, and Psychoanalytic Theory and is currently wrapping up a manuscript on the history of Latinx health in the fields of psychiatry and epidemiology. He is also working on a manuscript that explores the question of race and ethnicity in affective neuroscientific research on the brain.

Introduction

Patricia Gherovici

Almost two and a half centuries after its independence, the United States still sees itself as a young country, freshly out of the shackles of British colonialism. On the streets of Philadelphia, where I live, I overhear this story being told to tourists who have come to explore the cradle of this nation and discover the shrines of democracy where the Declaration of Independence was signed and the Constitution was written. Many of them leave with the idea that all that colonial history is behind us and that the era of an "American Empire" belongs to the past vagaries of a young republic. If they made a detour in their carefully calibrated itinerary and visited the heart of Philadelphia's barrio in North Philly, which few tourists ever do and most residents would never recommend, it would become evident that just a quick ride away from the Liberty Bell, the legacy of colonialism is alive and well. In those impenetrable zones of our late capitalism, one still sees the lasting effects of America's colonial history, of its interventionism in Latin America, as well as the usual post-colonial consequences – urban diaspora and ghettoization.

This collection co-edited with Chris Christian explores the effects of this ongoing phenomenon on people living in the barrio and on the culture around the mental health treatment they have available to them. Let us begin by understanding the word "barrio." In Spanish the word is quite anodyne, meaning simply "neighborhood." The word often connotes an affectionate connection with one's place of origin, it may even mean "home." In the U.S., "barrio" usually refers to a Spanish-speaking quarter, often a crowded inner-city section with many people living in poverty – the equivalent of the vernacular "hood" or ghetto. A quick detour through the origin of "ghetto" is illuminating. The term comes from Venice, dates back 500 years, and refers to the place where the Jewish community was compelled to live in residential segregation (Liberman, 2009). In that first ghetto, housing was limited, overcrowded, and unsanitary (Shulvass, 1973). Jews had to return to the ghetto by sunset because the gates were locked until dawn. The etymology of the word has been disputed; some interpretations link it to the Hebrew word *get*, the act of separation or divorce, while other conjectures link it to the iron foundries that were there. Whether or not the Hebrew origin is accurate, this meaning would add "a sardonic twist" to the situation of the ghettoized Jewish community in early modern times (Jütte, 2015, p. 55). As a metaphor, "divorce" describes quite well the multiple situations by which whole communities still find themselves pushed into a secluded estrangement in closed urban spaces as a result of social, legal, or economic pressure.

Contemporary barrios in the United States are defined by language borders that are invisible to the outside observer but experienced as impassable by their inhabitants. Barrios are racialized enclaves that function like socio-linguistic islands. These marginalized locations, spatially separate and socially distant, become harsh environments, haunted by crime resulting from the parallel economy of the drug trade, with an increasing presence of fundamentalist religions, family fragmentation, extreme poverty, and violence. It is well known that this type of residential segregation has negative socioeconomic consequences for minority groups. Often these communities experience their disadvantaged spatial locations as a hindrance to overcome (Chavez, 1991; Dávila, 2004). This is why many scholars, activists, and policy makers challenge the use of the word barrio, deeming it a troublesome notion that perpetuates exclusion and marginalization.

Why then try to insert psychoanalysis in such a controversial location? While it is uncontestable that unequal urban development and unjust wealth distribution create these forlorn urban spaces, our collection purposely places psychoanalysis in the barrios, a term that we want to pluralize so as to include various similarly economically challenged locations inside and outside the United States borders. We argue that it is worth disputing common assumptions about psychoanalysis, often presented as a treatment that can only be practiced with middle- and upper-middle-class patients. With this supposition, psychoanalysis in the United States has itself been ghettoized, a contention that is made forcibly by Antonio Viego in this collection. This interdisciplinary volume moves beyond stereotypes and assumptions to show that psychoanalysis is not only possible but also much needed in the barrios.

The old American ideal of assimilation in a melting pot, a process that harmonically fuses all ethnicities into one homogenous culture, has been supplanted by the reality of a mosaic of small communities, a "tossed salad" juxtaposing distinct groups with "ingredients" that can co-exist but do not actually mix or integrate. Although its immigration policies have recently changed significantly, the United States is a nation built by immigrants, a country that historically has hosted and protected foreigners and defended freedom of religion while protecting and pursuing democratic ideals. Nevertheless, this project has not been fully realized.

Let us take the example of the Puerto Rican population, one of the main groups that compose the community of North Philadelphia; their plight dramatically illustrates the situation of the so-called Hispanic population at large because their realities expose the contradictions of a country waking up from an unrealized American Dream of social mobility; here is a country that does not think of itself as "colonial" but has colonies, and Puerto Rico is one of its most painful examples; it is a country that proudly imagines itself as a model of integration but divides its population into ethnic groups like cloistered units, a country that maintains "third world" inner-city enclaves within a "first world" nation.

In the current political climate more than ever, it is important to discuss the civil rights of members of minority groups, including their rights to mental health and well-being. According to the U.S. Census Bureau update of 2012, approximately 38.3 million people or 13% of U.S. residents ages five years and older living in the United States spoke Spanish at home. By 2013, the numbers showed that United States had the fifth largest Spanish-speaking population in the world, and by 2015 it moved up to the number two spot behind Mexico with 56.6 million Hispanic people, making those of Hispanic origin the nation's largest ethnic or racial minority (17% of the nation's total) (U.S. Census Bureau, 2016). A recent report by the renowned Instituto Cervantes research center estimated that presently 52.6 million people in the United States speak Spanish (Burgen, 2015). The report adds that there are 41 million native Spanish speakers in the United States plus 11.6 million people who are bilingual. Of all the immigrants currently living in the United States, almost half (47%) are Hispanic (Flores, López, & Radford, 2017; Pew Research Center, 2016).

"Welcome to Amexica!" announced the cover of *Time* magazine on June 11, 2001. Perhaps a more proper portmanteau could have been "MexicUS." According to U.S. Census Office estimates, by 2050 the white population will not be the majority group. Hispanics will have become the first (that is, most numerous) minority group, and approximately 138 million people or a quarter of the United States population is expected to be Spanish-speaking and of Hispanic descent. Given this projection, "It is not hyperbole to suggest that the future of the nation and its economy depend on the well-being of Latinos," concludes *Latinos: Remaking America* (Suarez-Orozco & Paez, 2002), a recent book produced by Harvard's Rockefeller Center for Latin American Studies. Moreover today, the word "bilingual" in the U.S. only means one thing – Spanish/English. This de-facto "Latinization" of the United States makes *Psychoanalysis in the Barrios: Race, Class, and the Unconscious* not just pertinent but urgent. Our focus in this collection is to highlight the utility of applying psychoanalytic concepts and practices with economically challenged Hispanic populations of the barrios.

Contrary to the common belief that poor people are so consumed with the pressures of everyday living that they can only benefit from symptom-focused and concrete interventions, this collection demonstrates that psychoanalysis facilitates the exploration of the unconscious realm that underpins crucial symptomatic behavior. Sharing vivid testimonies of psychoanalytic cures with people from the barrios, this book argues that psychoanalytic principles can be applied with beneficial results to clinical work with Latino patients who are affected by poverty. Taking as a point of departure the barrio context, this volume captures the complexities introduced by differences of culture, class, gender, language, ethnicity, and race.

Psychoanalysis in the Barrios: Race, Class, and the Unconscious defines an ethical position that has liberatory and emancipatory potential. In the American context, poor, minority patients are infantilized – many mental health providers believe that economically disadvantaged ethnic minorities lack direction in their lives, and that the task of the clinician is to guide them (Gelman, 2003; Gherovici, 2003, 2013). This perspective repeats and perpetuates the inequities of society. The psychoanalytic approach involves treating people as subjects while making productive use of conflict. Our stance is not a purely humanistic gesture of respect for the other. Psychoanalysis uses language production as its material so as to allow patients to face a certain subjective division. By making patients enter the dynamism of subjectivity by which they become true grammatical subjects and regain agency, a psychoanalytic sensibility offers an increased responsibility. In the end, patients, even when they have to face the dire conditions of life in the barrio, feel empowered and act in ways that afford them equal treatment.

In contrast to the experience in many Latin American countries, where psychoanalytic clinical work is practiced with populations of all social strata, in the United States psychoanalysis has been practiced almost exclusively in a classical milieu, which has meant that those who can take advantage of it are from the upper class. In the United States, rigid class boundaries have prevented experiments like those conducted in countries in Latin America. In light of what can amount to structural discrimination, this book documents the efficacy of psychoanalysis in so-called "Hispanic ghettos" by providing evidence that psychoanalysis and psychoanalytic psychotherapy can be successfully practiced in the barrios.

For quite a long time (Gherovici, 1995–1996, 1996a, 1996b, 1997a, 1997b, 1998, 2001, 2003, 2004, 2013), under the heading of "Freud in the barrio," I have been arguing for a more socially responsible practice of psychoanalysis, one that does not forget that the origins of our profession were quite radical, as documented by Elizabeth Danto (2005).[1] As early as 1918, having witnessed the devastation of World War I and fully aware of the magnitude of its destructive impact on the underprivileged classes, Freud appealed to the conscience of society when he stated the obvious: the poor have as much a right as the rich to benefit from help provided by psychoanalysis. Here is his passionate plea:

> [I]t is possible to foresee that at some time or other the conscience of society will awake and remind it that the poor man should have just as much right to assistance for his mind as he now has to the life-saving help offered by surgery; and that the neuroses threaten public health no less than tuberculosis, and can be left as little as the latter to the impotent care of individual members of the community. When this happens, institutions or out-patient clinics will be started . . . whatever form this psychotherapy for the people may take, whatever the elements out of which it is compounded, its most effective and most important ingredients will assuredly remain those borrowed from strict and untendentious psycho-analysis.
>
> (Freud, 1919, pp. 167–168)

Freud was in fact proposing a "psychotherapy for the people" whose structure and composition would follow the usual model of "strict and untendentious psychoanalysis." When he gave this eloquent call for social justice, was Freud stating the obvious – both poor and rich have the right to "strict and untendentious" psychoanalysis?

Freud's social activism and his commitment to the treatment of the poor and the working classes have been erased not just from the collective memory but, most importantly, also from psychoanalytic history. In the years between the two world wars, many analysts made psychoanalysis available to students, artists, craftspeople, unemployed workers, farmers, domestics, laborers, and public school teachers in clinics open to all. Freud's initiative was so persuasive that many medical students traded free treatment in exchange for training. Helen Deutsch, who was in charge of the Vienna Psychoanalytic Society's Training Institute, spoke of a "spirit of reform" (Danto, 2005, p. 3). Max Eitington, who made possible the establishment of the first free clinic in 1920, the Berlin Poliklinik, considered Freud's idea of treatment being available regardless of class as "half as prophecy and half as challenge" (Danto, 2005, p. 3). About 20 clinics opened all over Europe, including Vienna, London, and Budapest. Other clinics followed in Zaghreb, Moscow, Frankfurt, New York, Trieste, and Paris. They were free of charge like the municipal schools and universities of Europe. Analysts at the time saw themselves as brokers of change – individual and social.

This radical Freudian initiative found an equivalent in New York City in 1945 when psychiatrist Fredric Wertham, director of the mental hygiene clinic at Queens General Hospital, prominent novelist Richard Wright, and Earl Brown, a staff writer for *Life* magazine opened a psychoanalytically influenced clinic in the basement of Harlem's St. Philip's Episcopal Church. The clinic was not technically free: those who could afford it were charged 25 cents for sessions and 50 cents for court testimonials. It was called Lafargue Clinic as a homage to a Latino figure, the Afro-Cuban physician and philosopher Paul Lafargue. Lafargue, was a mixed-race Cuban "proudest of his Negro extraction," as he said when asked about his origins (Derfler, 1991, p. 15). He was also Karl Marx's son-in-law and the author of the notorious essay "The Right to Be Lazy" (1883).

Unhappily, in 1959, the Harlem clinic was forced to close, relocating to another place and minimizing the psychoanalytic influence, mostly because of McCarthysm and witch-hunting. Wertham was a German Jewish émigré close to Marxism who advocated for a socially conscious and uncompromising practice of psychoanalysis. Wright met Franz Fanon and James Baldwin in Paris (Zaretsky, 2015, p. 74). Wright and Wertham shared Fanon's radical revolutionary position about the emancipatory power of the unconscious (Mendes, 2015, pp. 16, 155–157). Wright believed that in the U.S., psychoanalytic treatment could undo the negative effects of segregation (García, 2012, pp. 49–74, 105–135; Mendes, 2015, pp. 35–37, 40–44). The impact of psychoanalysis was not just palliative: Wright believed in the potential of psychoanalysis to rethink "race." Psychoanalysis would usher in new strategies of academic enquiry leading to an anti-racist clinical approach capable of overcoming segregation (García, 2012). With uncompromising psychoanalysis as "an essential frame and method" (Mendes, 2015, p. 103), the Lafargue Clinic challenged in practice the racism of psychiatric services that failed to take into account the psychic consequences of oppression in the assessment and treatment of poor African-Americans.

After such socially responsible and progressive origins, it is quite surprising to see that for decades the discussion of class and gender inequality, racism, and ethnic discrimination in psychoanalysis has all but disappeared. Is it because those ideologically charged issues do not matter any longer for the type of psychoanalysis that is practiced in the U.S.? Eli Zaretsky (2005) has noted the substantive difference between European psychoanalysis and the form that developed in the United States where it quickly "became a method of cure and self-improvement" (p. 67). It took a more marketable shape when drenched "in the optimistic and pragmatic spirit that has in many ways transformed it," as Philip Cushman (1995, p. 148) observes. Indeed, psychoanalysis became a method for personal improvement available only to those who could afford it. Today, most psychoanalytic training institutes in the U.S. offer training that is all but inaccessible to everyone but the wealthy. Candidates in training are hampered by the prospect of incurring hefty student loans. This situation de facto prevents even middle- and upper-middle-class individuals who might otherwise undergo training from taking the time and investing money to do so.

Historically, in its professionalization, American psychoanalysis has disregarded the political implications of the practice, focused on developing as a narrow and very lucrative (Hale, 1995) medical sub-specialty (Turkle, 1992), completely divorced from politics and seemingly impermeable to the pressures of history. Dagmar Herzog (2017) shows how removed from Freud's initial project was the variation of psychoanalysis that developed in the United States. The depoliticization of psychoanalysis in this country has been amply documented by historians such as Nathan Hale (1995) and Russell Jacoby (1983). Zaretsky's (2015) fascinating exploration reframes this general attitude as the political conformity of American psychoanalysis. In the rest of the Americas, psychoanalysis had a very different development. It was considered eminently political. Psychoanalysts were often radicalized, and the psychoanalytic discourse as a whole was embraced by left-wing intellectuals as a tool for social transformation, as Nancy Hollander notes in her chapter in this collection.

Let us now move back to the barrio. I often share an anecdote that gives a poignant sense of my experience as a psychoanalyst working with a typically disenfranchised population in such a setting. My daily commute to the clinic where I worked in North Philadelphia took me on a tour of the barrio. I would often walk where the street is narrow and has a roof created by the iron structure of the elevated railways of the EL subway line. This giant rusty carcass is the only reminder of the existence of the sky beyond. Inside the darkened box underneath beats the life of the barrio. The scene of my anecdote is a just few blocks away from the Bloque de Oro, on Kensington Avenue, where fast food shops serve their customers from behind bullet-proof windows and almost all surfaces are covered with graffiti. The mornings are quiet, and at that hour it is hard to imagine the nature of the night in that same location – of the night with hurried drug-dealers, junkies, and prostitutes and their customers moving between shadows and artificial lights. During the day, the streets on Kensington are deserted, removed from the bustle of 5th Street with its hair salons, pork butchers, *bodegas*, restaurants of *criolla* food, the *botánicas* selling spiritualism material, and the sweet smell of Puerto Rican bakeries spreading on the sidewalk. Each morning, I would descend from my subway stop to the sunless empty sidewalks to walk among discarded appliances, abandoned cars, and all sorts of uncollected garbage. One morning, I was surprised by the presence of crowds on the street. Gone were the abandoned cars, the old fridges, and rusty washing machines. The corner shop had a new bright sign. The neighbors jostled on the sidewalk not to miss anything. There was excitement in the air. All this agitation was triggered by the making of *Twelve Monkeys*, a movie inspired by Chris Marker's famous science fiction film *La Jetée* (Marker, 1962) constructed almost entirely from still photos, telling the story of a post-nuclear war experiment in time travel. There they were in Philadelphia's barrio – Bruce Willis, Madeleine Stowe, and Brad Pitt.

Everyone was thrilled. The science fiction film that was in progress took place in a dystopian future: humanity had disappeared from the surface of the earth and only a handful of survivors remained in desolate undergrounds. Deadly viruses and pollution had made the surface of the planet uninhabitable. This drab street of the barrio had been chosen as the ideal backdrop for this end-of-the-world scenario. Our barrio was going to represent the planet after the annihilation of humanity. But to represent a post-apocalyptic world we had to clean up the barrio! What I would like to underline here is not that the decay of these social locations defies the imagination, but rather that they needed to be painted over to become visible.

For almost 30 years now, starting in 1990 to be precise, I have been using my clinical experience as a psychoanalyst in the barrio to illustrate the reach of psychoanalysis beyond class boundaries.[2] Psychoanalysis, I found, was being reinvented in the barrio, a social location where one encounters all the hurdles one can expect when dealing with marginalized groups: the challenges of precariousness, vulnerability, and violence.[3] This community provides a context to explore the limits of the application of the American community mental health model and see how much more productive and democratic a psychoanalytic approach can be. Usually, the mental health services available to the Hispanic community attempt to persuade – or even force – the patient to adhere to the model of capitalist productivity.

Unhappily, since I first discovered the North Philadelphia barrio, the conditions have not changed much. Poverty continues to be extreme (U.S. Census Bureau, 2017) with three generations of unemployed people often present in a family. According to Ericksen (1986), Puerto Ricans are much worse off than Blacks, Whites, or other Hispanics. A study from CUNY Hunter's Centro, the Center for Puerto Rican Studies (2016), confirms that no improvement has been visible: they conclude that the situation of the Puerto Ricans in Pennsylvania shows a lower employment rate than the stateside Puerto Rican average, and that it is close to the employment rate of those in the island (but before Hurricane Maria destroyed most of the economy.) One in three Puerto Rican families in Pennsylvania lives in poverty. Since most of Philadelphia's barrio population is unemployed and since it is highly unlikely that they will find any work, one cannot imagine how they could join the productive segment of the U.S. population. It is in this context that the concept of "productivity" takes an ironic ring and naturalizes the drab reality of class boundaries. There is a parallel or underground economy in which drug-dealing is considered a respected type of "work." For the North Philadelphia community, productivity acquires a new dimension: instead of producing goods, people produce symptoms.

However, community mental health centers can and do actually operate as a site for social control. This social endeavor has severe political implications not only clinically but also culturally. Currently, the imposition of "managed care" privileges cognitive therapy and behavioral approaches as the only possible efficient therapeutic modality. It treats the psyche as if it were a malfunctioning organ in need of reeducation. At the exact opposite of the spectrum, psychoanalysis offers an ethical model that is not utilitarian.

Rather than adapting, psychoanalysis addresses and confronts the subject with reality in all its raw manifestations. Education does not transform the unconscious. Instead of forcing patients to "normalize" their symptoms, psychoanalysis makes the symptoms "productive" by allowing patients to find subjective meaning in them. As a counterpart to a capitalist model of production, psychoanalysis, considered by Jacques Lacan as the very symptom of capitalism, encourages the symptom to produce meaning rather than commodities. When patients recognize that their subjectivity has been expressed in symptoms, we often have a productive moment of emergence, the birth of a singular truth unleashing a new sense of agency. Psychoanalysis can impact individuals and society if it effectively releases changes in subjective positions brought about by the emergence of an unconscious knowledge.

When we talk about the Hispanic barrio, we need to be aware of the complexities of the label. Indeed, "Hispanic" is a problematic and contested verbal construct that conflates categories of language, race, and class. Beyond an allegedly common language, Hispanics are not a homogeneous group. For the purpose of exposing its contradictions and symptomatic function, discussed by Joshua Javier Guzmán in his essay in this collection, we will retain the word "Hispanic," keeping in mind that it is a loaded political term often used as a segregation device. Aware of the paradoxes of this racialized and racist category, the U.S. Census concedes, "Hispanic origin can be viewed as the heritage, nationality, lineage, or country of birth of the person or the person's parents or ancestors before arriving in the United States. People who identify as Hispanic, Latino, or Spanish *may be any race*" (U.S. Census, Hispanic Origin).[4] In my experience as a psychoanalyst working with a predominantly Puerto Rican, inner-city community in Philadelphia's barrio, I was surprised to discover that for the so-called "Hispanic" population, the notion of "race" was used to mean "poor," a notion that I will expand on in my chapter. Furthermore, most sociological studies agree that richer Hispanics, once away from the ghetto, lose most of the characteristics typically associated with being Hispanic (McKay, 1985, p. 3).

In what has been described as "cultural racism," poverty is seen as an immutable cultural feature (Marger, 2009, pp. 25–26). Then the economic disadvantage of marginalized minorities is naturalized and traced to a people's way of life; thus socioeconomic disparity is ascribed to a failure to conform to a productive work ethic and to obey institutional authority. With this subtle form of racism, a set of behaviors and characteristics is projected onto a group to justify their situation not only as immutable but also as divorced from social conditions. In a similar manner, it is often assumed that essential cultural features function like biological determinations that make poor people bad candidates for psychoanalysis or psychoanalytic therapy. If it is clear that in the "Land of Opportunity" upward social mobility for racialized, disenfranchised communities is becoming more and more unlikely, then one may wonder if other forms of movement are available to poor people. For community mental health centers that serve inner-city populations, the available treatment stagnates in a mechanized ritual: sessions are used to straighten up behaviors, re-educate, persuade, and domesticate. Replicating the morass of class, after many years in treatment, most patients do not experience any changes. The emphasis of the treatment is placed on the implementation of low-cost standardized techniques that produce few results other than offering social buffering.

If publications like those of Rafael Javier (1990), Javier and Herron (1992), Herron and Javier (1996), Altman (1995, 2010), Lewis Aron and Karen Starr (2013) make strong cases for the usefulness of psychoanalytic interventions with the urban poor, their position remains an exception. I have explored elsewhere the way authoritative Spanish-speaking mental health practitioners dismiss psychoanalysis as an "elite" treatment, all the while presenting a portrait of class determination as an "essential" cultural feature (Gherovici, 2003; 2013). The issues revolving around race, language, and culture play a major role in these controversies; yet they should not exclude considerations of the way in which the unconscious functions in the psyche of the poor. It seems to me that the purported unsuitability of psychoanalysis for poor minority groups also exposes political conflicts, and that these have had important clinical consequences. The idea that psychoanalysis is not useful for dealing with the "real" problems of the poor is often based on the belief that only the "real world" can provide a solution to these problems and that this solution must be sought by political and economic means. This position reflects less a reality than a symptom of the dominant culture. It also reveals the opinion, even prejudice, that caregivers have vis-à-vis the minorities they care for. More disturbingly, this kind of prejudice has encroached on therapeutic models. Javier (1990) has observed that the application of psychoanalysis to the urban poor has been a subject of heated controversy. Surveying the literature, one discovers that even "liberal" authors seem to believe in a questionable "psychogenesis of poverty" (Herron and Javier, 1996).

Such a construction confuses the contingencies of situations created by poverty with a causal explanation relying on the psyche of the poor. It is a variation on the old truism: "If the poor are poor, it is because they deserve it." But it gets modified into: "If the poor are poor, it is because they desire it unconsciously." Some authors misappropriate the findings of anthropologist Oscar Lewis (1968) about what he called a "culture of poverty,"[5] (p. 188) and rush to the conclusion that poverty would entail adaptive psychic features then deemed essential, like an orientation to the present, a lack of sophistication, an inability to project oneself into the future, and very poor insight. Taken together such characteristics would render psychoanalysis impracticable (Allen, 1970; Costantino, Malgady, & Rogler, 1986; Malgady, Rogler, & Costantino, 1987; Minuchin, Montalvo, Guerney, Rosman, & Schumer, 1967; Rogler, Malgady, Costantino, & Blumenthal, 1987; Ruiz, 1981; Sarbin, 1970; Sue & Sue, 1977). Here one can see how a social tautology ("the poor are poor") has been transformed into a pseudo psychic determinism ("the poor want to be poor.") Consequently, any reference to psychoanalysis will be derided as an unaffordable luxury. Psychoanalysis is seen as a therapy of choice applicable to those who are supposedly more psychologically sophisticated, in fact restricted to the upper classes who can afford it.

To challenge the common reproach that psychoanalysis is long and expensive, hence is not for the bedraggled, poorer sections of the population, I would contend that this is a myth invented by American practitioners in the 1950s. We know that Freud insisted on short-term treatments. Intensity was the key for the success of early psychoanalytic cures. This determined the high frequency of the sessions. Indeed, Freud would see his patients every day, six days a week. What was "long" for the creator of psychoanalysis meant six months in some rare cases, a year at most. The transformation of psychoanalysis into an endless endeavor was a shrewd money-making strategy manufactured in the New World. The idea that psychoanalysis was an exclusive treatment, the so-called "Park Avenue practice," was another distortion aimed at generating incomes on a par with the highest-paying medical specialties (Lionells, 1999, p. 16). Of course, the longer a psychoanalysis lasted, the more profitable it would be. Today most practitioners of psychoanalysis have taken distance from this classical restrictive model. One could even claim that a treatment with patients lying on the couch five times a week talking about their childhood to a mute analyst for decades should not be called Freudian psychoanalysis. What I wish to address here is the prejudice internal to psychoanalysis itself. This raises the question as formulated by Bertram P. Karon (2002) in "Analyzability or the Ability to Analyze?" Karon argues that this is the wrong question to ask. The right question would be "What needs to be done?" – which would entail, among other changes, to provide psychoanalytic treatment for disenfranchised populations (p. 121).

If we start from the idea proposed by Lacan that there is only one resistance, that of analysts themselves, it must be recognized that psychoanalysts are partly responsible for the difficulties encountered in the practice of psychoanalysis among minorities. In the end, what makes a psychoanalytic cure possible is the will of the analyst to offer a space where the analysand's unconscious can be heard.

When one talks of a psychoanalytic treatment in a mental health clinic, other issues are introduced such as the use of interpretation, timing of sessions, frequency, money, face-to-face versus the couch, etc. Freud believed that any line of therapy that recognizes the unconscious processes of transference and resistance as starting point can rightfully be called psychoanalytic. A clinical practice that would take into account unconscious processes requires many adjustments that, though challenging, are not impossible. Nonetheless, the important fact is that analysts have to be clear about their role in transference and remain vigilant to the interference that the institution may present to the process. Necessary changes in the way therapy is practiced in mental health clinics should address the wide implications of many of the bureaucratic requirements in place. For instance, they request patients to sign a treatment plan that functions like a contract coercing the patient to "comply," "by following" specific tasks in order to achieve certain goals established by the therapist. Periodically (usually every 2 or 3 months), the treatment plan is revised, the patient's performance is evaluated, and a new treatment plan contract is written and signed.

This commodification of mental health practices has the potential of triggering many negative effects, namely an obsessive pursuit of symptom suppression and adaptation to social mandates. I recall the wise comment of a depressed patient who was asked to sign a form that was part of the regular intake procedure in which he was to promise that he was not going to take his own life during the course of the treatment. He told me, "Then, I will die a liar." The absurdity and futility of these pedagogical strategies and the implications of such emphasis on adaptation in terms of individual freedom, especially for individuals of a minority culture or a lower socioeconomic class, are too obvious.

Although most current forms of talk therapy derive from Freud's invention, in the United States psychoanalysis developed in a manner adapted to a cultural juncture that emphasized the ego as the agent of adaptation – the unconscious was Americanized. The importance placed on adaptation determined that both American psychoanalysis and other forms of talk therapy move away from the unconscious to stress adaptation and normal development. A type of treatment that focuses on interpreting unconscious desire and undoing repression seems to offer an option that resonates better with the struggles of minority groups. Psychoanalysis not only deals with unconsciously repressed conflict. It also encourages the exploration of fantasy, giving dream-life great importance. Free association expands the imagination and opens up a space of futurity beyond the constraints of the repetition. A capacity to imagine is crucial in developing the ability to envisage a different future, so as to then construct new realities. This is of great importance for people located at the margins. A free play with the imagination is an essential factor in rebuilding someone's personal life, and one hopes it will also enable change at a social level. As Ruha Benjamin observes, "Social change requires novel fictions that reimagine and rework all that is taken for granted about the current structure of society" (Benjamin, 2016) Psychoanalysis, instead of enforcing adaptation to oppressive social conditions, makes for subjective agency.

Psychoanalysis in the Barrios: Race, Class, and the Unconscious begins by tracing the advent of Freud in Latin America. First, the threat that the new "plague" – a term half-jokingly used by Freud to refer to the arrival of psychoanalysis in the U.S. in 1909 – represented. Psychoanalysis was for many Latin American dictatorial regimes an ideological foe. This was linked to the flourishing of psychoanalysis in major cities in South America. However, in North America, psychoanalysis could not reach segments of inner-city populations. Despite what appears to be a limited reach in inner cities, psychoanalysis has provided a useful theoretical framework for clinical practice in such locations, like no other, for understanding symptoms, expanding meaning, appreciating intersectionalities that include sex and gender, and creating potentiality through its praxis.

Psychoanalysis in the Barrios: Race, Class, and the Unconscious is divided into four sections. In the first section, "Freud with a Spanish Accent: The Latin American Experience of the Psychic Being Political," the authors explore the political impact that Freud has exerted not just in the field of Latin American psychoanalysis but also on the culture at large of these countries. Mariano Plotkin opens this section with "Freud and the Latin Americans: A Forgotten Relationship." This chapter unearths Freud's little-known correspondence with Latin American authors, psychiatrists, and intellectuals and highlights the elements that contributed to the creation of a specifically Latin American psychoanalysis. In Chapter 2, "Psychoanalysts Bearing Witness: Trauma and Memory in Latin America," Nancy Hollander explores how in Argentina psychoanalysis, which was aligned with the Left, was adopted not just by clinicians but also by intellectuals and artists whose political affiliations were anti-fascist and anti-establishment. In Argentina, a brutal military regime put an end to this radicalization of left-wing intellectual life. Under circumstances of state terror, the question was whether analysts could remain outside of the political struggles or become agents of social change. Finally, in Chapter 3, "Dying to Get Out: Challenges in the Treatment of Latin American Migrants Fleeing Violent Communities," Ricardo Ainslie, Hannah McDermott, and Crystal Guevara explore the case of Juan, a severely traumatized survivor, and assess the psychic consequences of forced migrations from Mexico and Central America all triggered by extreme violence. Drawing on clinical material, they illustrate how a psychoanalytic understanding of imposed migration and its attendant traumas can yield new vistas.

The second section is "Pathology of Otherness: Diagnosis in the Barrio." Here the authors examine the hegemony of the medical model on psychiatric diagnosis and some of its alienating effects on subjectivity. Christopher Christian opens this section with Chapter 4: "The Analyst as Interpreter: *Ataque de Nervios*, Puerto Rican syndrome, and the Inexact Interpretation." Christian looks at how labels such as Puerto Rican syndrome and panic attacks came to replace the more localized term *ataque de nervios* and how the psychiatric nomenclature can act like Edward Glover's "inexact interpretation," providing symptomatic relief by virtue of distancing the subject from the true nature of their anxiety. Such relief is inevitably accompanied by an experience of self-alienation. Contributing to current debates on normalcy and pathology in Chapter 5, "The Anxiety of Citizenship or the Psychotic as Citizen," Alfredo Carrasquillo shows how a diagnosis of psychosis can be used by the practitioner as a shield against the anxieties created by listening to a patient's hallucinations and dreams, defensively rendering them as unintelligible and meaningless. He uses the example of an innovative treatment program in Québec for people with psychosis to prove that psychoanalysis should not hesitate to treat madness. In Chapter 6, "Eating Brains: Latinx Barrios, Psychoanalysis and Neuroscience," Antonio Viego reads critically Oliver Sacks's account of his treatment of José, a man diagnosed with autism. Viego points out Sacks's inconsistencies and shows how the medical gaze pathologizes otherness while revealing crucial aspects of the implications of the term "Latinx."

Diagnosis is not the only form of social control. In the third section, "The Latino Queer Body: Mourning, Melancholia, and the Law," the essays by Jennifer Lambe, Ben Sifuentes-Jáuregui, Licia Fiol-Matta, and Joshua Javier Guzmán describe the regulation and control of the Latino/a body by the state and institutions like psychiatrists, the medical establishment, and public opinion. In this section, the authors explore the historical and political conditions that create the context in which particular Latino/a bodies are viewed and defined. In Chapter 7, "Visible Pleasure and Sex Policing: State, Science, and Desire in Twentieth-Century Cuba," Lambe traces the evolution of exhibitionism in Cuba as a psychiatric, criminological, and popular notion. Lambe argues that visibility itself was at issue in the efforts to police the public display of sexuality. Moreover, this unease with looking exposed the scientific-bureaucratic gaze. Sifuentes-Jáuregui in Chapter 8, "Melancholia and the Abject on Mango Street: Racialized Narratives/Psychoanalysis" provides an original analysis of strategies of identity formation in Sandra Cisneros's *The House on Mango Street*. Very often individuals within barrio communities seek to define themselves by constructing a racialized identity, and thus Sifuentes-Jáuregui investigates how reading Chicano narratives contributes to the construction of a Latino/a self. He also teases out the implications of this process for psychoanalysis. In Chapter 9, "Chencha's Gait: Voice and Nothing in Myrta Silva," Fiol-Matta takes the example of the life and work of iconic guarachas singer Chencha/Myrta Silva to reveal, in the artist's queer performance completely merging song and singer, the hidden presence of the unattainable object of desire, the psychoanalytic object *a* embodied in the voice. Also considering queer subjectivities and performances, Guzmán's Chapter 10, "Beside Oneself: Queer Psychoanalysis and the Aesthetics of Latinidad," discusses the figure of the "Latina/o subject" as a problem for aesthetics and psychoanalytic queer criticism. An analysis of the life and work of Chicano poet and scholar Arturo Islas, who died of AIDS complications in the 1990s, throws light on the complexities of the notion of Latinidad.

In the fourth section, "The Clinical Is Political," Carlos Padrón, Daniel José Gaztambide, and I explore the political possibilities generated by the psychoanalytic process. Padrón in Chapter 11, "The Political Potentiality of the Psychoanalytic Process," discusses the contributions of Hans Loewald in the context of the psychoanalytic treatment of Antonio. He illustrates the never completed state of potentiality fostered by psychoanalytic praxis that nevertheless can grant a sense of authorship and legitimacy to the analysand. In Chapter 12, "Treating Borderline Personality Disorder in El Barrio: Integrating Race and Class into Transference-Focused Psychotherapy," Gaztambide outlines an integration of cultural difference, race, class, and identity into transference-focused psychotherapy. This psychoanalytic treatment for borderline personality disorder uses a systemic lens borrowed from liberation psychology to address socioeconomic and political inequality. In Chapter 13, "Psychoanalysis of Poverty, Poverty of Psychoanalysis," I revisit the Puerto Rican syndrome taken as a social allegory of the paradoxical position of colonial subjects and discuss an overlooked historical event that took place during the Korean War at the time when the syndrome was invented. The racism of psychiatry exemplified in the Puerto Rican syndrome is linked to the existing bias against the practice of psychoanalysis with low-income populations. I use several clinical vignettes to argue for the usefulness, pertinence, and emancipatory potential of psychoanalysis with barrio populations.

Psychoanalysis in the Barrios: Race, Class, and the Unconscious breaks new ground by challenging the undemocratic character of current mental health practices, which is quite pronounced for Latino patients. The current inequality in access to psychoanalytic treatment has ideological and political implications. This collection seeks to reopen the discussion so as to break the invisible borders surrounding the ghettos in which psychoanalysis finds itself.

This collection is an interdisciplinary volume with essays by distinguished international scholars and clinicians that bridge the gaps between disciplines including psychoanalysis, queer studies, anthropology, urban studies, sociology, literature, and history. It argues for the pertinence and usefulness of psychoanalysis with populations of Latinx origin living under economically oppressive circumstances.

Psychoanalysis in the Barrios: Race, Class, and the Unconscious covers material that will appeal to readers in clinical practice, psychology, cultural, and Latino/a studies, queer studies, urban studies, anthropology, and sociology. This project was inspired by the highly visible and successful documentary *Psychoanalysis in el Barrio*, winner of the PEP 2015 Video Grant (Christian, Reichbart, Moskowitz, Morillo, & Winograd, 2016). The film challenges the not-uncommon notion that Hispanic patients affected by poverty can only benefit from therapies that rely on concrete or medicalized interventions. The documentary was initiated by my co-editor, Christopher Christian, and features myself, as well as Ricardo Ainslie, Carlos Padrón, and Daniel José Gaztambide, authors in this collection. The film premiered in New York City in April 2016 with an enthusiastic audience of over 300 people. It continues to elicit great interest in the discussion of the practice of psychoanalysis in nontraditional social locations. We hope that the reader of this collection can join the enthusiastic response of the film's audience, all those who greeted the first screening by clapping and laughing loudly; our intention here is less to bring psychoanalysis back into the barrio than to celebrate the barrio and bring it back into a renewed psychoanalysis.

I wish to thank Marco-Antonio Coutinho Jorge, Molly-Anne Rothenberg, and Benigno Trigo for their generous invitations to share my work in progress: "Sigmund in the Barrio: A Psychoanalyst's Experience in Inner-City Philadelphia," Corpo Freudiano Escola de Psicanalise, Rio de Janeiro, Brazil, August 24, 2010; "Freud and Lacan in the Barrio: Clinical Work with Marginalized Populations," The Edward H. Knight Fund Public Lecture, New Orleans Psychoanalytic Center, November 19, 2010; and "Sigmund in the Barrio: How Can Psychoanalysis Deal with Race?" lecture co-sponsored by the Robert Penn Warren Center for the Humanities, Afro-Hispanic Review, Department of Philosophy, Department of French and Italian, Department of Spanish and Portuguese, and the Department of English, Vanderbilt University, October 3, 2012. Some of the ideas discussed in this introduction were presented in "The Politics of 'Associated' Madness: Psychoanalysis in the Barrio," Critical Refusals, International Herbert Marcuse Society, Fourth Biennial Conference, University of Pennsylvania, October 27, 2011.

Notes

1 For an assessment of Danto's comprehensive work on the free clinics, see Joanna Ryan's chapter, "Asking Questions of History," in *Class and Psychoanalysis: Landscapes of inequality* (p. 19–35). New York, NY: Routledge, 2017.
2 See Gherovici 1996a; 1996b; 1996c.
3 Imagine my surprise when during my work in the barrio clinic I encountered the Puerto Rican syndrome, a diagnosis that I discuss in this collection (see Chapter 13) as does my co-editor Chris Christian (see Chapter 4). The label was invented by U.S. Army doctors in the 1950s to diagnose Puerto Rican soldiers coming from the Korean War front who were suffering from mysterious symptoms for which their psychiatric knowledge could give no explanation or offer any treatment. The manifestations described by the syndrome ranged from suicidal gestures to pseudo-epilepsy, from rage outbursts to catatonia, from amnesia to convulsive attacks and happened to be an exact repetition of the most classical form of hysteria, one long considered eradicated. This form of hysteria with recalcitrant bodily symptoms was none other than the one that guided Freud in the creation of psychoanalysis and allowed for the discovery of the unconscious.
4 Emphasis added.
5 This is how Lewis sums it up: "by the time slum children are aged six or seven, they have usually absorbed the basic values and attitudes of their subculture and are not psychologically geared to take full advantage of the changing conditions or increased opportunities that may occur in their lifetime" (Lewis, 1968, p. 188).

References

Allen, V. L. (1970). Personality correlates of poverty. In V. L. Allen (Ed.), *Psychological factors in poverty* (pp. 242–266). New York, NY: Academic Press.
Altman, N. (1995). *The analyst in the inner city: Race, class and culture through a psychoanalytic lens*. Hillsdale, MI and London: The Analytic Press.
Aron, L., & Starr, K. (2013). *A psychotherapy for the people: Toward a progressive psychoanalysis*. New York, NY: Routledge.

Benjamin, R. (2016). Racial fictions, biological facts: Expanding the sociological imagination through speculative methods. *Catalyst: Feminism, Theory, Technoscience*, *2*(2), 1–28. https://catalystjournal.org/index.php/catalyst/article/view/28798/21397

Burgen, S. (2015, June 29). US now has more Spanish speakers than Spain – Only Mexico has more. *The Guardian*. Retrieved May 10, 2018 from www.theguardian.com/us-news/2015/jun/29/us-second-biggest-spanish-speaking-country

Centro (2016). Puerto Ricans in Pennsylvania, the United States, and Puerto Rico 2014. Center for Puerto Rican Studies, Hunter, CUNY, Centro DS2016US-6 released April 2016. Retrieved September 17, 2018 from https://centropr.hunter.cuny.edu/sites/default/files/PDF/STATE%20REPORTS/9-PA-PR-2016-CentroReport.pdf

Chavez, L. (1991). *Out of the barrio: Toward a new politics of Hispanic assimilation*. New York, NY: Basic Books.

Christian, C., Reichbart, R., Moskowitz, M., Morillo, R., & Winograd, B. (2016). Psychoanalysis in El Barrio. [Documentary] *PEP Video Grants*, *1*(2), 10. United States: PEP Web.

Costantino, G., Malgady, R., & Rogler, L. (1986). Cuento therapy: A culturally sensitive modality for Puerto Rican children. *Journal of Consulting and Clinical Psychology*, *54*, 639–645.

Cushman, P. (1995). *Constructing the self, constructing America: A cultural history of psychotherapy*. Indianapolis, IN: Addison Wesley.

Danto, E. (2005). *Freud's free clinics: Psychoanalysis and social justice 1918–1938*. New York, NY: Columbia University Press.

Dávila, A. (2004). *Barrio dreams: Puerto Ricans, Latinos, and the neoliberal city*. Berkeley, CA: University of California Press.

Derfler, L. (1991). *Paul Lafargue and the founding of French Marxism, 1842–1882*. Cambridge, MA: Harvard University Press.

Ericksen, E. (1986). *The state of Puerto Rican Philadelphia: Research on Philadelphia and the Greater Delaware Valley region*. Philadelphia, PA: Institute for Public Policies Studies, Temple University.

Flores, A., López, G., & Radford, J. (2017, September 18). Facts on U.S. Latinos, 2015: Statistical portrait of Hispanics in the United States. *Pew Research Center Hispanic Trends*. Retrieved from www.pewhispanic.org/2017/09/18/facts-on-u-s-latinos-trend-data/.

Freud, S. (1919). Lines of advance in psycho-analytic therapy. In J. Strachey (Ed.), *The standard edition of the complete psychological works of Sigmund Freud, Volume XVII (1917–1919): An infantile neurosis and other works* (pp. 157–168). London, England: Hogarth Press.

García, J. (2012). *Psychology comes to Harlem: Rethinking the race question in twentieth-century America*. New Studies in American Intellectual and Cultural History. Baltimore, MD: Johns Hopkins University Press.

Gelman, C. R. (2003). Psychodynamic treatment of Latinos: A critical review of the theoretical literature and practice outcome research. *Psychoanalytic Social Work*, *10*(2), 79–102.

Gherovici, P. (1995–1996). The ghetto sublime hysterics. *Bien Dire*, *2–3*, 5–21.

Gherovici, P. (1996a). Recuerdos del futuro: histeria raza y el ghetto hispano. In *1895–1995, Estudios sobre la histeria cien años después* (pp. 33–43). Buenos Aires: Ediciones Kline.

Gherovici, P. (1996b, November). The Puerto Rican syndrome. *Journal for the Psychoanalysis of Culture and Society*, *2*, 182–186.

Gherovici, P. (1996c, November). Sigmund dans le Barrio. *Scansions*, Numéro Spécial 6/7 "L'avenir de la Psychanalyse", 7.

Gherovici, P. (1997a). Blocking the Hispanic unconscious: Subjectivity and subjection. *Clinical Studies: International Journal for Psychoanalysis, 2*(2), 23–37.

Gherovici, P. (1997b). The Hispanic La Raza: Psychoanalysis and losing (the) race. *Clinical Studies: International Journal for Psychoanalysis, 3*(1), 55–71.

Gherovici, P. (1998). Le ghetto contre-attaque: la production hysterique dans le barrio portoricain aux Etats-Unis. *La clinique lacanienne. Revue internationale, 3,* Encore? l'hysterie, 135–150.

Gherovici, P. (2001). Between meaning and madness: The altered states of Hispanics in the U.S. In A. Molino & C. Ware (Eds.), *Where id was: Challenging normalization in psychoanalysis* (pp. 149–163). London and New York, NY: Continuum.

Gherovici, P. (2003). *The Puerto Rican syndrome.* New York, NY: Other Press.

Gherovici, P. (2004). Un Freud francés con acento español. *Imago Agenda,* 22–24.

Gherovici, P. (2013). Let's beat up the poor. *CR: The New Centennial Review, 13*(3), 1–28.

Hale, N. (1995). *The rise and crisis of psychoanalysis in the United States: Freud and the Americans, 1917–1985.* Oxford: Oxford University Press.

Herron, W. G., & Javier, R. A. (1996). The psychogenesis of poverty: Some psychoanalytic conceptions. *Psychoanalytic Review, 83*(4), 611–620.

Herzog, D. (2017). *Cold War Freud: Psychoanalysis in an age of catastrophe.* Cambridge: Cambridge University Press.

Jacoby, R. (1983). *The repression of psychoanalysis: Otto Fenichel and the political Freudians.* New York, NY: Basic Books.

Javier, R. A. (1990). On the suitability of insight-oriented therapy for the Hispanic poor. *American Journal of Psychoanalysis, 50*(4), 305–318.

Javier, R. A., & Herron, W. G. (1992). Psychoanalysis, the hispanic poor, and the disadvantaged. *Journal of the American Academy of Psychoanalysis and Dynamic Psychiatry, 20,* 455–476.

Jütte, D. (2015). The place of music in early modern Italian culture. In R. Davies (Ed.), *Musical exodus: Al-Andalus and its Jewish diasporas.* Lanham, MD: Rowman & Littlefield.

Karon, B. P. (2002). Analyzability or the ability to analyze? *Contemporary Psychoanalysis, 38,* 121–140.

Lewis, O. (1968). The culture of poverty. In D. P. Moynihan (Ed.), *On understanding poverty: Perspectives from the social sciences.* New York, NY: Basic Books.

Liberman, A. (2009). *Why don't we know the origin of the word ghetto?* OUPBlog: Oxford University Press's Academic Insights for the Thinking World. Retrieved from https://blog.oup.com/2009/03/ghetto/.

Lionells, M. (1999). Thanatos is alive and well and living in psychoanalysis. In R. Prince (Ed.), *The death of psychoanalysis.* Northvale, NJ: Aronson.

Malgady, R. G., Rogler, L. H., & Costantino, G. (1987). Ethnocultural and linguistic bias in mental health evaluation of Hispanics. *American Psychologist, 42,* 228–234.

Marger, M. (2009). *Race and ethnic relations: American and global perspectives.* Belmont, CA: Wadsworth Press (first edition 2006).

Marker, C. (1962). *La Jetée.* France.

McKay, E. (1985). *The National Council of La Raza, cultural relevance: An Anglo's guide to working effectively with Hispanics.* Handout.

Mendes, G. (2015). *Under the strain of color: Harlem Lafargue clinic and the promise of and antiracist psychiatry.* Ithaca, NY: Cornell University Press.

Minuchin, S., Montalvo, B., Guerney, B., Rosman, B., & Schumer, F. (1967). *Families of the slums*. New York, NY: Basic Books.

Pew Research Center. (2016). *[Graph illustrations of median household income, poverty rate, and median household net worth]. Latinos lag behind U.S. public on income and wealth and have higher poverty rates*. Retrieved from www.pewhispanic.org/2016/06/08/latinos-increasingly-confident-in-personal-finances-see-better-economic-times-ahead/ph_2016–06–08_nsl-economy-04/.

Rogler, L. H., Malgady, R. G., Costantino, G., & Blumenthal, R. (1987). What do culturally sensitive mental health services mean? The case of Hispanics. *American Psychologist, 42*, 565–570.

Ruiz, R. (1981). Cultural and historical perspectives. In D. Sue (Ed.), *Counseling the culturally different* (pp. 186–215). New York, NY: Wiley.

Ryan, J. (2017). *Class and psychoanalysis: Landscapes of inequality*. New York, NY: Routledge.

Sarbin, T. R. (1970). The culture of poverty, social identity, and cognitive outcomes. In V. L. Allen (Ed.), *Psychological factors in poverty* (pp. 29–46). New York, NY: Academic Press.

Shulvass, M. A. (1973). *The Jews in the world of the renaissance*. Leiden: Brill and the Spertus College of Judaica Press.

Suarez-Orozco, M., & Paez, M. (Eds.). (2002). *Latinos: Remaking America*. Berkeley, CA: University of California Press.

Sue, D. W., & Sue, D. (1977). Barriers to effective cross-cultural counseling. *Journal of Counseling Psychology, 24*, 420–429.

Turkle, S. (1992). *Psychoanalytic politics: Jacques Lacan and the French Revolution* (2nd ed.). New York, NY: Free Association Books.

U.S. Census Bureau. (2016). Facts for features. *Hispanic Heritage Month 2016*. Newsroom (media portal). Retrieved from www.census.gov/newsroom/facts-for-features/2016/cb16-ff16.html.

U.S. Census Bureau. (2017) [Demographic data table]. *Quick facts: Philadelphia County, Pennsylvania*. Retrieved from www.census.gov/quickfacts/fact/table/philadelphiacountypennsylvania/PST045216.

U.S. Census Bureau. (2016) [Library of data points regarding Hispanic people]. *Hispanic Origin*. Retrieved from www.census.gov/topics/population/hispanic-origin.html.

Zaretsky, E. (2005). *The secrets of the soul: A social and cultural history of psychoanalysis*. New York, NY: Vintage.

Zaretsky, E. (2015). *Political Freud: A history*. New York, NY: Columbia University Press.

Section I

Freud with a Spanish accent

The Latin American experience of the psychic being political

Chapter 1

Freud and the Latin Americans
A forgotten relationship

Mariano Plotkin[1]

In 1938, soon after the German annexation of Austria, Freud left his native Vienna for his exile in London. He was to die there one year later, in September 1939. Pressed to save his own life as well as the lives of his immediate family – though he did not succeed in saving his sisters, who died in the Shoah – Freud could, nonetheless, take with him his cherished collection of antiques and a good portion of the 3,600 titles and 4,500 volumes of his personal library (Davies & Fichtner, 2006). One can assume that, given the conditions of his departure, he took with him only those books that, for one reason or another, he considered particularly valuable. He left behind, for instance, most books that were not directly dealing with psychoanalysis or other topics of immediate interest to him. The volumes he would leave behind were sold to a book dealer, and they eventually found their way to the Augustus C. Long Health Sciences Library at Columbia University as a separate archive known as the Freud Library. A small number of books were held in private hands and others are today housed at the Library of Congress in Washington, DC.

It is hardly surprising that an intellectual of Freud's stature took pains to select and take with him a portion of his library. More surprising, perhaps, is the fact that 33 of the books he took to London were authored by Latin American doctors or intellectuals (he left behind another 25 books written by Latin Americans). However, perhaps even more surprising, is that 13 of the books he decided to keep were written in Portuguese by Brazilian authors (Plotkin & Ruperthuz, 2017). While it is well known that Freud could easily read Spanish – he had learned it in his youth so that he could read *Don Quixote* in its original language[2] – he openly confessed many times that he could not read Portuguese. Why, then, did he take those books to London, books that not only had he not read, but also he would not have the ability to read? What was the place of Latin America in Freud's vision of the world? The goal of this chapter is to map out the complex relationship between Freud and Latin America. Freud was interested in spreading psychoanalysis around the world and was ready to make concessions in terms of tolerating theoretical deviations. However, he had difficulties in considering people who were not European (or North American) as equals. The analysis of the correspondence he kept with some Latin American doctors and intellectuals (in this chapter I will analyze only a small but relevant portion of it) shows Freud's difficulties in coming to terms with what he perceived as the "exotic world." Freud entered into the depth of the (European's) unconscious, but it seems that he was not able to totally accept the cultural "other."

Although Freud never set foot in the region, and in spite of the fact that his own references to Latin America throughout his *Complete Works* can be counted on the fingers of one hand, not only did the founder of psychoanalysis establish a circuit for the exchange of books, publications, and photographs with doctors and intellectuals of the subcontinent, but he also maintained correspondence with some Latin Americans. Among them, Peruvian doctor Honorio Delgado stands out. Freud and Delgado had a personal friendship and kept up a sustained, although patchy, exchange of letters that lasted for almost 20 years.[3] Freud referred many times to Delgado as his "first foreign friend." Delgado was one of the earliest biographers of Freud in any language, publishing *Sigmund Freud* in his native Peru in 1926 (Delgado, 1926). The volume would later be translated into Portuguese and published in Brazil (Delgado, 1933). Freud himself read the book and corrected a few factual errors in the first edition. As Elisabeth Roudinesco points out, however, in reference to the number of times that Freud's father had been married, it seems that Delgado, who claimed that Jacob Freud had been married three times, was indeed right, while Freud, who insisted that his father only married twice, appears to have been (whether consciously or not) wrong (Roudinesco, 2014).

Young Peruvians like Delgado – he was in his 20s when he first wrote to Freud and had just published his dissertation of 1918 devoted to psychoanalysis – but also Brazilians, Argentines, Chileans, and Mexicans who were doctors, lawyers, intellectuals, and even students felt attracted to Freud's ideas. Many of them sent their own writings and composed letters to the founder of psychoanalysis. In some cases, that gave origin to more sustained exchanges.

In Latin America, the reception of psychoanalysis among medical and intellectual circles took place earlier than in most other parts of the world. Already in 1899, that is to say *before* the publication of *Interpretation of Dreams*, Dr. Juliano Moreira from Bahia, Brazil, was including Freud's works on hysteria (in German) in the bibliography for his courses at the School of Medicine of Bahia. In 1914, Genserico Aragão de Souza Pinto wrote a dissertation on psychoanalysis for the School of Medicine of Rio de Janeiro (Stubbe, 2011). There, he mentioned psychoanalytic treatments that had been carried out by other doctors in the city since several years earlier. By the 1920s, psychoanalysis was discussed, accepted, practiced, or dismissed (which indicates that it was actually known) in cities such as Buenos Aires, Rio de Janeiro, São Paulo, Lima, and Santiago de Chile. Even in Mexico, where the reception of psychoanalysis was weaker and took place later than in other Latin American countries, the first dissertations on psychoanalysis were written as early as the 1920s (Plotkin & Ruperthuz, 2017; Capetillo Hernández, 2012).

By the 1930s, psychoanalysis had also made its way into popular culture. Popular magazines as well as widely read newspapers in Argentina, Brazil, and Chile not only published articles on psychoanalysis but, in some cases, included columns in which readers were invited to submit their dreams which would be analyzed by "expert psychoanalysts" (Plotkin, 2007). Freud became a well-known international figure in many major Latin American cities. The possession of a letter written by Freud, or one of his books with a handwritten dedication, or – even more importantly – one of his autographed photographs, soon became a sign of belonging to a prestigious international community.

Psychoanalysis was therefore known and discussed across Latin America since the 1910s or even earlier, but what did Freud make of Latin America? His contacts with the region also started early, even before the invention of psychoanalysis. In the early 1880s Freud, who could not find a job in Vienna, was advised by the prestigious doctor Hermann Nothnagel – who in 1897 would recommend Freud for a professorship at the University of Vienna – to immigrate to Buenos Aires. Argentine doctor Roberto Wernicke had been a student of Nothnagel in Vienna and, therefore, there was already a possible contact in the South American city (Plotkin & Ruperthuz, 2017). Many years later, towards the end of his life, Freud would again receive invitations to immigrate to Buenos Aires, as well as to Santiago de Chile and Mexico City.

A few years after deciding not to follow Nothnagel's advice to move to Argentina, Freud published his controversial work on the therapeutic uses of cocaine (Freud, 1974). Incidentally, this work was cited as early as 1885 by Chilean doctor César Martínez in a dissertation titled "Contribución al estudio de la cocaína" (Martínez, 1885; Ruperthuz, 2015). Freud's text, *Über Coca*, starts with a long discussion of the many uses, both therapeutic and ritual, of the coca plant and its by-products in ancient Latin America. Among Freud's sources for the book stand out the works of Paolo Mantegazza, an Italian neurologist and physiologist who had done extensive fieldwork in northern Argentina, where he married a local woman.

In spite of these early contacts of Freud with the continent, for most of his life he considered Latin America an exotic region. In the best cases, Latin America was conceived of as a potential land of mission for the diffusion of psychoanalysis and, in the worst case, as a place to send undesirable people. In October 1920, in an ironic tone, he suggested to Italian psychoanalyst Edoardo Weiss that a certain individual, who remained unnamed but whom Freud obviously did not appreciate, could be sent to exile in South America (Freud & Weiss, 1979).

Freud was interested in the dissemination of his ideas *urbi et orbi*, and Latin America was no exception. He was aware of the early entrance of psychoanalysis to the region. However, for him the continent was an essentially exotic place, and this is perhaps why he showed a certain leniency towards the "deviations" committed by Latin American doctors, leniency that he did not show when the "deviants" lived and worked in more central places (i.e., in Europe). Only in a private letter did Freud complain to Delgado about the fact that the latter had included Adler's picture ("Adler's grimace," in Freud's words) alongside of his own (Freud's) at the end of the biography written by the Peruvian.[4]

The place of the "exotic" in Freud's thinking was complex. As Ranjana Khanna has pointed out, psychoanalysis originated and developed as a "colonial" discipline (Khanna, 2003). The Freudian association between the minds of neurotics and "primitive people," on the one hand, and children, on the other hand – particularly in works like *Totem and Taboo* – placed psychoanalysis in the same epistemological universe as ethnology, the other "colonial science." As Khanna points out, psychoanalysis and ethnology responded "to the same global political relations" (Khanna, 2003, p. 67). Furthermore, the "link" between children, the "primitive," and the neurotic was unidirectional. It was the clinical experience that allowed Freud to "understand" the mind of a Maori chief and not the other way around.

The difficulties that Freud experienced in dealing with the "exotic other" emerged clearly in his correspondence. For instance, in a letter dated November 30, 1911, to Sándor Ferenczi, he referred to the writing of *Totem and Taboo*, commenting, "The book on the Totem is giving me an enormous work. I am reading thick volumes without being really interested in them, given the fact that I already know what the end result is. My instinct tells me so" (Freud & Ferenczi, 1999). We can easily find similar reflections in his letters to Jung and to other close collaborators. The contact with the "other," therefore, was more "intuitive" than empirical. The conclusions did not depend on experience. This kind of knowledge, therefore, was placed outside the *Weltanschauung* in which Freud so dearly wanted to locate psychoanalysis – that of science.

Interested as Freud was in propagating psychoanalysis, he was in contact with doctors and intellectuals from "exotic" areas, such as the Far East and Latin America. As an enlightened scientist, he was drawn to archeology and antiques, with a strong interest in the objects associated with these regions. However, his personal letters show that he was not particularly patient with their people. He did not seem impressed, for instance, by the visit of prestigious Indian writer and philosopher Rabindranath Tagore in 1926, and even less by the visit of University of Calcutta philosophy professor Surendranath Dasgupta, shortly after. Freud immediately wrote to Ferenczi pointing out that his "need to see Indians was for the moment completely satisfied" (Hartnack, 2001, p. 138). Christiane Hartnack emphasized that Freud showed little interest in the theoretical developments of his Indian follower, Girîndrashekhar Bose, which were based on the specificity of Indian cultural phenomena. When Bose sent Freud a carved ivory statuette of Vishnu for his antique collection, the founder of psychoanalysis showed his appreciation for the present, but also made clear that the gift would have a place of honor on his desk only because it served as a reminder of the progress made by psychoanalysis and of its "proud conquest" of foreign countries and cultures (Hartnack, 2001, p. 1).

But what about Latin America? A search through the volumes of the *Standard Edition of the Complete Psychological Works of Sigmund Freud* immediately reveals that in all the 24 volumes, only three Latin Americans appear with their full names: Garcilaso de la Vega ("El Inca"; 1539–1616), whose *Comentarios reales de los Incas* Freud had already cited in his studies on cocaine; Chilean doctor Germán Greve (1869–1954); and his friend Honorio Delgado (1892–1969) (mentioned twice). Also very telling is the way in which Freud narrates the occasion when, according to him, psychoanalysis was discussed for the first time in the continent. In his *On the History of the Psychoanalytic Movement* of 1914, Freud wrote, "A physician from Chile (probably a German) spoke at the International Congress at Buenos Aires in 1910 in support of the existence of infantile sexuality and commended highly the effects of psycho-analytic therapy on obsessional symptoms" (Freud, 1966 [1914], p. 30). Only in a footnote does Freud identify the supposedly Chilean-German doctor as Germán Greve, a Chilean doctor born in Valparaíso in 1869. It is noteworthy, however, that by the time Freud wrote this piece he had known Greve for many years. In fact, three years earlier, in 1911, Freud himself had written an extensive commentary on Greve's paper for the journal *Zentralblatt für Psychanalyse*. But the story had started even earlier. In 1894, Greve had participated in the Conference of German Naturalists and Physicians that took place in Vienna. Among those who attended the meeting were prestigious doctors such as Otto Binswanger, Auguste Forel, Constantin von Monakow, Richard von Krafft-Ebing . . . and Sigmund Freud, who in the official picture of the participants to the conference appears standing just five persons away from Greve (Plotkin & Ruperthuz, 2017)!

Indians and semi-anonymous Chilean doctors, all seemed to be part of an undifferentiated mass of exotic people with whom Freud, nonetheless, interacted. Even his friend Honorio Delgado appears to have been of value for Freud only as long as he could operate as some kind of a psychoanalytical ambassador to Latin America.

Freud's Latin American relations

Freud's closest relation in Latin America was Delgado. Not only did they keep up a lasting correspondence, but Delgado also achieved the status of a semi-insider in Freud's inner circle of collaborators and was internationally recognized as such. He was invited to participate in official psychoanalytic gatherings, and his works were reviewed by psychoanalysts of the stature of Ernest Jones and Karl Abraham, among others.

Delgado had been born in Arequipa, Peru, in 1892. In 1915, at age 23, he published his first text on psychoanalysis in the newspaper *El Comercio de Lima*. His dissertation of 1918 was devoted completely to psychoanalysis. He sent a copy of it to Freud, who responded quickly and as a result pursued their epistolary exchange. Unlike most Latin Americans (with the exception of some Brazilians) who approached Freud's ideas through the works of French commentators, Delgado, who was married to a German woman, had access to Freud's works in the original language. Freud appreciated this and on more than one occasion showed his pleasure for Delgado's "high level of understanding" of psychoanalysis. This appreciation, however, stands in an apparent conflict with the fact that Delgado openly combined Freud's ideas with those of Alfred Adler. From the very beginning of their association, Freud and Delgado created a space for the transnational circulation not only of letters, but also of publications, photographs, and presents. Delgado even sent presents to Freud's grandchildren and, on at least two occasions, went with his wife to visit the Freud family in Vienna. Freud exchanged photographs with his Peruvian friend and asked him to submit contributions to the international psychoanalytic journals. At the same time, he routinely sent Delgado copies of his latest publications.

Beyond Freud's personal sympathy for Delgado and the Peruvian's admiration for the Viennese master, there were more concrete interests at play. For Delgado, the ability to show a personal proximity to Freud and his inner circle was important for consolidating his position as a psychiatrist in the emerging Peruvian – and by extension, Latin American – psychiatric field. Being in possession of Freud's letters, photographs, and publications placed him (at least in the eyes of other Latin Americans) in the position of an "insider" to the international psychoanalytic movement. Freud, on the other hand, was interested in maintaining a friendship with Delgado because of the prominent position that the latter occupied – in spite of his young age – in the Latin American psychiatric field and the level of recognition he enjoyed throughout the region. Moreover, Delgado and his mentor Hermilio Valdizán were the publishers of a prestigious journal, *Revista de Psiquiatría y Disciplinas Conexas*, that soon became a vehicle for the circulation of psychoanalytic ideas, not only in Peru, but also in Latin America at large. In a letter to Delgado, Freud expressed his frustration upon learning that the journal had ceased its publication in 1924. Thus wrote a very disappointed Freud,

> Dear Colleague: With regret, I have learned that your *Revista* has been discontinued and I would like to know the reasons, and if you do not think to compensate us with another publication. We were very proud that your journal served so exceptionally our cause.[5]

This journal was of outmost importance for Freud because it also opened its pages to other European psychoanalysts. As Karl Abraham commented to Ferenczi in 1920,

> In the Peruvian Revista de Psiquiátrica [sic] I have found a review of your book, my dear Ferenczi. I cite a passage: "A new book from the pen of this brilliant clinical psychologist is a happy event for those who are interested in scientific psychiatry." Are you satisfied with this? Unfortunately, this is, at the same time, one more piece of proof that no one is a prophet in his own land.
>
> (Wittenberger & Tögel, 2002, p. 188)

Nonetheless, Delgado was not taken *totally* seriously by the members of Freud's inner circle. In a circular-letter of the "Secret Committee"[6] dated in December 1920, Otto Rank pointed out, ironically,

> Delgado has sent a brief article for the Homage [to Freud]; from all those promised, this is the only one that has arrived in due time: from Peru!! However, it became weaker as a result of the long trip; nonetheless we beg you, dear Abraham, to translate this piece, which is only a few pages long, although it is written very poetically.
>
> (Freud & Abraham, 2001, p. 183)

A "very poetically" written piece that had, moreover, "bec[o]me weaker as a result of the long trip" did not seem very promising as a scientific article. Abraham – similarly to Jones – used a similar patronizing tone in his reviews of Delgado's work published in the *Zeitschrifft für Psychoanalyse* and the *International Journal of Psycho-Analysis*. While both European psychoanalysts praised Delgado's efforts in the diffusion of psychoanalysis in remote lands, they did not miss the opportunity to point out that the Peruvian's understanding of the Freudian system was far from complete. In particular, they criticized Delgado's eclectic combination of Freud's doctrines with those of Adler.

Delgado's case shows both how prominent a Latin American could be within Freud's inner circle and the limits to that prominence. While he was accepted by Freud's disciples because of his personal relationship with "the Professor," he was never considered an equal. It seems that Freud's interest in the Peruvian psychiatrist derived from Delgado's potential role as an ambassador of psychoanalysis in Latin America and not so much from Freud's appreciation for Delgado's ideas (Plotkin & Ruperthuz, 2017). Perhaps, had he analyzed the exchange between Freud and Delgado, French anthropologist Marcel Mauss may have understood this relationship as stemming from a system of gift exchange similar to those that he studied in Polynesia in the 1920s (Mauss, 2009). Those systems, according to Mauss, worked outside of, and predated, the establishment of a market-based economic system and constituted specific forms of social hierarchies and reciprocal obligations. After the completion of the exchange, the objects exchanged maintained a close association between the donors. The gifts carried the identity of the donor and a part of his/her essence. For Delgado, the possession of a present sent by Freud was perceived as some sort of an emblem that granted him legitimacy within the emerging psychoanalytic universe in Latin America. For Freud, the possession of Delgado's and other Latin Americans' publications and presents was valuable insofar as those objects bore testimony of the success of psychoanalysis in remote lands. This could explain Freud's zeal to keep the Latin American books when he left for his exile. It is worth recalling that, in his exchanges with Latin Americans, Freud hardly discussed any theoretical or clinical issue. The circulation of letters and other symbolic objects was valuable for what they represented – they somehow carried with them the essence of the donor – and not so much for their actual content.

Psychoanalysis for everybody:
Gastão Pereira da Silva

Although the exchange between Freud and Delgado provided benefits for both parties, this was not always the case in Freud's interactions with Latin Americans, as is exemplified by the trajectory of Brazilian doctor Gastão Pereira da Silva (1896–1987), whose possession of a letter from Freud became a tool for gaining legitimacy within the incipient Latin American psychoanalytic universe of the 1930s. It also shows the asymmetry existing in the relations between Freud and the Latin Americans.

Evidence suggests that Brazil was probably the first country in Latin America where psychoanalysis was known and discussed (Plotkin & Ruperthuz, 2017). Brazil also boasted the earliest attempts at institutionalizing psychoanalysis in the region. As early as 1927, a group of doctors, artists, and intellectuals of São Paulo created the short-lived *Sociedade Brasileira de Psicanálise* (Brazilian Society of Psychoanalysis), which received provisional recognition from the International Psychoanalytic Association (IPA). The society published a single issue of its journal, the *Revista Brasileira de Psychanályse*, which was duly sent to Freud and which he took with him to London in 1938. Among the members of this Brazilian association were Dr. Durval Marcondes, who would later be one of the founding members of the psychoanalytic profession in São Paulo; Dr. Julio Porto Carrero, a psychiatrist and criminologist active in Rio de Janeiro, who throughout his career published a large number of works on psychoanalysis and translated several of Freud's works into Portuguese; and Dr. Juliano Moreira, the first physician who discussed psychoanalysis in his native Bahia, among others. The society also attracted several avant-garde artists who showed an intellectual curiosity for psychoanalysis, but who did not intend to make a profession out of it. By the 1930s, there were active groups of people interested in Freud's ideas in different parts of the country.

There was one individual, however, who did not participate in any of these attempts at institutionalizing psychoanalysis but who nonetheless played a crucial role in the popular diffusion of Freud's thought in Brazil: Dr. Gastão Pereira da Silva. This doctor, active in Rio de Janeiro, was a self-taught devotee of psychoanalysis who was very committed to its dissemination. Throughout his long life, he published a large number of books on the topic; the first one, *Para comprender Freud*, was reissued 17 times during his long life. Pereira claimed to have written almost 100 novels with psychoanalytic content. As noted earlier, throughout the 1930s and 1940s, several popular magazines and newspapers in Latin America included a section on the psychoanalysis of dreams. Pereira da Silva, however, went even further than others did in this area. He published an impressive number of articles on psychoanalysis in popular magazines such as

O Malho and *O Carioca*, where he ran a column on psychoanalysis of dreams (Marcondes, 2015). In the 1940s, he also ran a popular radio show that focused on the interpretation of dreams. In 1940, Pereira da Silva wrote an apologetic book on Brazilian president Getulio Vargas's dictatorship based on his own idiosyncratic reading of Freud's *Group Psychology and the Analysis of the Ego* (1920). In this text, Pereira combined Freud's theories with those of Gustave Le Bon. We should remember, however, that *Group Psychology* starts with a critical discussion of Le Bon's ideas and that Freud was convinced that his own focus on the libidinal nature of human relationships had superseded Le Bon's theories of crowd psychology. According to Pereira da Silva, Vargas was the only politician who was able to capture the Brazilians' unconscious (Pereira da Silva, 1940). Overall, it could be argued that Pereira da Silva's works combined psychoanalysis, self-help, and sexology: a mixture that seems to have been very successful in Brazil at that time (Russo, 2002), at least among those who had access to the written media, though they represented a small minority of the Brazilian population.[7]

Pereira da Silva's case demonstrates how psychoanalysis developed not only as a therapeutic technique, but also as a cultural artifact located at the crossroads of the lettered and popular cultures. While Pereira did practice psychoanalysis – although he always claimed that he lived *for* psychoanalysis, never *from* psychoanalysis – he did not belong to the increasingly institutionalized psychoanalytic circuits of Brazil. As a (failed) candidate for membership to the prestigious Brazilian Academy of Letters, he belonged to the cultivated literary circles of Rio de Janeiro, but his trajectory was aimed at the popularization of psychoanalysis, in a way that transcended its reception in medical and lettered groups. However, he was in the possession of a valuable object that he used to get legitimacy among all those interested in psychoanalysis: a personal letter from Freud.

In many of his numerous publications, and even in interviews given to the media, Pereira da Silva mentioned or even included fragments (without revealing that they were just fragments) of the letter that Freud wrote to him in 1934 (Plotkin & Ruperthuz, 2017). Pereira manipulated the letter, presenting it as evidence of the respect and appreciation that Freud supposedly had for him. What follows is my own translation into English of Pereira da Silva's translation into Portuguese of Freud's letter (originally written in German), as he presented it in an interview he gave shortly before his death (*Revirão*, 1985):

I owe you much for having sent me your previous book, *Para comprender Freud*, and the most recent one, *A Psicanálise em 12 Lições*, as well as for all your efforts in favor of psychoanalysis, and also for your participation in the translations that you have done together with your friend, Dr. Ninitch, thus introducing that literature [on psychoanalysis] in your country. My name is still little known in Brazil, and only your effort and that of your friend Ninitch will make it better known.

Freud's letter also made reference to an autographed photograph that included the following handwritten note: "Remembering my own struggle against the bitterest resistances, I wish you the most satisfactory success." And then: "I give you with pleasure the autographed photography. I don't know what interest you may have in an image of the ugly physiognomy of an old man aged 78." In Freud's reference to his own old age, it is possible to perceive a certain ironic tone that seems to be absent from the rest of the letter.

The complete letter in German, which I was able to locate at the Freud Archive in the Library of Congress in Washington, DC, actually reads quite differently, and by comparing the original with Pereira's version, his manipulation becomes evident.

First of all, in the original letter Freud did not mention the titles of the two books that Pereira had sent him. Moreover, right after the paragraph translated above, there was another one (significantly omitted by Pereira da Silva) which reads as follows (my translation from German):

> And unfortunately I am not in the position of showing gratitude in the manner you wish. Since one year ago or more I have had no intention of writing references, introductions or recommendations after their number has exceeded the allowed number. In your particular case, there is, moreover, the additional obstacle that I do not read Portuguese, and therefore can only express some benevolent phrases. But you should not lament. My name is still little known in Brazil, and only your effort and that of your friend Ninitch will make it better known.[8]

As is easily seen here, the tone of the whole letter was very different from what Pereira da Silva wanted people to believe. The substantial omission in Pereira da Silva's translation was Freud's refusal to write a reference or letter of recommendation that the Brazilian doctor had clearly requested from him. The "additional obstacle" that Freud mentions shows, moreover, not only that he had not read the books that Pereira da Silva had sent him, but also that he would probably never read them. The remark that his name was unknown in Brazil was not only untrue – and Freud knew it well, for he had been in contact since the 1920s with other Brazilian doctors and anthropologists interested in psychoanalysis – but, in the context of the whole letter, it also looks as an ironic point aimed at reinforcing the lack of interest that Freud had for his correspondent. However, in the hands of Pereira da Silva, this letter became a kind of emblem that provided him legitimacy and a place of privilege in the emerging hierarchy of the Brazilian psychoanalytic world. Pereira claimed that he had received other letters from Freud, but these have never been located.

Alexander Lipschütz: A European scientist in Chile

So far, we have seen two paradigmatic cases of letter exchanges between Freud and Latin Americans. In the case of Honorio Delgado, this exchange was the result of a system of mutual benefits between the Peruvian and the founder of psychoanalysis. Each had something to gain in the exchange in addition to the personal affection that each seemed to feel for the other. In the case of Pereira da Silva, the relationship was largely unilateral. For Pereira da Silva, the possession of a personal letter written by Freud (and his photograph as well) became a crucial piece of evidence of his supposedly high standing within the psychoanalytic world. However, as becomes clear when Pereira's version of the letter is compared with the original, Freud showed very little interest in his correspondent. The gains in the relationship were only for Pereira.

The case of a European scientist established in Chile, who also exchanged a few letters with Freud, presents another epistolary dynamic between Freud and one of his followers in Latin America. Physiologist Alexander Lipschütz (1883–1980), born in Estonia but active in Germany and Austria, was already a well-known scientist in 1926 when he immigrated to Chile, where he became known as Alejandro Lipschutz. Back in Europe, Lipschutz (I follow here the Chilean spelling of his name) had done important work on the endocrine glands of mammals, showing the effects of implanting the sex glands of male and female guinea pigs into guinea pigs of the opposite sex. In 1919, Sándor Ferenczi called Freud's attention to Lipschutz's experiments (Freud & Ferenczi, 1999, p. 231), and Freud seems to have followed this work with interest. In the 1920s, Freud even cited Lipschutz's works in *Psychogenesis of a Case of Homosexuality in a Woman*, in the fourth edition of *Three Essays on Sexuality*, and in *Beyond the Pleasure Principle*. In Chile, Lipschutz became interested in psychoanalysis and wrote several pieces on it and on Freud. In 1938, he even tried to convince Freud to seek exile in Chile (Vetö & Sánchez, 2017).

Lipschutz's epistolary relationship with Freud started in 1927, when he sent him the text of a lecture written in Spanish that he had given in Chile. Freud did not associate the name of Lipschutz with that of the European scientist. Thus, he replied with a letter in which he thanked Lipschutz for the text (which could not be located and whose title is not mentioned), pointing out that his knowledge of Spanish had allowed him to understand it without any problem.[9] He continued, "You are a physiologist, which I, in my young years, wanted to become. Only the understanding advice of my revered teacher Ernst Brücke, who knew about my poor material conditions, took me to other paths." Freud ends his letter by expressing his satisfaction for Lipschutz's knowledge of psychoanalysis and saying that, if other people in Chile had a similar level of expertise, then he had nothing to fear about the fate of his discipline around the world.

Four years later, in 1931, Freud wrote another letter to Lipschutz. This second letter contains some noteworthy points. By then, Freud suspected who his correspondent was. Therefore, Lipschutz, who in the first letter was addressed as "Dear Colleague," in the second one became "Respected Professor." Freud continued his letter by pointing out that he was then on vacation and, therefore, was not in the position of checking if the Alexander Lipschütz he was addressing his letter to was the same person he had cited "several times" in his own works, and from whose book on the implantation of glands published in 1919 he (Freud) had learned so much. Freud was not aware that Lipschutz had moved to Chile. The second point of interest of this letter lies in its focus on one of Freud's pet topics: the resistances that psychoanalysis generates in society. Apparently, Lipschutz had mentioned in his letter the resistances that his own research on physiology was generating in Chile. Freud immediately associated Lipschutz's preoccupations with his own, but emphasized, at the same time, the supposed specificities of psychoanalysis. While for Freud it was absolutely natural that his own doctrine tended to awaken resistances, since it destroyed illusions and prejudices, he showed perplexity for those that Lipschutz's research might have generated. In the myth of origin that Freud and his immediate followers had constructed for psychoanalysis, resistances were not part of a normal reaction to just any new form of knowledge, which, in this specific case, also threatened well-established hierarchies within the psychiatric profession around the world. For Freud and his disciples, the very concept of resistance was only applicable to psychoanalysis, and this was due exclusively to its supposedly disruptive nature and to the effects that the truth it revealed had on society, in analogy to the resistances emerging in patients during the therapeutic work.

Finally, Freud went back to another one of his obsessions: the compatibility (or lack thereof) between psychoanalysis and biology. He expressed his satisfaction to learn that Lipschutz, like Freud himself, did believe that the conclusions of psychoanalysis were not incompatible with those of endocrinology, "as if the psychic process could be explained directly by the effect of the glands, or if the intelligence of the psychic mechanisms could replace the knowledge of the underlying chemistry."

Thus, we see from the letters between Freud and Lipschutz that once Freud recognized in his correspondent a prestigious European scientist, his tone changed completely. Not only did it become less formal (Freud recognized Lipschutz as a peer), but Freud also delved into certain concrete aspects of Lipschutz's work in a way that was not common in the letters he wrote to other Latin Americans.

Letter from a young Argentine student

Unlike the extensive correspondence that Freud kept with his European followers and collaborators, the exchanges he maintained with Latin Americans avoided clinical or theoretical discussions. Latin Americans in general wrote to Freud to express their admiration for the master; Freud usually replied by thanking them politely for the texts that they sent him and encouraging his interlocutors to keep on working on psychoanalysis. To some extent, this was true even in his letters to Honorio Delgado. In a correspondence that lasted for almost 20 years, one cannot find a single theoretical or clinical discussion; Freud made specific references to the content of Delgado's work only to correct some supposedly factual mistakes present in the biography.

To my knowledge, the only case in which Freud did indulge in some kind of theoretical discussion with a Latin American correspondent is not found in any letter addressed to one of his admirers or to an aspiring psychoanalyst, but rather in one written in response to a young medical student from Buenos Aires.[10] Although the student, Cayetano Paglione, appreciated Freud's ideas, he also criticized some of them, and Freud felt compelled to respond to those criticisms. The exchange is noteworthy because this is one of the very few cases in which we have both sides of the correspondence – the letter originally written in Spanish by Paglione and boldly addressed on the envelope to "Dr. Freud, Viena" (he did not actually know Freud's street address), and Freud's response in German. The very fact that a letter addressed to "Dr. Freud, Viena" reached its addressee bears witness to the level of recognition that Freud enjoyed in 1935 in his native city and beyond.

Paglione started his letter by expressing his admiration for Freud. However, immediately after, he questioned what he considered to be the incomplete character of Freud's theory of dreams. Paglione remembered having read "something very acceptable" on dreams – he would not say exactly what it was – according to which certain vibrations produced in the brain were the common source of dreams and memories. Paglione also criticized the concept of the death instinct, which he considered to be a mere "superstition or predestination." According to Paglione, this was the only portion of Freud's theory that was based on prejudices, rather than on the result of actual empirical research. The young student ended his letter by wishing that psychoanalysis would extend its scope of applications and could therefore address a large variety of aspects of human life.

Freud's response, written in German, in his usual Gothic handwriting, addressed both points of criticism. Regarding dreams, Freud determined that the theory of brain vibrations was "completely a-psychological and therefore incompatible with our analytic findings on dreams." More interesting, however, was the refutation he offered to the criticism of the death instinct. In this case, Freud did not use psychological arguments. The problem, according to him, was that Paglione had ignored the fact that the death instinct was an "organic force," and its interest for psychoanalysis as an object of study derived from its psychological manifestation. Specifically, Freud pointed out that the acceptation of the existence of a death instinct was current knowledge among the biologists. Once again, as in the case of his letter to Lipschutz, Freud wanted to underline the compatibilities existing between psychoanalysis and biology.

At the end of his letter, Freud emphasized the need for having previous experience in psychoanalysis as a precondition for a proper understanding of his ideas. He also pointed out that he had no knowledge of the edition of his work that Paglione mentioned in his letter. Apparently, it was a Chilean edition of a book titled *La libido y la psicoanálisis* (1934), boasting a prologue by Waldo Frank. It seems that it was one of the many pirate editions of Freud's works that enjoyed a broad circulation in Latin America. Although Freud's *Obras completas* translated by Luis López Ballesteros had been available in Spanish for a decade, many people, like Paglione, approached Freud's works through a parallel circuit of editions that, in most cases, were commercialized without the author's knowledge and consent.[11]

Conclusions

The place of Latin America in the development of psychoanalysis in its triple character as a theory of the mind, a therapeutic technique, and a broadly defined cultural artifact located at the crossroads of lettered and popular culture has been largely overlooked by the general histories of psychoanalysis. This chapter is a contribution to filling this gap by focusing on one specific aspect of Freud's biography that also has been largely ignored: his personal contacts with Latin Americans. Although Freud's Latin American correspondents were very few in number compared to those in Europe or North America, these epistolary exchanges shed light on the ways in which psychoanalysis was received in the region and on Freud's thoughts and feelings about both the reception of psychoanalysis in Latin America and on the place that Latin America occupied in the development of psychoanalysis as a transnational system of ideas and beliefs. Today, some countries in the region, such as Argentina and Brazil, are considered international centers for the production, circulation, and consumption of psychoanalysis, particularly the cities of Buenos Aires, São Paulo, and Rio de Janeiro. Spanish and, to a lesser extent, Portuguese have been accepted as semi-official languages for the discussion of psychoanalysis. Though the place of psychoanalysis in Latin American urban culture has a long history, only in recent decades did scholars begin to explore it. Today, there is an active scholarship on different aspects of the history of psychoanalysis in various Latin American countries.[12] However, with a few exceptions (Bosteels, 2012; Damousi & Plotkin, 2009; Damousi & Plotkin, 2012; Gallo, 2010; Plotkin & Ruperthuz, 2017), that scholarship has been "national" in character. In other words, as a rule, research on this topic has addressed the way in which psychoanalysis developed in specific countries rather than in Latin America in general. Moreover, the general histories of psychoanalysis, as well as Freud's biographies, have largely overlooked the role of Latin America in the development of psychoanalysis and in Freud's own life.[13] In this contribution I have selected a few exchanges between Freud and Latin Americans that illustrate the different patterns of reception of psychoanalysis in the region as well as the perceptions that Latin Americans had of Freud and his work, on the one hand, and how Freud conceptualized the development of his system of thought in "exotic lands," on the other. I hope that this chapter constitutes a step forward in the process of bringing Latin America back to the general historiography on psychoanalysis.

Acknowledgements

I thank Piroska Csúri for her comments on this text. This research was partially funded by a Pluriannual Project from CONICET (Argentina), PIP 1122013 0100024CO, and by PICT 2013–2770, and by a PUE (CONICET): 229201601 00005CO.

Notes

1 Portions of this article are based on *Estimado Dr. Freud: Una historia cultural del psicoanálisis en América Latina* (Plotkin & Ruperthuz, 2017).
2 Freud studied Spanish together with his friend Eduard Silberstein. Parts of the letters they exchanged between 1871 and 1881 were written in crude Spanish (Boehlich, 1990).
3 The correspondence between Freud and Delgado was first published by Álvaro Rey de Castro (1983).
4 Letter from Freud to Delgado, October 2, 1926. Freud wrote textually, "Nur die reproduction der Adler-Fratze hätten Sie mir esparen können." (Delgado, 1989, p. 537).
5 Letter from Freud to Delgado, March 20, 1925 (Delgado, 1989, p. 536).
6 The "Secret Committee" was created by Ernest Jones in the wake of the conflict between Freud and Jung. Patterned after secret lodges, it consisted of a group of Freud's most loyal disciples who were ready to defend the psychoanalytic cause against enemies both from within and from without.
7 As late as 1955, over 50% of the population was illiterate.
8 The letter is housed at the Freud Archive, Library of Congress, Washington, DC, Folder 19.
9 The letters are found in the Freud Archive, Library of Congress, Box 36, Folder 32. The letters from Freud were also published in Spanish in Lipschutz (1958).
10 I want to express my gratitude to Horacio Tarcus for giving me access to the letters that his father exchanged with Freud.
11 For an extended discussion on the circulation of Freud's ideas in Latin America, see Plotkin and Ruperthuz (2017).
12 Brazil is probably the country that has the largest number of scholars working on different aspects of the history of psychoanalysis, including not only historians, but also anthropologists and sociologists. It is impossible to list the large number of works on the topic. In Argentina and Chile, as well as in Mexico and Colombia, there are also research groups working on the history of different aspects of the "psychoanalytic world." Some of these contributions can be found in the online journal *CulturasPsi/ PsyCultures*: www.culturaspsi.org
13 See, for instance, Makari (2008) and Zaretsky (2004). See also the recent biography of Freud by Elisabeth Roudinesco (2014), where the mention of Freud's relationships with Latin Americans is limited to Delgado's biography of Freud. Apparently, these otherwise fine pieces of scholarship have largely ignored Latin America.

References

Boehlich, W. (Ed.). (1990). *The letters of Sigmund Freud to Edouard Silberstein (1871–1881)*. Cambridge, MA: Belnak Press.

Bosteels, B. (2012). *Marx and Freud in Latin America: Politics, psychoanalysis and religion in times of terror*. New York, NY: Verso.

Capetillo Hernández, J. (2012). *La emergencia del psicoanálisis en México*. Xalapa, Mexico: Universidad Veracruzana.

Damousi, J., & Plotkin, M. (Eds.) (2009). *The transnational unconscious: Essays in the history of psychoanalysis and transnationalism*. London, England: Palgrave-Macmillan.

Damousi, J., & Plotkin, M. (Eds.) (2012). *Psychoanalysis and politics: Histories of psychoanalysis under conditions of restricted political freedom*. New York, NY: Oxford University Press.

Davies, J. K., & Fichtner, G. (Eds.) (2006). *Freud's library: A comprehensive catalogue*. London, England and Tübingen, Germany: The Freud Museum/Edition Diskord.

Delgado, H. F. (1926). *Sigmund Freud*. Lima, Peru: C. F. Southwell.

Delgado, H. F. (1933). *A vida e a obra de Freud*. Rio de Janeiro, Brazil: Marisa.

Delgado, H. F. (1989). *Freud y el psicoanálisis. Escritos y testimonios*. Introducción, compilación y notas por Javier Mariátegui. Lima, Peru: Universidad Peruana Cayetano Heredia Fondo Editorial.

Freud, S. (1966 [1914]). On the history of the psychoanalytic movement. In S. Freud (Ed.), *The standard edition of the complete psychological works of Sigmund Freud* (vol. XIV). London, England: The Hogarth Press.

Freud, S. (1974). *Cocaine papers*. New York, NY: Stonehill.

Freud, S., & Abraham, K. (2001). *Correspondencia Completa (1907–1919)*. Madrid, Spain: Síntesis.

Freud, S., & Ferenczi, S. (1999). *Correspondencia Completa (1917–1919)*. Madrid, Spain: Síntesis.

Freud, S., & Weiss, E. (1979). *Problemas de la práctica psicoanalítica. Correspondencia Freud-Weiss*. Barcelona, Spain: Gedisa.

Gallo, R. (2010). *Freud's Mexicco: Into de wilds of psychoanalysis*. Cambridge, MA: MIT Press.

Hartnack, C. (2001). *Psychoanalysis in colonial India*. Oxford, England: Oxford University Press.

Khanna, R. (2003). *Dark continent: Psychoanalysis and colonialism*. Durham, NC: Duke University Press.

Lipschutz, A. (1958). *Tres médicos contemporáneos: Pavlov, Freud, Schweitzer*. Buenos Aires, Argentina: Losada.

Makari, G. (2008). *Revolution in mind: The creation of psychoanalysis*. New York, NY: Harper, 2009.

Marcondes, S. (2015). *Nós, os charlatães. Gastão Pereira da Silva e a divulgação da psicanáilse em O Malho (1936–1944)*. M.A. Thesis. Casa de Oswaldo Cruz-Fiocruz.

Martínez, C. (1885). Medicina: contribución al estudio de la cocaína Memoria de prueba para optar al grado de Licenciado en Medicina. *Anales de la Universidad de Chile*, 257.

Mauss, M. (2009). *Ensayo del don. Forma y función del intercambio en las sociedades arcaicas*. Buenos Aires, Argentina: Katz editores.

Pereira da Silva, G. (1940). *Getulio Vargas e a psicanálise das multidões*. Rio de Janeiro, Brazil: Zelio Valverde.

Plotkin, M. (2007). Sueños del pasado y del futuro. La interpretación de los sueños y la difusión del psicoanálisis en Buenos Aires (1930–1950). In S. Gayol & M. Madero (Eds.), *Formas de historia cultural*. Buenos Aires, Argentina: UNGS-Prometeo.

Plotkin, M., & Ruperthuz, M. (2017). *Estimado Dr. Freud. Una historia cultural del psicoanálisis en América Latina*. Buenos Aires, Argentina: Edhasa.

Revirão. (1985). *Gastão Pereira da Silva*. Brazil: Rio de Janeiro.

Rey de Castro, Á. (1983). Freud y Honorio Delgado. Crónica de un desencuentro. *Hueso Húmero*, *15–16*, 5–76.

Roudinesco, E. (2014). *Freud en son teps et dans le nôtre*. Paris, France: Éditions de Seuil.

Ruperthuz, M. (2015). *Freud y los chilenos. Un viaje transnacional (1910–1949)*. Santiago, Chile: Pólvora Editorial.

Russo, J. (2002). A difusão da psicanálise no Brasil na primeira metade do século XX. Da vanguarda modernista a radio-novela. *Estudos e Pesquisas em Psicologia*, *2*(1), 53–64.

Stubbe, H. (2011). *Sigmund Freud in den Tropen. Die erste Psychoanalytische Dissertation in der portugiesichsprachigen Welt (1914)*. Aachen, Germany: Shaker Verlag.

Vetö, S., & Sánchez, M. (2017). Sigmund Freud and Alejandro Lipschutz: Psychoanalysis and biology between Europe and Chile. *History of the Human Sciences*, *30*(1), 7–31.

Wittenberger, G., & Tögel, C. (2002). *Las circulares del "Comité Secreto"* (2 vols.). Madrid, Spain: Síntesis.

Zaretsky, E. (2004). *Secrets of the soul: A social and cultural history of psychoanalysis.* New York, NY: Vintage Books.

Chapter 2

Psychoanalysts bearing witness

Trauma and memory in Latin America

Nancy Caro Hollander

It is March 2016 and I am once again in Buenos Aires, this time to participate along with my Argentine psychoanalytic colleagues in events to mark the 40th anniversary of the military dictatorship that disappeared, tortured, and murdered 30,000 Argentine men, women, and children. At the moment, I am in the office of the Grandmothers of the Plaza de Mayo, speaking with its gracious and energetic president, 86-year-old Estela Carlotto. We have had many conversations over the years, but this time we are being filmed for a video whose purpose is to convey to U.S. citizens the nature of the psychosocial impact of state terror and the contributions of psychoanalytic activists to the reparation of individual and group trauma. After describing the history of the Grandmothers' decades-long search for their disappeared grandchildren, Estela passionately asserts the importance of remembering and grieving the past: "When political crimes are denied and forgotten," she says emphatically, "they are repeated." Her warning about the danger of social amnesia – *olvido* – reflects the political stance of the human rights movement that has struggled on behalf of memory – *memoria* – to challenge the state's policies of amnesty for the former torturers and its rationale that forgetting about the past is necessary for national reconciliation. Until the election of Nestor Kirchner in 2003, this governmental strategy of impunity left intact traumatic wounds in the body politic, which are revived during each political and economic crisis that threatens to destabilize daily life.

As I converse with Estela, buoyed by her contagious resilience, I am simultaneously aware of a vaguely melancholic feeling floating along the edges of my attentiveness to our exchange. This is a familiar experience, for like so many Argentines, I lost loved ones to the torturers' weapons. Reminiscent of what Anne Alvarez calls "the thinking heart" (2017), my emotional identification with the pain of survivors informs my intellectual interrogation about the dynamics and goals of state terror and its tenacious psychological hold on those who lived through it as well as their progeny who suffer its unresolved legacy. I am also inspired by the example of those Argentine psychoanalysts who have over the past half-century dedicated their energies to community activism during the most extreme of social situations. This chapter tells their story, one that I believe can serve as a model for psychoanalysts in general as we witness growing economic inequities and authoritarian movements that threaten social stability and psycho-logical welfare in the Global North as well as the Global South.

The psychosocial dynamics of authoritarianism

The state terrorist regimes that took power in Latin America's Southern Cone during the 1970s strove to eliminate the progressive political movements that had since the late 1960s mobilized millions in support of a radical redistribution of power and resources. The case of Argentina is illustrative of the pattern in which the state protected the elite-dominated status quo by marshaling the entire apparatus of military, legal, education, medical, mass media, and religious institu-tions to impose an insidious culture of fear on the populace. The hegemonic tools of the terrorist state – the soldiers, tanks, submachine guns, hooded kidnappers, torturers, electrical prods, the disappeared, the torture victims – were utilized to annihilate the mind's capacity for critical thought, thereby securing adaptation to military rule for a time. The entire society, not only the men, women, and children whose raped, tortured, and massacred bodies were the victims of human rights abuses, was the target of state terror. One of the Argentine generals expressed the junta's goals succinctly: "First," he warned ominously, "we are going to kill all of the subversives; then their collaborators; then their sympathizers; then the indif-ferent; and finally, the timid" (Hollander, 2010, p. 91).

The armed forces and paramilitary organizations attacked groups and individu-als they labeled as "subversive," but they also randomly detained and kidnapped apolitical citizens in their homes, at their workplaces, and on the streets in order to impose a terrifying and unpredictable social reality and to splinter public ties. While the state denied the existence of secret concentration camps and its policy of disappearing tens of thousands of citizens, selective release of torture victims functioned as a warning to others about what could befall them if they resisted authoritarian rule (Argentine National Commission on the Disappeared, 1986). As the population was terrorized into silence and isolation, behavior became char-acterized by inexpressiveness, inhibition, and self-censorship (Hollander, 1997, pp. 111–119).

A minority of politically conservative Argentines benefited from the military's economic policies and accepted its ideological justification that the disappear-ances, torture, and murder were necessary to defend Western Christian civilization threatened by a political opposition defined as a cancer on the body politic. Their identification was facilitated by unconscious defenses, including the projection of disavowed aggression onto the disappeared and murdered, whose annihilation could thus be justified. However, the majority of citizens experienced the military project as a threat to civilization and became victims of the military's doctrine of "collective guilt." Daily life became inscribed with persecutory anxiety, reflected in a pattern of hyper-vigilance and the creation of a false self to hide one's disaf-fection with the regime. It became too risky to trust co-workers and neighbors, and children were admonished not to tell classmates about their personal lives or make eye contact with strangers on the street or in the subway. Intimidated progressive activists were driven to disavow their deeply held belief systems and former political commitments. Dissociation of aspects of the self also occurred at an unconscious level as individuals disavowed the part of their personalities that threatened annihilation because of affinity for the politics and values of the victims of arbitrary repression (Hollander, 2010). Identification with the aggressor was an unavoidable outcome among those who became passive bystanders, watching silently as the soldiers and death squads ruthlessly snatched people out of restaurants, classrooms, offices, factories, and even their own homes, disappearing them into thin air. "*Habrá hecho algo*" (He or she must have been up to something) became a frequently noted reaction, one that denied any identification with the disappeared and simultaneously lent a veil of rationality to the state's repressive actions so as to quell the terror that one could be the next victim of completely arbitrary political acts.

Within the ongoing traumatic impact of the culture of fear, healthy mourning for losses suffered was impossible. Those whose loved ones were disappeared experienced a politically imposed phenomenon that Argentine psychoanalysts call "frozen grief" (M. Langer, personal communication, León, Nicaragua, June 14, 1983). Families were caught in an anguishing contradiction: they could not mourn without risking intense guilt, for without proof of death, to give up searching for the lost loved one and to go on with one's life was tantamount to a kind of murder. But to maintain the mental representation of the disappeared, to keep him or her alive, imposed a profound form of mental suffering. Not knowing about the individual's actual fate produced an intra-psychic elaboration that included fantasies of the possible torments to his or her mind and body, fantasies based on knowledge of the state's (disavowed) concentration camps and other centers of torture. Obsessive rumination about the terrifying fate of the loved one caused acute anxiety and could result in the wish to free the victim from suffering through the fantasy of his or her death, a wish that produced intense guilt feelings. For families caught in this dilemma, living intimately with the fantasy of the tortured, disappeared loved one was itself a psychological torture that had no resolution.

Psychoanalytic activism in times of terror

Community activism among psychoanalysts in Argentina began in the late 1960s as they joined other intellectuals in adapting the critical ideas of Sartre, Althusser, Fromm, and Marcuse to an analysis of the increasingly polarized political conditions of Argentina (Hollander, 1997, p. 62–78). Some training analysts and many candidates also grew increasingly critical of the Argentine Psychoanalytic Association (APA) for its hierarchical structure, internal power struggles, and lack of response to increasing police and paramilitary repression, especially in light of the growing vocal opposition among many social sectors, including other professionals. Those analysts who participated in social projects in impoverished working class and immigrant communities were direct witnesses to the paramilitary intrusion into daily life. Their provision of psychological services to diverse populations in non-traditional settings was exciting, but at times threatening as well. The military and police presence was increasingly intimidating as these analysts worked alongside other social activists to address the structural and institutional sources of the class, race, and gendered oppression that fostered psychological disease among the poor and marginalized populations they were attending. Their experience taught them that the social questions facing all Argentines must be taken up within the APA as part of the legitimate concerns of psychoanalysis (Hollander, 1990).

The APA's leadership insisted on the need to maintain neutrality in the interest of value-free scientific inquiry as well as in clinical technique. The dissidents critiqued the neutrality principle, arguing that scientific inquiry was always organized by the ideological frame of the investigator and that everything about the psychoanalyst, including her language, demeanor, clothing, address, consultation room, and fees, represented a specific insertion within class and culture, negating the possibility of neutrality, even in the transference relationship. These progressive analysts' views reflected an international movement within psychoanalysis during the era of France '68, the failed Czech revolution of the same year, the U.S. anti-war movement, and more. In the early 1970s, during two International Psychoanalytic Association (IPA) meetings, a number of candidates and their teachers and analysts organized several counter-congresses to address the urgent social issues provoked by a world in turmoil. But it was the Argentines, including some of the most prestigious training analysts, who in 1971 broke with their IPA-affiliated society in order to develop a psychoanalytic praxis they considered to be more responsive to the psychosocial realities of Argentina. For a brief period, they were able to put their radical theory into practice through the creation in 1972 of an autonomous institute, the Research and Training Center, that provided an unprecedented opportunity to non-medical mental health professionals to obtain formal psychoanalytic training. The innovative training program included classes in psychoanalytic theory and radical social theory, with a clinical practicum whose patients came from the radical, grassroots labor unions. These analysts also offered psychoanalytic psychotherapy to working-class people in public hospitals and clinics that aimed to integrate psychoanalysis with progressive political goals.

Thus it was that following the military coup, psychoanalysts and other mental health professionals were a specific target of state repression. Although they were viewed as containers of their patients' secrets and thus an important source of potential information regarding the "subversive" opposition to the social order, they were targets as well, because they were identified with the ideas of Sigmund Freud. Unable to abide by political and philosophical pluralism, the terrorist state rejected the modern age with all of its contradictions. As the military succinctly put it,

Argentina has three main enemies: Karl Marx because he tried to destroy the Christian concept of society; Sigmund Freud, because he tried to destroy the Christian concept of the family; and Albert Einstein, because he tried to destroy the Christian concept of time and space.

(Timmerman, 1982, p. 130)

Some psychoanalysts were disappeared, and along with the thousands of other disappeared, they were tortured. Within this general environment of intimidation, the majority of psychoanalysts, like the citizenry in general, withdrew into an isolated social and professional life, supporting the APA, which refused to publicly criticize the state's extreme human rights violations.

However, the practice of psychoanalysis was seriously compromised. In the culture of fear, free association became untenable because unguarded thoughts and feelings threatened to reveal information that might be potentially dangerous to the patient and/or the analyst. The analytic function became more difficult to provide, for when patients spoke of traumatic personal situations arising from the politically repressive environment, analysts' ability to listen was compromised by associations to their own concerns, conflicts, and fears produced by the same conditions. Too often analysts took shelter in their own or their patients' denial about threats emanating from external reality, preferring to find refuge in interpretations that focused on infantile sources of anxiety or on the transference relationship. The extreme social situation in which these psychoanalysts practiced revealed the inevitable convergences between psychic and social reality, a theme that would attract increasing attention within the profession throughout the world in subsequent decades.

However, a network of dissident psychoanalysts chose to practice a psychoanalysis that addressed the dialectical relationship between social and psychic reality. They held that it was important to recognize their own anxieties and symptoms of ongoing trauma so that they could be more effective in understanding those of their patients. They aimed to responsibly balance the professional mandate to focus on patients' subjective reality with the concomitant need to provide reality testing to individuals whose denial of external danger put them at risk (J. C. Volnovich, personal communication, Buenos Aires, Argentina, August 13, 1990).

Those who treated the direct victims of state terror – survivors of torture and families of the disappeared – concluded that in conditions of such extreme political polarization, they could be effective only if their patients knew of their opposition to military rule. They embraced a therapeutic perspective defined as "ethical non-neutrality." These analysts collaborated with human rights activists who were aiding poor and working-class communities, many of whose members had been disappeared. Argentine psychoanalyst Julia Braun, whose adolescent son had been disappeared, describes how the only thing that helped her bear the anguish of her loss was to participate with other health professionals in a progressive church project in a poor immigrant community, where she offered individual and group psychotherapy to the many families suffering from the same kind of "frozen grief" as she. Although her project was designed to bring professional help to the impoverished parishioners, Braun experienced it as a profound source of mutual support, a kind of therapeutic community. This activism permitted Braun to escape her isolation through a courageous alliance with the victims of the armed forces. It also provided a source of continuity with her son, because she was with people who shared his values and political commitments. "We experienced a sense of gratification and mutual appreciation.... And it was, as well, a profound source of reparation. I could help them with their losses in a way that I couldn't help the loved one whom I myself had lost" (J. Braun, personal communication, Buenos Aires, Argentina, October 7, 1994).

Three other Argentine psychoanalysts – Diana Kordon, Dario Lagos, and Lucila Edelman – were also convinced that their psychological survival of state terror lay in their willingness to act in concert with their ego ideal, which meant an active commitment to human rights and opposition to military rule. They formed a Team of Psychological Assistance (Equipo) to work with the Mothers of the Plaza de Mayo, the first human rights group in the country (distinct from the aforementioned Grandmothers of the Plaza de Mayo), to challenge the "silence rule" of the military regime. According to Edelman, their identification with the Mothers' struggles to locate their disappeared children and grandchildren made it possible for them to develop this unique therapeutic team effort on their behalf (Kordon & Edelman, 1986). These psychoanalysts helped the Mothers organization deal with basic questions, such as what to tell the children whose parent or parents had been disappeared; how to deal with problems that emerge in the couple relationship of parents of a disappeared loved one; or how to help parents tolerate the uncertainty and anguish of not knowing about the fate of their disappeared children and grandchildren. They created small groups composed of the families so they could participate together in the elaboration of these and other issues. The Equipo members have observed the salutary effect of participants' activism in the Mothers organization, the value of which lies in the Mothers' refusal to accept the terms of the terrorist state. Their discourse articulates the existence of a responsible party that has disappeared their children, and they demand an accounting of the guilty. Kordon and Edelman suggest that the Mothers' organization sheds light on the relationship between political resistance and mental health, noting that these women have been more able to work through the traumatic loss of their loved ones in part because their activist group has become a privileged relationship, giving a new meaning to group links beyond the family.

> The struggle for peace and justice means another type of relationship with the [child] . . . the ego ideal system has been altered: to be a mother now means 'to fight for all our children' or 'to fight for life'
> (Kordon & Edelman, 1986, p. 63).

Kordon argues that involvement in the Mothers organization is potentially healing because loss is no longer individualized, detached from its historical context, but is now part of the collective process that produced it and can now potentiate its reparation. "The Mothers' transcendence of isolation and their commitment to act as historical agents are essential to the resolution of the pathological effects of social trauma." The Equipo members also point out that their own political activism, which often required manic defenses to ward off the terrors that might have otherwise immobilized them, permitted them to find strength in the solidarity of the group and rescued them from the sense of helplessness that accompanied an isolated and passive endurance of state terror.

In neighboring Chile, Elizabeth Lira and her colleagues braved potential retribution from the Pinochet dictatorship by treating its victims in the psychiatric and medical section of The Catholic Foundation of Social Aid (FASIC), where they offered psychological treatment to ex-prisoners, families of the disappeared, and torture victims. They recorded testimonies by hundreds of people who had been illegally imprisoned and tortured. "It was so sad, men and women so young: twenty, twenty-two year olds . . . so destroyed. I had a hard time psychologically containing both for them and for me something that was almost uncontainable" (Hollander, 1997, p. 136). The FASIC therapists read about the Holocaust and began an ongoing dialogue with therapists from other countries who practiced under similar conditions in order to elaborate a psychosocial analysis of state terror.

For Lira and her colleagues, treatment issues were connected to the struggle to end the dictatorship. Their patients' participation in the testimonials project was meaningful because the reality of their experiences could be confirmed by their therapist-witnesses, a central component in the elaboration of trauma. Analysts and patients shared in a political act by sending these testimonials to international human rights organizations and the United Nations to expose and denounce the dictatorship. In 1983, Lira and her colleagues assembled two volumes of articles detailing their psychoanalytic observations and, using pseudonyms for their safety, distributed copies clandestinely in human rights congresses (Lira, 1994). After forming the Latin American Institute of Mental Health and Human Rights (ILAS) in 1988, Lira commented that her psychoanalytic training had proved essential to her work:

> I came to realize that behaviorist treatment models were of no use in addressing those affected by state terror . . . only a psychoanalytic conceptualization of the psychic apparatus and psychoanalytic clinical techniques could make our therapeutic work effective. But I also became convinced that the patient's relationship with the analyst under these conditions needed to be thought of as more complex than simply a matter of transference. In fact, the patient-therapist relationship was often a transformative one, in which the patient learned to be able to depend on the analyst, not only for psychological support, but for practical help in resolving problems related to basic necessities, like finding work, locating housing, and searching for the disappeared.
>
> (Hollander, 2010, p.147)

When working with victims of state terror, the notion of neutrality appeared totally irrelevant to Lira, who insists that her patients' knowledge of her opposition to the military dictatorship was fundamental to the working alliance. Without such assurance, she asks, how would victims of state terror be able to speak, thinking the therapist might be on the side of the enemy? "It is this shared context that permits the patient to risk entering into the treatment and disclosing traumatic experiences related to torture and forced disappearances. In this sense, the therapeutic relationship is itself reparative" (Lira, 1994).

Uruguayan psychoanalysts who treated survivors of torture and families of the disappeared noted similar experiences. Former president of the Uruguayan Psychoanalytic Association, Marcelo Viñar, known among his colleagues for his opposition to military rule, was arrested and interned in a prison infamous for its torture of prisoners. His experiences as a captive were illustrative of what he terms the "demolition of the psychic apparatus" produced by modern torture techniques that include the imposition of states of traumatic helplessness as well as the humiliation that comes from one's complete dehumanization (M. Viñar, personal communication, Montevideo, Uruguay, October 10, 1990). Viñar's own experience, including the difficult aftermath of states of depression and compromised capacities to resume life as usual with family, friends, and colleagues, magnified by the travails of exile, helped him to understand the plight of the torture survivors he subsequently treated.

Those psychoanalysts in Argentina, Chile, and Uruguay, who were pursued by the military and forced into exile, lived for a time in other countries where they continued their human rights work (see Hollander, 2010). They offered their clinical skills to victims of state terror in the exile communities, contributed to the growing literature analyzing the psychological effects of social trauma, and participated in the international campaigns to denounce the illegal and immoral military governments that held their populations hostage. When from the mid-1980s these dictatorships gave way under domestic and international pressures for a return to democratic governance, psychoanalysts came home from exile. They faced the dual demands of reconstituting their personal and professional lives and taking part in the struggles for social and psychological reparation.

The culture of impunity and psychoanalytic witnessing

The psychic vicissitudes produced by state terror have endured during the decades following the military's return to the barracks. As indicated earlier, in Argentina as well as in Chile and Uruguay, until recently, post-dictatorship governments endorsed policies of immunity for former perpetrators. In so doing, they refused to bear witness to survivors' experience of state organized repression, thereby compromising their potential for working through traumatic losses. Loss and the mourning process require recognition by others, an acknowledgement that the experience is real. While psychoanalysis, following Freud, Klein, and others, has tended to conceptualize mourning as a private task, every documented human society has evolved public mourning rites, customs, and codes that acknowledge loss (Leader, 2008). Mourning provides the possibility of integrating the reality of a loss or a traumatic shock through processes of remembering and symbolization in dialogically mediated doses (Krüger, 2017). Mourning, in this sense, is a social strategy whose witnessing function can potentiate the binding of communities, the absence of which produces an illusory and fragile group cohesion founded on repression and denial. Alexander and Margarete Mitscherlich argued that in post-war Germany, the resistance to mourning was motivated in part by the wish to avoid the affective experience of group self-devaluation (1975). While this was true as well in the case of the Southern Cone countries, resistance to mourning had political motivations. The heirs to military rule were the same elites who had traditionally held power, and they had little motivation to recognize the suffering imposed by military policies whose goal had been to secure their political, social, and economic privilege. The politicians who represented them in government either identified with the former military perpetrators or were too intimidated to risk offending them. Thus the new democratic governments repudiated responsibility for the state's extreme human rights violations, thereby endorsing forgetting – *olvido* – as an ideological and discursive strategy. In contrast, human rights organizations struggled to rescue memory – *memoria* – of those whose rights had been violated and for the legal and social accountability of the perpetrators. But in the Southern Cone, as in most post-conflict societies, the asymmetry of power has determined whose voices may be heard, who may speak and who may become objects of shared mourning – whose lives are, in other words, grievable (Butler, 1997). In this context, the disappeared are signifiers that represent a past (systemic) violence that continues to be performed in the present. The culture of impunity disappeared the narratives of survivors, thus impeding their capacities to disentangle current reality from the horrors of the past and to mourn losses so as to sustain intimate attachments that render the precariousness of life tolerable. Survivors' psychic wounds are unavoidably inherited by subsequent generations who are occupied by their parents' unmetabolized traumas.

In the absence of social witnessing, psychoanalysts became a primary resource for understanding the psychosocial legacy of state terror. They have noted that with the end of the dictatorships in the Southern Cone, people continued to experience profound distrust of one another. Torture survivors were held in suspicion that because so many had died in custody, they must have betrayed others to assure their own survival. Those who stayed during the dictatorship felt suspicious of friends and comrades who had gone into exile, resentful that they had freed themselves from living in terror to pursue their personal ambitions in other countries. Those who returned from exile looked with suspicion on those who had stayed and survived while so many had died. As Marcelo Viñar has pointed out, the continued fracturing of social ties was inevitable (M. Viñar, personal communication, Montevideo, Uruguay, August 11, 1990).

In Argentina, those psychoanalysts who had been community activists before and during the dictatorship continued their efforts to be socially useful. For example, when the government transitioned into constitutional rule in 1983, Julia Braun was appointed by the Argentine Ministry of Health to be the director of a special psychological service for the victims of military repression. Her appointment represented the first time a psychoanalyst had assumed a leadership position within the Ministry. Although it was short-lived, Braun initiated a number of group therapy interventions for families of the disappeared. She also provided treatment opportunities for schoolchildren whose cumulative traumatic symptoms were exacerbated by the ongoing right-wing violence aimed at intimidating human rights activists in their efforts to seek judicial indictments of the military.

Psychoanalysts who continued to work with survivors reported various symptoms reminiscent of what Haydée Faimberg (1988) calls "the telescoping of generations," when the failures of the parental generation to resolve the wounds of its own history become an internalized part of subsequent generations' identity. For example, Chilean psychoanalysts have noted that a pathogenic aspect of state terror lay in its unleashing of extraordinary violence upon the civilian population, problematizing the normal healthy development of aggression. They observe that the victims of persecution have tended to experience the psychic equivalence between aggressive impulses and destruction, thereby associating normative aggressive feelings within an intimate relationship with an actual threat of death of oneself and/or the other. In such cases, the tendency to maintain an illusory conflict-free object relationship that reinforces omnipotence and feelings of unreality dominate the internal world and the perception of external reality (Lira, 1994). When not resolved, the narcissistic defense against aggression and the confusion provoked by ordinary feelings of frustration and hatred in love relationships are enacted with the next generation. Children are vulnerable to internalizing their parents' dissociated hatred, which then functions as an internal reservoir of negativity directed against the self.

During military rule, some parents who were overwhelmed by daily fears of becoming victims of the random acts of state violence turned to their children to navigate a threatening world. Tasked precociously with the obligation to become their parents' protectors, these children had to assume complementary ego functions and thereby sacrifice their own need for protection. Psychoanalysts report that in adolescence and adulthood such patients develop rigid false-self structures in order to defend against what has been introjected from their parents' dissociated feelings of loss, destruction, and death (Becker & Diaz, 1998).

Kordon, Edelman, and Lagos have continued to work with the Mothers of the Plaza de Mayo, organizing psychotherapy groups and "groups of reflection" to provide an opportunity for people to come together to deal collectively with their subjective reactions to state terror. In 1990, they created an organization called The Argentine Team of Psychosocial Work and Investigation to study and treat the sequelae of state terror, including the psychological complications faced by adolescent children of the disappeared, whose symptoms increasingly appear as the result of personal psychopathology rather than the product of powerful social processes. For example, children born after the end of military rule have often been subjected to parental demands that they stay closely connected to family, lest their normal urges toward separation rekindle terrors related to involuntary losses experienced during the original traumatic period. When loved ones have been disappeared, children are potentially under pressure to replace the lost and always idealized objects, representing them in their attitudes and behavior. Perhaps the most dramatic manifestation of this socially induced family pathology is that these children are also called upon to make the past disappear by living out their parents' aspirations that were cut off when their lives were derailed by state organized violence (Becker & Diaz, 1998). In such families, the normal tasks in adolescence of separation and individuation and the achievement of one's own identity are compromised. Moreover, children whose parents were disappeared frequently experience conflicts between the conscious acceptance of their parents' imposed fate and feelings of hostility and reproach for having been "abandoned" by them, expressed in their aggressive attitudes toward family members caring for them, as well as in transference relationships in the clinical setting (Kordon & Edelman, 1986). In other cases, children who had too early been forced to assume the role of adult to replace a disappeared parent formed personalities structured for over-adaptation. As adolescents, especially among boys, they have manifested a proclivity toward extreme empathic responsibility for their families at the cost of their own youthful needs for exploration, experimentation, and pleasure in peer relationships beyond the family.

Kordon has reported that children whose parents were disappeared and were raised by their grandparents reveal other traumatic sequelae. These families often represented the "crossing out" of a whole generation, especially when the grandparents established a direct parent-child relationship with their grandchildren. Although the grandparents' conscious intent was to protect the children from feeling different from their peers, in actuality it often revealed unconscious wishes to deny the deaths of their own children and/or to substitute their grandchildren for their disappeared sons and daughters, thus abrogating the need to mourn their loss. Kordon points out that such children, as they grow up, have frequently manifested confusion about parental images and family roles or self-negating adaptations to the unconscious demands of their grandparents.

Juan Carlos Volnovich is among the psychoanalysts who have worked with the Grandmothers of the Plaza de Mayo to develop strategies to help the biological families and their restituted grandchildren deal with the complex emotional challenges of the reunification process. Volnovich has provided therapeutic interventions as well as psycho-educational guidance for the Grandmothers who help families navigate the secondary trauma potentially experienced by young people who must deal with the reality of their perverse histories and the complex opportunities and demands implied in the encounter with families for whom they hold such profound significance (J. C. Volnovich, personal communication, Buenos Aires, July 14, 2008; Carlotto, 2016).

Neoliberal crisis and psychoanalytic community activism

Much of Latin America today is dominated by a neoliberal political economy with patterns of impunity in every domain: corrupt politicians oversee a privatized free-market system that enriches a super-wealthy elite while it unravels whatever is left of the social programs in housing, healthcare, education, and working conditions won throughout the decades prior to the era of state terror. The impunity of deregulation and downsizing imposed by structural readjustment policies of the International Monetary Fund and World Bank provoke rising rates of unemployment and poverty. Neoliberal ideology emphasizes a consumerist ethic that identifies aspirations for a better life with the consumption of commodities: desires for peace, stability, opportunity, democracy, equality, love, gratification, and self-esteem are depicted as attainable through the purchase of products. However, even as commercialized discourse stimulates yearnings to benefit from consumer culture, neoliberal capitalism drives ever downward the economic capacity of the majority to do so. Deteriorating life conditions stimulate anxiety among middle- and working-class people about the present and future for themselves and their families. The resulting frustration, insecurity, anger and, inevitably, self-blame tend to collapse the capacity to understand the mystifying and destructive impact of systemic sources of psychological distress. Recourse to defenses of denial, splitting, projective identification, and displacement is manifested in the social violence that comes not only from the criminality exercised by those in power, but also from the aggression that is manifested amongst the powerless themselves.

However, history offers opportunities for people to exercise agency on behalf of challenging the dominant ideological discourse and of acting in solidarity with one another. One such possibility occurred in 2001 when the Argentine people suffered a traumatic event that reactivated the unresolved psychological sequelae of state terror. Argentina had been the poster child of neoliberalism, but its constantly rising GDP had hidden dangerous systemic contradictions indicative of its essential weakness. In a dizzying matter of days in December, a series of crises culminated in the complete collapse of the economy. By the millions, people were suddenly losing jobs, their life savings, access to social security and other public services, and the ability to feed their families. For many, this crisis represented the return of the repressed in the sense that societies, much like individuals, revise past events at a subsequent time and experience the present in light of the past. Earlier trauma, in a process Freud called *nachträglichkeit* or afterwardness (Laplanche, 1999), is resignified in light of the present, when it can assume even more disturbing significance or provide an opportunity to create a new and different meaning through the exercise of reparative action not possible earlier. So it was that the Argentine people, the majority of whom had been terrified into silence during state terror, this time found the capacity to raise their voices in collective opposition to the corrupt state that had caused this ontological crisis. Pushed to the extreme of endurance, they could let themselves recognize that the same powerful forces responsible for state terror now threatened their very survival through the imposition of a destructive economic model. Day and night, men, women, and children participated in massive demonstrations demanding accountability and refusing to accept the legitimacy of the state. They brought down three consecutive short-lived governments. As money disappeared from circulation, neighbors organized community-based flea markets in which they bartered essential goods and services in order to survive. They gathered spontaneously in the city's plazas to hold discussions about the crisis and what ordinary people could do to challenge a dysfunctional state. Workers occupied factories abandoned by their owners who fled the country, taking their capital with them. Middle-class professionals enthusiastically offered their skills in efforts to facilitate the success of these factory occupations (Hollander, 2004). Psychoanalysts Silvia Yankelevich and Cesar Hazaki, who are associates of the magazine *Topia: A Journal of Psychoanalysis, Society and Culture*, offered their assistance to workers who had occupied a small bread factory called Grissinopoli. As the workers struggled to continue production after their boss, who had not paid their wages for months, had abandoned the country, they were confronted with multiple problems, including anxieties related to their assertive challenge to traditional property rights and the authority of the state. Yankelevich made herself available to the women, many of whom experienced psychosomatic symptoms stimulated by their defiance of cultural norms by living in the factory with their male counterparts. They also had to navigate their husbands' hostile jealousy and their anguish at having to leave their children in the care of others. Many of the male workers suffered conflict and guilt because in the factory they had food and had a roof over their heads while their impoverished families were left to manage on their own. Both Yankelevich and Hazaki employed a "psychoanalysis without the couch," making interventions informally with workers who sought them out to unburden themselves during lunch breaks or in the hallways of the factory. The analysts also served as resources for the workers when they needed help during court negotiations over their legal rights to the abandoned factory. Both analysts frequently assisted the workers in developing new capacities to function in a group, to deal directly with conflicts as they arose, and to resolve differences that emerged in the context of learning to administer a factory. They also helped the workers launch the factory's cultural center, whose programs attracted other workers and their families as well as supportive middle-class professionals. They established various liaisons with the surrounding community, an example of which were the cultural center's popular Saturday night free movies and popcorn for the neighborhood children and adolescents. These experiences aided the workers' growing awareness of their importance as a model to others in the neighborhood and contributed to their increased individual and collective self-esteem (S. Yankelevich, personal communication, Buenos Aires, Argentina, November 11, 2003; Hazaki, 2002).

By 2003, these grassroots threats to established power sparked the election of a progressive government that implemented important political and economic reforms even while it co-opted much of the radical challenge to the existing system. Over the subsequent decade, the state instituted a formal challenge to impunity by embracing the discourse and demands of the Mothers and the Grandmothers of the Plaza de Mayo. It officially recognized the 30,000 disappeared, as well as the plight of survivors and the need for accountability of the perpetrators (Hollander, 2010). Trials have in part accomplished at last a social witnessing of survivors' narratives and punishment of the culprits. Public monuments and libraries, often in former concentration camps, have been constructed to document the terrorific policies of the military, providing sites of collective mourning. The Parque de la Memoria, situated along the Rio de la Plata estuary in Buenos Aires, is ringed with somber walls that bear the names of most of the 30,000 disappeared, serving as a symbolic register of past trauma in the service of avoiding its repetition.

However, Argentina remains a society divided, and the 2015 election brought to power a right-wing president whose policies include antipathy toward the human rights movement as well as regressive economic policies of austerity. The massive demonstration in which I participated in March of 2016 that observed the 40th anniversary of the military coup brought together 300,000 men, women, and children in Buenos Aires' Plaza de Mayo, who demonstrated in solidarity with the era's new disappeared – those beleaguered by economic, political, and social disempowerment. The progressive psychoanalysts who rallied carried a massive banner that proclaimed, "We believe that the promotion of the general wellbeing and of people's rights should be the principle objective of government. We do not want the function of mental health professionals to continue to be the reparation of the victims that the concentration of capital has left strewn along the road."

Psychoanalysts in the Southern Cone have carved out a space for community activism under the most extreme social situations of authoritarian governance and economic catastrophe. My colleague and friend, Argentine psychoanalyst Juan Carlos Volnovich, presciently remarked to me some years ago that psychoanalysts throughout the world would do well to pay attention to political and economic events in his country. Argentina is like the canary in the mine, he said, in that the systemic contradictions of neoliberal capitalism will come to produce economic crises and the dialectic of political authoritarianism and radical resistance in the Global North as well as the Global South. So it is that U.S. neoliberal domestic and foreign policy has created its own crises of unending wars, torture policies, repression of civil liberties, and the 2008 recession. The progressive response, including the election of our first Black president and the Occupy movement, has given way to a conservative backlash that elected an authoritarian president with a right-wing agenda, producing in turn a massive grassroots resistance. Our polarized political culture is a reflection of deepening economic and social inequities that generate collective anxieties whose effect is being increasingly felt within our profession. More practitioners are becoming aware that the social and psyche are recursively linked, and many are engaged in projects that reach out to diverse communities most affected by othering and the politics of austerity. As we take up theoretical and clinical issues related to class, racial, ethnic, sexual, and gendered oppression, we may choose, like our Argentine colleagues, to embrace a principle of ethical non-neutrality as we reach out to more diverse communities, learning from them in ways that help us become more relevant and useful. And like Argentine psychoanalysts, we may find ourselves protesting the need for us to keep repairing the psychological damage produced by our increasingly unjust social order.

References

Alvarez, A. (2017). *The role of emotion in thinking and the problem of deficits in the internal object*. Invited paper presented at the International Visiting Scholars Conference, Psychoanalytic Institute of Northern California, Berkeley, CA, April 22, 2017.

Argentine National Commission on the Disappeared (1986). *Nunca mas*. New York: Farrar, Straus, and Giroux.

Becker, D., & Diaz, M. (1998). The social process and the transgenerational transmission of trauma in Chile. In Y. Dannieli (Ed.), *International handbook of multigenerational legacies of trauma* (pp. 435–446). New York, NY and London, England: Plenun Press.

Braun, J. (1994, October 7). *Personal communication*. Buenos Aires, Argentina.

Butler, J. (1997). *The psychic life of power*. Stanford, CA: Stanford University Press.

Carlotto, E. (2016, March 21). *Personal interview*. Buenos Aires, Argentina.

Faimberg, H. (1988). The telescoping of generations. *Contemporary Psychoanalysis*, *24*, 99–117.

Hazaki, C. (2002). *Grissinopoli: Crónica de una lucha obrera. Produciendo realidad: las empresas comunitarias – Grissinopoli, Río Turbio, Zanón, Brukman, Gral. Mosconi*. Buenos Aires, Argentina: Topia Editorial, 25–38.

Hollander, N. (1990). Buenos Aires: Latin Meca of psychoanalysis. *Social Research*, *57*(4), 890–919.

Hollander, N. (1997). *Love in a time of hate: Liberation psychology in Latin America*. New Brunswick, NJ: Rutgers University Press.

Hollander, N. (2004). Argentine economic meltdown: Trauma and social resistance. *Mind and Human Interaction*, *13*(4), 227–235.

Hollander, N. (2010). *Uprooted minds: Surviving the politics of terror in the Americas*. New York, NY: Routledge.

Kordon, D. & Edelman, L. (1982). Observaciones sobre los efectos psicopatologicos del silenciamiento social respecto de la existencia de desaparecidos. In Kordon, D., Edelman, L. et al. *Efectos psicológicos y psicosociales de la represión política*. Buenos Aires: Sudamericana-Planeta. (1986).

Krüger, S. (2017). Unable to mourn again? Media(ted) reactions to German neo-Nazi terrorism. In L. Auestad (Ed.), *Shared traumas, silent loss, public and private mourning* (pp. 59–76). London, England: Karnac.

Laplanche, J. (1999). *Essays on otherness*. London, England: Routledge.

Langer, M. (1983, June 14). *Personal communication*. León, Nicaragua.

Leader, D. (2008). *The new black*. London, England: Hamish Hamilton.

Lira, E. (Ed.). (1994). *Psicología y Violencia Política en América Latina*. Santiago, Chile: ILAS.

Mitscherlich, A., & Mitscherlich, M. (1975). *The inability to mourn: Principles of collective behavior.* New York, NY: Grove Press.

Timmerman, J. (1982). *Prisoner without a name, cell without a number.* New York, NY: Vintage Books.

Viñar, M. (1994, October 10). *Personal interview.* Montevideo, Uruguay.

Viñar, M. (1990, August 11). *Personal interview.* Montevideo, Uruguay.

Volnovich, J. C. (2008, January 3). *Personal interview.* Buenos Aires, Argentina.

Volnovich, J. C. (1990, August 13). *Personal communication.* Buenos Aires, Argentina.

Yankelevich, S (2003, November 11). *Personal communication.* Buenos Aires, Argentina.

Chapter 3

Dying to get out

Challenges in the treatment of Latin American migrants fleeing violent communities

Ricardo Ainslie, Hannah McDermott, and Crystal Guevara

In this chapter, we explore the intersection of migration and trauma via three clinical vignettes that capture the complex nature of the psychological experience of immigrants fleeing violent communities as well as the therapeutic challenges that emerge in treatment. The three cases we present reflect work with individuals who experienced significant personal and social trauma in their lives prior to making the decision to migrate. All three came from impoverished communities in Mexico where violence was rampant and where community violence was overlaid onto personal experiences of familial deprivation, conflict, and loss. While economic opportunities no doubt played a role in their decisions to migrate, the overwhelming character of their experiences in their home communities were also decisive in these deliberations. Further, though these patients presented for treatment due to concerns in their daily lives at the present, the violence of their pasts was for each a crucial and defining aspect of therapy and the seemingly unrelated concerns they presented.

The context of modern immigration

The population of immigrants in the United States has exploded, growing fourfold since the 1960s (Pew Research Center, 2016a). Today there are more than 42 million immigrants living in the United States, almost two-thirds of them from Mexico (Pew Research Center, 2016a), with roughly eight million immigrants classified as "unauthorized" (Pew Research Center, 2016b). What is often missed in explorations of the psychology of immigration and therapeutic work with immigrants is the fact that many, especially those coming from Mexico, Central America, and Africa, are coming from communities ravaged by violence. This means that in addition to the more familiar themes that we associate with the psychological experience of migration, such as loss and mourning (Ainslie, 1998; Akhtar, 2011; Grinberg & Grinberg, 1984; 1989) and the stressors of encountering a new and unfamiliar culture (Ainslie, Tummala-Narra, Harem, Barbanel, & Ruth, 2013; Akhtar, 1996), clinicians working with immigrant populations must increasingly be aware of, and sensitive to, the very real possibility that their patients have witnessed and/or been victims of unspeakable violence in their communities of origin, including victimization through domestic violence, criminal organizations, or violence that is state sponsored (see Holland, 2006 and Volkan, 1993).

Such realities have increasingly blurred the historic convention of distinguishing between immigrants and refugees as motivated by different considerations. Historically, refugees have been understood to be individuals fleeing political violence and catastrophic circumstances, whereas immigrants have been viewed as driven by economic hardship. Increasingly, however, immigrants are fleeing communities in countries that have devolved into civil war, or where broad swaths of those countries are, for all intents and purposes, ungovernable failed states with no rule of law. People who leave countries facing such conditions are likely to have been motivated to leave their communities of origin driven by both economic concerns and by the cataclysmic social conditions where violent crime, including high murder rates, is rampant. People fleeing countries experiencing such violence and tumult arrive in places like the United States and Western Europe having been immersed in extremely traumatic experiences yet without the protections afforded by refugee status. Treatment providers are unlikely to consider the traumatic experiences that these individuals have experienced, as they fail to appear on most standard assessments (Kaltman, Green, Mete, Shara, & Miranda, 2010).

Considering that these patients fall into the space between categorizations of "immigrant" and "refugee," it is important that their unique constellation of needs be recognized. In the following cases, we wish to illustrate the complexity of therapeutic work with these immigrant patients, especially when that complexity is shaped by a confluence of personal and collective trauma and the utility of psychoanalytic frameworks for meeting their needs.

Case #1

Sylvia was a Mexican woman in her late 40s, a mother of five who had lived in the United States for about 15 years. She was connected to counseling services through the Texas crime victims' compensation program. Four months previously, Sylvia was the victim a nearly fatal attack that left her with significant physical and emotional scars. Sylvia was born and raised in what she described as a poor and very rural community made up of small farms, outside of Nuevo Laredo, Mexico. Sylvia's community of origin can be characterized as "violent" because of the violence perpetuated within it, but, perhaps more importantly, because of the failure of systems to provide justice and protection to those, like Sylvia, who were victimized. The events of her early life and the failure of her community to hold and protect her were recurrent themes in our work, nearly half a century later.

Sylvia was the youngest of 11 'children and described her early childhood as marked by poverty and the sense that her family did not have sufficient resources. She reported that her father had left the family before she could remember. In her early childhood, before the age of 5 or 6, Sylvia was sexually abused by her maternal uncle, though she had limited memories of this event. Yet, the difficult conditions of her early years were cushioned by the love of her mother, a woman who reportedly worked tirelessly and lovingly to support her children.

However, Sylvia life's changed dramatically around age 9 when her mother was murdered by a spurned would-be lover. Sylvia alternately recalled being told this news by her eldest sister and discovering it by seeing a photograph of her mother lying in a pool of blood in the newspaper, an image that haunted her. There was never justice for Sylvia's mother; her killer was never prosecuted and continued to live in the community. Following her mother's death, Sylvia was sent to an orphanage run by nuns for the remainder of her childhood, an experience she described as "cold," "hungry," "cruel," and loveless. Although she maintained contact with her siblings, Sylvia recalled that after her mother's death she was "alone" in the world. Despite her negative experiences at the orphanage, she developed a strong Christian religious conviction.

In her late teens, Sylvia met and married her husband. Through this marriage, she achieved financial stability that she had sorely needed. She and her husband had five children, and motherhood came to be a central aspect of Sylvia's identity. However, from the beginning the marriage was tempestuous, abusive, and violent. Sylvia reportedly experienced severe episodes of depression, attempting suicide at least twice during their marriage. After more than 15 years together, Sylvia left her husband, although they did not divorce. She reported that living alone with her children outside Nuevo Laredo for the following few years was the happiest time of her life, in which she finally felt she had a place of her own. However, after her elder daughter immigrated to the United States, Sylvia was persuaded to move as well, first to Laredo and then to a larger city in central Texas.

Moving in with her elder daughter's family, including three young children, and Sylvia's youngest, still-teenaged, daughter, she found herself overwhelmed with childcare responsibilities and with little of the freedom she had enjoyed during the years after her separation. In particular, she felt restricted by her financial dependence on her daughter and son-in-law. As a result, Sylvia sought employment to provide herself with more independence and the sense of purpose she missed from working. She secured a job as a bartender at a bar in a blue-collar, Spanish-speaking neighborhood. Although Sylvia felt ashamed about working at a "low class" bar, which was at odds with her identity as a mother, she reportedly loved working as a bartender: the money, the camaraderie with her co-workers, and the chance to listen to her customers and give them advice.

The attack that precipitated Sylvia's seeking therapy occurred before her regular shift at work. Her memories of the attack were limited; she recalled clearly getting out of the car to go to work that evening and receiving a call, which she later saw as portent, from her son-in-law encouraging her to stop working and to leave her job. Sylvia couldn't recall what instigated the attack itself, except that the coworker who attacked her had caused problems before, and she recalled a "flash" of memory of the other woman jumping across the bar at her "like an animal," smashing a bottle and attacking Sylvia's face, body, and hands with the broken end. Sylvia recalled seeing herself, her body as if from above, lying in a pool of blood.

Four months after the attack, Sylvia presented to her first session at the community mental health agency where I was a practicum student as extremely dysregulated, unable to fill out her paperwork, quick to disassociate, hyperventilate, and experience panic attacks, suicidal and desperate for someone to talk to about how poorly she felt. Sylvia bore scars on her face, wrist, and arm and along her thigh running from her waist to her knee. These scars, she felt, were mocking reminders of what she had been through. The depth and relentlessness of Sylvia's despair and its embodied presentation, howling sobs, quick and shallow breathing, hunched posture, and ceaseless pacing, affected and overwhelmed me. Sylvia reported symptoms associated with complex PTSD: chronic suicidal ideation, tumultuous interpersonal relationships, a fragmented sense of self, flashbacks, panic attacks, and a pervasive sense of loss of safety, meaninglessness, and despair.

Sylvia's transference toward me was idealizing and very, even overly, positive. She called me her "beautiful, studious angel" and would tell me that therapy was the only place in which she could be herself. In my countertransference, I often felt a sense of helplessness, that treating her was wrestling a windstorm. Yet I also found her charming, sharp and funny, and abidingly strong. Her presentation was so turbulent, so easily, seemingly almost willingly, dysregulated, that our sessions were fragmented and our progress slow. In addition, despite her praise for therapy, Sylvia had chronic difficulty getting to session and arriving on time. She acknowledged that she was her own biggest barrier to treatment: failing to fill the car with gas, putting off leaving her house, forgetting to check her voicemails.

Despite our uneven progress, Sylvia was immensely compelling and her case filled with meaningful interplay between her present and past. From the beginning of treatment, Sylvia introduced her presenting issues as not just the recent assault that had nearly taken her life but also, and even more so, her unresolved feelings revolving around the death of her mother. The two events were so inextricably intertwined that at moments I could not tell which of the two she was talking about or whether the thoughts and feelings she expressed referred to both. I came to understand that these two events meant the same thing to Sylvia, the loss of safety in the world, and were symbolized by the same image of Sylvia and/or her mother lying, dying in a pool of her own blood.

She repeated constantly the question "why?" Why had this happened to her? she asked. Why had God permitted that her mother be taken, that her own life be threatened? Her fears about her own potential loss of life were transfigured into a persistent, nagging suicidal ideation, held back only by her deep conviction that suicide was punishable by an eternity in hell and by Sylvia's sense that her suicide would do to her children what her own mother's death did to her. She alternated between asking why she hadn't fought back, even killing her coworker, and asking why her coworker hadn't done them both a favor and finished the job. Between furious questions of "why," she would raise her head, smile slyly, and ask me "Am I crazy?" or crack a dark joke. Despite the chaos

Sylvia brought into the room, in these moments of stillness I felt connected to her, admiring her strength, her humor, feeling deeply for all that she had been through.

The line between reality and dream, in addition to that between past and present, was often blurred by Sylvia's frequent experiences of portentous dreams, visitations, visions, nightmares, and flashbacks, experiences that often featured the key figures of her mother and her attacker. This symbolic content played an important role, helping me to see through content that was often difficult to parse. Sylvia reported experiencing visitations from her mother in her dreams. She had experienced similarly mystical dreams in the past, including dreams foretelling the deaths of two of her brothers. In the visitations, her mother appeared and offered her love and comfort. Yet Sylvia seemed unable to accept the love and comfort her mother offered her. Sylvia described her mother's arms reaching out to embrace her but the thought of the embrace, rather than providing comfort, re-awoke her sense of fear and provoked extreme emotional dysregulation.

As therapy progressed, it became apparent that in all her relationships Sylvia experienced similar difficulty accepting the love she craved; in her relationships with her children and with befriended neighbors, bids for love and attention turned to bitter fights. Fights, particularly those with her children, in turn produced bitter self-recrimination for proving her failure as a mother. In session with me, she invested in and praised our relationship, sometimes leaving needy, breathless voicemails only to fail to show up for the appointment and thereby the care she sought.

A key metaphor from our treatment came from Sylvia's visions of two dolls, the good, beautiful doll and the ugly, bad, unlovable doll. Sylvia reported that these two dolls had been two of her few possessions when she lived in the orphanage. She identified herself as the ugly doll, thrown to the floor, undeserving of love. She fragmented herself into "the ugly doll" and the "good mother." I came to appreciate her tempestuous presentation as the result of spending her week denying the "ugly doll" in order perform the role of the "good mother," only to vent the pain, hate, and suffering of her denied self in the consultation room with me. Sylvia would gesture to a corner of the room and tell me she was seeing the doll, lying there, unable to be picked up, and she would spew verbal abuse at it.

In many ways, that is how our therapy ended: my care and regard for her could not convince Sylvia to pick the doll up, to use her capacity as the "good mother" to care for the part of herself who needed mothering the most, model it though I tried. After eight months of therapy, I moved agencies and brought Sylvia to the new agency as my client. In our first session she was desperate to see me and I was relieved she had made it, half expecting the change of venue to shatter her already tenuous attendance record. But she missed our second session, later citing a new job that conflicted with our time. I detected a familiar pattern: a job was significant progress for Sylvia, yet it became the barrier to further treatment. In our third session, she broke into a tirade of racist insults, turning to me and noting, "I've offended you, haven't I?" Sylvia didn't return my calls after she missed the next appointment. I didn't have the opportunity to ask her if she was trying to push me away or to pick up the doll again.

Case #2

Working in a primary care setting often proved challenging due to the time and session restrictions, even as it provided opportunities to access and provide integrated treatment for underserved patients.

Gloria was a 26-year-old mother of three who had emigrated from Mexico. Gloria's primary care physician referred her for therapy when she presented with concerns of depression and "anger management difficulties." The clinic provided Gloria with psychiatric consultation for anti-depressants, one-on-one counseling sessions with her therapist, and parent-child therapy with another psychologist – all in one location.

Gloria had migrated to the United States eight years earlier with her husband and oldest daughter after the violent murder of her sister-in-law. Gloria still recalls the trauma of witnessing her sister-in-law's dead body in the family dining room, her home's white walls stained with blood. Her sister-in-law's murder remains unsolved. In addition, Gloria's family faced recurring threats from local gangs. Gloria described being "hunted" by local gang members who were seeking to extort families and small businesses in the community. Leaving everything behind, Gloria and her family fled the corruption and violence that defines contemporary life in many Mexican communities.

Gloria had seen therapists at the community clinic on two previous occasions prior to this course of therapy. Since her initial visit in 2009, clinic psychiatrists had diagnosed her with depression; unspecified, then major depressive disorder, generalized anxiety, with a possible personality disorder. Over the years, Gloria had been on a variety of anti-depressants, but none seemed helpful and she therefore was reluctant to stay on her medications. Significantly, Gloria's two former therapists had described her as a "guarded" patient who assiduously avoided speaking about her previous life in Mexico.

Gloria returned to therapy for a third time, now presenting with concerns that she was experiencing distressing difficulties feeling close to her three young children; her eldest daughter had to come with Gloria and her husband, while the two younger girls were born in the U.S. Gloria feared that her daughters would see her as a "bad mother."

This time Gloria's experience in therapy was markedly different from the prior two therapies. She appeared to be highly motivated and very engaged with therapy. For example, although she lived 40 minutes away from the clinic and had very limited resources, she never missed an appointment and always arrived early. Her only absence was a three-week hiatus during major Immigration and Customs Enforcement (ICE) raids in the community, which resulted in her feeling that it was too unsafe to leave her home. She often had to bring her 2-year-old toddler to her sessions, but preferred that to having to miss an appointment.

During parent-child sessions, I observed that Gloria's children appeared to adore her. They were often affectionate toward her, but she was very rigid and unable to reciprocate their overtures. Gloria could observe herself, and in her individual therapy appointments she reported that she was painfully aware of what was taking place but felt unable to respond. The circumstance left her feeling deeply frustrated. In her individual sessions, she voiced the wish to be able to be more responsive, to find this "genuine love," a love she said she had never felt. "It has to be genuine," she would say.

Another complication in her treatment was that it was clear that Gloria did not respond well to the short-term, Cognitive Behavioral Therapy modality that was the clinic's primary approach to therapy; it was too directive and did not fit well with what I could sense she needed. My supervisor and the clinic allowed me to approach this therapy with a non-structured, narrative focus. This was a big change for Gloria, but she responded to it well, as reflected in her dedication to the work we were doing together.

In Gloria's prior two treatments she had been very reluctant to talk about her past experiences, but in the current therapy she was gradually able to bring her past into her therapy. Gloria found a way to connect with me and reveal her vulnerability and I learned quickly that the therapy sessions were providing her with a space to show the vulnerability she was hesitant to reveal to the outside world.

As we slowly delved deeper, Gloria began to discuss how her own mother had abandoned her in infancy because she was a product of rape. Her mother left her with her maternal grandparents in rural town in Mexico. Gloria described her grandmother as a very cold and distant woman. Thus, no one filled the emotional void left by her mother's abandonment and rejection. In addition, Gloria reported that her grandfather had sexually exposed himself to Gloria and her cousins at an early age. Gloria was also sexually abused by an older male cousin and a family friend between the ages of 8 to 12. At one point she had attempted to tell her mother and her grandmother about these experiences, but nothing was ever done to protect her.

Gloria was, for a long time, not able to understand how these experiences had impacted her emotional life and, in turn, her ability to connect with her children and others. She reported that as a child she had never felt a bond with anyone in her family, and gradually she came to see that this was the pattern that she was now repeating with her own children and husband.

Gloria felt a tremendous amount of guilt about her difficulties in these relationships. This included her mother, whom she attempted to re-engage, but continued to feel as if nothing was there. She described this effort as a formality born out of *respeto* (respect) for her mother, but lacking the real emotion she desired. There were many variations. She also felt guilty that she had never allowed her sister-in-law, the one who had been murdered in their home prior to Gloria and her family leaving Mexico, to get close to her, a connection she knew her sister-in-law had very much wanted. Gloria felt haunted by her relational failures at every turn, failures that left her feeling depressed and full of self-criticism. "There's nothing good about me," she would say in her appointments.

Gloria had succeeded in erecting an emotional wall around herself, beginning with her maternal abandonment, her grandmother's cold indifference, and the sexual abuse that had victimized her. Her sister-in-law's murder was simply the final blow. For Gloria, to be vulnerable was to expose herself to profound loss and anxiety. It was too much to risk.

We took it session by session. The therapy focused closely on the therapeutic relationship, constantly reflecting on what was taking place between us. There was an obvious pattern in which she would reach out to me in some way, only to immediately pull back into her defended, guarded position. It was evident that our relationship was enormously important to her (and, in countertransference, I felt very maternal and caring toward her). Even though we were close to the same age, in the transference I became the mother that did not reject her or abandon her, but rather the "good object" that stood with her, was interested in her, and that "genuinely" cared about her. At times when she felt hopeless that she could not "mend" or that she was just "a bad mother," I reassured her that I was here for her and that I would not give up on her; that I would carry the hope for her until she could carry it herself. The therapeutic alliance became the primary therapeutic tool upon which she leaned. This was the reason she never missed appointments and the reason she arrived early, eager to start the day's therapy.

In one session, when she'd been bringing in the many sad and traumatic aspects of her childhood and reflecting on the many facets of the abandonments she'd experienced, she became flooded with emotion. She said she feared she was incapable of loving others like a mother should love her children or a wife should love her husband. She couldn't find that tender place within herself from which she knew such feelings came. She was acutely aware in that session of the wall she had built and the emotional cost to her of such protection from vulnerability. It was one of the few times I saw her cry in the 11-month treatment.

I was a practicum student at this clinic and I was to rotate to another site at the end of the year. An extremely difficult moment in the therapy centered on the termination. It was the clinic's policy that Gloria could be transferred to another therapist, but Gloria's response was what one could have anticipated given her history of abandonment and given that she'd finally allowed herself to feel close to me. Even as Gloria expressed her dismay, we were able to reflect on how our therapeutic relationship had shown her that she could, indeed, feel close to others and the implication of this for her relationship with others. We also explored what she valued about our relationship, and the fact that although she might be scared about the termination, she would have these genuine moments as a reminder of what she could have with others in her life. I, too, felt a great deal of sadness in the termination as well as some guilt: I was abandoning her as she'd been abandoned by others whom she needed and relied upon. However, this loss was different. We both knew it and, most importantly, we could talk about it – something that had never been possible before. Gloria's story was a journey of grief, guilt, abandonment, and trauma – all which had plagued her ability to connect with others, especially her own children. However, it was clear that she'd made significant strides in working through these feelings by the time I left the clinic.

Case #3

Arturo was referred by local nongovernmental organization (NGO) as a young man "struggling with his transition to life in the United States," as well as symptoms of depression and anxiety. The appointments were carried out in Spanish, both patient and analyst being native speakers. Arturo was 19 years old and dressed in ill-fitting work clothes furnished as uniforms by his place of employment. He was slight in height and frame, and he avoided eye contact. He seemed frail and quite vulnerable. In the initial appointment, Arturo appeared quite dissociative, and it was with great difficulty that he attempted to describe his situation. One of the things he discussed was that he suffered from great anxiety and felt very isolated and alone, notwithstanding some sources of support: a girlfriend and her family, as well as the church that they all attended. Arturo was not a religious person, but this church community was very welcoming of people in his circumstance and it was through the church that he had met his girlfriend and her family. People in the church community actively reached out to him and had helped him find work, and he described his girlfriend and her family as embracing of him (they were American citizens of Mexican ancestry).

Notwithstanding the efforts to support him, Arturo was acutely aware of the fact that he experienced great difficulty allowing his girlfriend, her family, and others in the church community to get close to him. He described himself as chronically feeling hyper-anxious, easily distracted, and very disconnected. The latter, in particular, was creating substantial conflict in his relationship with his girlfriend, a circumstance that worried him considerably. He was afraid that he was going to lose his girlfriend, yet he found it difficult to behave in a way that met her needs within the relationship. This was reproduced in the sessions, as he found it difficult to relax and connect with me, sharing his experiences only with great difficulty, skittish in his eye contact, and requiring a great deal of effort to draw him out. In the countertransference, I experienced him as "orphaned" (the image had come to mind for me during our first appointment), and notwithstanding his avoidant, detached style, there was nevertheless a pull toward wanting to take care of him that may have been the same quality that helped his girlfriend, her family, and the church community reach out to support him as well. He was likeable even though he kept himself at a remove.

Prior to his migration to the United States, Arturo, his mother, and two younger siblings had lived in a poor, working-class neighborhood in the border city of Nuevo Laredo, Tamaulipas, across the Rio Grande River from Laredo, Texas. Arturo's mother was a poorly paid public school teacher. Arturo's father had abandoned the family when Arturo was six and it had been years since he had had contact with him. Nuevo Laredo was a dangerous city, especially in neighborhoods such as the one where Arturo and his family lived. More than a decade into the raw violence that has swept parts of Mexico and claimed close to two hundred thousand lives, Tamaulipas remains one of the most violent and ungovernable areas in the country.

In the first appointment, Arturo indicated that he'd "had to leave Mexico," without further elaboration. It wasn't until his second appointment that the reasons for his leaving were fleshed out. When he was 15 years old, Arturo and two friends had left his house where they'd been playing video games and walked to the corner store to buy a soda. As the boys emerged from the store, a group of men brandishing guns forcibly seized them, placed bags over their heads, and bound their hands with duct tape. They were subsequently beaten while being held in a room in a safe house somewhere in the city. Neighbors witnessed Arturo's kidnapping and immediately notified Arturo's mother. The kidnappers soon contacted her, demanding an exorbitant ransom that she was unable to pay.

Nuevo Laredo was under the control of the Gulf Cartel and their armed wing, a group of ex-military gone to the dark side known as Los Zetas (the Zetas would soon split off from the Gulf Cartel and become the most feared cartel in Mexico). The streets of the city had been a bloody battleground since the early 2000s, when the Sinaloa Cartel had attempted to seize control of Nuevo Laredo, which was prized because of its easy access to United States drug markets, given that the border crossing at Laredo, Texas is, by a significant margin, the busiest truck crossing on the U.S.-Mexico border with approximately two million trucks per year (U.S. Department of Transportation, 2016). The result was open warfare in the city streets, including an ambush of federal forces as they arrived to reduce the violence, the murder of a newly elected mayor within hours of assuming the post, and attack on the city's newspaper with bazookas and AK-47s. But in the poor neighborhoods, local gangs terrorized defenseless civilians with assaults, kidnappings, and extortions. It is likely that Arturo was the victim of just such a local gang; at least that was his own theory.

The three boys were kept in the safe house for a week. In the interim, Arturo's mother contacted her brother who, according to Arturo, had "communication" with the Zetas or a street gang that was closely affiliated with them. Through his contacts, Arturo's uncle arranged for his release, without payment. On the day he was let go, the kidnappers entered the room where the boys were being held, sacks still over their heads and hands now zip tied. They took off the bag over Arturo's head and, in that moment, the kidnappers executed the two other boys with a gunshot to the head. Perhaps they acted out of frustration: their kidnapping was unraveling, as none of the boy's families had money and they'd now been forced to free one of them. Whatever the cause, the violence was reflective of what has become commonplace in a handful of Mexican states where drug-related violence runs unabated – communities where ordinary citizens live under constant threat and high levels of vulnerability with no recourse (law enforcement is either non-existent or in collusion with the criminals who victimize the citizenry).

A terrified Arturo made his way home and told his mother what had he'd endured over the course of that week and about the assassination of his two friends in front of him. Arturo and his mother believed that he continued to be at risk, so they immediately pulled together a bag of his clothes and a little cash, and Arturo made his way across the Rio Grande River, illegally crossing into the United States. He remained in Laredo for 18 months, living with an aunt before making his way to San Antonio, where employment was more plentiful and where he had another relative. He spent two years in San Antonio before moving to Austin where he was now working in the service industry.

I only saw Arturo for five sessions. During each, the sense that this was a very traumatized young man remained salient. I understood his avoidant quality as clearly defensive – a product of the overwhelming trauma of his kidnapping. That trauma was in turn overlaid on a familial history of poverty, neglect, and abandonment. Arturo found every session difficult, and yet he seemed to also value them, as he put considerable effort into getting to appointments. He worked six days a week, and public transportation to my office was difficult to manage given that he lived and worked at the other end of the city from my office – it took Arturo an hour and a half each way to make his appointments. The focus of our brief contact was to help him understand that the difficulties he was experiencing in allowing his girlfriend, her family, and others in his church community to get closer to him were rooted in the overwhelming violence he'd experienced, layered over a family where there had been little affection or closeness – three children abandoned by their father with a single mother who worked and had no alternative but to leave them at home alone until she returned from work each day. His mother had no emotional reserves left to give much to her children in terms of love and affection beyond keeping the household afloat financially on her meager income. Without a doubt, his anxiety and depression were partly shaped by these experiences, although the overwhelming nature of his kidnapping and the death of his two friends was a specific, traumatic event and pivotal in driving him to leave home. It had also left a deep and as yet unprocessed psychological wound. After the fifth session, Arturo left me a voicemail saying he would not be able to make his appointment the next few weeks due to work conflicts and illness in his girlfriend's family. He said he would check back with me when he was ready to resume, but I did not hear from him again.

In my view he had used these sessions, in part, as a place to share his history with another person who listened to it with empathy and understanding. That, alone, was meaningful. These were experiences that lived within him that prior to these appointments had not been shared with anyone else. He'd been alone with them for years. While his presentation was emotionally quite flat and detached, it was not dissociated. He *wanted* to tell me what he'd lived through. My stance was to be receptive and, where appropriate, to suggest the connection between these experiences and his current struggles – gingerly and in ways that were "useable."

Similarly, four years after his kidnapping, Arturo had never discussed this experience with anyone, save with his mother the day of his release. He voiced relief to have a place where he could talk about it. Remarkably, he had not seen the connection between this traumatic experience and the difficulties he was having allowing himself to get close to his girlfriend and to others.

Everyone who had contact with Arturo, including the NGO that referred him for treatment, thought that he was just one more undocumented immigrant fleeing economic hardship for a better life in the United States. The caseworker's description that he was "struggling with his transition to life in the United States" only captured his circumstance in the most superficial terms (partly, of course, because Arturo himself had not shared with her a fuller picture of his background and the experiences he'd endured given their traumatic character). None imagined that Arturo had survived a profoundly traumatizing horror as a young teenager.

Discussion

The literature on the psychology of the immigrant experience rarely enters the terrain of trauma, and yet increasing numbers of immigrants are driven to leave their countries of origin because they live in communities ravaged by violence, often violence that has affected them directly. It is our view that clinicians working with immigrant populations should always be alert to the possibility that their patients arrive with both personal and collective experiences of trauma that may create significant therapeutic challenges. In addition, some of these patients' current conflicts may activate or deeply resonate with prior trauma that they have experienced. Arturo's difficulties relating to his girlfriend, her family, and his church community were clearly a product of the profound trauma he had experienced as an adolescent prior to leaving Mexico. This is also clear in Sylvia's fusion of the near-lethal attack at her place of work in the United States post-migration, with the murder of her mother when she was a child, as reflected in the collapsed symbolic representation of seeing her bloodied self as at one with the image of her mother's bloodied body, as well as in her therapist's struggle to distinguish the emotional reference points ("is she talking about herself, her mother, or both?"). For clinicians working with immigrant patients who come from conflict-laden communities and who have experienced overwhelming violence in addition to substantial personal/familiar conflict, the emotions are often difficult to distinguish and, indeed, as with Sylvia, are at times fused.

Similarly, Gloria's struggle with her attachment to her children and others in her current life was an extension of her mother's abandonment and rejection from the very beginning of Gloria's life. Gloria's grandmother's coldness and emotional neglect meant that she was unable to fill the vacuum created by the loss of her mother and, instead, further exacerbated the impact of this early maternal abandonment. Finally, her extended experiences of sexual abuse as a little girl also played a role in fostering her protective detachment. This detachment, with such deep roots in Gloria's childhood, was now surfacing as a conflict-laden concern, as she struggled to feel close to her three children, her husband, and others in her current, post-migration life.

Immigrant patients with multiple personal and social traumas often require therapeutic approaches that are more flexible and relationally driven and where there is a focus on creating a space within which these patients can eventually discuss and explore the traumatic content that so haunts them, in addition to exploring other life experiences. For example, Sylvia entered therapy in a state of acute crisis, dysregulated to the point that she could not fill out the paperwork during intake. However, her therapist succeeded in creating a therapeutic space within which Sylvia could eventually feel safe enough to explore her mother's murder and the near-lethal attack that had been the impetus for her seeking therapy. The turbulent character of some of the sessions was offset and absorbed, to some extent, by the positive, idealizing transference that Sylvia developed toward her therapist, and it helped sustain the therapy during these difficult times. Similarly, Gloria had previously seen two therapists who viewed her as guarded and closed-off before finding a therapist who was willing to set aside the time-limited CBT framework that her agency preferred for a more open-ended, non-directive narrative approach, where attention to understanding Gloria's life-defining experiences and how these surfaced within the therapeutic relationship was the focus of the work.

It is our observation that psychodynamic approaches that are characterized by this open-endedness, with attention to creating a "useable" therapeutic space and where the observation of transference and countertransference elements helps to shed light on and facilitates the use of the therapeutic relationship in constructive ways, are all key to working with immigrant populations who have experienced trauma. But just as importantly, such accepting, unstructured, narrative-based approaches appear to be more culturally sensitive to the needs of people for whom time-limited, overly structured, directive therapeutic approaches are not a good fit.

Finally, all three cases illustrate the brittle nature of the therapeutic frame when working with immigrant patients with multiple traumatic experiences. Sylvia and Gloria both responded with great difficulty to their terminations, and neither was able to follow her therapist to the therapist's new site, despite good working alliances and despite the therapists' best efforts to continue the work. The break in the continuity of the work was simply too much for these two patients. In the case of Arturo, simply being in therapy posed an extreme hardship given his long work hours and the inordinate amount of time it took him to reach his appointments. Nevertheless, in retrospect, his therapist felt that he should have been more thorough in addressing Arturo's challenges in making It to appointments Perhaps such an exploration might have provided some strategies for facilitating his continuation. On the other hand, it is also possible that the appointments were themselves challenging, emotionally, for Arturo given that the process challenged his defenses. Nevertheless, Arturo's treatment also exemplifies another common feature of work with such immigrants: the fact that they work long hours (often at more than one job), frequently with the pressure of earning enough money to help support family in their country of origin, all the while earning low wages. Such conditions can sometimes make therapeutic commitments difficult to sustain.

However, as seen in these three cases, the logistical difficulties posed by treatment for immigrant patients are not a prescription for overly structured or time-limited approaches, but rather require clinicians to develop and use flexible, relational approaches to reach through the structural barriers that may appear to "wall off" these clients. In addition, psychoanalytic frameworks provide critical tools for working with these populations on a variety of levels. First, they provide an indispensable theoretical lens for conceptualizing these patients' experiences and their impact on their sense of themselves and others, as well as the psychological resources, including defenses, that they have available to manage them. Second, psychoanalytic approaches lend themselves to the kind of open-ended, narrative-based engagements that immigrants from Latin America (and probably elsewhere) find more palatable, engaging, and culturally familiar. This is especially important when contrasted with interventions focusing exclusively on behavior change or the alteration of thoughts as is common in CBT treatments, which tend to be somewhat ahistorical and less interested in broader life contexts and experiences that may help explain the origins of the patient's feelings and struggles. Psychoanalytic approaches not only create a context that invites these broader cultural and historical elements into the treatment, it sees these as indispensable to therapeutic understanding.

References

Ainslie, R. C. (1998). Cultural mourning, immigration, and engagement: Vignettes from the Mexican experience. In M. Suárez-Orozco (Ed.), *Crossings: Immigration and the socio-cultural remaking of the North American space* (pp. 283–300). Cambridge, MA: Harvard University Press.

Ainslie, R. C., Tummala-Narra, P., Harem, A., Barbanel, L., & Ruth, R. (2013). Contemporary psychoanalytic views on the experience of immigration. *Psychoanalytic Psychology, 30*(4), 663–679.

Akhtar, S. (1996). "Someday . . ." and "if only . . ." fantasies: Pathological optimism and inordinate nostalgia as related forms of idealization. *Journal of the American Psychoanalytic Association, 44*, 723–753.

Akhtar, S. (2011). *Immigration and acculturation: Mourning, adaptation, and the next generation.* New York, NY: Jason Aronson.

Grinberg, L., & Grinberg, R. (1984). A psychoanalytic study of migration: Its normal and pathological aspects. *Journal of the American Psychoanalytic Association, 32*, 13–38.

Grinberg, L., & Grinberg, R. (1989). *Psychoanalytic perspectives on migration and exile.* New Haven, CT: Yale University Press.

Holland, N. (2006). Negotiating trauma and loss in the migration experience: Roundtable on the global woman. *Studies in Gender and Sexuality, 7*, 61–70.

Kaltman, S., Green, B. L., Mete, M., Shara, N., & Miranda, J. (2010). Trauma, depression, and comorbid PTSD/Depression in a community sample of Latina immigrants. *Psychological Trauma Theory, Research, Practice and Policy, 2*(1), 31–39.

Pew Research Center. (2016a). Retrieved from www.pewhispanic.org/2016/04/19/statistical-portrait-of-the-foreign-born-population-in-the-united-states-2014/.

Pew Research Center. (2016b). Retrieved from www.pewhispanic.org/2016/11/03/size-of-u-s-unauthorized-immigrant-workforce-stable-after-the-great-recession/.

United States Department of Transportation. (2016). *Bureau of Transportation Statistics, table 1–54: U.S.-Mexican border land-freight gateways: Number of incoming truck or rail container crossings.* Retrieved from www.rita.dot.gov/bts/sites/rita.dot.gov.bts/files/publications/national_transportation_statistics/html/table_01_54.html.

Volkan, V. D. (1993). Immigrants and refugees: A psychodynamic perspective. *Mind and Human Interaction, 4,* 63–69.

Section II

Pathology of otherness

Diagnosis in the barrio

Chapter 4

The analyst as interpreter

Ataque de nervios, Puerto Rican syndrome, and the inexact interpretation

Christopher Christian

In her first visit to a psychotherapist, upon being asked to explain what brings her in to treatment, the prospective patient, a Puerto Rican woman, begins to tremble and falls to the floor, overcome by what appears to be a seizure – as if to say, "I'll show you what brings me in." She spontaneously lays bare the affliction that troubles her. She kicks and screams and in doing so, she violently expresses something that she will not or, for unconscious determinants, cannot articulate any differently. Her symptoms have been described by different terms, including hysteric fits, *ataques convulsives*, the Puerto Rican syndrome, and *ataque de nervios*. The patient experiences all the telltale signs of an *ataque* as now catalogued by the *DSM-5* (American Psychiatric Association, 2013). These include episodes of shouting and screaming; incoherence; and the loss of muscular control that can often lead to falling, experienced by a Latina. Despite how familiar and familial these symptoms may be, she remains unaware of what her symptoms mean. In therapy, she will work to translate them into a new idiom.

One can think of psychotherapy as a series of interactions between a clinician and a patient through which, over an extended period of time, they jointly develop a language that allows them to verbalize the patient's experience, understand it, and ultimately transform it. In this endeavor, words are privileged (Rizutto, 2015). "Nothing takes place between them (patient and analyst)," Freud (1926b) wrote, "except that they *talk* to each other" (p. 187). Even before the treatment method was coined by Freud as *psychoanalysis*, Anna O had already famously referred to it as the *talking cure* (Breuer, 1893). *Ataques*, like its kith and kin hysteria, poses a challenge to the aims of the talking cure insofar as action and somatization replace talk – the patient's communication cannot be confined to speech.

In his search for a form of treatment for hysteria, Freud soon encountered that the edict given to the patient to say whatever comes to mind, an instruction known as the *fundamental rule of psychoanalysis* (Freud, 1912), was soon met by some internal resistance in the patient. The seemingly simple task was impossible to carry out fully. Freud also recognized that there were other roads to the unconscious. Somatic expressions of conflict spoke a language of their own. In his famous case history of Fräulein Elisabeth, Freud writes that her leg pains "joined the conversation" by aching at particular moments, speaking to the unconscious conflicts that lay behind her overt physical symptoms. The analyst was like a detective, discovering clues as they attempted to decipher the hidden story behind the patient's complaints. A mortal, Freud (1905) wrote, cannot keep a secret:

> If his lips are silent, he chatters with his finger-tips; betrayal oozes out of him at every pore. And thus the task of making conscious the most hidden recesses of the mind is one which it is quite possible to accomplish.
>
> (pp. 77–78)

Symptomatic acts, as described by Freud, betrayed conflictual unconscious wishes about which the conscious mind appeared to know very little. The man whose paralysis could not be accounted for by an organic cause was, nonetheless, understood to be communicating his conflictual wish to leave his family. The daughter who could not move her arm communicated the ambivalence with which she held an impulse to strike out in anger. In the case of Dora, Freud (1905) observed that her playing with her purse represented a conflicted sexual wish.

> Dora's reticule [a square purse], which came apart at the top in the usual way, was nothing but a representation of the genitals, and her playing with it, her opening it and putting her finger in it, was an entirely unembarrassed yet unmistakable pantomimic announcement of what she would like to do with them – namely, to masturbate.
>
> (p. 77)

Freud likened the unconscious to a "foreign language" (Freud, 1923, p. 112). The task of the psychoanalyst was to serve as an interpreter, expanding the meaning of the patient's symptoms. An important question regarding this process of interpretation arises then: Between what languages or registers are interpretations (or links) to be made? Freud initially sought to interpret the contents of the unconscious. Repressed thoughts and upsetting experiences that were cordoned off from consciousness in the unconscious were thought to be at the root of the patient's symptoms. To relieve these symptoms, the analyst needed to bring the repressed material into the light of day. In this quest to access the repressed material in the unconscious, Freud believed that dreams served as the royal road, and he had hoped that the treatment of a case of hysteria would illustrate the "central importance of dreams" in clinical practice (Freud, 1905 [1901], p. 433). Dreams themselves required interpretation from the manifest content of the dream to the latent content of unconscious wishes.

As clinical practice evolved, it became more apt to think of the analyst's task as translating the patient's symptoms and complaints into the language of intrapsychic conflicts and compromise formations. Just as important as the elucidation of repressed material was the elucidation of the modes by which such material was kept out of awareness. Ego psychology and defense analysis focused on interpreting the patient's unconscious modes of self-protection (A. Freud, 1936; Brenner, 1981; Gray, 1996).

With the increased medicalization of psychoanalysis, particularly in the United States, other interpretations took the form of translating a physical symptom into a diagnostic label. A patient, for instance, describes feeling butterflies in his stomach and the therapist refers to this experience as *anxiety*. Ostensibly these interpretations aim to give the patient insight into seemingly inexplicable feelings, sensations, thoughts, and behaviors. However, as we will see, some types of interpretations could serve other functions, including that of alienating both patient and clinician from the *true* source of anxiety.

In this chapter, I offer some observations on *ataque de nervios*. I will review how the term was introduced into Western psychiatry and discuss the significance of the term "Puerto Rican syndrome" used as a referent to *ataque de nervios*. I will examine some cultural determinants of *ataques*, including the need for a witness. I then explore the connection between *ataques*, hysteria, and conversion disorders. And, finally, I consider how *ataque de nervios*, much like hysteria, is rooted in sexual impulses, but moreover how *ataques* can also serve as a culturally sanctioned means for both expressing and disavowing aggression in women.

Puerto Rican syndrome: On the use of a diagnostic label

Ataque de nervios (translated as attack of nerves) came to the attention of Western psychiatry in the 1940s and 50s, as a large number of Puerto Rican men began serving in the military. The condition was at the time labeled, perhaps with intended prejudice, the Puerto Rican syndrome. One of the earliest descriptions of the syndrome was offered by Ramón Fernández-Marina in 1961 in the journal *Psychiatry*. His brief article is important not only because it introduced *ataque de nervios* to the psychiatric literature, but because it did so in Freudian terms. In this piece, Fernández-Marina also describes what he saw as a bias in American psychiatry evidenced by a neglect among psychiatrists to diagnose schizophrenic thought processes in their Puerto Rican patients. Why, Fernández-Marina wondered, were psychiatrists so quick to use the new term "Puerto Rican syndrome" to diagnose their Puerto Rican patients, without detailing the schizophrenic thought processes that were clearly manifested in the hysteric attacks of these patients? He hypothesized that by employing the label Puerto Rican syndrome, the psychiatrist convinced himself that he need not look any further. The diagnosis served to foreclose a more nuanced evaluation of the patient and betrayed a prejudice against a culture that was deemed, according to Fernández-Marina, as "primitive, superstitious, and generally ignorant" (Fernández Marina, 1961, p. 80).

In her book *The Puerto Rican syndrome*, Gherovici (2003) ponders a similar question in regards to the adoption of the term "Puerto Rican syndrome." According to Gherovici, the term became a label that even psychiatrists on the island embraced, denoting the need to fit *ataques* into a new, sterile, psychiatric nomenclature. For psychiatrists on the island, the term distanced the medical doctor from the more familial term *ataques*. As epidemiological studies conducted in Puerto Rico (Guarnaccia, Canino, Rubio-Stipec, & Bravo, 1993) have shown, *ataque de nervios* was hardly considered a psychiatric illness by the general population. The phenomenon and its treatment were as familiar to Puerto Ricans as say stress, headaches, and aspirin were to the Western layperson. *Ataques* were a culturally accepted and easily recognized response to stress. So, it was puzzling that island psychiatrists embraced the imported English term Puerto Rican syndrome for what had hitherto been a domestic expression of distress (Gherovici, 2003). Similar to Fernández-Marina, Gherovici concludes that the use of the term served a defensive function. In adopting it, these psychiatrists rendered pathological a normative phenomenon with which they were culturally and personally familiar, but from which they needed to distance themselves.

Paul Verhaeghe (2004) illustrates some fundamental differences between medical diagnoses and clinical psychodiagnostics in his book *On Being Normal and Other Disorders: A Manual for Clinical Psychodiagnostics*. In medical diagnoses, the physician notes individual symptoms that allow him to arrive at a broader diagnostic category. That is to say, the physician goes from the particular to the universal. The specific symptoms of headache, muscle aches, tiredness, loss of appetite, and swollen and tender salivary glands under the ears on one or both sides (parotitis) in a young child, for instance, point to a more general category of the mumps. In psychodiagnostics, by contrast, symptoms cannot be understood independent of how they refer to the unique aspects of the person's present and past relationships. The clinician must work downward from the broader category to $n = 1$. Symptoms must be contextualized in order to render them sensible. The symptoms are inevitably a referent to a relationship with someone.

In the case of Puerto Rican syndrome, the symptoms have been de-contextualized on different levels, creating a state of alienation for the subject. On one level, there is the cultural and geographical dislocation of *ataques* when they occur outside of the patient's familiar cultural setting. In such cases, they afflict a woman[1] in a place where those around her are unfamiliar with the signs of her affliction. When a woman is overcome by an *ataque* in the barrio, it is easily recognized as a sign of distress. A spectator may ask what brought it on but will never need to ask what it is. When an *ataque* affects a woman outside of the barrio – outside of her cultural milieu – the unfamiliar witness, which is quite often part of the medical establishment, is left dumbfounded, helpless, and frightened; thus, the need to give "it" a diagnostic label whereby in the act of calling "it" something, be it panic attacks or Puerto Rican syndrome, "it" is contained and rendered less threatening, even if misrecognized.

Fernández-Marina and Gherovici pointed to a motivation in the clinician to apply medical terminology in an effort to distance themselves from the patient (or from familiar aspects of the patient with whom the clinician identifies). Yet we also see a motivation on the part of the patient to embrace the new terminology, one that serves the function of what Glover (1931) once described as the "inexact interpretation."

> [T]he patient seizes upon the inexact interpretation and converts it into a displacement-substitute. This substitute is not by any means so glaringly inappropriate as the one he has chosen himself during symptom formation and yet sufficiently remote from the real source of anxiety.
>
> (p. 400)

The inexact interpretation, Glover (1931) believed, would bring about symptom relief "depending on an optimum degree of psychic remoteness from the true source of anxiety" (p. 400). The diagnosis, like the inexact interpretation, is employed defensively. In the guise of explaining something, it moves the subject away from the particular wishes, impulses, and conflicts that are at the heart of the subject's anxiety. It is not uncommon to hear a patient refer to her episodes as "my attacks" or "my condition," denoting a degree of warmth and even affection for her diagnosis. *Ataques* express feelings that ought *not* be known directly, such as aggressive impulses and sexual desires. They are experienced as uncanny and mystical in nature, speaking to something that is outside the subject. Psychiatric terminology – be it terms like panic attacks, hyperkinetic seizures, or the now defunct term Puerto Rican syndrome – inevitably erases the patient's subjectivity. And paradoxically, as Glover suggests, herein lies its value for the patient. Unconsciously, the patient is motivated to not recognize herself and be misrecognized by medical terminology.

The need for a witness

In her novel, *A Candle in the Sun*, Edith Roberts (1937) colorfully captures the spectacle that an *ataque* is meant to be, as she describes the crowd that is drawn to Doña Concepción's house when she bursts into an *ataque* upon learning that her son is marrying a woman from the United States.

> Doña Concepción was having an *ataque*. The four-poster rocked with it. The whole house vibrated to it. . . . When two hundred and ten pounds of irrational femininity bursts into hysterics, reverberations are apt to reach the public.
>
> (Roberts, 1937, p. 9)

An important and defining feature of *ataque de nervios* is the need for a spectator. In a classroom discussion of *ataques* with a group of undergraduate psychology students, the majority of whom were Latinx and familiar with the symptoms, I asked the students about their understanding of *ataques*. One question threw into sharp relief the main difference between an *ataque* and a panic attack, a diagnostic entity with which *ataques* are often confused: I asked, "Would a person ever suffer an *ataque de nervios* when she was alone?" The pointed response from one student was "Why would you waste an *ataque*?" It succinctly spoke to the fact that *ataques* are a performance meant to be witnessed.

> This brought the number of persons in, or nearly in, Doña Concepción's spacious bedroom up to around twenty, had anyone thought it unusual enough to count them.
>
> (Roberts, 1937, p. 14)

Some clear distinctions have been drawn between *ataques* and anxiety diagnoses, such as generalized anxiety or panic attacks. First, an *ataque de nervios* occurs at a culturally appropriate time, which can include a funeral, the scene of an accident, or during a family altercation (Guarnaccia, Good, & Kleinman, 1990; Oquendo, Horwath, & Martinez, 1992). Second, a precipitant is always present. These can include a sudden loss, a divorce, a separation such as a child going away to college, and/or a verbal or physical altercation with a family member (Liebowitz et al., 1994). These precipitants are in line with the situations of danger enumerated by Freud (1926a) and referred to by Brenner (1982) as the calamities of childhood. They include loss of the object, loss of the object's love, castration or bodily damage, "and the various aspects of superego punishment subsumed under the headings of punishment, guilt, remorse, self-injury and penance" (Brenner, 1982, pp. 163–164). Even for a person who has suffered many *ataque de nervios*, each episode is preceded by one such stressor (Guarnaccia, Lloyd, & Rogler, 1999). Unlike an un-cued panic attack, there is no such thing as an un-cued *ataque de nervios*. Guarnaccia et al. (1999) believe that an *ataque* enlists the support of the person's social network, which is related to a third important distinction of an *ataque de nervios*: It has never been found to occur when the person is alone.

The importance of the presence of an observer as a necessary condition for an *ataque de nervios* was something I came to recognize in one of my earliest clinical experiences with *ataques*. It took place during my clinical internship year at a major metropolitan hospital, where I was charged with co-leading a psychotherapy group. On one occasion, when my co-therapist, the senior clinician, was absent, a new patient attended the group for the first time. Within a few minutes of arriving, this patient began to tremble, collapsed to the ground, writhing and kicking, and knocking over the chairs in the room. The meeting had to be cut short to re-stabilize the patient. Within an hour, the patient was calm enough to go home. The following week, she attended the next scheduled group meeting, to which my co-leader had now returned. Within the first ten or fifteen minutes of that meeting – and much to my appreciation, for I did not want my colleague to be spared the stress that I had endured while he was on vacation – the patient re-enacted the whole episode. What became clear to me then was the importance for the patient to have both group leaders witness her in the throes of her symptoms.

Although *ataques* are undoubtedly a performance, a problem arises when the act is performed before the wrong audience, one who cannot understand their role or what the *ataque* is meant to communicate. The psychiatrist, the therapist, and other health professionals become, unwittingly, the wrong audience insofar as the language that they use to decipher the *ataques* represents a foreign dialect, often influenced by psychiatric discourse, which ultimately contributes to the patient's sense of alienation. The patient who adopts her psychiatrist's term "panic attacks" to replace the native term *ataques* is, for better or worse, no closer to understanding what afflicts her and why. The idea that a symptom can both communicate and disguise the intra-psychic conflicts that lay at its source was at the heart of Freud's earliest ideas about conversion disorders.

Ataque de nervios, hysteria, and conversion disorders

The term "conversion" was introduced by Freud in his paper *The Neuropsychoses of Defence* (1894) to explain how a repressed experience becomes manifested in the body. Freud proposed that when a sexual memory is repressed, the libido that is detached from that memory is transformed into what he called "something somatic" (Freud, 1894, p. 49) so as to *discharge* the excitation. This need to discharge excitation was explained by Freud's *principle of constancy*. According to this principle, every experience has a "quota of affect" (Breuer & Freud, 1893–1895, p. 166) that needs to be expelled in order to preserve the health of the organism. Conversion, of course, was a central feature of hysteria. Thus, the process of acquiring hysteria entailed first and foremost an act of repression. Freud (1894) writes that in cases of hysteria,

> an occurrence of incompatibility took place in their ideational life. . . . their ego was faced with an experience, an idea or a feeling which aroused such a distressing affect that the subject decided to forget about it because he had no confidence in his power to resolve the contradiction between the incompatible idea and his ego by means of thought-activity. In females incompatible ideas of this sort arise chiefly on the soil of sexual experience and sensation.
>
> (p. 47)

But in addition to repression, there needed to be a discharge of the sum of excitation that was initially associated with the objectionable idea before it was repressed. As Freud put it,

> the incompatible idea is rendered innocuous by its sum of excitation being transformed into something somatic. For this I should like to propose the name conversion.
>
> (p. 49)

Somatization becomes what Freud called a *mnemic* symbol: that is, memories of pains through which the body processes the traumatic experience. Now and then, certain experiences or impressions similar to the initial traumatic event or idea re-establish the link between the idea and the original excitation, and another conversion is developed. The subject experiencing a conversion disorder could either "work over the idea associatively" or try to "get rid of it in hysterical attacks" (Freud, 1894, p. 50). So, talking about the idea, a process that entailed not only recollection but also abreaction, was one way of bringing about a discharge of excitations. Freud would in time recognize that elevating an unconscious event, experience, or a repressed wish to consciousness was not sufficient for symptomatic relief. The repressed content needed to be integrated into the patient's personality.

Fifteen years after the publication of *The Neuropsychoses of Defence*, in his condensed paper, *Some General Remarks on Hysterical Attacks*, Freud (1909) puts forth a second theory: Hysterical attacks can be understood as representing an unconscious fantasy. He relates the *mnemic* representation of the attack to the process of condensation discussed in dream work, whereby the motoric innervation that marks an attack can represent *multiple* aspects of a past traumatic experience or conflictual fantasy. Often the nature of the experience or fantasy being represented in the attack can become obscured by the fact that the patient can play out *multiple roles* of the different objects represented in the repressed material. This is illustrated in his paper *Hysterical Phantasies and their Relation to Bisexuality* (1908), in which a patient, Freud describes, "tore off her dress with one hand (as the man) while she pressed it to her body with the other (as the woman)." The pantomime in the attack may also represent the opposite of the conflictual wish, such as the case when a longed-for embrace is represented by drawing the hands backward until the hands meet over the spinal column. Freud (1909) writes,

> It is possible that the well-known *arc de cercle* which occurs during attacks in major hysteria is nothing else than an energetic repudiation like this, through antagonistic innervation, of a posture of the body that is suitable for sexual intercourse.
>
> (p. 230)

Apropos of Freud's idea of an attack representing multiple roles, or conflicting impulses, I recall a colleague's description of a case in which a patient, who was also being treated in group therapy, began experiencing an *ataque* marked by intense heat rising in her body. The patient left the group and entered a bathroom, afraid that she would need to undress in response to the suffocating heat. Significantly, though, the patient left the door of the bathroom open, and thus remained exposed to the other patients in the waiting room. When her therapist, noticing that the patient was undressing, offered to close the door, she responded, "*no, no, no déjela abierta*" (no, no, no, leave it open).

A key point in Freud's paper, *Some General Remarks on Hysterical Attacks*, is that the attack is designed to take the place of autoerotic satisfaction. Many of the

Figure 4.1 The circular arc – *"arc de cercle,"* Paul Richer, Études cliniques sur l'hystéro-épilepsie ou grand hystérie (Paris, 1885).

movements in hysterical attacks, Freud argues, denote elements of sexual activity, and the onset of the attack is marked by a surge in libido, where now the attack serves as a substitute satisfaction.

> Already in ancient times coition was described as a "minor epilepsy". We might alter this and say that a convulsive hysterical attack is an equivalent of coition . . . hysterical attacks, like hysteria in general, revive a piece of sexual activity in women which existed during their childhood.
>
> (Freud, 1909, p. 234)

A contemporary, even if unconventional, illustration of Freud's claim of a hysterical attack as a "piece of sexual activity" comes from Luis Rafael Sánchez's (1976) Puerto Rican novel *La guaracha del Macho Camacho*. La Madre is a character in the novel who longs to be the next Iris Chacón, a vedette, a star of Puerto Rican television, whose performances in scantily clad attire titillated Puerto Rican audiences every Saturday night during the 1970s and 80s. La Madre says:

> *Y las dos veces que me he perdido el show de Iris Chacón en la televisión me han comentado que le pusieron la cámara en la barriga y esa mujer parece que se iba a romper de tanto que se meneaba, como si fuera una batidora eléctrica, como si fuera una batidora eléctrica con un ataque de nervios.*
>
> And the two times that I missed seeing the show of Iris Chacón on television they've told me that they placed the camera on her belly and that that

woman looked like she was about to break from how much she was shaking, like she was an electric blender, like she was an electric blender with an *ataque de nervios*.

(Sánchez, 1976, p. 18; translation mine)

The above passage does as much to signal how Iris Chacón's dancing is like an attack of hysteria as it does to comment on how an *ataque de nervios* is a sensuous act. When La Madre describes Iris Chacon's erotic dancing, it brings to her mind an *ataque de nervios*. The passage incidentally also points to the pervasiveness of an *ataque de nervios* in Puerto Rican culture. Everybody knows what La Madre is talking about.

Returning to the evolution of Freud's ideas about the hysterical attack, we see that Freud moved away from the explanation proffered in his paper *The Neuropsychoses of Defence* (1894), where he explains an attack as a sum of excitations or a quota of affect needing discharge, to a psychological explanation whereby, as Laplanche and Pontalis (1973) summarize it, "what specifies a conversion symptom (or hysteria) is their symbolic meaning" (p. 90).

Ataque de nervios – a form of Puerto Rican hysteria

A remarkable feature about Fernández-Marina's paper is its description of *ataque de nervios* as a form of a hysterical attack – albeit different from those described by Breuer and Freud – one that is uniquely Puerto Rican. It is rooted in the child-rearing experiences and cultural practices of Puerto Ricans, taking into account their particular geographic location. According to Fernández-Marina, Puerto Rican families are large and live together in crowded conditions where, because of the tropical climate, infants are scantily clad, all of which contributes to tactile overstimulation of the infant's exposed skin by many objects. Fernández-Marina writes that the Puerto Rican infant is subject to

almost constant fondling, caressing, and handling by older siblings, grandmothers, aunts, and neighbors as well as by the mother. Frequently, the father, wishing to show off his son as a *macho completo* (complete he-man) will play with the infant's genitals.

(p. 82)

As an example of overstimulation, Fernández-Marina gives a father openly touching his son's genitals as a public celebration of the boy's virility. As Fernández-Marina was well aware, *ataques* is mostly a phenomenon that affects women. Yet it would have been quite different for Fernández-Marina to use as an example of overstimulation the touching of the girl's genitals, making obvious that such touching was sexual and suggesting that *ataques* were rooted in early experiences of sexual molestation of children, thus rendering them a pathological phenomenon rather than a normative one.

In addition to the excessive stimulation, Fernández-Marina claimed that the infant who is raised in close quarters is often consequently exposed to the primal scene. As an adult then, she employs the *ataques* as a device for achieving a vicarious orgasm. Fernández-Marina's Freudian adaptation of conversion hysteria, thus, leads to the following formulation of the elements of the *ataque de nervios* in adults: First, a traumatic childhood sexual experience, which can include overstimulation, is registered, then repressed. As an adult, a memory of the experience is triggered, and now enacted in the form of an *ataque de nervios*. The *ataque* both gives expression to the affects tied to the original experience and occludes the actual memory being enacted, with its attendant autoerotic gratification.

Ataques as disavowed expression of aggression

The emphasis thus far placed on repressed sexual experiences as etiological in the development of *ataque de nervios* among Puerto Rican women omits a feature of *ataques* that is most evident to anyone who has witnessed the phenomenon: mainly the unmistakable presence of aggression. Among the main dimensions identified in *ataque de nervios* by Guarnaccia et al. (1996) is a behavioral dimension consisting of aggressiveness, which can include aggression towards the self as well as passive and active suicidal ideation and/or attempts. A*taques de nervios* thus allow for the expression of aggression (Oquendo et al., 1992) among women in a culture where gender roles stress self-sacrifice and suffering as a feminine archetype. The term *Marianismo* (Collier, 1986; Cofresí, 2002) has been used to designate this pattern of behavior that conforms to a traditional female role of submissiveness in Hispanic cultures. Drawing on the iconography of the Virgin Mary, the feminine ideal is obedient, dependent, timid, docile, sentimental, and gentle (Comas Diaz,1988); and Latinas are expected to "show resignation in the face of adversity, abuse, or neglect" (Cofresí, 2002, p. 441). In this patriarchal context, a*taques* provide a culturally sanctioned way of simultaneously expressing and disavowing aggression. The woman who is overcome by an *ataque* is thought to lack agency to the point of losing control over her own body. She is not thought to be doing something but rather is seen as experiencing something happening to her.

Dissociation versus repression

Ataque de nervios touches on a debate in the history of psychoanalysis that has to do with the difference between repression and dissociation. At the inception of psychoanalysis and present in Breuer and Freud's work in the *Case Histories of Hysteria* were some fundamental disagreements about the nature of hysterical phenomenon. On the one hand, Breuer contended that hysteria was acquired during *hypnoid* states, marked by a split in consciousness. This idea of a split in consciousness placed Breuer's view in line with the views of Janet and Charcot. Freud, on the other hand, emphasized the *defensive* function of conversions. In order for a defense to take place, the patient had to recognize and repress an objectionable impulse or register a traumatic impression, and subsequently bar it from consciousness. Dissociation, by contrast, ensued when an experience had not been fully formulated into awareness. One oft-cited difference between repression and dissociation is that in dissociation there is an alteration in perception during overwhelming trauma that distorts the encoding of the event.

The DSM-IV (American Psychiatric Association, 2000) defines dissociation as a "disruption in the usually integrated functions of consciousness, memory, identity, or perception" (p. 477) and includes such symptoms as amnesia, fugue, multiple personality, depersonalization, and trance. Bromberg (1996) describes dissociation as an adaptive function "when one's overarching sense of self cannot hold two incompatible modes of relating to the same object at the same time" (p. 233). According to Bromberg (1996), dissociation results from self-states that lack linguistic symbolization, marked by impressions that cannot be rendered "thinkable." It is the alteration in perception at the time of the traumatic incident that accounts for a profound deficit in the encoding and integration of the experience, including its attendant charged affects. An unformulated experience, the mark of dissociation, differs from a concrete experience that is formulated, registered, and then barred from consciousness, which is the mark of repression.

We see then how *ataque de nervios* raises questions that tap into longstanding debates in psychoanalysis dating back to the original riddles posed by cases of hysteria at the turn of the century. Are *ataques* best understood as un-integrated self-states resulting from traumatic experience that have not been fully registered and lack symbolic elaboration? Are they manifestations of repressed sexual impulses being discharged somatically? Are they culturally sanctioned modes of at once expressing and disavowing aggression? And, are these explanations mutually exclusive?

Conclusion

While hysteria may have disappeared as a psychiatric diagnosis in the *DSM*, it is alive and kicking in the barrios. Yet, one would not know it judging from the scarcity of psychoanalytic works addressing *ataques*. The remarkable exception is, of course, Gherovici's seminal volume, *The Puerto Rican syndrome*. It is interesting to note that a syndrome from the barrio, much like conversion disorders at the inception of psychoanalysis, continues to perplex psychoanalysis and challenge our notions of mental functioning, the role of symptoms, impulses, and defense. Notwithstanding, psychoanalysis represents the best explanatory model for understanding and treating conversion and, by extension, *ataque de nervios*. Most contemporary psychoanalysts would agree that like conversion and hysteria, the etiology of *ataque de nervios* is not limited to repressed sexual experiences and wishes, but that an *ataque* can originate from repressed sexual as well as aggressive experiences and traumas. And it can give expression, via its symptoms, to repressed sexual as well as aggressive impulses and wishes.

In fact, it is more apt to say that *ataques* can simultaneously give expression to and defend against knowledge of an infinite variety of conflictual impulses and wishes. What specifies a conversion symptom (or an *ataque*) is its symbolic meaning.

It is also safe to say that both repression and dissociation play a part in the development of *ataque de nervios*. We can see how trauma overwhelms the ego functions of perception and memory, resulting in experiences that are un-integrated into a core sense of self and remain instead as split-off self-states or states of dissociation. But trauma can also trigger conflicted feelings and fantasies about self and other, and internalized object relations, both of which are repressed. Both features, repression and dissociation, contribute to *ataque de nervios* as a symptom representing a compromise formation – that is, a symptom that may gratify certain wishes, aggressive and sexual, while defend-ing against knowledge of such wishes. A very brief illustration is the case of a female patient whose first session was the basis for the introduction of this chapter. This patient described, and in sessions exhibited, a*taque de nervios* that were marked by dissociation, whereby she would go into trance-like states and would experience amnesia as to her actions following an *ataque*. But in addition to dissociation, the *ataques* were also marked by repression and unconscious identifications. In the course of her treatment, this patient recovered a memory of her father, out of control and needing to be constrained in a "straitjacket." This scene was likely to have been overlaid with other scenes and experiences. The accuracy of the memory is less important than the fact that her own *ataque de nervios* represented an identification with her out-of-control father, which had been repressed.

What makes *ataque de nervios* a distinct form of conversion hysteria is that it is modeled on features of Latino culture, including the role of a community in responding to distress. The fact that *ataques* require a witness not only ensures that it succeeds as a communicative act, enlisting support, but also ensures that the syndrome survives through intergenerational transmission. An *ataque* is there-fore always modeled on someone else's experience. Today's audience is tomor-row's performer. Identification is critical in the survival of *ataques* as cultural phenomenon.

Finally, psychoanalysis teaches us that general categories and diagnostic labels can sometimes have limited use, and in some cases rather than expand under-standing can in fact contribute to a defense against knowing. We can see how in today's market-driven delivery of mental health treatments, with an emphasis on expediency, diagnoses like panic attacks come paired with ready-made treat-ment plans. The diagnosis takes precedence over the patient's unique experi-ences, circumstances, and life history. The way back to the center of the patient's subjective experience is to situate the symptoms in the context of the person's impulses, wishes, desires, fears, and unconscious identifications. In therapy, the challenge rests in interpreting the symptoms back into a language that was known all along, but which the patient needed to forget. In the course of psychoanalysis, the paradoxical motivation for forgetting and adopting a new language in the service of misrecognition, be it the language of somatic experience or the medical terminology imported from without, is elucidated. The history of the term Puerto Rican syndrome bears witness to the motivation for forgetting and for misrecognition – a motivation that is not the patient's alone but can be shared by the medical and psychiatric establishment.

Acknowledgements

A passage from the book *Candle in the Sun* appears courtesy of Lilly Library, Indiana University, Bloomington, Indiana. The image *arc de cercle* by Paul Richer appears courtesy of the Musée d'Histoire de la Médecine, Paris.

Note

1 Despite *ataque de nervios* coming to the attention of Western psychiatry via male soldiers, *ataques* is most often seen in women.

References

American Psychiatric Association. (2000). *Diagnostic and statistical manual of mental disorders: DSM-IV-TR*. Washington, DC: American Psychiatric Association.

American Psychiatric Association. (2013). *Diagnostic and statistical manual of mental disorders* (5th ed.). Arlington, VA: American Psychiatric Publishing.

Brenner, C. (1981). Defense and defense mechanisms. *Psychoanalytic Quarterly, 50*, 557–569.

Brenner, C. (1982). *The mind in conflict*. Madison, CT: International University Press.

Breuer, J. (1893). Fräulein Anna O, case histories from studies on hysteria. In *The standard edition of the complete psychological works of Sigmund Freud, Volume II (1893–1895): Studies on Hysteria* (pp. 19–47). London, England: Hogarth Press.

Breuer, J., & Freud, S. (1893). On the psychical mechanism of hysterical phenomena. In *The standard edition of the complete psychological works of Sigmund Freud, Volume II (1893–1895): Studies on hysteria* (pp. 1–17). London, England: Hogarth Press.

Bromberg, P. M. (1996). *Standing in the spaces: Essays on clinical process trauma and dissociation*. Hillsdale, NJ: Analytic Press.

Cofresí, N. I. (2002). The influence of marianismo on psychoanalytic work with Latinas: Transference and countertransference implications. *The Psychoanalytic Study of the Child, 57*, 435–451.

Collier, J. F. (1986). From Mary to modern woman: The material basis of marianismo and its transformation in a Spanish village. *American Ethnologist, 13*(1), 100–107.

Comas-Diaz, L. (1988). Cross-cultural mental health treatment. In L. Comas Diaz & E. E. H. Griffith (Eds.), *Clinical guidelines in cross-cultural mental health*. New York, NY: John Wiley & Sons, Inc.

Fernández Marina, R. (1961). The Puerto Rican syndrome: Its dynamics and cultural determinants. *Psychiatry, 24*, 79–82.

Freud, A. (1936). *The ego and the mechanisms of defense*. New York, NY: International Universities Press.

Freud, S. (1894). The neuro-psychoses of defence. In *The standard edition of the complete psychological works of Sigmund Freud, Volume III (1893–1899): Early Psycho-Analytic Publications* (pp. 41–61). London: Hogarth Press.

Freud, S. (1905). Fragment of an analysis of a case of hysteria (1905 [1901]). In *The standard edition of the complete psychological works of Sigmund Freud, Volume VII (1901–1905): A case of hysteria, three essays on sexuality and other works* (pp. 1–122). London: Hogarth Press.

Freud, S. (1909). Some general remarks on hysterical attacks. In *The standard edition of the complete psychological works of Sigmund Freud, Volume IX (1906–1908): Jensen's 'Gradiva' and other works* (pp. 227–234). London, England: Hogarth Press.

Freud, S. (1912). Recommendations to physicians practising psycho-analysis. In *The standard edition of the complete psychological works of Sigmund Freud, Volume XII (1911–1913): The case of Schreber, papers on technique and other works* (pp. 109–120). London, England: Hogarth Press.

Freud, S. (1923). Remarks on the theory and practice of dream-interpretation. In *The standard edition of the complete psychological works of Sigmund Freud, Volume XIX (1923–1925): The ego and the id and other works* (pp. 107–122). London, England: Hogarth Press.

Freud, S. (1926a). Inhibitions, symptoms and anxiety. In *The standard edition of the complete psychological works of Sigmund Freud* (vol. XX, pp. 75–175). London, England: Hogarth Press.

Freud, S. (1926b). The question of lay-analysis: Conversations with an impartial person. In *The standard edition of the complete psychological works of Sigmund Freud* (vol. XX, pp. 183–250). London, England: Hogarth Press.

Gherovici, P. (2003). *The Puerto Rican syndrome*. New York, NY: The Other Press.

Glover, E. (1931). The therapeutic effect of inexact interpretation: A contribution to the theory of suggestion. *International Journal of Psycho-Analysis, 12*, 397–411.

Gray, P. (1996). Undoing the lag in the technique of conflict and defense analysis. *Psychoanalytic Study of the Child, 51*, 87–101.

Guarnaccia, P. J., Canino, G., Rubio-Stipec, M., & Bravo, M. (1993). The prevalence of ataques de nervios in the Puerto Rico disaster study: The role of culture in psychiatric epidemiology. *Journal of Nervous and Mental Disease, 181*, 157–165.

Guarnaccia, P. J., Good, B., & Kleinman, A. (1990). A critical review of epidemiological studies of Puerto Rican mental health. *Journal of Psychiatry, 147*, 1449–1456.

Guarnaccia, P. J., Lloyd, R., & Rogler, L. H. (1999). Research on culture-bound syndromes: New directions. *American Journal of Psychiatry, 156*, 1322–1327.

Guarnaccia, P. J., Rivera, M., Franco, F., & Neighbors, C. (1996). The experience of ataques de nervios: Towards an anthropology of emotions in Puerto Rico. *Culture, Medicine and Psychiatry, 20*(3), 343–367.

Laplanche, J., & Pontalis, J. B. (1973). *The language of psychoanalysis* (D. Nicholson-Smith, Trans.). New York, NY: W. W. Norton.

Liebowitz, M. R., Salman, E., Jusino, C. M., Garfinkel, R., Street, L., Cardenas, D. L., . . . Klein, D. (1994). Ataque de nervios and panic disorder. *American Journal of Psychiatry, 151*, 871–875.

Oquendo, M., Horwath, E., & Martinez, A. (1992). Ataques de nervios: Proposed diagnostic criteria for a culture specific syndrome. *Journal of Culture Medicine Psychiatry, 15*, 367–376.

Rizutto, A. M. (2015). *Freud and the spoken word: Speech as a key to the unconscious* (1st ed.). London, England: Routledge.

Roberts, E. (1937). *Candle in the sun.* New York, NY: The Bobbs-Merrill Company.

Sánchez, L. R. (1976). *La guaracha del macho Camacho.* Buenos Aires, Argentina: Ediciones de la Flor.

Verhaeghe, P. (2004). *On being normal and other disorders: A manual for clinical psychodiagnostics.* New York, NY: The Other Press.

Chapter 5

The anxiety of citizenship or the psychotic as citizen

Alfredo Carrasquillo

In his work on the history of madness, Michel Foucault showed how modernity was constructed around the exclusion of the madman as the other of rationality. The politics of otherness at stake legitimized the confinement of the madman and served as a value system to categorize and stigmatize human beings according to their ability to be rational and to obey social and cultural commands (Foucault, 1967; 2000).

As psychiatry and medical research have evolved, new explanations for the etiology of psychosis have emerged, but they seem to be consistent and share the very same imaginary structure of interpretation about madness that Foucault was able to grasp – namely, the person with psychosis is a deficient and lacking human being, and what is more, a potentially dangerous madman (Foucault, 1967). Nowadays, the explanation tends to inscribe that condition in the genetic wiring or the neurological particularities of the brains of individuals with psychosis: they are impaired because they come with broken mental equipment. Hence, at least for now, there is nothing we can do to repair what cannot be fixed. Hegemonic treatments – pharmacological treatments and hospitalizations, that is to say – serve to contain symptoms supposedly for the benefit of the patient, but clearly as well – or even more, it is honest to admit – to make sure the psychotic is not a social risk for their community and is not an unbearable burden for their family and their clinicians.

If psychosis as a mental condition is inscribed from the outset in the very genetic or neurobiological composition of the brain of the person with psychosis, it is easy to understand why psychiatric discourses today still legitimize, as in the very origins of modernity and even before, their subjective destitution and captivity as an object of medical and legal intervention and disciplinary action. In most societies, there is a prevalent legal and medical framework that infantilizes people with psychosis so that just like in the case of a child, they are in the custody of rational and capable adults; they are objects to be disciplined and controlled. Given that they are impaired and lack the capabilities to discern and make rational choices (as if neurotics had that sustained capacity!), the system legitimizes their destitution from the position of subject and their repositioning and objectification as *infans* in its very etymological original: unable to speak (Abrevaya, 2000; Carrasquillo, 1997).

The ethical choice at stake has political implications insofar as that destitution implies that people with psychosis are not fit to make their own life choices and to live and serve with the rights and responsibilities of a citizen. Consequently, and beyond discussions between different paradigms and approaches to the understanding of psychosis, the hegemonic psychiatric perception of psychosis, with its legitimation of the subjective destitution of people with psychosis, is a human rights issue that is being insufficiently addressed and denounced.

Aside and beyond the medical rationale that informs such an understanding and approach, it is worth exploring, as some anthropologists have done, what operates in promoting such a perspective. It is my contention that most psychiatric approaches to people with psychosis, just like the very physical disposition of psychiatric institutions inscribed in the heritage of the asylum and the panopticon, are built as protections against something, not clearly articulated, that is feared. Very recently, Spanish philosopher Adela Cortina proposed the concept of *aporofobia* to name what she defines as the fear of the poor or fear of poverty (Cortina, 2017). Most probably, there is a need to articulate a concept that could serve to name the fear of madness or the fear of psychosis. We know, however, that instead of naming a fear of otherness on the side of the clinicians, what conventional psychiatry does is to create a new disorder and include it in the most recent version of the *DSM*. That was the case, in our cultural context, as some researchers have shown, of the Puerto Rican syndrome (Gherovici, 2003).

In *Strangers to Ourselves*, a beautiful account of different historical stages in which humanity has constructed perceptions of otherness, Julia Kristeva leads to Freud and interrogates how human beings try to locate what is rejected or obscene of the human condition in the field of the other. What Freud teaches, she suggests, is that the foreign inhabits us. That our very humanity is inhabited by the other scene and that there is something "other" and "foreign" inside ourselves and not merely in others (Kristeva, 1991). Drawing on both Kristeva's conclusion and on Lacan's concept of *extimité* – that internal otherness that seems foreign to the narrative of the ego of the subject (Miller, 2010) – we should wonder if clinicians, by fearing what comes up in the phenomenological manifestations of psychosis and delusions, are fearing the emergence of otherness and of the unspeakable Real that is present and operating in their very subjective constitutions (García, 2011).

If this is the case, then perhaps we can make sense of the hegemonic and conventional psychiatric approaches to psychosis – complete with their construction of an organic deficit, hospitalizations, and pharmacological straitjackets rather than treatment for the benefit of the patient – as a defensive response to that unbearable otherness that clinicians cannot face as it reflects their own internal otherness.

While the antipsychiatry movement of the 1960s and other political responses to the inadequacies in the dominant approaches to management of psychosis were quite effective in denouncing human rights violations against individuals with psychosis, they were unable to comprehend the psychotic experience well enough to develop an alternative clinical intervention plan. They remained trapped in a romantic understanding of the need to create a free space for the deployment of the psychotic experience, not quite understanding the suffering at stake, for the person with psychosis, in such spaces of freedom and openness to delusions (García, Basaglia, & Basaglia Ongaro, 1972; Laing & Esterson, 1967; Szasz, 1973). Even when they made a strong case against prevailing approaches in psychiatry and honored the particularities of the psychotic experiences, their approaches failed to develop an alternative direction of the treatment and a deeper understanding of the psychotic experience to provide people with psychosis with a grounding that is not merely that of delusions (Apollon, 1999; Basaglia et al., 1978).

So if as clinicians we do not support the dominant practices, which rob individuals with psychosis of their autonomy and subjectivity, but we also do not want to celebrate "freedom" as a solution without any accompanying clinical strategies, we need to find ethical ways to respond, in the clinic, to the psychotic particularities and experiences (Downing & Mills, 2017; Lombardi, La Tessa, & Skiadaressis, 2012).

That is exactly what a group of clinicians did in Québec City in 1982. They made an ethical choice to provide young people with psychosis access to a clinical treatment in a middle-class neighborhood in the city rather than in a hospital setting. The treatment was provided under a key principle: patients will always be acknowledged in their subjective positions – never objectified – as citizens with rights and responsibilities who have ownership over their clinical treatment, a treatment that occurs in the community and includes a series of strategies – artwork, excursions, trips – to bring back the *usager*[1] into the social link.

This treatment program has evolved, with observations of its progress being integrated into it, to improve the patient experience in the "388."[2] For example, clinicians have learned that they cannot place themselves in the position of what Lacan called "the subject supposed to know" (Apollon, 2010). Clinicians instead sustain the absence and place themselves in the position of a student willing to learn about the psychotic experience, the patient's personal history, and especially those forgotten elements of both the patient's experience and history that come up as recollections in dreams. Dreams become a central element of the clinical experience with patients with psychosis, one that delusions attempted to cover up. Both the clinician and the analysand end up in a shared quest for *savoir*, for a new knowledge different from the misplaced certainty offered by delusions (Bergeron, 2010).

Such a repositioning of the clinician to make transference possible – transference understood as love of unconscious *savoir* – is not a mere tactic to gain commitment from the patient. It has a deeper ethical and epistemological implication: on the one hand, that there is something to learn from psychotic experiences, in particular hallucinations and what they conceal and, on the other hand, that people with psychosis cannot be silenced with medications. Instead, it is in their very discourse which lies their capacity to produce for themselves a new *savoir* and a new way of relating to the world and to their experience. The challenge for the clinician, then, is to listen with true interest and to learn without fear. The challenge of listening without fear implies that not all clinicians are equipped to serve as analysts for people with psychosis. A level of clinical experience – that starts, as we know, in the very analyst's personal *travail de cure* – is required to be able to listen effectively to the experience and accounts of a patient with psychosis.

Whereas the dominant psychiatric understanding suggests that psychoanalysis is counter indicative for the treatment of psychosis, several psychoanalysts and schools from different continents – just like the 388 in Québec City – have developed clinical and theoretical approaches that take us way beyond what Jacques Lacan (1975; 1984) called "a question preliminary to any possible treatment of psychosis" (Abrevaya, 2000; Lombardi et al., 2012). In fact, contemporary Lacanian psychoanalysis allows us to explore ways we can structure a clinical setting and a framework for a treatment of psychosis that does not limit patients with psychosis to the position of objects of medical intervention and control, but that insists on their positioning as subjects responsible for their actions and, as such, recognizes and sustains them in the position of citizens with rights and responsibilities in relation to the social link (Bergeron, 2013). In the clinical setting in particular, the analysand is invited to do some work – tough work, as *usagers* of the 388 attest (Potvin & Bergeron, 2013) – but work that allows them to speak again and to regain a desire to live and to explore other possibilities (Cantin, 1999).

Why are models such as the 388 relevant for us in the barrios? These novel approaches open a space to explore both how psychoanalysis is a clinical option for some of the most disenfranchised among the poor – namely Hispanic people with psychosis – and how it can open a new ethical space for the patient's desire to transform the social link, with all its political implications, instead of silencing it with physical or pharmacological confinements which end up being politically and socially repressive. This is perhaps especially true in the present moment during the Trump presidency, when the Hispanic is constructed as the enemy to be excluded and whose citizenship puts the nation at risk. Any ethical and clinical response to create a space for the voice of the Hispanic "other" is an important political and ethical act.

The value of the experiences, investigations, and observations of clinicians at the centre psychanalytique de traitement pour jeunes adultes psychotiques in Québec City, 36 years after its opening, aside from its direct impact in facilitating the transformation of the lives of many *usagers*, (Potvin & Bergeron, 2013) is that it has produced a unique understanding of psychosis, the psychotic experience, and the conditions that make a psychoanalytic treatment of psychosis possible. Thirty-six years later, the clinical experience is built and structured around key theoretical and ethical premises worth exploring, as they underscore the recognition of the person with psychosis as citizen and speaking being and not as object of clinical intervention to be silenced with pharmacological interventions.

Each year the 388 has served an average of 90 patients with psychosis who are between 18 and 35 years old. The Center is a project of GIFRIC, the Groupe

Interdisciplinaire Freudien de Recherches et d'Interventions Cliniques et Cul-
turelles, a nongovernmental organization created in 1977 by a transdisciplinary
group of around 30 mental health practitioners and professionals from the broad
human sciences. The center, not without very complicated struggles throughout
its history, receives public funding to support its operations and services, but is
granted fiscal and administrative autonomy that currently protects its clinical and
ethical model of services and interventions.

Each *usager*, who must make a personal demand for their treatment at the center, is part of a multidisciplinary clinical team that also includes a psychiatrist, a
psychoanalyst, clinical *intervenants*, and a social worker. The clinical team establishes and agrees upon the objectives of a treatment plan and coordinates the treatment and psychosocial evolution.

The central component of the clinical plan is psychoanalytic treatment, a regular and ongoing clinical space in which the analysand is invited to speak about
their psychotic experience, about things and experiences they have never spoken about before, and about things that cannot be expressed or that are censored
in other contexts. As Bergeron explains, it is important that from the very first
interview with an analyst, the analysand be engaged in the clinical process as
co-responsible for the clinical experience. The analysand enters into a symbolic
payment agreement with the analyst and commits to bringing written accounts
of any dreams to the sessions. The dream, says Bergeron, is an answer to the
analyst's *desire-to-know*: "Thus, in treatment, the dream will function as the
psychotic's 'ticket to ride' to subjectivity and individuality" (Bergeron, 2002,
pp. 73–74).

Aside from operating as a symbolic payment and contributing to the commitment to the experience, dreams "prove valuable because, with the signifiers they
offer, they are the best clinical tool for gaining access to the analysand's history"
(Bergeron, 2002, p. 74), a personal history that gradually, as it articulates a different narrative, allows the psychotic to interrogate delusional certainties and to
step out of them and out of the repetitive crisis they prompt. Jointly with such
an interrogation of the delusional certainties, the psychoanalytic experience aims
to create the conditions for the analysand to renegotiate a space as citizen in the
community and in relation to the social link. The new narrative that comes out of
dreams will become a new base to support a new existence that will limit the psychic power of delusions and voices over the acts of the subject. Two logics are
gradually confronted in the dream work, namely the logic of delusions and the
subjective history as it is rearticulated with pieces coming up in the dream work
production (Cantin, 2010).

Bergeron (2002) explains:

> In delusion, signifiers are "absolute" and words have only one closed mean-
> ing. In the dream, by contrast, signifiers open up other signifiers. The dream,
> moreover, yields signifiers which recall events that marked the psychotic's
> life because they operated a rupture in that life by remaining non-represented,

unassimilable, and unspeakable. These memories derived from dream-work, then, uncover gaps, loose threads in the fabric of the delusion and thereby put the delusion into question.

(p. 74)

As a result, Bergeron (2002) adds, "the psychotic's history will be based on signifiers that will allow access to his or her truth as a human subject marked by lack," a process that will create the conditions for a subjective repositioning of the analysand, away from being an enslaved object of an imaginary other and into a subjective stance filled with new possibilities aligned to their unconscious quests.

To support such a subjective repositioning, the 388 also provides support throughout the treatment, both for the *usager* and their family. The center has clinical personnel available 24/7, every day of the year, so that the patient is partnered in keeping daily activities and responsibilities, but also to support the patient when a psychotic break or decompensation takes place. The very logic of the treatment at the 388 expects and understands several breaks or decompensations will take place as part of the experience. During these junctures, the analysand can stay at the center (they have seven beds available for that) and continue the clinical work preventing hospitalization, unless the patient chooses to go to the hospital, a subjective choice that would be respected (Apollon, Bergeron, & Cantin, 1990).

The 388 also has a program of art studies – distinct from art therapy – via which *usagers* work and study with local artists and learn and practice music, ceramics, theater, writing, and painting, with the end goal of finding ways to express what cannot be expressed or transmitted via signifiers. A program of cultural, recreational, and social activities allows participants to travel in and outside Québec City, visit art exhibits, and take part in sports activities and special projects, all of it with the purpose of nurturing their integration with the community, preventing isolation, and creating new social and significant bonds with others.

Family members are supported with the aim of making sure they support the treatment and improve their interactions with their family member who is facing difficulties and undergoing clinical treatment. Counseling, support, and information is provided, especially in junctures of crisis when family members get even more concerned (Apollon et al., 1990).

Something that differentiates the experience of the 388 from many other models is that all members of the multidisciplinary team must undergo their own psychoanalytic cure. Also, all members of the team share the same theoretical and ethical perspective to make sure that no matter who the staff member is, the handling and interactions of all clinical staff – even administrative staff – are guided by the same principles. The clinical teams meet on a weekly basis and get the clinical supervision needed both to solve clinical problems and to make sure team members are able to listen adequately to their patients (Apollon et al., 1990).

Clinical teams and the whole 388 experience are guided by a series of working hypotheses for treating patients with psychosis (Apollon et al., 1990):

1   The patient can be treated outside a hospital setting, even during psychotic breaks and psychotic decompensations.
2   It is possible to treat a patient in the community, that is to say, in a normal social setting.
3   It is possible to articulate a psychoanalytic treatment of psychosis.[3]
4   Patients see themselves as objects alienated in front of the exigencies of an all too powerful other. Thus, it is important to address them as subjects capable of implicating themselves and of taking charge of themselves, and not to treat them or approach them as objects of medical intervention to which we can apply biochemical or psycho-education methods.
5   The reconstruction of the social link for patients goes through the reorganization of their relationships with others and with society.
6   All members of the clinical teams must have a joint clinical perspective and approach to patients.
7   There must be an administrative and information system to support the clinical work.

Innovation and the articulation of new ethical responses to contemporary clinical, social, and cultural challenges have been a key element of the 388 experience. Thus, their work builds on the teachings and legacies of Sigmund Freud and Jacques Lacan, but articulates new answers, building on the *savoir* produced in the clinical experience itself. It also takes advantage of Apollon's training and work both as a philosopher and anthropologist that began decades earlier in Haiti and France (Apollon, 1976). The writings and teachings of psychoanalysts Willy Apollon, Danielle Bergeron, and Lucie Cantin attest and transmit those new answers and their implications for a psychoanalytic understanding of the clinic of psychoses (Apollon, 1999; Apollon et al., 1990; 2008; 2013).

An ethical principle operates through the treatment at the 388. Its aim is not to contain symptoms, prevent delusions, or offer chemical straitjackets to patients. The aim is to create the conditions for patients with psychosis to gain full responsibility for their lives and futures, for living with and among others, and for their responsibility as citizens in society capable of contributing to society beyond their particular interests. The repositioning of patients in the clinical experience makes this possible. No longer are they objects of an imaginary other, controlled from the outside and having no free will or control of their lives, but rather they are in charge of their own lives and able, as a result of dream work and consistency in the clinical experience, to put limits to the jouissance of the imaginary others who have previously ruled their lives.

The evaluation component of the different research efforts at the 388 (Cantin, 2008) shows different manifestations of the results of the model: *Usagers* regain autonomy and are able to live on their own; they are able to get back to work and stop depending on government support; and the use of medications and the recurrence of hospitalizations are dramatically reduced. These results are possible because as Robert Hughes and Kareen Ror Malone (2002) clearly noted, the patient "is not regarded as an object of care, but rather treated as a subject of speech." And as such, as Apollon underscores, the model offers a listening space for patients' signifiers, so their delusions can take on a meaningful structure rather than remaining as unstructured, often frightening forces in patients' lives (Apollon, 2010, p. 73).

Bergeron (2002) explains:

> The framework of the psychotic's treatment must from the outset be anchored on the side of the symbolic Father, where castration, as we have said, is the law for all. The treatment must sever the psychotic from his or her imaginary relationship with that other being who dictates every action.
>
> (p. 73)

What does this clinical model for the psychoanalytic treatment of people with psychosis show us? What importance, if any, does it have for the reflections about the pertinence of psychoanalysis as a clinical and ethical tool in the Hispanic barrios?

Rethinking the position and possibilities of repositioning of the person with psychosis, as the experience of the 388 shows, has clinical and ethical implications. But it also has political implications. An individual who has been freed from the insurmountable demands of an imaginary other, who has come to understand the defects of the symbolic universe, is an individual with social and political agency – a citizen among other citizens. Furthermore, that individual may then be uniquely qualified to see and relate to the defects in the symbolic universe in a way that neurotics usually cannot articulate and may fulfill a particular social role that is consistent with what Bergeron calls the "utopia of the psychotic" (Bergeron, 2008). It is compelling to consider what effects might occur if as clinicians we take seriously the *savoir* that the person with psychosis can articulate about the human condition and about our symbolic universe (Apollon, 1999).

The continued positioning of psychoanalysts in the field of medical knowledge and science would interfere with full exploration of these points. The role of contemporary psychoanalysis in the field opened up by Freud and Lacan is precisely to assess the dimension of the Real in the human experience, a dimension that is foreign and cannot be grasped by science and medical discourse. Hence, the field of psychoanalysis is that of analytic *savoir* and its transmission, not the field of medical or scientific knowledge that attempts (and fails) to reduce the human to the biological. It is from the ethics and particularities of psychoanalytic practice and *savoir* that psychoanalysts can contribute to the conversation, both regarding the clinical experience and with issues related to our ways of relating and living together in the social link.

There, psychoanalysts have a political role to play. If, as Éric Laurent says, marginalized individuals are excluded from economic relations, psychoanalysis creates a space for them in a field from which they are not excluded, namely, the field of language. If they are speaking beings, Laurent says, they can speak and as such, they can produce solutions (Laurent, 2008). As clinicians, we must decide if we stand on the side of exclusion and political and social repression or if we intend to address the treatment of psychosis as a human rights issue in our Hispanic barrios, just as our colleagues from Québec have done at the 388 with their French-speaking patients.

The hegemony of Donald Trump and his discourse and violent gestures against Hispanics attempt to create anxiety about Hispanic citizenship to legitimize exclusions and persecution against immigrants. Hispanic people with psychosis are doubly excluded and silenced for being Hispanics and having psychosis. Creating clinical spaces for their speech, in which they are not objectified but acknowledged as subjects and as citizens, is both an ethical and political response that explains why psychoanalysis must have a place in our barrios.

Notes

1 *Usager* (literally, user) is the term used at the 388 to name their participants, patients or analysands. It underscores the active role or agency of the psychotic in the clinical experience.
2 The "388" refers to the number of the street in the address where the Center (Centre psychanalytique de traitment pour jeunes adultes psychotiques) is located in Québec City.
3 Granted that certain theoretical and technical transformations are necessary for the psychoanalytic treatment of psychosis (Apollon, 1999; Cantin, 2009).

References

Abrevaya, E. (2000). *La locura como pasión: Freud, Lacan, Winnicot, Foucault*. San Juan: Postdata.
Apollon, W. (1976). *Le Vaudou: Un espace pour les "voix."* Paris, France: Galilée.
Apollon, W. (1999). *Psychoses: l'offre de l'analyste*. Québec, Canada: GIFRIC.
Apollon, W. (2010). Clínica psicoanalítica de las psicosis. *Intervalo*, 91–114.
Apollon, W., Bergeron, D., & Cantin, L. (1990). *Traiter la psychose*. Québec, Canada: GIFRIC.
Apollon, W., Bergeron, D., & Cantin, L. (2008). *La cure psychoanalytique du psychotique*. Québec, Canada: GIFRIC.
Apollon, W., Bergeron, D., & Cantin, L. (2013). *Un avenir pour le psychotique*. Québec, Canada: GIFRIC.
Basaglia, F., Langer, M., Caruso, I., Szasz, T., Verón, E., Suárez, A., & Barrientos, G. (1978). *Razón, locura y sociedad*. México: Siglo XXI editores.
Bergeron, D. (2002). *After Lacan: Clinical practice and the subject of the unconscious*. Albany, NY: State University of New York Press.
Bergeron, D. (2008). Utopie et psychose: la quête du transcendant. In W. Apollon, D. Bergeron, & L. Cantin (Eds.), *La cure psychoanalytique du psychotique* (pp. 295–326). Québec, Canada: GIFRIC.

Bergeron, D. (2010). La producción del cuerpo psicótico y sus consecuencias clínicas. *Intervalo*, 115–132.

Bergeron, D. (2013). Les conditions d'efficacité de la cure analytique avec le psychotique. In W. Apollon, L. Cantin, & D. Bergeron (Eds.), *Un avenir pour le psychotique: Le dispositif du traitement psychanalitique* (pp. 35–47). Québec, Canada: GIFRIC.

Cantin, L. (1999). Preface. In W. Apollon (Ed.), *Psychoses: l'offre de l'analyste* (pp. 11–14). Québec, Canada: GIFRIC.

Cantin, L. (2008). Comment penser une évaluation d'un traitment psychanalytique de la psychose. In W. Apollon, D. Bergeron, & L. Cantin (Eds.), *La cure psychanalytique du psychotique: Enjeux et stratégies* (pp. 87–120). Québec, Canada: GIFRIC.

Cantin, L. (2009). An effective treatment of psychosis with psychoanalysis in Québec City, since 1982. *Annual Review of Critical Psychology, 7*, 286–319.

Cantin, L. (2010). ¿Qué nos enseña la psicosis sobre la clínica del síntoma? *Intervalo*, 133–150.

Carrasquillo, A. (1997). La infantilización del otro. In *Actas del Coloquio sobre lo Infantil*. San Juan, PR: Taller del Discurso Analítico.

Cortina, A. (2017). *Aporofobia, el rechazo al pobre: Un desafío para la sociedad democrática*. Barcelona, Spain: Paidós Ibérica.

Downing, D. L., & Mills, J. (2017). *Outpatient treatment of psychosis*. London: Karnac.

Foucault, M. (1967). *Historia de la locura en la época clásica*. México: Fondo de Cultura Económica.

Foucault, M. (2000). *Los anormales*. Buenos Aires, Argentina: Fondo de Cultura Económica.

García, C. (2011). ¿Antipsicótico es lo mismo que odio y repudio al psicótico? *Cruce: Crítica Socio-Cultural Contemporánea, 1*.

García, R., Basaglia, F., & Basaglia Ongaro, F. (1972). ¿Psiquiatría o ideología de la locura? Barcelona, Spain: Anagrama.

Gherovici, P. (2003). *The Puerto Rican syndrome*. New York, NY: Other Press.

Hughes, R., & Ror Malone, K. (2002). Introduction. In W. Apollon, D. Bergeron, & L. Cantin (Eds.), *After Lacan: Clinical practice and the subject of the unconscious* (pp. 1–34). Albany, NY: State University of New York Press.

Kristeva, J. (1991). *Extranjeros para nosotros mismos*. Barcelona: Plaza & Janés.

Lacan, J. (1975). De una cuestión preliminar a todo tratamiento posible de la psicosis. In J. Lacan (Ed.), *Escritos 2* (pp. 513–564). México: Siglo XXI editores.

Lacan, J. (1984). *El seminario de Jacques Lacan: Libro 3: Las psicosis 1955–1956*. Buenos Aires, Argentina: Paidós.

Laing, R., & Esterson, A. (1967). *Cordura, locura y familia: Familias de esquizofrénicos*. México: Fondo de Cultura Económica.

Laurent, E. (2008, July 9). Hemos transformado el cuerpo humano en un nuevo dios. *La nación*.

Lombardi, G., La Tessa, M., & Skiadaressis, R. (2012). *La clínica del psicoanálisis: Las psicosis*. Buenos Aires, Argentina: Atuel.

Miller, J.-A. (2010). *Extimidad*. Buenos Aires, Argentina: Paidós.

Potvin, M., & Bergeron, D. (2013). Le point de vue des usagers. In W. Apollon, D. Bergeron, & L. Cantin (Eds.), *Un avenir pour le psychotique: Le dispositif du traitement psychanalytique* (pp. 169–189). Québec, Canada: GIFRIC.

Szasz, T. (1973). *El mito de la enfermedad mental*. Buenos Aires, Argentina: Amorrortu editores.

Chapter 6

Eating brains

Latinx barrios, psychoanalysis and neuroscience

Antonio Viego

There is an interesting error made in revered British neurologist Oliver Sacks's 1985 case study, "The Autist Artist" (Sacks, 1998) regarding the calculation of the number of years a new patient, José, "said to be hopelessly retarded" (p. 214), spent allegedly sequestered by his family in the home's cellar. In fact, Sacks writes that "for fifteen years he scarcely emerged from the house" (p. 221). Earlier we are told that what brings José to the hospital where Sacks will first see him are the violent, destructive seizures he suffered at 21 years of age – the most recent one, a "fit" of "rage of a sudden, unprecedented, and frightening violence . . . in which objects were smashed" (p. 222). Either José was 23 when Sacks first sees him or there are some miscalculations made as to the number of years José spent at home or as to his age when the illness first set in. This makes the first object Sacks asks José to draw – a pocket watch – particularly interesting. One might say that the case study itself gets the time wrong or doesn't know how to tell time or that something about José's case scrambles a certain temporal order.

Sacks's case study, centered as it is on "José," presents a capacious holding frame in this essay for several points of discussion that together serve to metaphorize a variety of conceptual preoccupations and promptings under the rubric "Latino/a barrios and psychoanalysis." These include the meaning of "psychoanalysis in the barrios" as well as its inverse, the meaning of "barrios in psychoanalysis." There are myriad questions inherent in this exploration. Can Lacanian psychoanalysis be understood as a "culturally affirming (barriological) spatial practice" (Villa, 2000)? In what ways do significant advances in neurobiology have an impact upon the questions raised in debates about "psychoanalysis in the barrio"? Do these compel psychoanalysts, philosophers, and theorists of subjectivity to pay attention to the biology of the brain (Johnston & Malabou, 2013, p. xv)? Finally, for those of us working at the intersection of Latina/o studies, psychoanalysis, neuro-psychoanalysis, and affective neurosciences, is it time to think about the impact that the mostly recent nominatory term, "Latinx," may have on our research, practices, clinics, and classrooms? Early in this case study, Dr. Sacks learns from hospital staff that José "is just a Xerox" (p. 217). Borrowing this X, I will explore whether José is productively imagined as a "Latinx" analysand.

Getting back to the details of the family's sequestration of José, they are scant, to say the least; it is as though José had disappeared from the world, from society. One should also keep in mind, in fact, that the reader is never told where in the world the events in the case study take place. There is a family home, a state hospital, and a clinic. Sacks reveals that José had been living in the cellar of the family home and would have remained there if not for the violent attacks that landed him in the hospital. "José had suffered from confusion and chaos – partly organic epilepsy, partly the disorder of his life – and from confinement and bondage, also both epileptic and existential" (p. 222). The case study takes a slightly odd turn at this point as Sacks appears to use as a point of departure the scene of José's admission to a state hospital in order to discuss the benefits of hospitals and asylums for some subjects; "Hospital was good for José, perhaps lifesaving, at this point in his life, and there is no doubt that he himself felt this fully" (p. 222).

Let's return first to Sacks's commentary on José's admission to the state hospital in order to enter into an exploration of the meaning of "psychoanalysis in the barrios." As I've already commented above, Sacks does not do the work of locating the familial home or hospital for us, whether they are in or in proximity to Latino/a barrios, or whether these sites are in the United States. However, I don't think this imperils the asking of questions that I have in mind here regarding the meaning of "psychoanalysis in the barrios." We continue to be greatly indebted to Patricia Gherovici's now classic study *The Puerto Rican Syndrome* (2003), in which she painstakingly details her experience as a Lacanian clinician whose practice is squarely located in the Puerto Rican barrios of North Philadelphia in the 1990s.

In what follows, I will review some of the establishing claims Gherovici makes early in that text, then compare those claims with another classic piece of critical race theory and American and Chicana/o Studies scholarship focused on the politics of space and place, Raúl Villa's, 2000 *Barrio Logos: Space and Place in Urban Chicano Literature and Culture*. Although these texts are referencing two different "Latino/a" barrios – one Puerto Rican and the other Chicano/a, or Mexican-American – a comparison is unquestionably still useful. My intent here is to have readers consider Villa's description of the practices that inhere in his notion of "barrioization" as occurring within the barrios that Gherovici invokes. Early in her text, Gherovici describes to her readers some of the obstacles one may find in dealing with marginalized groups: "urban poverty, alcoholism, drug addiction, disintegrating families, and the most extreme violence, encountered on a daily basis and manifesting itself in the most aberrant forms" (p. 21). Next, I would like us to consider Villa's working definition for "barrioization," one he understands as composed of a set of complex dominating social processes that although originating outside of the barrios

was not imposed without significant response by the Mexicanos living within, and acting on behalf of, their developing social milieus. The situating powers of the landscape, law, and media effects have been regularly, if not uniformly, contested or circumvented by Chicanos. Barrio residents have consciously and unconsciously enacted resistive tactics or defensive mechanisms to secure and preserve the integrity of their cultural place-identity within and against the often hostile space regulation of dominant urbanism.

(p. 5)

I want to think about these terms, "psychoanalysis" and "barrios," separately, first to impose on myself the necessity of asking questions of each before settling on the presence of one in the other, as in "psychoanalysis *in* the barrios." We want to create the opportunity for "psychoanalysis" to question, to ask what it is it thinks it is getting "in" to. This means having a working understanding of what a "barrio" is beyond only images and experiences of community degradation, disenfranchisement, and disintegration. We are afforded here the privilege of having at our disposal a fairly robust history of critical, theoretical, and artistic accounts of "barrios," "barriology," and "barrioization" dating back to the Chicano Movement in the late 1960s, specifically to the work of the artist collective *Con Safos* in East Los Angeles, for whom the term "barriology" keyed a "playful but serious promotion of the cultural knowledge and practices particular to the barrio" (Villa, 2000, pp. 6–7). As has been noted by key Chicano historians like Richard Griswold del Castillo, "barrios" have provided a feeling of "home," a "geographical identity," of sorts, to marginalized, dispossessed, and poor Chicano/as (1979, p. 150). At the same time, "barrios" have always been seen as more than spaces of communalism and security that provide the means for expressly affirming cultural practices. Writing in 1979, Griswold del Castillo remarks that at the same time "barrios" represented "a place of familial warmth and brotherhood, it was also a place of poverty, crime, illness, and despair. To this day, Chicanos continue to feel ambivalent about the barrio" (p. 140). Again, although it's obvious that Gherovici, Griswold del Castillo, and Villa are remarking on different Latino/a barrios informed by and expressive of different cultural traditions and subjected to non-identical forms of ongoing disenfranchisement, I would like to retain what is still relevant across these different descriptions to illustrate certain shared commonalities between Puerto Rican barrios in Northeast Philadelphia in the 1990s and Chicano/a barrios in the 1960s–90s. Villa writes, "Nevertheless, many of the cultural practices produced and exercised in the barrios have tended toward positive articulations of community consciousness, which contribute to a psychologically and materially sustaining sense of 'home' location" (2000, p. 5). I would like to underscore the latter part of Villa's remark, specifically those practices exercised in barrios contributing to a "psychologically . . . sustaining sense of 'home' location." How can psychoanalysis be practiced in Latino/a barrios while remaining alive and listening to the ambivalence that Griswold del Castillo notes above?

When it comes to the mental health model most commonly made available in Latino/a barrios, Gherovici reminds us that in most cases,

> the mental health services available to the Hispanic community are geared toward simply symptom suppression. This model is functionalist, based on the idea of correcting symptoms with the goal of helping – or even forcing – the patient to comply with the model of capitalist productivity.

> (p. 21)

I want to ask my reader again to hold this passage in mind while working through the following set of claims made by Villa, claims made on the heels of a spirited grappling with Michel de Certeau's *The Practice of Everyday Life*. He writes,

> Manifesting alternative needs and interests from those of the dominant public sphere, the expressive practices of barrio social and cultural reproduction – from the mundane exercises of daily-round and leisure activities to the formal articulation of community defensive goals in organizational forums and dis- cursive media – reveal multiple possibilities for re-creating and re-imagining dominant urban *space* as community-enabling *place*. Thus, they contribute to a cumulative "anti-discipline" that subverts the totalizing impulse of the dominant social space containing the barrios. Collectively, these community- sustaining practices constitute a tactical ethos (and aesthetic) of *barriology* ever engaged in counterpoint to external barrioization.

> (p. 6)

If we take another look at what Gherovici states mental health services for Latino/as are geared to – "simply symptom suppression" with a goal toward plug- ging the Latino/a patient back into the machine of capitalist productivity – we can see that this approach runs counter to what Villa notes is defining of the "expres- sive practices of barrio social and cultural reproduction" – that they manifest alternative needs and interests from those of the dominant public sphere. Read- ing Gherovici and Villa in concert here, we might note that there is a species of mismatch between the needs and general ethos of barrio culture and the routine approach of most mental health services, whose primary goal is to adequately adjust the subject to the needs of capitalism which most often requires temporary symptom reduction.

In an effort to continue cobbling together what I am calling a call and response between Gherovici's and Villa's meditations on "barrios," I want to return to a section in Gherovici's first chapter of *The Puerto Rican Syndrome*, where she is providing background regarding both her particular psychoanalytic orientation and her arrival in Northeast Philadelphia. She notes that coming "from a devel- oping Latin-American culture" and being a Lacanian psychoanalyst today in the

United States "means being a minority within a minority" (p. 3). This is perhaps one way of understanding the meaning of "barrios in psychoanalysis" insofar as Lacanian psychoanalysis continues to be an outsider to the list of preferred psychoanalytic treatments available in the United States.

> Feeling myself disenfranchised as a minority, since after all I was a Lacanian psychoanalyst, I found myself working in the middle of a much more disenfranchised community. Lacan, for many critics in North American circles, is known as the "French Freud" and considered to be elitist; his take on psychoanalysis is seen as abstract intellectual pursuit closer to literary theory than to clinical practice. Anyone with such training may look like an unlikely candidate to offer any useful clinical contribution, especially given the practical concerns raised by "ghettoized" Latino populations. My clinical work in the *barrio* has led me to conclude that psychoanalytic practice itself has been "ghettoized."
>
> (p. 3)

As strange as it might read to some (and I know I have not and likely will not draw out all of the specificities of Lacanian psychoanalytic theory), the basic anti-functionalist model a Lacanian psychoanalytic orientation generally follows, one that does not seek to "correct" and "fix" symptoms with an eye toward adjusting the patient (analysand) so that he or she might fulfill the needs of capitalist productivity, is consonant with the motives and practices expressed within Latino/a barrios where people are having to operate the tension between external "socially deforming (barrioizing) and culturally affirming (barriological) spatial practices" (Villa, 2000, p. 8). Lacanian psychoanalysis in the barrios should not be taken to mean, in any strict sense, the preservation of barrio spaces as spaces of desirable living. I turn to Villa again,

> If the barrio is a complex and contradictory social space for its residents, the motives for defending its territorial and cultural integrity against external disruption must be similarly variegated. The nature of these complexities begs the question: Why is this vulnerable urban milieu so important to Chicanos?
>
> (Villa, 2000, p. 8)

Putting a finer point on this, one may say that what one's clinical work as a Lacanian in the barrio leads one to believe is that the functionalist approach, in particular, should be avoided in barrio settings unless, that is, one is precisely aiming to produce psychologized Latino/a subjects who absorb more than question the "totalizing impulse of the dominant social space containing the barrios" (Villa, 2000, p. 6) and that subsequently find themselves less skilled at developing what Villa calls "the tactical ethos (and aesthetic) of *barriology* ever engaged in counterpoint to external barrioization" (p. 6). In an interview with famous Chicano/a literary artist, Ernesto Galarza, author of the seminal 1971 novel *Barrio Boy*, offers,

> the preservation of a barrio is not the ultimate answer to anything. It's the same sort of thing you get when people talk about preserving a way of life. It's a pretty meaningless phrase. . . . Now there are always sentimental reasons for wanting to help people not lose their homes. These are powerful feelings but they don't give you much of an intellectual idea of what's going on.
> (Quoted in Barrera & Vialpando, 1974, p. 13)

A clinical approach that is functionalist, that is concerned with the psychological adjustment and re-alignment of subjects to and with the dictates of a preconceived agreed upon social, cultural, political reality, does little to answer Galarza's question of what is, intellectually speaking, going on.

So far I have been speaking mostly of "psychoanalysis" and "Lacanian psychoanalysis" as potentially *in* the barrios. Taking into account what's going on, as it were, in current psy-sciences, theoretically and clinically speaking, it would be irresponsible to not talk about the important, relatively recent, advances made by neurobiology that demand psychoanalysts, psychologists, philosophers, and theorists of subjectivity to pay attention to the biology of the brain. Philosopher and psychoanalyst Adrian Johnston captures this view sharply when he writes,

> I explore the future of psychoanalysis as it is enriched and carried forward by these same sciences. Despite this division, we agree that neither psychoanalysis nor the neurosciences (nor philosophy, for that matter) can remain unchanged in passing through these ultimately unavoidable disciplinary intersections. . . . ignoring the impressive advances of neurobiology lands the theorist of subjectivity in either metaphysical dogmatism of factual error – intellectual bankruptcy either way.
> (Johnston & Malabou, 2013, p. xv)

Embedded in that discussion is yet another preoccupation, one not necessarily germane to the history of psychoanalysis but crucial to the history of nomenclature in Latinx Studies, whose history has unfolded more or less in tandem with the historical shift toward "the neurologization of self" and one very germane to our discussion above – the speedy rise and adoption of the nominatory term, "Latinx" over "Latino" in the twenty-first century. I would like to take this opportunity to shrilly propose that anyone working in what Robyn Wiegman has termed "identity knowledge" fields – where "knowledges are animated by political desires that each has sought quite explicitly to know itself and to assess its self-worth by situating its object relations as a living habit of – and for – social justice" (2012, p. 4) as in Latinx Studies and African-American Studies, for example – can no longer ignore neurobiological research on the brain, research that is, if not changing entirely, adding new ways of thinking about subjectivity and identity in the twenty-first century. In this next section, I hope to follow through on my earlier proposal that we read José as a Latinx subject who has been removed from, as Sacks intimates, a precarious and dangerous home situation vaguely described as a barrio and housed in a hospital where he will receive neuro-psychological treatment. To do this, I would like to return to Sacks's 1985 case study, "The Autist Artist," to follow Sacks's reported treatment of José.

During the initial visit, Sacks asks José to draw a pocket watch. This was in keeping with Sacks's practice of asking patients to draw, both to assess "various competencies, but also as an expression of 'character' or 'style'" (p. 215). Sacks describes José's drawing as one of "remarkable fidelity." He'd put in

> every feature . . . , not just "the time" (though this was faithfully registered as 11:31), but every second as well, and the inset seconds dial, and, not least, the knurled winder and trapezoid clip of the watch, used to attach it to a chain. The clip was strikingly amplified, though everything else remained in due proportion.
>
> (Sacks, 1998, p. 215)

Upon closer inspection he noticed that the figures were of different sizes, shapes, even style –

> some thick, some thin; some aligned, some inset; some plain and some elaborated, even a bit "gothic." And the inset second hand, rather inconspicuous in the original, had been given a striking prominence, like the small inner dials of star clocks, or astrolabes.
>
> (p. 215)

Both Sacks's stopwatch and José's rendition of it are included as part of a single image early in the text of "The Autist Artist"; Sacks's stopwatch is on the left-hand side and José's drawing of it is on the right. Before I go on to say more about José's drawing, I would like to inform readers why this image, along with others drawn by José, is not included in this essay. After asking the publishers of Sacks's text, Simon & Schuster, for permission to reproduce these images, I was told that it would cost Routledge, the publishers of *Psychoanalysis in the Barrios*, $2000. Individual drawings by José could be purchased at the rate of $250 per drawing. My editors and I decided that using the images would be cost prohibitive. After conducting what research I could into the matter of whether José or his family were compensated monetarily for the use of his drawings, I have concluded that they were not. I had considered drawing approximations of José's images but decided I did not want to join what most would consider a disturbing, unjust dynamic of exploitation. In a passage late in the case study, Sacks informs the reader that José's "current 'job' is hand-printing sundry notices for the ward" (p. 232) and that there were any number of employment opportunities as a draftsman open to José given his skill, "but, alas, he will do none, unless someone very understanding, and with opportunities and means, can guide and employ him" (p. 232). It would appear that Simon & Schuster did ostensibly employ José for his drawings but did not monetarily compensate him for his work.

It is not only because watches and clocks generally come to dominate work days that José's drawing may seem appropriately chosen as the first image to showcase his drafting talents in the case study. His drawing calls up the images of soft, melting, pliable clocks in Salvador Dalí's 1931 painting, "The Persistence of Memory," invoking for this reader the question of time and futurity in Latinx Studies. A fairly ubiquitous move in Latinx Studies scholarship regards remarking on the enormous growth of the Latinx population in the U.S. Next, triumphalist claims are made about how this demographic explosion promises that Latinx subjects will enjoy increased power, electoral and otherwise, in the future. In short, Latinidad is mostly theorized in terms of the future, as something yet to come, and that somehow never arrives. Latinx is a future tense ontology. Cristina Beltran's introduction to *The Trouble with Unity* usefully presses its readers to think about the implications of this Latinx moment that never seems to arrive. Art historians routinely discuss how Dali's soft watches create "a haunting allegory of empty space in which time is at an end" (de la Croix & Tansey, 1980, pp. 831–832). I read José's soft watch as communicating a very similar allegory about "empty space" where time has come to an end in the endless contemporary pronouncements made about Latinx futurity, where the future of Latinx power never quite arrives.

José's seizures continued throughout the weekend but were brought under relative control thanks to the anticonvulsants Sacks had prescribed. Despite the fact that Sacks was no longer technically needed for his neurological advice, he nonetheless felt an urge to see José again: "I was still troubled by the problem presented by the clock and felt an unresolved mystery about it. I needed to see him again" (p. 216). Throughout the case study, Sacks presents José as an enigma, a mystery, a conundrum, an ontological and epistemological question. "What then was José, I had to ask myself. What sort of being? What went on inside him? How had he arrived at the state he was in? And what state was it – and might anything be done?" (p. 220).

I would like to borrow Sacks's preceding questions in order to inquire of these same issues about "Latinx." Specifically, I would like to think about the explosive emergence of "Latinx" in concert with the ascendance of the neurosciences and in the context of the neurologization of contemporary notions of self and of the subject. By way of example, a few students in my spring 2016 seminar, "Brains, Everywhere" struggled to see the relevance of this topic to Latinx Studies and Latinxs, given that the seminar had been cross-listed with The Program in Latino/a Studies of the Global South. In the seminar, I tracked the history of the last three decades of "neuro-revolution," which has given rise to a "neuro-society," "neuro-cultures," and "neuro-subjects." A key question in the seminar was how might the introduction of this "neuro" factor affect meaning in disciplines that were previously "neuro-free." This presented the opportunity to examine how the growth of a neurological perspective in these disciplines might create opportunities for different fields to potentially engage each other's research to ask broad questions about "personhood/subjectivity," knowledge, "mind/body," "self/ego," "emotion/affect." I thought the reasons for the seminar's relevance to Latino/a Studies was obvious. Why wouldn't this "neuro-revolution" and the production of "neuro-subjects" or "the neuro-consolidations of selfhood" (Bassiri, 2016, p. 45) be relevant to those of us working in Latino/a Studies? Employing the term "Latinx," some of my students appeared to want an explanation of some specific, substantive content about "Latinx" that made the course worthy of the cross-listing. Wanting to avoid invoking and deploying "Latinx" as if it were simply an extension of "Latino/a," I initially struggled to answer, as I had to consider what "Latinx" *is* or *does* before considering what the "Latinx" relevance of the material might be. There is an element of the Lacanian "Real" in the "X"; it cannot be made to make sense and it disrupts attempts at fixed meaning; it is the trauma that cannot be delivered in speech. It seems relevant that the ascendance of "Latinx" is taking place concurrently with the ascendance of the neurosciences. The notion of the "neurological self" currently circulating and the emergence and circulation of a term like "Latinx" are both signs of the general indeterminacy that marks the moment with respect to conceptualizations of the human subject. I would like, nonetheless, for us to consider the notions of self and subjectivity implied by the term "Latinx" and how "Latinx" might, for example, either illustrate, challenge, or ignore "the neurological consolidations of selfhood" (Bassiri, 2016, p. 45) that are allegedly becoming dominant today. An examination of the signifying labor performed by the term "Latinx" can serve to connect these issues raised by the "neuro-revolution" to, among other things, questions of race raised by "psychoanalysis in the barrio." As it stands, the brain as an object of study in this research goes unmarked with respect to sex, gender, race, ethnicity, etc.

Up to now, I have refrained from engaging in the still thorny debates regarding the use of "Latino" in cultural, scientific, technical, you name it, texts and studies. I do so now because I'd like to offer the reader a description of how this nominatory term is used in "Latino Psychology" and "Latino Psychiatry." The problems with the use of the term that continue to be rehearsed are the same. "Latino" unrigorously groups together significantly different – in terms of culture, language, politics, history, etc. – Latin American and Caribbean origin groups; sometimes, Central Americans are left out entirely. I will quote at length here from Ernestina Carrillo's in *The Latino Psychiatric Patient*:

> The challenge for clinicians working with Latinos in psychiatric settings is to learn how to tie the broad, general information about Latino culture and to apply it to the circumstances of the individual patient without making oversimplified, stereotypical assumptions.
>
> (p. 37)

Putting aside the difficulty of knowing when it is that one's working with "broad, general information about Latino culture" doesn't in fact inspire "oversimplified, stereotypical assumptions" about said Latino cultures, I want to draw our attention to the language of evaluation and measurement either explicitly referenced or metaphorized in this approach. We need to be careful that we not reproduce the currently popular logic that seeks "evaluation" and "measurement" as goals in and of themselves. For those readers working in colleges and universities with spirited assessment offices, in particular, you might have noticed that we more often than not appear to be measuring measurement and evaluating evaluation. Éric Laurent's (2014) sharp *Lost in Cognition* devotes attention to discerning how this obsession with measurement and evaluation shores up an ideology that we see comfortably ensconced in cognitive psychology and other currently dominant therapeutic paradigms.

> Cognitivist net-speak has spread quickly, coinciding with a generational shift amongst psychiatrists and psychologists. It is now looking to become more firmly entrenched. The common ideology, or rather the common hope, of academic psychology today is to try to reduce the subject of psychology to a system of learning.
>
> (p. x)

"Lacanian psychoanalysis in the barrio" cannot help but work against these trends. Mercifully.

Let me describe what is currently characterized as the "neurobiologization of the self" by turning briefly to Nikolas Rose and Joelle M. Abi-Rached's excellent *Neuro*. Rose and Abi-Rached attempt to illustrate the idea shared currently by a number of affective neuroscientists and neuroscientifically informed philosophers that the "self is an illusion created by our brain" (p. 200), by turning specifically to German philosopher, Thomas Metzinger, and his *The Ego Tunnel*:

> nobody has ever been or had a self: conscious experience is a creation of our brains, an internal construct in what he terms "the ego tunnel," which also creates "an internal image of the person-as-a-whole," which is "the phenomenal ego, the 'I' or 'self' as it appears in conscious experience" (Metzinger, 2010, pp. 1–12).
>
> (p. 201)

They sharply capture the questions this view of self-hood raises for the social and human sciences:

> Many ... regard this neurobiologization of the self as the most challenging feature of contemporary neuroscience. It seems to threaten the very conception of the human being that lies at the heart of their work: the idea that personhood is a matter of internal mental states – consciousness, intention, beliefs, and the

life – existing in a uniquely human psychological realm of mind, embodied in a self-conscious subjectivity, and created in a world of meaning, culture and history.

(Rose & Abi-Rached, 2013, p. 201)

What would a Latinx Studies critical approach look like here? Can Latinx Studies carry the "neuro" prefix? What would a Latinx Psychoanalysis look like? Just how profound is the correspondence Catherine Malabou notes in the following passage:

"Brain events" are intimately linked with our identity. We may even say that they constitute them. That is why there is a profound correspondence between the brain and subjectivity, between the brain and the "inner life." We have to understand today the way in which the brain "produces" our subjective mental life.

(Johnston & Malabou, 2013, p. 28)

Francisco Ortega and Fernando Vidal claim that brain imaging has been absolutely crucial for the "neurologization" of the human and social sciences and of our cultures more generally. The development of "electroencephalography" in the 1930s convinced some brain researchers that the recorded waves would offer direct insights into mental life (Ortega & Vidal, 2011, p. 13). Where is the Latinx subject to be possibly located in this? As Claudia Milian importantly reminds us, "The Latinx horizon hits up against so many daily uses in a way that Latino/a does – or did – not" (Milian, 2017, p. 4). The signifier called up here – what is hit up against – "x-ray" creates an associative link between "Latinx" and "brain imaging," not to mention, then, notions for what constitutes truth, evidence in a regime of the scopic. I think I feel some of the same unease that Nicole Guidotti-Hernández (2017) cops to; she struggles "with the easy and uncritical transition in discourse" that the term appears to perform and that most put into the service of performing. What amounts to policing, once again, the borders of this term, I would like to propose for now that Latinx not be understood as a term marking a transition from a previously known and agreed upon substance, "Latino/a." I don't want to deny that it emerges in complicated ways from "Latino/a" but it also kills off its maker. At least, it should. Ideally, anyway. The "eks"'s aural reconfiguration of "Latino/a" challenges the primacy accorded the visual register in the cultures where it reigns: one hears Latinx; one cannot say that one sees Latinx. One might say the angle of vision changes with "Latinx" and so it makes possible, quite literally, new ways of seeing and listening for Latino studies scholars and psychoanalysts alike. But as a term it does not make a substance miraculously appear that would definitionally represent it. Some have noted rather woefully that the term seems to have a built-in dehumanizing effect. That's not quite right. It has, to be more precise, a built-in other-than-humanizing effect. R. Galvan writes, "Its verbal texture distorts the established rhythm and sound of Latin in favor of eks making audible and consequently visible unseen bias created by the revised expression" (Galvan, 2017, p. 5). We need to be alive to the explosive plasticity of the term. It is, or should be, for anti-psychologistic uses; it announces gaps and fissures and breaks and splits. Latinx is not ego psychological; it is an illustration of the irreducibility of the brain to the mind, a point that has been the rather consistent critique made by Lacanian psychoanalysts of the affective neuroscientific work of scientists and philosophers like Antonio Damasio and Thomas Metzinger. Rather than think "Latinx" has got it right – made a space for every subject – we should understand it as the impossibility of doing so, even in the very attempt to do so. "Latinx" is to "Latino/a" what "psychoanalysis" is to "psychology."

Although we were not reading any material that could be said to contain "Latino" or "Latina" content in my "Brains, Everywhere" seminar, we encountered somewhat late in the semester "José," the autistic young man whose case study I opened with and that closes neurologist Oliver Sacks's *The Man Who Mistook His Wife for a Hat and Other Clinical Tales*. Was "José" going to stand in for the previously noted lack of Latinx content? We had paved the way for his arrival in some ways through our readings of Catherine Malabou's *What Should We Do with Our Brain?* and *The New Wounded: From Neurosis to Brain Damage*. The term "new wounded" was bandied about; we felt like we could think with it.

> They are, as the term indicates, victims of various cerebral lesions or attacks, head trauma, tumors, encephalitis, or meningoencephalitis. . . . In addition, we might think of the patients whom psychoanalysis has attempted to cure without success: schizophrenics, autistics, victims of Tourette's syndrome.
>
> (Malabou, 2008, p. 10)

The figure of the "immigrant" emerged in our discussion as a potential member of Malabou's "new wounded" contingency when we considered Malabou's later, more capacious definition of the "new wounded that would include all disenfranchised subjects who are victim to trauma and systemic violence and mistreatment. Although Malabou is skeptical about classical psychoanalysis' ability to treat subjects who have suffered brain trauma, she is generally supportive of neuro-psychoanalytic treatment, of approaches to trauma that understand neuronal disturbances at the same time they understand "neuronal disturbance in other terms than pure and simple physiological lesions" (pp. 10–11). Returning to my opening discussion, I think we can include Latinx barrio residents as members of the "new wounded" contingency.

Given that Oliver Sacks represents precisely the approach Malabou privileges, I would like to return to his case study and walk the reader through his treatment of José, one whose narrative of progress is contingent on Sacks's particular interpretations of what José's drawings mean. In their conceptualization of "Latinx," Fiol-Matta and Gómez-Barris (2014) write, "the 'x' turns away from the dichotomous, toward a void, an unknown, a wrestling with plurality, vectors of multi-intentionality, and the transitional meanings of what has yet to be seen" (p. 505). I see the analytic work in my reading of Sacks's case study below as an attempt to track what the "X" points us toward, which is to say, among other things, the moments of rupture, silence, and socio-political and ethno-racial familial trauma that so often unfold in barrio settings.

Sacks wanted to review José's entire chart given that he'd only been given a "consultation slip" that was not very informative. Upon their second meeting in a clinic at the same hospital, Sacks reports that the "dull, indifferent look, the mask" José had previously possessed was gone. This "indifference" (along with "disaffected," "blank") routinely appears in the affective neuroscientific litera-ture's description of patients with severe brain damage. Sacks tells José he has been thinking about him and would like to see more drawing. He hands José a copy of *Arizona Highways*, noting that its illustrations were useful for conducting neurological tests with his patients. He asks José to draw the cover image – an "idyllic scene" of two people canoeing on a lake at sunset with mountains in the background.

Once again, Sacks is impressed by José's rendition. For Sacks, it offered strong evidence that José was not merely copying the image but providing something additional: "The tiny figures, enlarged, were more intense, more alive, had a feel-ing of involvement and purpose not at all clear in the original" (Sacks, 1998, p. 217). Sacks describes all of José's drawings as more profound version of the originals; whatever the original image appears to do or want to do, José's versions do more of it.

Then, Sacks, turning to another page in *Arizona Highways*, asks José to draw a trout.

After these drawings, Sacks felt like he now "had something to go on" (Sacks, 1998, p. 219).

> The picture of the clock had startled me, stimulated my interest, but did not, in itself, allow any thoughts or conclusions. The canoe had shown that José had an impressive visual memory, and more. The fish showed a lively and distinctive imagination, a sense of humor, and something akin to fairy-tale art. Certainly not great art, it was "primitive," perhaps it was child-art; but, without doubt, it was art of a sort. And imagination, playfulness, art are pre-cisely what one does not expect in idiots, or *idiots savants*, or in the autistic either. Such at least is the prevailing opinion.
>
> (Sacks, 1998, p. 219, emphasis in original)

Sacks is still, up to this point, at a loss for precisely how to diagnose José. Sacks asks himself, "What then was José, I had to ask myself. What sort of being? What went on inside him? How had he arrived at the state he was in? And what state was it – and might anything be done" (Sacks, 1998, p. 220). At this point the case study begins to feel a bit like a detective story, "I was both assisted and bewildered by the available information – the mass of 'data' that had been gathered since the first onset of his strange illness, his 'state'"

(Sacks, 1998, p. 220). Again, mystery, uncertainty, and doubt provide the affective framework for Sacks's experience of José. Sacks is trying to understand why José would excel the way he does in drawing but cannot seem to produce speech. One wonders at the form of sociality that could be possible here, and it is certainly on Sacks's mind – he feels he is both communicating somehow through the drawings with José and simultaneously feeling shut out. Sacks begins to ask himself questions about the violent seizures and what they might mean and reasons why they invariably affected José's temporal lobes. Sacks reminds the reader that the temporal lobes are classically associated with not only the auditory capacities of a person but also the perception and production of speech. He cites another doctor's assessment of the matter, that José was not only considered to be "autistic" but that he also likely had a temporal-lobe disorder that interfered with his ability to recognize speech sounds, speak, and understand speech. What remained to be explained, an explanation that psychiatry and neurology could not offer, was José's loss or regression of speech. Following a period of normal development, José had stopped speaking to others altogether at age 8. There is an interesting parenthetical comment included after Sacks's statement that José had been "normal" up until the age of eight: "(or so his parents avowed)." This comment captures Sacks's implicit criticism of the family, a criticism that becomes more explicit later. Sacks does not trust the family's account. José's family, in the end, is made to carry the lion's share of the blame for José's condition. We do not know what his family might have been struggling with at the time. Did José have access to clinics such as the one Patricia Gherovici practiced in? Would the familial shame around José's condition – Sacks implies as much – have prevented them from seeking help at a clinic just as they'd apparently avoided seeking help at a hospital, until it seemed absolutely necessary?

Despite this loss of speech, one capacity "was apparently 'spared' – perhaps in a compensatory way enhanced: an unusual passion and power to draw" (Sacks, 1998, p. 220). We learn at this point that drawing was a skill possessed by several in the family and that José had shown a talent for it from a very young age. His father was an avid sketcher; his older brother was a successful artist. With the onset of his illness, José suffered 20–30 major seizures a day, innumerable "little seizures," falls, blank and dreamy states. His loss of speech combined with a general emotional and intellectual regression put José in a "strange and tragic state" (Sacks, 1998, p. 221). He was taken out of school, returned to the family permanently with diagnoses of "retardation," "aphasia," "epileptic," and "autistic." By the age of nine, José had dropped out of school, society, and, to use Sacks's term, "reality."

Then Sacks begins to describe his third encounter with José, a meeting whose details are meant to illustrate the benefits of José's treatment at the hospital (as opposed to the family home where he was sequestered in a cellar, as Sacks intimates). Unlike the other visits, this time Sacks appears unannounced, "without warning," in José's admission ward. Once more, a drawing is produced. It is the symbolic currency of these drawings that sustains whatever social bonds might exist between Sacks and José. I am discussing all of the drawings here because I would like the reader to see the kind of narrative Sacks appears to intend to provide with them, a somewhat linear, developmental narrative that displays in the end a better outcome for José, evidence of the fact that he's getting better, and that each drawing supersedes the 'previous one in its evidentiary status as a sign of improvement. In his account of this third encounter, Sacks appears to encourage the reader to ask after the form of sociality between these two subjects. The second meeting amounts to a kind of fishing trip between father and son out on a canoe. Sacks wants José to return to the trout he had drawn earlier, asking him to do it from memory.

> What would he draw now? He closed his eyes for a moment – summoning an image? – and then drew. It was still a trout, rainbow-spotted, with fringy fins and a forked tail, but, this time, with egregiously human features, an odd nostril (what fish has nostrils?), and a pair of ripely human lips. I was about to take the pen, but, no, he was not finished. What had he in mind? The image was complete. The image, perhaps, but not the scene. The fish before had existed – as an icon – in isolation: now it was to become part of a world, a scene. Rapidly he sketched in a little fish, a companion, swooping into the water, gambolling, obviously in play. And then the surface of the water was sketched in, rising to a sudden, tumultuous wave. As he drew the wave, he became excited, and emitted a strange, mysterious cry.
>
> (Sacks, 1998, pp. 223–224)

Has José imagined here for the first time the possibility of a kind of sociality, the existence of an other, if not an Other? Sacks proceeds to ask some questions about what the symbolism might mean. In fact, he asks himself first if these fish can be read symbolically. What he considers to be most important about the drawing, in the end, is the fact that José drew it on his own initiative, impulse, not on Sacks's suggestion.

What happens next reveals Sacks's fear of José's potential aggression. Sacks asks a question about the possible meaning of the waves, "In his drawing as in his life hitherto, interaction had always been absent. Now, if only in play, in symbol, it was allowed back. Or was it? What was that angry, avenging wave?" (Sacks, 1998, p. 224). So, Sacks introduces the possibility that this drawing may represent José's real attempt at a form of sociality and attempt to address an other but he's not sure – "or was it?" – and it's the existence of the waves in the drawing that appear to make Sacks question his original assertion. It's Sacks obviously who thinks to characterize the waves in the drawing as "avenging" and "angry." We won't expound upon all of the different ways we might read not only the waves but the fish (gulping, in a panic, in play, etc.). On the heels of the sentence ending with "angry, avenging wave," Sacks reports that he chose to end the "free association,"

> best to go back to safe ground, I felt. . . . I had seen potential, but I had seen, and heard, danger too. Back to safe, prelapsarian Mother Nature. I found a Christmas card lying on the table, a robin redbreast on a tree trunk, snow and stark twigs all around. I gestured to the bird, and gave José the pen.
>
> (Sacks, 1998, pp. 224–225)

José draws the robin, using a red pen for its breast. Sacks notices that the robin's feet seem to be "gripping" the branch, perhaps done so by José in order to underscore the "grasping power of hands and feet." But what most strikes Sacks about the drawing are the flowers that José has added. The scene on the on card was a wintry one, the branch a "dry winter twiglet" (p. 225); José draws blooms at the end of these winter twigs effectively for Sacks turning "winter into spring" (p. 225).

Let's think about what Sacks proposes these drawings represent. The two spotted trouts immersed in water crowned by an "angry, avenging wave" suggested an attempt to forge a social bond of some sort, but the wave that Sacks quite literally reads as another character in the picture board story makes him wonder whether this question about sociality and the existence of an other is even credible. The drawing of the robin, in the end, for Sacks is important because of the transformation of seasons that José magically effects with the inclusion of blooms – from winter to spring. One cannot help but think here of the – what to call it? – agency and autonomy of the artist here. In the first drawing that José will be allowed to create from his own memory, Sacks experiences something threatening, José's anger, and so stops the exercise and asks that José draw instead an image Sacks provides, here, the opening flap of a Christmas card. The details José adds on his own cannot be tolerated and are read in a very exaggerated way, it seems. Then the waves. Are they so threatening? Angry? Why would José have had reason to have drawn anything to connote "avenging," and wouldn't it be important to hear him tell us why? I have been at pains to imagine how this case study metaphorizes something about Latinx. I will risk offering here that the "X" represents what needed to go missing in Sacks's account of the first drawing that, to Sacks, is not present in the second, replacement drawing, as it were: violence, aggression. Virtually every dictionary definition of bloom will include among its first five entries, "a rapid and excessive growth." José's drawings cannot be accepted by Sacks, it seems, as communicating anger, protest, anything that's not affirming. At this point as Sacks moves on to tell us that the medical treatment that José received in the hospital

> had improved, it could not be doubted, his physiological potentials for speech. For José, there had always been two issues to contend with: both the fact of speech impairment due, ultimately, to frontal lobe damage and also

the refusal to speak, a fact that could not be rationalized either neurologically or psychiatrically.

(p. 225)

"A double malignancy of disease" is the phrase Sacks uses to characterize the coupling of the two.

In the final section of the case study, Sacks moves from the specificity of José's case to more general claims about "autistic" subjects and their relationship to the "particular" versus the "universal." First, we are told that on what amounts to the fourth and final encounter between Sacks and José that José had been moved to a "quieter ward." Sacks goes to meet José and is taken aback at what seems like José's transformed demeanor, "he waved his hand lustily as soon as he saw me – an outgoing, open gesture. I could not imagine him having done this before. He pointed to the locked door, he wanted it open, he wanted to go outside" (Sacks, 1998, p. 228). Sacks tells the reader that José led the way downstairs and into an "overgrown, sunlit garden" (p. 228). Sacks reports that this is likely the first time José has "voluntarily" gone outdoors since the age of eight, since the onset of the still only mysteriously explained "illness" and that upon entering this garden José takes out a pen he had brought himself and not acquired from Sacks and begins drawing a dandelion. "This, I think, is the first drawing from real life that José had done since his father took him sketching as a child, before he became ill" (p. 228).

Sacks thinks it's a "splendid drawing, accurate and alive. It shows his love of reality, for another form of life" (p. 228). Sacks's interpretations are at times a bit fanciful, something I can appreciate somewhat, but he's a bit too willful in his need to read certain images for what can only be called its "good" content – its positive, affirming content – and the evidence is often dubious. How is this flower, singular as it is, not a sign of a kind of regression from a previously symbolizable sociality that Sacks saw illustrated in the drawing of the two trout? The single flower also might be read as divorced from reality. Previously, Sacks read José's rendering of the robin and the blooms at the end of wintry twigs as transforming the seasons. Here we have a single flower floating in space, unmoored. Sacks tells the reader that the flower is reminiscent of those one finds in

> medieval botanies and herbals . . . even though José has no formal knowledge of botany, and could not be taught it or understand it if he tried. His mind is not built for the abstract, the conceptual. That is not available to him as a path to truth. But he has a passion and a real power for the particular – he loves it, enters into it, he re-creates it.
>
> (p. 228)

Sacks proceeds to make some comments about the "autistic person" that may sound outdated to readers in 2017, like "the abstract, the categorical, has no interest for the autistic person – the concrete, the particular, the singular, is all" (p. 229).

The case study ends with an appeal of sorts, regarding what it would take to make José a proper laboring subject. Before this is made more explicit, Sacks hones in on what he considers the final questions:

> is there any "place" in the world for a man who is like an island, who cannot be acculturated, made part of the main? Can the "main accommodate," make room, for the singular? . . . Specifically: what does the future hold for José? Is there some "place" for him the in the world which will *employ* his autonomy, but leave it intact?
>
> (p. 231, emphasis original)

The closing question is interestingly worded. Sacks's term "employ his auton-omy" hardly needs "employ" to be italicized as it is in the original to still cre-ate the impression that Sacks understands the fact of alienated labor. However, the phrase, "but leave it intact" where "it" refers to "autonomy" (of the laborer) makes one wonder why it might be specifically with José that this be left intact, and what that would mean in terms of labor and alienation and capitalism. The questions of labor, work, and employment are often front and central in case stud-ies on brain-wounded subjects. Descriptions in case studies always take up with the topic of the labor that the brain-traumatized subject in question can no longer perform. Sacks's parting words on José inform us that

> he has carved exquisite lettering on tombstone. He is current "job" is hand-printing sundry notices for the ward, which he does with the flourishes and elaborations of a latter-day Magna Carta. All this he could do, and do very well. And it would be of use and delight to others, and delight him too. He could do all of these – but, alas, he will do none, unless someone very under-standing, and with opportunities and means, can guide and employ him.
>
> (p. 232)

José, I might have informed the reader earlier, is never identified in this 1985 case study that was originally published in *The New Yorker* as "Latino" or "His-panic" or "Latin American." The family, instead, one might say, seems charged with signifying some species of ethnoracialized, cultural otherness. Some of us may recognize in the family's eventual turning away of a social worker, a tutor, and state hospital medical attention other distancing, life-sustaining strategies practiced by immigrant families. What remains shrouded in mystery, in addition to José's diagnosis, are the 15 years he spent sequestered in the family home. Again and again, Sacks tells us of the missing documentation of these years in the medical chart. One could say that José himself is a partial document from the perspective of the medical gaze. I had hoped to employ Sacks's case study in order to metaphorize some feature of "Latinx" and to imagine something like "psychoanalysis in Latinx barrios" and I have been drawn to the void, the gulf separating Sacks from José, José from the barrios, Latinx from Latino/a. I don't think Sacks knows what to do with the anger he's willing to concede is perfectly understandable for José to feel. As the "new wounded," to return to Malabou's term above, José's case must be interpreted in light of both the wound that attends the brain damage and also that which attends the experience of socio-political trauma as a disenfranchised ethnoracialized subject, the experience in the barrios that Villa details so well for us. Sacks's inability and refusal to metabolize José's anger, in effect, can be read as a refusal to fully document José's history. Sacks in some ways perpetuates the failures of documentation which are failures, let's be clear, to historicize the subject's life starting the moment he tells José to stop "free associating." In what remains of my essay, I'd like to offer a species of meta-phorization of José's anger as well as offer a visual analogue of sorts of "Latinx."

While collecting my name badge for a "Neuroscience and Emotion" workshop I was attending at Duke in the fall of 2015, I came across a huge bowl of pins on the registration table that read: "I Love Brains" (see Figure 6.1).

Figure 6.1 Pin distributed to attendees at "Neuroscience and Emotion" workshop at Duke University in October 2015

Figure 6.2 Spanish language pin made available by Duke Institute for Brain Sciences in Fall 2016

In the pin above that began to circulate sometime at Duke University in the spring of 2016, the heart shape when interpreted in Spanish takes on additional meaning, which is to say that the heart shape is able to call up the signifier, "desire" (see Figure 6.2).

The English language version seems clear enough to most, "I Love Brains." In Spanish, the heart shape is roughly analogous to "*quiero*" and could mean "love" or "want." There are some of us who still remember the racist Taco Bell advertisement campaign featuring a chihuahua (1997–2003) who would mouth the words, "*Yo quiero Taco Bell*." I am one of those people and so I can't help but read "*Yo quiero cerebros*" as announcing the appetite one might have for brains, "*frituritas de seso*." This is a pin for brain-eating agents. Perfect. In another essay (Viego, 2013), I have claimed that the Latino/a subject as characterized in contemporary psychotherapeutic and epidemiological literature is somewhere between life and death, a zombie, too alive in the health studies literature, too depressed and anxious in the psychotherapeutic literature (37–39). Zombies, you might have noticed, are partial to brains.

Acknowledgements

Brief parts of this essay appear in a short piece called "Latinx and the Neurologization of Self" in *Cultural Dynamics* Volume 29, Issue 3, August 2017, pp. 160–176. Copyright 2017 by SAGE Publishing.

References

Barrera, M., & Vialpando, G. (Eds.). (1974). *Action research in defense of the Barrio: Interviews with Ernesto Galarza, Guillermo Flores, and Rosalío Muñoz*. Los Angeles, CA: Aztlán Publications Pamphlet Series.

Bassiri, N. (2016). Who are we, then, if we are indeed our brains? Reconsidering a critical approach to neuroscience. In J. De Vos & E. Pluth (Eds.), *Neuroscience and critique: Exploring the limits of the neurological turn* (pp. 41–61). New York, NY: Routledge.

Carrillo, E. (2001). Assessment and treatment of the Latino patient. In A. G. Lopez & E. Carrillo (Eds.), *The Latino psychiatric patient: Assessment and treatment* (pp. 37–53). Washington, DC: American Psychiatric Publishing.

de Certeau, M. (2011). *The practice of everyday life*. (S. F. Rendell, Trans.). Berkeley, CA: University of California Press.

de la Croix, H., & Tansey, R. G. (1980). *Gardner's art through the ages*. New York, NY and London, England: Harcourt Brace Jovanovich.

Fiol-Matta, L., & Gómez-Barris, M. (2014). Introduction: *Las Américas Quarterly*. *American Quarterly*, *66*(3), 493–505.

Galvan, R. (2017). EE/UU: Exquisite expression/unsettling utterance. *Cultural Dynamics*, *29*(3), 186–192.

Gherovici, P. (2003). *The Puerto Rican syndrome*. New York, NY: Other Press.

Griswold del Castillo, R. (1979). *The Los Angeles barrios, 1850–1890: A social history*. Berkeley, CA: University of California Press.

Guidotti-Hernández, N. M. (2017). Affective communities and millennial desires: Latinx, or why my computer won't recognize Latina/o. *Cultural Dynamics*, *29*(3), 141–159.

Johnston, A., & Malabou, C. (2013). *Self and emotional life: Philosophy, psychoanalysis, and neuroscience*. New York, NY: Columbia University Press.

Laurent, É. (2014). *Lost in cognition: Psychoanalysis and the cognitive sciences* (A. R. Price, Trans.). London, England: Karnac Books (Original work published 2008).

Malabou, C. (2008). *What should we do with our brain?* (M. Jeannerod, Trans.). New York, NY: Fordham University Press (Original work published 2004).

Malabou, C. (2012). *The new wounded: From neurosis to brain damage* (S. Miller, Trans.). New York, NY: Fordham University Press (Original work published 2007).

Metzinger, T. (2010). *The Ego tunnel: The science of the mind and the myth of the self*. New York, NY: Basic Books.

Milian, C. (2017). Extremely Latin, XOXO: Notes on Latinx. *Cultural Dynamics*, *29*(3), 121–140.

Ortega, F., & Vidal, F. (2011). Approaching the neurocultural spectrum: An introduction. In F. Ortega & F. Vidal (Eds.), *Neurocultures: Glimpses into an expanding universe* (pp. 7–28). Frankfurt am Main, Germany: Peter Lang.

Rose, N., & Abi-Rached, J. M. (2013). *Near: The new brain sciences and the management of the mind*. Princeton, NJ: Princeton University Press.

Sacks, O. (1998). *The man who mistook his wife for a hat and other clinical tales*. New York, NY: Simon & Schuster.

Viego, A. (2013). The nightgown. *CR: The New Centennial Review, 13*(3), 29–52.

Villa, R. H. (2000). *Barrio logos: Space and place in urban Chicano literature and culture*. Austin, TX: University of Texas Press.

Wiegman, R. (2012). *Object lessons*. Durham, NC: Duke University Press.

The Latino queer body

Mourning, melancholia, and the law

Chapter 7

Visible pleasure and sex policing

State, science, and desire in twentieth-century Cuba

Jennifer Lambe

With the disarming simplicity of a doo-wop vibe, "*Siempre hay un ojo que te ve*," a 1993 Cuban song by Juan Carlos Alfonso y su Dan Den promises its addressee that someone is always watching her. The singer chronicles his habit of seeking out his love object, wherever she happens to be, to admire her from afar (Alfonso, 1993, track 3). But this story of a persistent watcher quickly verges into creepy territory; allegory is afoot. When the singer assures his love object that she cannot hide from his gaze, that it's impossible for her to pass by *"inadvertida"* (without notice), it is clear that he is invoking other, not quite lustful, modes of looking. The eyes of the voyeur, one of which adorns the album's uncanny cover, are a metonym for a watchful state (see Routon, 2010).

There are pleasures in looking and pleasures in being seen. Yet the insistent gaze also insinuates mastery and its vulnerability; it is "an assertion of power and privilege, but . . . an acknowledgement of anxiety as well" (Metzl, 2004, p. 417). Desire and authority are bound up together in the visual terrain of subject formation, perpetually vulnerable to fixation and deviation. In Freud's classic formulation of opposed and ambivalent perversions, voyeurism was thus evidence of the "narcissistic organization of the ego," with the gaze upon the self the most primary register of erotic looking (1957 [1915], p. 31).

Lacan theorized this connection as even more fundamental. In his work, the desire to see and be seen gives rise to both consciousness and disavowal, as in the "satisfaction of a woman who knows that she is being looked at, on condition that one does not show her that one knows that she knows" (Lacan, 1981). Lacan thus locates individual looking in more expansive fields of visibility, similarly shot through with libidinal urges. More than a few commentators have identified fruitful overlap between Lacan's "scopic drive" and Foucault's "panoptic gaze" (Krips, 2010). Per Foucault, this is a "pleasure that comes of exercising a power that questions, monitors, watches, spies, searches out, palpates, brings to light; and on the other hand that kindles at having to evade this power, flee from it, fool it, or travesty it" (1990 [1976], p. 45). In the reciprocity of entwined gazes, desire and punishment collide, converting the viewer and viewed alike into fulcra of knowledge production.

Gazes, then, do not exist in a vacuum; they are defined by angles and aims. At the nexus of looking, knowing, and desiring, this paper takes as its object the *ofensa a la moral* (or "crime against morality"), an opaque category of policing that dots the archival record of early republican Cuba. The so-called crime of immorality, adapted from Spanish colonial law and retained through the reform-ist Social Defense Code of 1936, implied a referent as culturally contingent as it was all-encompassing: decency. In turn, the various uses to which the law was put point to evolving notions of moral violation. Invariably, however, its applications converged on the untoward articulation of visibility and sexuality, where public erotic acts and utterances threatened social norms. In this, it aligned with other purported violations of social and sexual propriety that transpired in the public sphere.

The mobilization of these categories drew on a vision of decency inflected by race, gender, and class. In Cuba – a former slave society in which wealthy white men had long counted on coerced access to female bodies – appropriate ways of seeing and desiring were shot through with relationships of power. Elsewhere in Latin America, scholars have pointed to the intersection of decency with the sacred cultural value of honor, possessed by men and threatened by women (Caul-field, 2000; Findlay, 2012; Johnson & Lipsett-Rivera, 1998; Twinam, 2001). At times, the *ofensa a la moral* (and its companion charges of *rapto*, or "seduction," and *escándalo público*, or "public scandal") were indeed wielded to reinforce the bounds of public and private activity for women and the threat posed to male honor by violations of the same.[1]

Yet the archive attached to this crime in early twentieth-century Cuba points to an ever-expanding landscape of public erotic life, one that bears little resemblance to an idealized notion of the aristocratic home as chaste fortress. Havana, the pre-eminent port city of the Americas, had long hosted a thoroughly "indecent" sexual culture that sprang from both the realities of male transience and the abuses of African slavery. This forced some groups (women of color, especially) to mobi-lize to gain access to the sexual values often denied to them (Morrison, 2015; Stolcke, 1974). But it left others alienated from the norms that morality policing purported to defend.

Here, I explore the diverse acts, practices, and desires targeted by decency enforcers in early twentieth-century Cuba. I focus in particular on police records of *ofensas a la moral* from 1928 to 1930, as the island catapulted toward politi-cal and social upheaval and a broad popular movement against dictator Gerardo Machado. The bulk of this paper explores several manifestations of Havana's shifting sexual culture in these years, especially male homosexuality, exhibition-ism, and voyeurism. Above all, I am interested in the fact of juxtaposition: What is It that made these offenses ontological kin? Overall, I argue that morality policing fundamentally turned on a problem of visibility, targeting sexual acts that occurred "out of place." Indeed, it was the very fact of visibility, whether embodied by men having sex with men or exhibitionists redirecting the sexual gaze onto themselves, that registered as both "immoral" (and, hence, criminal) and potentially "queer."

In this, it may seem only natural that a psychiatric perspective would enter the conversation on sexual crime. After all, in many contexts, scientific and criminological surveillance of sexuality emerged together as complementary approaches to the erotic margins of society. This is certainly the case for exhibitionism and homosexuality, two of the most prevalent offenses in my archive, around which a durable sexological and medical corpus has been built. Yet psychiatric expertise is largely absent from the history I trace here, and psychoanalytic discourse even more so. Where it enters, it does so belatedly and as an adjunct to other discourses around sexual crime.

As a result, this chapter necessarily speaks in two voices. On one hand, it traces a long tradition of intellectual production around sexuality and visibility, in dialogue with both the classic psychoanalytic paradigms referenced above and the more specific psychiatric work attached to exhibitionism. Nonetheless, an exclusively theoretical voice cannot capture the social embeddedness of sexuality, particularly where it is seen to threaten social boundaries. As the Cuban case suggests, the enforcement of sexual morality is only intelligible in sociohistorical context: specifically, the ways in which class and policing interact to make some bodies especially visible and hence vulnerable to prosecution and, eventually, diagnosis. Even so, the archive of sexual crime remains, in other ways, a repository of surfeit meaning – of desires, instincts, and feelings that cannot be accounted for through a kind of reductive social determinism.

This chapter thus locates the history of morality crime where social structures meet erotic effects. It is centrally concerned with the ways in which visibility rendered some sexual acts verboten while also, in their very juxtaposition, making them archivally legible. In the annals of morality crimes, we thus find a constant interplay of entangled gazes – of neighbors and transients, police and citizens, psychiatrists and the arrested men increasingly understood as "ill," as well as the historian who connects them in an unwieldy chain of archival affinity.

Moral crimes

> Those who should in any way offend modest or good morals by acts of grevious [sic] scandal or enormity, not expressly included in other articles of this code, shall incur the penalties of *arresto mayor* and public censure.
>
> (Title IX. Crimes against Chastity Chapter III.
> Crimes of Public Scandal, *Article 457*)[2]

The ambiguous history of "crimes against morality" represents a legal palimpsest, forged across several generations of sexual and social values. Like many elements of twentieth-century Cuban juridical culture, this provision made its way to the island in the form of the liberal and reformist Spanish Penal Code of 1870, which, among other things, made provisions for individual rights (Cleminson, 2016). After Cuban independence (1898), the 1870 Code was maintained with few modifications during the U.S. military occupations of the island that followed (1899–1901, 1906–1909), a surprising fact given the interventionist aims of those governments.[3] It was not until 1936 that the island finally moved away from the preceding legal regime, in the form of the Social Defense Code ("Código de Defensa Social"), which was put into practice two years later.

Even so, the fact of formal stagnancy during the preceding 60 years does not necessarily signify stasis in juridical application. We might instead conceive of the history of these legal categories as a record of cultural translation, as laws designed for one context were adapted to the first colonial and then neocolonial context of an island on the other side of the Atlantic Ocean. Even if the penal code remained relatively unaltered over the course of this period, its actualization in practice undoubtedly evolved. Indeed, in the Spanish context, the so-called crimes against "*honestidad* (morality)" date back much further than 1870, yet were mobilized in response to ever-shifting social threats.

This is particularly relevant when considering a crime that was defined by its ambiguity. Compared to its companions in Title IX of the legal code ("*delitos contra la honestidad*," or crimes against morality), which included seduction, rape, abduction, and corruption of minors, there was no positive – i.e. prescriptive – content to be found in Article 457, which cryptically proscribed offenses against "*el pudor* (modesty)" or "*las buenas costumbres* (good morals)." Already in the English translation provided above, crafted by the U.S. occupying government in 1900, we find a suggestive *mis*translation. The original Spanish clearly separates "*pudor*" from "*buenas costumbres*," highlighting the distinct etymology (social and linguistic) of *pudor* in the "honor/shame" cultures of the Spanish-speaking world. In English, in contrast, both nouns (*pudor* and *buenas costumbres*) have been rendered as adjectival adjuncts ("modest," "good") to the underlying construct of "morality." Meanwhile, in practice, the law was usually condensed into the shorthand of "*ofensas a la moral.*"

These various interpretations of "morality" crimes remind us that criminal codes were built on slippery processes of translation, from mother country (Spain) to colony (Cuba), nineteenth to twentieth century, and even Spanish to English under U.S. occupation. The most evasive course of adaptation, however, can be found in enforcement: turning legal principle into policing practice. This returns us to the obscurity of the construct itself: *What*, exactly, is outlawed here? As I will discuss below, moral crimes, which were frequently paired with "public scandal," offended in their very visibility. The exteriorization of definitionally "private" (read: sexual) acts was thereby cast as a violation of public decency.

In Cuba, the problem of morality crime emerged out of the specific social and political context of the early twentieth century, especially the impact of class, gender, and racial structures on sexual mores. The island had long witnessed a demographic imbalance between men and women, stemming in part from the labor required to fuel the sugar economy and the brutal conditions therein.[4] Wartime deaths during the final independence struggle against Spain (1895–98) had brought these proportions to a more equal level in some provinces, particularly those that had seen extensive fighting. Nonetheless, by 1907 male predominance had again become marked.[5] This was particularly true of the rural areas that continued to be powered by agriculture. The male population would only grow throughout the 1910s and 20s, with an influx of immigrants to work in the burgeoning sugar sector. The city of Havana, an important point of migrant entry and a final destination in its own right, was unique among the island's urban areas in its high proportion of male residents.[6]

By the 1910s and 20s, Havana had also witnessed the emergence of a cosmopolitan consumer culture, financed by a massive sugar boom and the expansion of companion sectors. Much of this development, however, was fed by graft and official malfeasance. The economic roots of progress would thus prove fragile, as were the political structures that sustained it. Throughout the 1920s and early 30s, Cubans would confront government corruption and economic setbacks due to fluctuations in the world market. These forces would come to a head in the repressive presidency of Gerardo Machado (1925–33; Pérez, 2012; Soto, 1985).

Such political and economic shifts would also contribute to the remaking of Havana's sexual culture. By the late 1910s, fueled by economic expansion and the emergence of a new leisure geography, traditional sexual roles and boundaries were being challenged by middle- and upper-class young people. As Lizabeth Lotz relates, the international archetype of the "modern woman" made her way to Havana's streets, where she helped to expand the bounds of sanctioned female behavior. Courtship practices and romantic relationships moved increasingly into the open, newly transacted in parks, movie theaters, and media outlets without the intercession of parents and chaperones (Lotz, 2010).

Inevitably, this provoked some anxiety. American influence on Cuban gender mores registered as particularly threatening given a broader context of U.S. tourism to the island. At the height of Prohibition in the United States, many Americans came to view their island neighbor as a sexual playground, where booze and cheap thrills could be more easily sought out. As Abel Sierra Madero has argued, these factors prompted efforts to modernize Cuban policing and legal structures and inspired a "crusade" against dandyism and effeminacy ("*pepillismo*") and female homosexuality ("*garzonismo*") (Sierra Madero, 2006).

This more ostentatious age of sexual display fomented media panic when enacted by the middle and upper classes. For non-elites, however, it was the police, the courts, and the social world of the neighborhood that would prove more central to the enforcement of sexual mores. It is impossible to measure, without companion evidence from other periods, if such moral policing truly expanded in these years and, if so, by how much.[7] Instead, I propose that we read the archival record as the reflection of a particular moment in the evolution of Cuba's sexual landscape. In this, visibility was itself at issue, as ordinary citizens and the police moved to combat the diverse manifestations of "immoral" public sexuality.

This vision of decency breached, differentially brought to bear on non-elite Cubans, was vast enough to accommodate all kinds of transgressions. In the nineteenth and early twentieth centuries, for example, "public" women were frequently prosecuted with reference to moral crime, in part because prostitution was never formally outlawed in Cuba (Sippial, 2013). By the early twentieth century, the law was also mobilized to target sexual crimes great and small. Under its auspices, policemen reported overly revealing clothing (Ofensas a la moral, 1913; 3a Estación, 1916), nudity (Ofensa a la moral, 1911), and public propositions (3a. Estación, 1915), while politicians moved to prevent bathing suits from being worn outside the beach (Escándalos en la playa de Marianao, 1914). Utilizing the same premise, municipal inspectors picked up sensual actresses for blowing kisses from the stage, only to be greeted by accusations of overreach by the press. "Crimes against morality are serious offenses," one account noted indignantly, "and shouldn't be confused with trivial ones, which are always pardonable in happy theaters" (La Camelia en el Juzgado, 1913). As Havana's network of "men only" theaters continued to expand, such sites became another node in the latent geography of indecency (Ibarra, 1994.)

In a similarly evocative case from 1930, charges were brought against a Havana entrepreneur who had been selling sweets wrapped in sexually suggestive poetry. Salvador Pasaron y López came to the attention of the police when several Cubans wrote to denounce the verses he had printed on his candy labels. Those wrappers inevitably made their way into the hands of children, who, according to one letter writer, "shouldn't read such things, as far from educating them it [perverted] them" (Prieto de Ferratti, 1930). In fact, Pasaron had seemed to court the inquisitive eyes of children by sponsoring a competition in which the boys and girls who collected the most wrappers would receive prizes. His candies were even printed with a stamp of government approval, which, he later clarified, was meant to apply to the contest only. As a result of the public outcry, Pasaron ultimately agreed to jettison the double entendres with which he had been marketing his candies, including the following, reproduced in police documentation:

1   Narciso finds a sausage, spilling drops of fat, and so Narciso says, the sausage seems quite sad.
2   Something strange is happening with Lara's watch, something strange and surprising, for when you wind it well, it dances and then stops.
3   That Christ you kiss so much makes me jealous inside; don't kiss him anymore, my love, kiss me, he's a saint, you'll pervert him.
4   Asleep with her mouth ajar, I put my finger in her mouth to see if she'd wake up, but I saw that she didn't even stir, so I stuck it in without fear.
5   She divorced Hernández because he was so very poor, and now she wants to find someone who has that much more.
6   Panchita has fallen in love with Justo's equipment, for her husband Pita's is too small, and can't give her enjoyment.
7   From that hole in the foot, Julia says he was born; but I know his true origins, don't believe it, José; I'm the author of that hole.

(Fiscal of the Audiencia de La Habana)

In a more serious vein, sexual acts between men were also a frequent target of morality enforcers.[8] Two aspects of this policing stand out. On numerous occasions, the "couple" who had been discovered included at least one boy (often under the age of 13). In these and other cases, one finds a fair amount of ambiguity around consent. Yet police rarely invoked laws related to rape or corruption of minors in charging the adult in question.[9] Rather, investigators often sought to establish whether either of the two partners could be considered a true "passive pederast," preferentially engaging in sexual activity with men as the "receiving" partner. Often, both individuals sought to prove that they had not in fact been so engaged, or that they had been forced to participate.[10] In assessing the truth of such claims, witnesses and third parties played a prominent role.

Most often, police officers themselves were most likely to catch couples in the act. This was true of a young black man found engaging in "carnal acts as a passive pederast" (Policía Nacional, 12a Estación, August 29, 1930). He was surprised on Marina Street by a policeman who arrested him while his partner fled; he later received a sentence of 180 days in jail. Two other men were discovered in the home of a woman, who insisted that she had found them with "their pants unzipped . . . showing each other their genitals" (Policía Nacional, Luyanó Subestación, November 16, 1930). When they ran off, she sent her 15-year-old son to capture them, and one allegedly tried to bribe him into silence. When confronted by police, the accused insisted that he had merely been trying to inquire after a room rental.

In the absence of private spaces in which they could pursue sexual relationships, men who had sex with other men found themselves scouted out in bus stations (Policía Nacional, 13a Estación, July 16, 1930), near the railroad lines (Policía Nacional, 11a Estación, December 6, 1928), behind parked cars (Policía Nacional, 12a Estación, September 2, 1928), and in remote sandbanks (Policía Nacional, 8a Estación, January 1, 1930) and parks. Many responded by attempting to flee capture, but those who were apprehended often insisted that they had been compelled to participate. This was undoubtedly true of some cases (Policía Nacional, 11a Estación, December 27, 1929), particularly those involving young children (Policía Nacional, Luyanó Subestación, July 23, 1929; Policía Nacional, 8a Estación, June 17, 1929).

Yet in others the insinuation of force was seen as potentially exculpatory and thus became the principal object of police investigation. One of the most extensive cases in police records deals with a 13-year-old boy who alleged that he had been raped by a 16-year-old known as "Rompe Coco" (Coconut Breaker/ Head Smasher) and a 17-year-old known as "Guampiro." The incident came to the attention of police because the boy's brother and friend had followed him to the railroad lines and come upon the three of them together. When caught, the boy insisted that, seven months before, Rompe Coco and Guampiro had threatened him with a stick and beaten him to force him to have sex with them. Since then, he alleged, they had continued to pursue him for sex, always under the threat of coercion, until the group was finally targeted by his brother.

The circumstances of the incident, together with the participation of the brother in uncovering it, generated extensive testimony, along with an examination of the boy's body by forensic experts. In addition to proving that he had been forced to have sex with Rompe Coco and Guampiro, the young man evidently also felt he had to disown any insinuation that he was himself a "passive pederast." Over and again, he claimed that he had consented to sex with the two individuals only because of the intimidation and violence to which they had subjected him. But the testimony of witnesses raised doubts on both counts. Indeed, it was the boy's own brother who maintained that, having spied on the three men from a safe distance, there had been no "act of protest" on the part of his brother (Testimony from Sumario 925 of 1929, December 31, 1929). Forensic experts had also concluded that there were signs in the "folds of [the boy's] anal mucus" that pointed to sexual activity in the past (Informe pericial, November 5, 1930). This evidence was supported by the testimony of a police investigator who, after interviews with the boy's neighbors, concluded that he was well known as a passive pederast and, moreover, that a "delinquent" with the alias of Joséito had repeatedly engaged in sexual acts with the boy.

The penalties assigned to Guampiro and Rompe Coco thus seem to accommodate some of the uncertainty attached to the case: Both were subjected to a fine rather than jail time. Strikingly, however, the court's verdict also absolved the young boy who had first appeared there as a victim. Though insufficient evidence existed to find him guilty of an "*ofensa a la moral*," his very inclusion in the sentencing speaks volumes about the overlapping prerogatives of sexual enforcement. That he had first come to the attention of the law thanks to his own brother; that he responded to his brother's allegations by accusing the others of coercion; and that he could not quite shake the insinuation that he himself was "indecent" – all of this reminds us that same-sex activity or desire was itself grounds for legal entanglement. And this was true regardless of the fact that the boy in question was only 13 years old.

The tangled web of witnesses, watchers, and offenders comes to a head in the most prevalent crime against morality. The police records from these years are full of men who peep, exhibit themselves, grab others, or, at times, all of the above. Sometimes, the uniquely Cuban term *rascabuchador* (literally, "stomach scratcher") was used to describe these individuals, whose defiance of public and private boundaries around sexual acts proved a constant nuisance (or worse) to their neighbors.[11] Most often, a language of moral condemnation was used in chronicling that menace; much more rarely, a discourse of illness appears. Sexual crimes of this kind thus seem to occupy a nosological gray zone, colored by the insinuation of abnormality but absent a full-fledged notion of psychiatric disease.

Take, for example, the case of a 37-year-old puppeteer, originally from Mexico, who was arrested by police for his voyeurism. The man, a "habitual *rascabuchador*," spent his nights "looking through doors and windows, to see families and *rascabucharlas*" (Policía Nacional, Arroyo Naranjo Subestación, November 18, 1930). In their investigation, police discovered that the puppeteer had run afoul of the law for such tendencies in the past. By popular judgment, he was an "individual of perverse habits who entertained himself by making indecent propositions to minors of both sexes in exchange for tickets to ride the horses" at the carousel (Policía Nacional, Arroyo Naranjo Subestación, November 18, 1930).

How were such acts interpreted by the detectives who investigated them? Here, the puppeteer's crimes are cast as evidence of sexual deviance. Just as often, however, it was a discourse of immorality that was used to characterize such acts, as in the case of a man who habitually peered through windows to try to catch people in their underwear (Report of Andrés Betancourt, Policía Nacional, Arroyo Naranjo Subestación, November 21, 1930), or another who stood naked in front of the open windows and doors of his house to exhibit himself to young girls (Policía Nacional, 13a Estación, October 2, 1930). A young *mestizo* mechanic managed to terrorize an entire neighborhood when he strolled through "with his pants all the way down and his genital organs in his hands," sometimes "masturbating and carrying out other immoral acts" (Policía Nacional, Luyanó Subestación, October 11, 1929). One woman even woke up to find a man who had been pursuing her standing next to her bed completely naked (Policía Nacional, Luyanó Subestación, October 7, 1928). Another group of young women suffered the constant attention of a patient in the venereal disease ward of the Salud La Benéfica Clinic, who insisted on standing in front of the window and, cackling, displaying his penis to them (Policía Nacional, 12a Estación, September 9, 1930).

But in only two cases out of the roughly 30 examined here was psychiatric illness presented as the underlying cause of such behavior. A young day worker, for example, was picked up in a public park for revealing his genitals, but police immediately classified him as "abnormal," with "disturbed mental faculties." They brought in two forensic doctors to assess his state of mind, both of whom concluded that he should be admitted for observation at the Hospital Calixto García. There, he was determined to be entirely sane and sent on to jail. Months later, he would be absolved for lack of evidence (Policía Nacional, 13a Estación, July 30, 1929). In only one case was a diagnosis of "exhibitionism" presented to explain the behavior of an unemployed 33-year-old who had the habit of standing behind a column, revealing his genitals, and masturbating in public. Detectives reached that conclusion after consulting with the Quinta de Salud del Centro Dependiente, which informed them that the individual in question had fled the clinic. He was ultimately returned there to continue his treatment for mental illness. Here, the discovery of a *preexisting* mental illness seems to be the only rationale behind its post facto assignation by police (Policía Nacional Secreta, April 4, 1929).

Pathological desires

> Yes, Ma'am, your son is crazy, but from the waist down!
> (Cuban psychiatrist, El problema social del exhibicionismo, 1970s)

From a comparative perspective, the absence of a medical voice in the records of morality crimes is perhaps surprising. Elsewhere, in the late nineteenth and early twentieth centuries, judicial enforcement and medical diagnosis worked in tandem to bring a new range of practices under the surveillance of the state. The sudden prevalence of public sexual display led in turn to new modes of diagnosing sexuality, including the category of "exhibitionism," first identified by French psychiatrist Charles Lasègue in 1877. As psychiatrists moved to bring sexual abnormality into their domain, policing also expanded, and it was not just exhibitionists who fell into the net. The panic around exhibitionism proved a convenient cover to simultaneously target men who had sex with other men (McLaren, 1999). Throughout Europe and the Americas, male homosexuality simultaneously emerged as a discrete category of psychiatric thinking, as overt and de facto criminalization waned in some places while expanding in others (on Latin America and Spain, see Ben, 2009; Galeano, 2016; González Pagés, 2010; Green, 2003; Huertas et al., 2016; Nesvig, 2001; Salessi, 2000).

In the discourses surrounding sexual perversion, however, a fundamental confusion persists: What was it that made exhibitionism or homosexuality both sick *and* dangerous? Angus McLaren argues that the category of exhibitionism condenses two seemingly antithetical anxieties. On one hand, we find a persistent insinuation of sexual danger attached to exhibitionism, the fear that such subjects might commit sexual violence against women. Nonetheless, at the same time, an opposing impulse seems even more primary: the suggestion that exhibitionists were somehow insufficient or inadequate men – perverts, and not rapists. The perversion of the exhibitionist lay in his inversion of the direction of the gaze. Per McLaren, the male exhibitionist, "who was supposed to be sexually active – was thereby rendering himself a passive spectacle for the female gaze" (McLaren, 1999, p. 205).[12] In this, he seemed to align himself with feminine patterns of sexual behavior. Little surprise, then, that there is a connotation of *queerness* attached to exhibitionism, which was actualized in everyday policing practices.

That queerness carries over to Cuban police records, where exhibitionism and voyeurism sit side by side with sexual acts between men. This association, however, was established primarily in practice, absent any overarching theory. The invisibility of medical expertise might be explained by virtue of the relative weakness of the psychiatric discipline at the time. Though the field had begun to institutionalize in the late nineteenth century, psychiatrists struggled throughout the first decades of the twentieth century to establish themselves as an authoritative social and medical voice (Lambe, 2017). Yet the very years covered by these records (1928–1930) represent a period in which psychiatric expertise had been brought increasingly to bear on the prosecution of crime, with celebrity physicians and lawyers drawing attention to the morbid underpinnings of criminal behavior (Lambe, 2014). Nonetheless, their presence is not felt in the area of decency crimes.

It was not necessarily for lack of trying. In 1910, Dr. Luis Perna, a prominent forensic psychiatrist, argued that exhibitionists should not be "punished as immoral" but rather treated as "mentally ill" and watched over by their families (p. 221). He made this plea while assessing one of the rare cases of exhibitionism to appear in the Cuban psychiatric literature: a 62-year-old cook who had "lost his devotion to his work, spending his time visiting houses in the neighborhood and bragging about his frequent amorous triumphs stemming from a genital vigor incompatible with [his] age" (p. 220). The individual in question had also been accused of exposing himself to young women – clear evidence, for Perna, of his underlying pathology. "It doesn't fit in the normal mold of human behavior," he opined, "that a poor old man would exhibit his rundown genitals, in which no youthful vestiges remain, and which would inspire not erotic desire or curiosity . . . but only disgust or pity" (p. 221). Perna's tone mirrors the contempt with which he assumes the cook's behavior would have been greeted but pairs it with a reading of Lasègue's work on the topic. He thereby bridges both colloquial and professional interpretations of his patient's "ridiculous" act.

Soon, however, Perna's perspective would move from the margins to the center of criminological practice. Cuba's 1936 Social Defense Code (Código de Defensa Social) explicitly reoriented attention away from punishment and toward prevention. In the words of prominent lawyer and physician José Agustín Martínez, the goal was to ground legal practice in "defending society, reeducating and readapting the offender, and indemnifying the victim" (Cuba, 1936, p. 8). No longer would retribution shape the exercise of justice: Rather, the foundation of the new legal regime was to be "punishment-treatment" (Cuba, 1936, p. 8). The central category for this generation of legal reformers, influenced by the work of Italian criminologist Enrico Ferri, was "dangerouness" – the future threat posed to society by the offender. This was to be assessed using the most innovative paradigms afforded by "physio-psychology" and "forensic Psychiatry" (Cuba, 1936, p. 11).

As Agustín Martínez would explain elsewhere, homosexuality was to be regarded as one such index of dangerousness – not a crime in itself, but rather a factor that had to be "obligatorily considered" in assessing the likelihood that an individual would commit a crime (Agustín Martínez, 1940, p. 129). In the coming years, homosexuality and other sexual "perversions" would also receive more serious attention from psychiatric professionals. Throughout the 1940s and 50s, Cuban psychiatrists expanded their efforts to treat homosexuality and gender inconformity, largely through psychotherapy and the reinforcement of social mores. Some even elaborated novel theoretical paradigms to accompany this work. Challenging the earthy emphasis of Freudian ideas about sex, Catholic psychiatrists, for example, developed a "rational" psychotherapeutic practice to treat homosexuality (Lambe, 2017, pp. 121–135).

This new psychiatric discourse, however, was strangely at odds with the Social Defense Code itself. Title XI not only preserved the language of decency policing (now categorized under "Crimes against Morality," or "*buenas costumbres*"), but also made its only explicit invocation of homosexuality (referred to as "pederasty") in a subsection on "public scandal." The language here is redolent of earlier legal epistemes, referring to anyone who "in a gravely scandalous way habitually commits acts of pederasty, as the active or passive partner, or makes a public show [*"haga pública ostentación"*] of that vice, or solicits or imposes on someone else to participate in it" (Cuba, 1936, p. 302). The Código thus maintained this crime alongside other offensively public acts, including obscene films, photography, and performances. Even as legal reformers moved toward a more psychiatric approach to sexual crime, then, they did not necessarily jettison the continued association of sexual criminality with visibility.

This tension would persist throughout the decades to come. In spite of broad-based advocacy for a more scientific (and psychiatric) approach to sexual crime, the implementation of the Código de Defensa Social, along with the projected rehabilitative facilities set to accompany it, remained shallow throughout the 1940s and 50s. In some ways, this was a function of structural obstacles. Whether under democratic governance (1940–1952) or another brutal dictatorship (1952–58), political corruption and instability put significant limitations on the extent of legal change that could be achieved.[13]

It would thus remain for the Revolution of 1959 to more vigorously take up sexuality and crime, now under the influence of Soviet models. Ultimately, this would bring renewed attention to both criminological and medical approaches to sexuality. Revolutionary psychiatrists, for example, revitalized a psychiatric campaign to treat homosexuality through aversion therapy (Lambe, 2017; Marqués de Armas, 2014). But psychiatrists were not alone in their efforts to target homosexuality; political imperatives would soon enter the conversation. From 1965 to 1968, homosexual individuals, religious believers, and political opponents were sent to work camps known as the Units to Aid Military Production (UMAPs) in the province of Camagüey. There, through the performance of manual labor, they were to be "treated" and reintegrated into society (Sierra Madero, 2016).

Eventually, professional and legal attention would turn to other sexual crimes as well. A 1970s roundtable, which brought together psychiatrists, lawyers, and judges, would culminate in the most sustained Cuban treatment of exhibitionism. Participants in the session expressed interest in precisely the dual nature of the diagnosis; exhibitionism, they argued, should be regarded as at once "an illness and a crime" (Hospital Psiquiátrico de la Habana, n.d., p. 3). Legally, it was covered in Article 488–2 of the revised Social Defense Code, which referred to "crimes against the normal development of sexual relations" (as distinct from homosexuality, covered in Article 488–1), defined as "offensive to *el pudor* or *las buenas costumbres*" (Hospital Psiquiátrico de la Habana, n.d., p. 23). In that category, it was joined, for example, by bestiality. But the defining attribute of exhibitionism remained its public nature, and, according to Cuban law, exhibitionism constituted a prosecutable crime *even in the absence of witnesses*. One is reminded here of the invisible eyes of the state, an omnipresent witness to sexual transgression.

This did not mean, however, that all exhibitionists should be treated equally. In each case, it was necessary, one participant elaborated, to "determine whether [the individual was] mentally ill and in need of treatment or an antisocial personality who should be punished" (Hospital Psiquiátrico de la Habana, n.d., p. 3). Finer distinctions still could be drawn: between "hypererotic subjects" (defined as anti-social) who engaged in "[acts] of sexual swagger (*bravuconería*)," the "mentally ill" for whom exhibitionism was but a secondary symptom, and finally those manifesting a distinct "sexual deviation" in which exhibitionism was itself the "essential" factor (Hospital Psiquiátrico de la Habana, n.d., pp. 6–7). This last group, psychiatrists added, was often characterized by "psychopathic personality" traits and presented the most common form of exhibitionism that came to their professional attention.

In claiming exhibitionism as a psychiatric problem, participants in this meeting sought to establish for it a distinct profile within both that field and the broader legal corpus. Yet it is worth noting a prominent thread uniting the emergent litera-ture on exhibitionism with the revolutionary approach to homosexuality. In more than one psychiatric publication, homosexuality was explicitly characterized as exhibitionist (Pérez Valdés, 1970)[14] or by way of the ad hoc category "*afocancia*," applied in the UMAP camps to measure an individual's degree of "ostentation" (Sierra Madero, 2016, pp. 334–336). Legally, this conflation came to a head in a 1973 law criminalizing the "*ostentación pública* (public ostentation)" of homo-sexuality. It was soon succeeded by a new penal code in 1979, which repurposed the category of "public scandal" to again outlaw homosexual "public ostentation" in addition to public or visible homosexual acts, voyeurism, and the dissemination of obscene materials (Zayas, 2011).

Here, we find evidence of the continued association between queerness, dis-play, and visibility. In many contexts, it was precisely this connection, often val-idated by the psychiatric field, that made police harassment such a prominent facet of the gay experience (Stewart-Winter, 2015), and even constitutive of pub-lic knowledge about homosexuality (Lvovsky, 2015). Cuban professionals also worked for this kind of accord between criminological and psychiatric knowledge in the management of sexual deviance. But the political stakes were too high to leave the problem to physicians alone.

Sexual abnormality, government officials and psychiatrists concurred, was out of step with the new revolutionary order. Moreover, by the late 1960s, many observers agreed that both psychiatric treatment and the UMAP camps had largely failed to achieve their goals in this respect (Lambe, 2017). Some, however, held out hope for a more political solution. Socialism, not psychiatry, would be the cure:

> In capitalist societies, where deviations and vices of all kinds proliferate, they are constantly on the rise. In socialist countries, by contrast, we can observe a constant decline. Here we can observe the influence of society as a whole on the potential sexual deviations; a correct education from infancy can help thwart the development of abnormal sexual conditioned reflexes that in our opinion constitutes the point of origin for sexual deviations.
> (Hospital Psiquiátrico de la Habana, n.d., p. 9)

This interpretation, which drew on the Pavlovian orthodoxy that came to characterize much psychiatric literature in Cuba by the 1970s, presumed expanding popular acceptance of psychiatric opinion. But it also articulated a fundamental connection between individual pathology and socio-political conditions. Like so many other things, "sexual deviations," doctors hoped, were a mere vestige of their capitalist past. On this score, they would certainly be disappointed.

Conclusion: Anxious eyes

In this, Cuban professionals recapitulated a debate that had begun a century earlier, as French and British psychiatrists struggled to understand the sudden prevalence of public sexuality. Though they tended to locate the origins of exhibitionism in individual pathology (degenerationist in the nineteenth century, psychodynamic in the twentieth), they also posed broader diagnostic questions: What was it about their society that had produced so many cases? As Angus McLaren (1999) points out, exhibitionism was not so much invented as exploited and shaped by the disciplines, which built on changing sexual and social mores. That convergence of social conditions and scientific development rendered the subject in question somehow symptomatic of both.

Some of this ambivalence was perhaps intrinsic to the science of sex. Tiffany Watt Smith has argued that the frequent (mis)rendering of Freud's *Schaulust* (literally, "pleasure in looking") as *scopophilia* or, worse, *scoptophilia* sprang from the constitutive ambivalence of scientific looking. In late nineteenth-century Europe, enthusiasm for "people shows" (*Völkerschau*), or displays of "primitive" men and women from the colonies, had provoked concern about *Schaulust*. In the resulting debates, an effort was made to wall off the "objective or studious gaze of the cultivated German" from the "visceral, overexcited pleasures of boisterous, uneducated, and work-class audiences" (Watt Smith, 2014, p. 25). This attempt to differentiate styles of looking, however, spoke to a broader unease: "Despite the many attempts to tease them apart, *Schaulust* lingered in scientific looking, not always an opposition to an ideal and restrained gaze, but sometimes part and parcel of the very techniques that defined objectivity itself" (Watt Smith, 2014, p. 25).

Ultimately, this returns us to the problem of visibility, intrinsic both to the pathology ascribed to public sexual acts and to the state and medical actors who exercised jurisdiction over them. Mikhail Shtern, a Russian sexologist exiled to the United States, would bring together these factors in his book, *Sex in the USSR* (1980). Drawing on years of surreptitious professional consultations in the late Soviet Union, Shtern asserted that political conditions had deeply shaped erotic effects. It was sexually disfiguring, he maintained, to have a "moral overseer constantly looking over your shoulder" (1980, p. ix). In a broad sense, the fact of state surveillance had generated a "split personality – the unresolvable contradiction between . . . publicly expressed attitudes . . . and behavior in private" (Shtern, 1980, p. vii). Yet the repressed inevitably reasserted itself, most notably in a "nationwide epidemic" of exhibitionism (Shtern, 1980, p. 163). For Stern, exhibitionism represented a reaction against sexual "restriction and surveillance," a "way of asserting oneself as an individual, a way of quite literally showing off one's virility and one's sexuality" (Shtern, 1980, p. 166).

Speaking to a very different context, in the late 1960s British psychiatrist Graham Rooth arrived at a similar conclusion after conducting a study of exhibitionism outside Europe and the United States. In his correspondence with some 24 colleagues in Latin America, Africa, and Asia, Rooth found little evidence of exhibitionism in any country but Turkey. Though all of the nations in question had passed laws against it, in few cases were they enforced; psychiatric consultation on the question was even more rare. In England, Germany, Canada, and the United States, in contrast, "indecent exposure" counted for something like one-third of all sexual crime. How to explain the difference? In his discussion of the findings, Rooth landed on one underlying commonality:

> Ultimately, the Victorian approach to nakedness and the mystery and guilt surrounding sex were associated with an overvaluation of the genitals amounting to a kind of negative veneration. The genitals became in some respects fetishes, in the broad anthropological sense, with an almost magical power of inspiring fear, interest, and excitement.
>
> (Rooth, 1973, p. 361)

We might be inclined, then, to identify a constitutive link between sexual "repression" – whether instantiated in uptight Western cultures or authoritarian socialist ones – and public "immorality," with the former constantly goading the latter into existence. Yet exhibitionism, and public sexual acts in general, represent less a conscious rejection of the state's gaze than its unconscious mirror, a scopic/libidinal excess generated by the microphysics of power. There is also an inescapably mundane foundation for this feedback loop between sex and visibility. Across all of these contexts, we find bodies that have not enjoyed access to the values and spaces that would shield them from scrutiny, legal or medical. Obliquely, Rooth reminds us that some of the queerness attached to public sexual acts is an artifact of precisely their embeddedness in social structures.

Decency and morality may be reinforced in private encounters. Yet they are constituted in the public sphere, where the state, science, and desiring subjects all collide, displaying their power by anxiously watching. For over a century now, observers of different stripes have struggled to interpret the practice of public sexuality and, in doing so, helped to reframe it as a social problem. In chronicling its existence, some have invoked a discourse of morality, others of perversion or illness. Yet neither approach fully captures what seems apparent from a distance: that exhibitionism is only illegal, or abnormal, by reference to a society that has defined it as such. Here, I engage this long conversation by uniting two (seemingly antithetical) approaches – historicist on one hand, psychoanalytic on the other. The tensions that emerge out of this juxtaposition, where transhistoricality and contextual specificity collide, raise the same questions confronted by many in the past: Is exhibitionism a symptom of individual or collective pathology? Is it culturally contingent or psychologically universal?

Tellingly, the answers I have found converge on the problem of the gaze. As I have argued, the *ofensa a la moral* was, at root, a crime of visibility. This produced an affinity of sorts between the category itself – as well as the diverse bodies that came to staff it – and those who later emerged to define it. In reading the margins of the island's sexual landscape, Cuban police, lawyers, and psychiatrists would be challenged by the ontological exuberance of their object, at once illness and crime, sick and offensive. It seemed to imply an uncomfortable social truth: that the social order they sought to uphold was not as straight as it might seem.

Notes

1 On gender, crime, and honor, see Beers (2004); Findlay (2012); Guy (1995); Huertas, Lucero, and Swedberg (2016); Piccato (2001, 2010); Salvatore, Aguirre, & Joséph (2001).

2 "*Delitos contra la honestidad.*"/"*Delitos de escándalo público*": "*Incurrirán en la pena de arresto mayor y reprensión pública los que de cualquier modo ofendieren el pudor ó las buenas costumbres con hechos de grave escándalo ó trascendencia, no comprendidos expresamente en otros artículos de este Código*" (Translation in Division of Customs and Insular Affairs, Cuba, & Puerto Rico, 1900, p. 96).

3 The U.S. entered the Cuban war for independence following the explosion of the USS *Maine*. Though the campaign spoke to imperialist aims, the Teller Amendment, passed in the immediate run-up to the intervention, prevented the U.S. from annexing Cuba outright. Even so, the Cubans were barred from the Spanish surrender to the Americans and from the peace negotiations that followed. In Paris, the U.S. and Spain transacted Cuba's future, which was to begin with a U.S. military occupation of the island (1899–1901). In one last imperialist insult, the U.S. military governor, Leonard Wood, maneuvered to force Cuban delegates to the island's first Constitutional Convention to accept the Platt Amendment, previously drafted by U.S. officials. This gave the U.S. nearly boundless authority to meddle in Cuban affairs and remained on the books until 1934.

4 The peak year of gender imbalance was registered in the Census of 1841, also a high point in the African-descendant and slave population of Cuba. These figures produced a crisis among the island's intellectual and economic elite, who raised concerns about the imminent "Africanization" of the island (Cuba. Oficina del censo, 1908, p. 202).

5 In 1887, the last year in which a Spanish census of the island was taken, males constituted 54% of the island's population (Cuba. Oficina del censo, 1908, p. 183). By 1899, in the first census conducted by the United States, that percentage had dropped to 51.8% (note that the male population actually dropped from 1887 to 1899, while the female population grew). The next U.S. census (1907) reflects disproportionate growth in the male population, with 52.5% of Cuba's 2,048,980 people male (Cuba. Oficina del censo, 1908, p. 214).

6 In 1907, the city of Havana's population was 52.9% male, compared to proportions under 50% in many other major urban areas (Cuba. Oficina del censo, 1908, p. 203). By 1931, the imbalance had diminished somewhat (51.1% male), though it remained one of the most male urban areas (Alonso, Chávez Alvarez, Cuba, & Dirección general del censo, 1979, p. 63). In 1931, rural areas remained highly skewed toward men; in the province of Camagüey, for example, males constituted 60.7% of the population in 1931 (p. 64).

7 Cuba's 1907 census, for example, recorded 1,537 crimes "*contra la honestidad*," 357 of them committed in Havana. This made "immorality" the third most common category of crime, after crimes against property (6,682) and crimes against people (1,969). (See Cuba. Oficina del censo, 1908, p. 133.)

8 On the history of homosexuality in Cuba, see Fowler Calzada (1998); González Pagés (2010); Marqués de Armas (2014); Sierra Madero (2002, 2006).

9 Age remains a thorny and understudied category in the history of sexuality, due perhaps to the intensity of recent political battles around homosexuality and pedophilia. For suggestive points of entry, see Cole (2000); Freedman (1987); Maynard (1997); Romesburg (2009); Rousseau (2007).

10 The purported absence of stigma attached to the "active" homosexual role in Latin America has been a frequent subject of scholarly inquiry. For a helpful summary of this work, see Nesvig (2001).

11 The Cuban popular vocabulary around exhibitionists and voyeurs is extensive and difficult to pin down in its evolution over time. "*Rascabuchador*" continues to be used as a more formal term for the people ordinary Cubans tend to call "*mirahuecos*," or Peeping Toms. Another word that is applied fairly broadly in discussing men who grope, watch, and exhibit themselves is "*jamonero*"; public masturbators are sometimes called "*pajusos*" and gropers "*panaderos*."

12 For a cognate debate on the gender politics of the gaze, see Mulvey (1999).

13 Twentieth-century Cuban history tends to be divided into three periods: the "neocolonial" First Republic that emerged out of the independence struggle (1902–1933); the Second Republic (1934–1958), which followed the broad-based Revolution of 1933; and the socialist revolutionary governments of Fidel and then Raúl Castro (1959–present). The Second Republic was itself split between the short-lived democratically elected (and corrupt) governments of the Auténtico Party and the administrations headed by Fulgencio Batista, both democratic (1940–44) and not (1934–1940 and 1952–1958).

14 A similar discourse was sometimes used to characterize the pathological roots of Afro-descendent religious practice (*Santería*); see Henriquez (1961).

Bibliography

Archival sources

Juzgado Correccional de La Habana, Secretaría de Gobernación, Archivo Nacional de Cuba, Havana, Cuba.

1 Letter from Rene Prieto de Ferratti to Fiscal of the Audiencia de La Habana, April 11, 1930, exp. 1050, leg. 208, num. 1522.

2 Fiscal of the Audiencia de La Habana, exp. 1050, leg. 208, num. 1712.

3 Policía Nacional, 12a Estación, August 29, 1930, exp. 1049, leg. 208, num. 323.

4 Policía Nacional, Luyanó Subestación, November 16, 1930, exp. 1051, leg. 208, num. 3569.

5 Policía Nacional, 13a Estación, July 16, 1930, exp. 1052, leg. 208, num. 1569.

6 Policía Nacional, 11a Estación, December 6, 1928, exp. 1055, leg. 208, num. 0840.

7 Policía Nacional, 12a Estación, September 2, 1928, exp. 1055, leg. 208, num. 0009.

8 Policía Nacional, 8a Estación, January 1, 1930, exp. 1051, leg. 208, num. 0001.

9 Policía Nacional, 11a Estación, December 27, 1929, exp. 1051, leg. 208, num. 4002.

10 Policía Nacional, Luyanó Subestación, July 23, 1929, exp. 1053, leg. 208, num. 2054.

11 Policía Nacional, 8a Estación, June 17, 1929, exp. 1053, leg. 208, num. 1616.

12 Testimony from Sumario 925 of 1929, December 31, 1929, Havana, Policía Nacional, 12a Estación, October 31, 1929, exp. 1051, leg. 208, num. 0134.

13 Informe pericial, November 5, 1930, Havana, Policía Nacional, 12a Estación, October 31, 1929, exp. 1051, leg. 208, num. 0134.
14 Policía Nacional, Arroyo Naranjo Subestación, November 18, 1930, exp. 1049, leg. 208.
15 Report of Andrés Betancourt, Policía Nacional, Arroyo Naranjo Subestación, November 21, 1930, exp. 1049, leg. 208, num. 12312.
16 Policía Nacional, 13a Estación, October 2, 1930, exp. 1049, leg. 208.
17 Policía Nacional, Luyanó Subestación, October 11, 1929, exp. 1052, leg. 208, num. 3137.
18 Policía Nacional, Luyanó Subestación, October 7, 1928, exp. 1055, leg. 208, num. 0310.
19 Policía Nacional, 12a Estación, September 9, 1930, exp. 1049, leg. 208, num. 3428.
20 Policía Nacional, 13a Estación, September 12, 1928, exp. 1055, leg. 208, num. 0109.
21 Letter from Alfonso L Fors to Sr. Juez. Corr. Sección Quinta, Policía Nacional, 13a Estación, June 19, 1929, exp. 1054, leg. 208, num. 1462.
22 Policía Nacional, 13a Estación, July 30, 1929, exp. 1053, leg. 208, num. 2159.
23 Policía Nacional Secreta, April 4, 1929, exp. 1054, leg. 208, num. 0825.

Periodicals

(1913, November 17). La Camelia en el Juzgado. *El Mundo*, 4.

(1915, June 15). Escándalos en la playa de Marianao. *El Mundo*, 14.

Henriquez, E. C. (1961). Convulsive and ecstatic crisis in fanatics and ignorant people. *Revista Archivos de Neurología y Psiquiatría Cubana, II*, 16–22.

(1911, March 27). Ofensa a la moral. *La Lucha*, 5.

(1913, November 8). Ofensas a la mora. *El Mundo*, 4.

Pérez Valdés, N. (1970, May–August). Dibujo de la figura humana en sujetos de conducta homosexual, siguiendo la técnica de Karen Machover. *Revista del Hospital Psiquiátrico de La Habana, XI*(2), 230–242.

Perna, L. (1910, August). Medicina legal – Informes diversos. *Archivos de Medicina Legal, 1*(8), 216–224.

(1916, January 10). 3a Estación. Capitán: Hidalgo. Zulueta y Refugio. *El Mundo*, 9.

(1915, October 26). 3a. Estación. Capitán Manuel Hidalgo. Refugio y Zulueta. *El Mundo*, 10.

Media

Alfonso, J. A. (1993). Siempre hay un ojo que te ve. [Recorded by Juan Carlos Alfonso y su Dan Den]. In *Siempre hay un ojo que te ve* [LP]. Havana: EGREM.

Secondary sources

Agustín Martínez, J. (1940). El homosexualismo y su tratamiento. In *Serie de conferencias sobre el Código de defensa social por el Colegio de Abogados de la Habana* (Vol. 56). Havana, Cuba: J. Montero.

Alonso, G., Chávez Alvarez, E., Cuba, & Dirección general del censo. (1979). *Memoria inéditas del censo de 1931*. Havana: Editorial de Ciencias Sociales.

Beers, M. (2004). Murder in San Isidro: Crime and culture during the Second Cuban Republic. *Cuban Studies, 34*(1), 97–129.

Ben, P. (2009). *Male sexuality, the popular classes and the state: Buenos Aires, 1880–1955.* Unpublished doctoral dissertation. University of Chicago, Chicago, IL.

Caulfield, S. (2000). *In defense of honor: Sexual morality, modernity, and nation in early-twentieth-century Brazil.* Durham, NC: Duke University Press.

Cleminson, R. (2016). Liberal governmentality in Spain: Bodies, minds, and the medical construction of the "outsider," 1870–1910. *Journal of Iberian and Latin American Studies, 22*(1), 23–40.

Cole, S. A. (2000). From the sexual psychopath statute to Megan's law: Psychiatric knowledge in the diagnosis, treatment and adjudication of sex criminals in New Jersey, 1949–1999. *Journal of the History of Medicine and Allied Sciences, 55,* 292–314.

Cuba. (1936). *Codigo de defensa social.* Havana, Cuba: J. Montero.

Cuba. Oficina del censo. (1908). *Censo de la República de Cuba bajo la administración provisional de los Estados Unidos.* Washington, DC: Oficina del censo de los Estados Unidos. Ann Arbor, MI: University of Michigan Library. Retrieved from http://name.umdl.umich.edu/AFP3877.1907.001.

Estados Unidos, Division of Customs and Insular Affairs, Cuba, & Puerto Rico. (1900). *Translation of the Penal Code in force in Cuba and Porto Rico.* Washington, DC: Government Printing Office.

Findlay, E. J. S. (2012). *Imposing decency: The politics of sexuality and race in Puerto Rico, 1870–1920.* Durham, NC: Duke University Press.

Foucault, M. (1990). *The history of sexuality* (R. Hurley, Trans.). New York, NY: Vintage Books.

Fowler Calzada, V. (1998). *La maldición: una historia del placer como conquista.* Havana, Cuba: Editorial Letras Cubanas.

Freedman, E. B. (1987). 'Uncontrolled desires': The response to the sexual psychopath, 1920–1960. *Journal of American History, 74*(1), 83–106.

Freud, S. (1957). Insticts and their vicissitudes. In *The standard edition of the complete psychological works of Sigmund Freud* (J. Strachey, Trans., Vol. XIV (1914–1916), pp. 109–140). London, England: Hogarth.

Galeano, J. F. (2016). Is he a "social danger"? The Franco regime's judicial prosecution of homosexuality in Málaga under the Ley de vagos y maleantes. *Journal of the History of Sexuality, 25*(1), 1–31.

González Pagés, J. C. (2010). *Macho, varón, masculino: estudios de masculinidades en Cuba.* Havana, Cuba: Editorial de la Mujer.

Green, J. N. (2003). *Beyond carnival: Male homosexuality in twentieth-century Brazil.* Chicago, IL: University of Chicago Press.

Guy, D. J. (1995). *Sex & danger in Buenos Aires: Prostitution, family and nation in Argentina.* Lincoln, NE: University of Nebraska Press.

Henriquez, E. C. (1961). Las crisis extáctico-convulsivas de los ignorantes fanáticos. (El santo). *Revista Archivos de Neurología y Psiquiatría, 11*(1).

Hospital Psiquiátrico de la Habana. (n.d.). *El problema social del exhibicionismo.* Havana: Ministerio de Salud Pública, Hospital Psiquiátrico de la Habana.

Huertas, L. E., Lucero, B., & Swedberg, G. J. (2016). *Voices of crime: Constructing and contesting social control in modern Latin America.* Tucson, AZ: University of Arizona Press.

Ibarra, J. (1994). *Un análisis psicosocial del cubano: 1898–1925.* Havana, Cuba: Editorial de Ciencias Sociales.

Johnson, L. L., & Lipsett-Rivera, S. (1998). *The faces of honor: Sex, shame, and violence in colonial Latin America.* Albuquerque, NM: University of New Mexico Press.

Krips, H. (2010). The politics of the gaze: Foucault, Lacan and Žižek. *Culture Unbound: Journal of Current Cultural Research*, *2*(1), 91–102.

Lacan, J. (1981). *The four fundamental concepts of psycho-analysis* (J. Miller, Trans.). New York, NY: W.W. Norton.

Lambe, J. L. (2014). *Baptism by fire: The making and remaking of madness in Cuba, 1857–1980.* Unpublished doctoral dissertation. Yale University Press, New Haven, CT.

Lambe, J. L. (2017). *Madhouse: Psychiatry and politics in Cuban history.* Chapel Hill, NC: University of North Carolina Press.

Lotz, L. M. (2010). *Leading the life of a modern girl: Representations of womanhood in Cuban popular culture.* Unpublished doctoral dissertation. University of North Carolina, Chapel Hill, NC.

Lvovsky, A. (2015). *Queer expertise: Urban policing and the construction of public knowledge about homosexuality, 1920–1970.* Unpublished doctoral dissertation. Harvard University Press, Cambridge, MA.

Marqués de Armas, P. L. (2014). *Ciencia y poder en Cuba: Racismo, homofobia, nación (1790–1970).* Madrid: Editorial Verbum.

Maynard, S. (1997). "Horrible temptations": Sex, men, and working-class male youth in urban Ontario, 1890–1935. *Canadian Historical Review*, *78*(2), 191–235.

McLaren, A. (1999). *The trials of masculinity: Policing sexual boundaries, 1870–1930.* Chicago, IL: University of Chicago Press.

Metzl, J. (2004). From scopophilia to survivor: A brief history of voyeurism. *Textual Practice*, *18*(3), 415–434.

Morrison, K. Y. (2015). *Cuba's racial crucible: The sexual economy of social identities, 1750–2000.* Bloomington, IN: Indiana University Press.

Mulvey, L. (1999). Visual pleasure and narrative cinema. In L. Braudy and M. Cohen (Eds.), *Film theory and criticism: Introductory readings* (pp. 833–844). New York, NY: Oxford University Press.

Nesvig, M. A. (2001). The complicated terrain of Latin American homosexuality. *Hispanic American Historical Review*, *81*(3), 689–729.

Pérez, L. A. (2012). *On becoming Cuban: Identity, nationality, and culture.* Chapel Hill, NC: University of North Carolina Press.

Pérez Valdés, N. (1970). Dibujo de la figura humana en sujetos de conducta homosexual, siguiendo la técina de Karen Machover. *Revista Del Hospital Psiquiátrico de La Habana*, *XI*(2), 230–242.

Perna, L. (1910). Medicina legal: Informes diversos. *Archivos de Medicina Mental*, *1*(8).

Piccato, P. (2001). *City of suspects: Crime in Mexico City, 1900–1931.* Durham, NC: Duke University Press.

Piccato, P. (2010). *The tyranny of opinion: Honor in the construction of the Mexican public sphere.* Durham, NC: Duke University Press.

Romesburg, D. (2009). "Wouldn't a boy do?" Placing early-twentieth-century male youth sex work into histories of sexuality. *Journal of the History of Sexuality*, *18*(3), 367–392.

Rooth, G. (1973). Exhibitionism outside Europe and America. *Archives of Sexual Behavior*, *2*(4), 351–363.

Rousseau, G. (2007). *Children and sexuality: From the Greeks to the Great War.* London, England: Springer.

Routon, K. (2010). *Hidden powers of state in the Cuban imagination.* Gainesville, FL: University Press of Florida.

Salessi, J. (2000). *Médicos maleantes y maricas. Higiene, criminología y homosexualidad en la construcción de la nación Argentina. (Buenos Aires: 1871–1914)*. Rosario, Argentina: B. Viterbo.

Salvatore, R. D., Aguirre, C., & Joséph, G. M. (2001). *Crime and punishment in Latin America: Law and society since late colonial times*. Durham, NC: Duke University Press.

Shtern, M., Shtern, A., Howson, M., & Ryan, C. (1980). *Sex in the USSR*. New York, NY: Times Books.

Sierra Madero, A. (2002). *La nación sexuada: relaciones de género y sexo en Cuba (1830–1855)*. Havana, Cuba: Editorial de Ciencias Sociales.

Sierra Madero, A. (2006). *Del otro lado del espejo: la sexualidad en la construcción de la nación cubana*. Havana, Cuba: Fondo Editorial Casa de las Américas.

Sierra Madero, A. (2016). "El trabajo os hará hombres": masculinización nacional, trabajo forzado y control social en Cuba durante los años sesenta. *Cuban Studies*, *44*(1), 309–349.

Sippial, T. A. (2013). *Prostitution, modernity, and the making of the Cuban Republic, 1840–1920*. Chapel Hill, NC: University of North Carolina Press.

Soto, L. (1985). *La revolución del 33*. Havana, Cuba: Editorial Pueblo y Educación.

Stewart-Winter, T. (2015). Queer law and order: Sex, criminality, and policing in the late twentieth-century United States. *Journal of American History*, *102*(1), 61–72.

Stolcke, V. (1989). *Marriage, class and colour in nineteenth-century Cuba: A study of racial attitudes and sexual values in a slave society* (2nd ed.). Ann Arbor, MI: University of Michigan Press (first edition 1974).

Twinam, A. (2001). *Public lives, private secrets: Gender, honor, sexuality and illegitimacy in colonial Spanish America*. Stanford, CA; Cambridge, MA: Stanford University Press; Cambridge University Press.

Watt Smith, T. (2014). *On flinching: Theatricality and scientific looking from Darwin to shell-shock*. Oxford, England: Oxford University Press.

Zayas, M. (2011, October 24). *Mapa de la homofobia*. Retrieved September 27, 2017 from https://manuelzayas.wordpress.com/mapa-de-la-homofobia/.

Chapter 8

Melancholia and the abject on Mango Street
Racialized narratives/psychoanalysis

Ben Sifuentes-Jáuregui

This essay is about the strategies of identification in Sandra Cisneros's *The House on Mango Street* (1989). How do Chicano/a subjects rehearse and articulate the Self? What are the limits on the Self to represent the group? What is the role of identification in the act of reading Chicano narratives? I want to consider specifically what the implications of psychoanalytic critique are for Chicano subjectivity and literature. And, vice versa, what does Chicano literature bring to psychoanalysis?

I begin with a prolegomenon on the limits of claiming an identity, questioning the desirability (or lack) to make certain claims of identity, and also theorizing the (im)possibility of speaking for the other. I find it important to situate myself as a critic with a particular theoretical perspective, thereby giving readers an idea from where I am speaking. Then, I proceed to discuss how in her foundational novel Cisneros negotiates some of the challenges of identity formation. I argue that *The House on Mango Street* presents a struggle to show a particular image of/within a Chicano community. Ultimately the protagonist, like the author, realizes that such a project of representation begins at home (vagueness intended).

The muteness of the father

First, I frame my comments with two perspectives on the limits of witnessing and the ability to narrate a traumatic event. Also, I want to keep in mind that these initial comments will enable me to approach comparatively the writing of and by Chicano subjects. In other words, let us consider how the narrative of trauma signifies on racialized subjectivities. I start off with a quote by Primo Levi, who talks about the obstacles present in bearing witness to the horrors of Auschwitz.

> I must repeat: we, the survivors, are not the true witnesses. [. . .] We survivors are not only an exiguous but also an anomalous minority: we are those who by their prevarications or abilities or good luck did not touch bottom. Those who did so, [they are . . .] the complete witnesses.
>
> (Levi, 1989, p. 83–84)

For Levi, the idea of a survivor is linked with the impossibility to know the Shoah fully. The survivor can never comprehend the horror; he or she cannot bear witness to it. Or, if they should know it, the violence of the event silences them; the horror makes them mute. This poignant insight has important implications for those who have witnessed other forms of racist violence – whether of different degree or kind. I don't want to flatten out or trivialize all forms of racism as having the same order; I just want to show the parallel ways of reading racist violence and its narratives.

I offer the following anecdote as example. In the early 1990s while living out East, I had the opportunity to teach in a gifted students program in California. When I told my father that I was going to spend a month in California, he was completely, vehemently opposed to the idea. I had never seen him oppose any of my work plans; much less with such force. My mother just said, "Don't worry. Go. He'll be fine." My father died in 1997; shortly afterwards, I was chatting with Mom and I remembered the incident, and I asked her whether she knew why he had reacted so negatively to my working in California. Her only guess – and I now believe it is very correct – was that when Dad was a 19-year-old, he got his papers, his "green card," and had gone to pick fruit in California, like so many young Mexican men of his generation. I remember as a child a picture of him bending over to carry a box of strawberries. Mom told me that Dad didn't like to talk about the two years he spent there, that afterwards he moved to Houston to look for work, before finally arriving and settling in Detroit. So, the story again, in 1955 around the time that the *bracero* program was being dismantled, my father, a young man, goes to California for two years, a period of his history which he would never want to share. He became "mute." All I can guess is that what might have happened in California then certainly influenced how he reacted to my news of teaching there. I suspect my father faced racist violence, which he would never want any of his children to experience at the very place he did. For him, the narrative of "getting out and 'forgetting' about it" was one of survival. His story of those two years died with him – all I experienced was an effect, a narrative aftershock of the "unsaid" that he might have experienced.

The impossible voice of the son

In a conversation between Gilles Deleuze and Michel Foucault, Deleuze comments that "[t]here is no denying that our social system *is totally without tolerance*; this accounts for its extreme fragility in all its aspects and also its need for a global form of repression."(Foucault & Deleuze, 1977, p. 209, emphasis added). In his understanding of cultural and social systems, Deleuze highlights the relation between the fragility or tenuousness itself of the social system, as well as the repressive force needed to maintain the system's centrality, autonomy, and authority. Deleuze locates in a total lack of tolerance for otherness the very thing which propels this dialectic between a system of fragility (an inflection of lack and desire) and its call for repression. In other words, what motivates (cultural, social, political) repression is a tacit awareness within the social system of its own fragile and temporary nature. Many systemic categorizations could be submitted to such a model – masculinity over woman, whiteness over racialized "others," and so on. The supposed priority of the first term (masculinity, whiteness) comes undone by its claim and very insistence for authority. Alongside this claim of authority comes a great deal of repression and silencing of the other. In this repressive context, speaking for the other is a continuation of the authorial claim of the *sujet-supposé-savoir*, and ultimately represents an aggressive imposition, a voice over another, a gagging of the other. Thus, Deleuze points out one of Foucault's theoretical achievements: "that only those directly concerned [those repressed] can speak in a practical way on their own behalf" (Foucault & Deleuze, 1977, p. 209). He clinches this point with that beautiful line: Foucault, he says, "teach[es] us something fundamental: the indignity of speaking for others" (Foucault & Deleuze, 1977, p. 209).

So, we come to a theoretical and ethical crossroad: On the one hand, Levi's insight about the limitations and near impossibility of bearing witness to ethnic and racial violence, and on the other hand, Foucault's call for dignity to allow the other to speak on her or his own terms. However, the question remains, what does the critic do to fulfill his desire to speak, to protest? If the critical narrative about racial violence can only show the contours of the experience, never its complete form and content, how do I tell a story about others? Does this mean I can only speak for myself? Already I've hinted that my narrative cannot presume to be complete: I cannot tell my father's story – first, because it never was revealed; second, because of the indignity of speaking for him, as him. The only story I can offer is one of the effects produced by the other's refusal to tell a story.[1] Mine is a narrative of melancholia; that is, my father's unsaid (and untold) story regulates any possibility of personally grasping a knowledge of the *petite histoires* that contribute to an Oedipal drama. Rather than thinking of a lost object, we encounter here a loss of knowledge, the awareness of a form of ignorance, that triggers melancholia as a series of other narrative possibilities and fantasies.

Again, I want to propose these coordinates as a framework to discuss Chicano literary production and the act of reading, which produces a particular subjectivity. How do we read Chicano literature without imposing and thereby reducing the radical potential of the literary thing? In other words, how do we avoid making such indignant statements as "Cisneros meant *exactly* this or that in her text"? Or, "so-and-so is a 'true' Chicano, whereas Richard Rodríguez isn't"? That is, how do we avoid falling into the trap of setting a litmus test for cultural and ethnic authenticity? Perhaps one way to circumvent this problem entails understanding what is meant by Chicano identity or, more precisely, *how* Chicano identities are formed.

Identifications[2]

Identities happen and are often hard to understand. In fact, much of the work in Latino/a Studies has struggled with the question of identity. Certainly, Cisneros's *The House on Mango Street* has been often set as the *urtext* for Chicana identity.[3]

Strategies for claiming an identity are many, although at times any effort to capitalize on the question of identity seems almost destined to be reduced to one of two tendencies. On the one hand, we have exercises that affirm an identity, to compact a community or group (yet, sacrifice the importance of a Self); on the other hand, we observe the valorization of the subject through a process of everlasting recognition, differentiation, or negation of the other. Both approaches to or conceptualizations of an identity seem to hinge on those two issues: Self and group – or a variation thereof, Self as/against/before . . . (the prepositions are endless) group. Diana Fuss (1995) theorizes the *very* process of identification – the internalization of the other, replacing a lost object from within – to swerve around the dilemma of having to choose among broader crystallizations of certain identities – the social, the political, the sexual, the national. Following Jean-Luc Nancy, Fuss defines identity as "'the Self that identifies itself.' Identification is the psychical mechanism that produces self-recognition. *Identification inhabits, organizes, instantiates identity*" (Fuss, 1995, p. 2).[4] For instance, we might agree that Chicano and Chicana identities are many and multi-faceted. However, and more precisely, the idea(l) of "Chicano" is deployed differently by everyone; in other words, how one might identify or not with this seemingly stable, identity of "Chicano" or "Chicana" will vary. That variation or fluidity is precisely the work of identification. Thus, Fuss (1995) warns us that

identification sets into motion the complicated dynamic of recognition and misrecognition that brings a sense of identity into being, it also immediately calls that identity into question.

(Fuss, 1995, p. 2)

This differentiation between identity (as a political goal) and identification (as the process to achieve such a goal) is central in our understanding of cultural and social politics. I would argue that the often-desired need for stability and cohesion in identity is regulated by a particularly conservative politic, whereas identification is the work of social and political coalition-building efforts, a different politic altogether. What is important to remember is that identities are never stable, nor are identifications ever complete. And, I argue further when discussing Chicano identities that some identities are fragmented, and identifications are interrupted and derailed. What happens when the very identity one wants for oneself is categorized as "too different" or "inferior," or the strategies of identification are seen as insufficient, inelegant, and subversive? What is one to do?

Broken identities

I began this essay with Levi's trauma narrative rather deliberately. My thesis is that some Chicano texts – and I include Sandra Cisneros's *The House on Mango Street* among this list – articulate a subject of trauma, that is, an identity or a subject who is fragmented, who has been violated and can only tell so much of her or his story. Furthermore, in the act of criticism, the critic almost seems compelled to "complete" this traumatic or fragmented subject and narrative; the critic wants to speak on the other's behalf. Yet, is that ever possible without being indignant?

If, in fact, Chicano subjectivity can be defined by her or his fragmentariness, as a broken figure, then *The House on Mango Street*'s protagonist-narrator, Esperanza, exemplifies this figuration of the subject *par excellence*. Esperanza's name, meaning hope, also signifies waiting – and by extension implies lacking. She tells us that "In English my name means hope. In Spanish it means too many letters. It means sadness, it means waiting. [. . .] It is the Mexican records my father plays on Sunday morning when he is shaving, songs like sobbing" (Cisneros, 1989, p. 10). Of the different characterizations that the child uses to illustrate her name, I would like to focus on the last one. Her name reminds her of her father's old records, of *boleros*, songs of passion and loss and impossible encounters. These songs, paradoxically, frame "like sobbing," a melodramatic love expression – they are excessive articulations of an impossibility. So is the narrator's name, Esperanza, an excessive desire for what might not happen. The melodrama of Esperanza's name points to a Manichean world of hope against perdition, of *jouissance* versus deep sadness. Furthermore, Esperanza tells us that it was also her great-grandmother's name. Because she didn't want to get married, her great-grandfather kidnapped her. She spent her life "the way so many women sit their sadness on an elbow" (Cisneros, 1989, p. 10). Esperanza can only sigh: "I have inherited her name, but I don't want to inherit her place by the window" (Cisneros, 1989, p. 11). This is a wonderful scene of identification, again, a narrative of how the Self brings the other within. Importantly, Esperanza's desire to have known her great-grandmother is followed by the refusal to accept the older woman's fate. Thus, as Freud points out, "identification is a partial and extremely limited one and only borrows a single trait from the person who is its object" (Freud, 1921, p. 107). Identification with the other is never complete; it involves a fragmentary relation, *yet it evolves psychically and narratively into a fuller expression of the Self*. Esperanza wants to rescue a part of her great-grandmother's story: she "[doesn't] want to inherit her place by the window."

I return to this image of a "woman sitting by the window" and take it as emblematic of a particular social and cultural condition traditionally assigned to women. The "woman sitting by the window" frames and captures so many traditional narratives of femininity: the woman waiting for her husband to come home, the woman trapped in her solitude, the woman longing to escape, the woman as a still, picture-perfect representation of passivity *qua* femininity, the woman as décor,[5] and a host of many other representations. For Esperanza this status of the "woman sitting by the window" is one considered as unwanted for herself. Esperanza wonders if her great-grandmother "made the best with what she got." This moment of wondering and wonderment is quite productive, because it rescues the older woman from her frozen silence and reanimates her, giving her imagination and creativity, also refunctioning the image to make it more identifiable for Esperanza herself. I suspect that Esperanza wants a particular version (or narrative) of her grandmother to survive for her and within her. She wants her, needs her as a figure of creativity and possibilities, not passivity. Consequently, we can see that Esperanza's identifications with her great-grandmother are specific: she identifies, not with her whole persona, but rather *with specific actions*. Identification isn't just how objects become internalized by the Self, but more specifically *how the other's actions are performed by the Self*. This detail changes how we can conceptualize "identification," not simply as an object relation, but as a performance that is repeated over and over again. Importantly this scene shows how Esperanza wishes to reinvent that part of her great-grandmother's history, which she deems necessary to her own history and identity. Once more, Esperanza's identity formation involves more than historical revision (testing the veracity of the "facts" that have been handed down to her and editing them), but rather refunctioning (in the Brechtian sense) certain images of the past. In other words, Esperanza replenishes that history with new meanings, refurbishing the interiority behind the historical names: Esperanza "inherits" her great-grandmother's name, but she does not want to "inherit" the one-dimensionality of her history, sitting by the window. There is a refusal here, a refusal to inherit willy-nilly a name or identity and be just what others tell her to be. This critical refunctioning serves as a powerful reminder of the writing of literature as a political practice for Chicano and Latino cultural and social transformations.[6]

Esperanza's name also implies a lack – and thus, a desire.[7] A desire for what? has been a question that has been answered over and over in criticism. Most obviously she wants a house. For the moment, I postpone this discussion about the house and ask a different question: May not Esperanza's desire well be a search for the Self? In fact, at the end of the vignette titled "My Name," Esperanza announces that "I would like to baptize myself under a new name, a name more like the real me, the one nobody sees. Esperanza as Lisandra or Maritza or Zeze the X. Yes. Something like Zeze the X will do" (Cisneros, 1989, p. 11). The first thing one notices here is how she wants to baptize herself differently. The re-signification of the Self is important because, behind it is a desire to have others know the "real" her, "the one nobody sees." The choice of names is equally interesting: The first two – Lisandra or Maritza – remind me of names from *telenovelas*; the preferred name, Zeze the X, plays with the idea of finality by doubling the letter *z*, also it is punctuated with "the X" as a marker on a map of the location of the booty, or *X* as the erasure of the Self or the impossibility of naming.[8] In other words, the name she chooses for herself repeats the very identity of the original name Esperanza, though from a different perspective. Esperanza marks the *hither* place of identity, a Self here and now looking elsewhere; Zeze the X (or any act of renaming, for that matter) points to a *telos*, the *thither* place of identity, the place of the Other, from where she can look (back) at herself anew.

This act of renaming also takes us to Freud's notion of the compulsion to repeat; I am talking specifically about the *fort/da* game he describes in *Beyond the Pleasure Principle* (Freud, 1920, p. 12–17). To recap, therein he tells about how a child stages an unpleasurable or traumatic event (his parents going to work) as a game with the purpose of repeating it. Freud argues convincingly that "[a]t the outset [the original trauma] he [his friends' child] was in a *passive* situation – he was overpowered [by the parents' departures]; but by repeating it [the trauma of departure, that is], unpleasurable though it was, as a game, he took on an *active* part" (Freud, 1920, p. 16). Repetition represents "an instinct for mastery" (Freud, 1920, p. 16); repetition allows the Self to imagine him or herself in an active position, rather than in a passive one. Thus, looking at Esperanza's restaging of her identity through the adoption of new names, she is in effect articulating a desire to master a new identity, which goes beyond role playing. She wants to name herself actively – with all the connotations that that action implies sexually, culturally, and politically.

The whole structure of *The House on Mango Street* operates with this movement as a regulating structure – from here to there and back, from passive to active and back. The text documents and narrates that movement, creating a spectrum for identification. I disagree with Ilan Stavans's (1996) description that the novel presents a cast of characters that

> is presented as real folks but, in truth, it is Manichean and buffoonish. Together they introduce a risky rhetoric of virtue that utilizes the powerless victim to advance a critique of the Hispanic idiosyncrasy, but that fails to explore any other of its multiple facets.
>
> (pp. 84–85)

While Stavans sees the text's Manicheanism as a reductive narrative strategy, I see it for all its dialectical potential. It also represents Cisneros's attempt and project to fill her novel with different histories, which form and inform the life of Esperanza herself. Briefly, if we take the theme of the "house" as the central motif in the novel, we realize that it is primarily discussed at the beginning and end of the text, leaving many chapters in between, where Cisneros gives a rapid picture retelling of the lives of many people: Nenny, Cathy, Meme Ortiz, Louie, Marin, Rosa Vargas and all her kids, Alicia, Darius, the nuns, Rachel and Lucy, Elenita, Geraldo No Last Name, Edna and Ruthie, Earl, the beautiful Rafaela, Sally, and Minerva. The brevity of the chapters is important here because it shows the impossibility of being able to tell the stories of others; it shows that Esperanza's retelling of each story is limited not only by what she can see, but also by what she can understand and know. It also shows that her identification with different friends and neighbors is partial. The tendency among some readers is to select and universalize some of the narratives – for instance, the story of Rosa Vargas as a critique of patriarchy (Quintana, 2012, pp. 67–69) or Rafaela's fate as an allegory of Chicano machismo and the oppression of Chicanas, or the vignette titled "Those Who Don't" as a return of the gaze within the context of racism and fear. While I find these different evaluations important, I don't want to read them simply as separate events, which we might flesh out as a way of returning the voice to those who cannot speak, but rather as identificatory moments that Esperanza herself experiences. Each chapter is part of her story and experience; it is her way of telling us something about herself, her way of looking forward and back at her life. Each vignette registers her identifications as ongoing processes of self-figuration, her movement from here to there. Piecing together these different vignettes allows for the rehearsal of an autobiographical retelling through the lives of others. Going back to the question of Esperanza's many lacks, we could argue that she is collecting others' stories and recycling them in the invention and finding of her own.

Melancholia on Mango Street

I now discuss the figure of the house. So much has been written about this metaphor that I hope to present something new to our understanding of it.[9] From the start, the house is not a place that Esperanza accepts as her own, as her place. She declares, "We didn't always live on Mango Street" (Cisneros, 1989, p. 3). In other words, Mango Street is not the place of origin, that place has been lost or, at least, displaced.

> Before that we lived on Loomis on the third floor, and before that we lived on Keeler. Before Keeler it was Paulina, and before that I can't remember. But what I remember most is moving a lot. Each time it seemed there'd be one more of us.
>
> (p. 3)

The place of origin traditionally and so powerfully insisted upon to determine one's identity is missing. In fact, this ideology of origins is rendered most visible in two separate scenes – first, when Esperanza meets her friends Lucy and Rachel. Right after exchanging names, the girls tell where they come from:

> We come from Texas, Lucy says and grins. Her was born here, but me I'm Texas.
>   You mean *she*, I say.
>   No, I'm from Texas, and doesn't get it.
>
> (p. 15)

In this exchange, Lucy commits some grammatical errors, which nonetheless highlight important conceptions about identity and origin. She states, "Her was born here, but me I'm Texas" thereby collapsing place and Self. When Esperanza tries to correct the subject of the first part of the sentence, Lucy misunderstands her and clarifies that she is from Texas, not her sister. Again, the repetition allows Lucy to insist on the priority of Self as an assignable place. Also, near the end of the text, we see this relation between place of origin and identity again when Esperanza tells us that

> I like Alicia because once she gave me a little leather purse with the word GUADALAJARA stitched on it, which is home for Alicia, and one day she

will go back there. But today she is listening to my sadness because I don't have a house.

(p. 106)

Importantly, for Esperanza, Alicia has a place in Mexico where she comes from, albeit romantic and mythic, a place she can call her own and where she can return to claim her identity. Guadalajara is a place you can mark on a leather purse and give as a memento. Esperanza cannot remember where she comes from; she only remembers "moving a lot."

"Moving a lot" keeps Esperanza from establishing a relation of belonging, and also makes identification more difficult, until finally there is the house on Mango Street. This house is supposed to crystallize her desire and relation to a place. But, the reality fails to satisfy the fantasy – the object is necessarily insufficient.

They [Mama and Papa] always told us that one day we would move into a house, a real house that would be ours for always so we wouldn't have to move each year. . . . And inside it would have real stairs . . . like the houses on T.V.

(p. 4)

The house itself is a fiction. More importantly it's the construction of desire created by Esperanza's parents – it's the speculation (*la esperanza*) of a winning "lottery ticket" for the father; it's also the material of the mother's bedtime stories. In fact, any house would unavoidably come up short to the fantasy house that the parents have drawn for Esperanza. Therefore, we aren't surprised to hear Esperanza's lament: "But the house on Mango Street is not the way they told it at all" (p. 4). I suggest that this difference between the two houses – the parents' fantasy, which becomes internalized as a child's expectation and the reality of Mango Street – produce a crisis in Esperanza's identity. If we consider that this child's notion of place is so intimately linked to her own identity, then the parents' imagined house (Imaginary) has left really a kind of imprint on Esperanza's own sense of Self. She expects to see the "perfect" house because it would be a complete representation of herself. However, the house where she ends up tears apart the fantasy and also replaces the idealized Self with an abject Self, leading to a narcissistic injury, which reminds us of what Freud (1917) called "an open wound" (p. 253),[10] the very figure of melancholia. Specifically, Freud states that melancholia refers to the state in which the Self reacts to the loss of a loved object, but it is a "loss of a more ideal kind." More precisely, the melancholic may be "aware of the loss which has given rise to his melancholia, but only in the sense that he knows *whom* he has lost but not *what* he has lost in him" (Freud, 1917, p. 245, emphasis in original). Thus, melancholia operates unconsciously.

Going back to Esperanza, the loss of the "house" is more than the loss of expectation and of the stories told by her parents. The lost house is also a loss of the Self insofar as the house is an exteriorization of her own sense of identity; this loss of Self will remain unconscious: she doesn't know *what* has been lost in her.

This exteriorization of Self would get dramatically and traumatically performed in a scene when a nun from her school sees Esperanza playing in front of her apartment on Loomis.

> Where do you live? she asked.
> There, I said pointing to the third floor.
> You live *there*?
> There. I had to look where she pointed . . . You live *there*? The way she said it made me feel like nothing. *There*. I lived *there*. I nodded.
>
> (Cisneros, 1989, p. 5)

When Esperanza first tells the nun that she lives "there," it is done in the most un-self-conscious manner. It is only after the nun, who stands in a position of authority, reacts and questions the place in a way that made the young girl "feel like nothing," that she sees her family's apartment home as something abject. It is the language of racism, in fact, that makes us "feel like nothing"; furthermore, racist language remakes not only the Self, but also the sense of the place. Esperanza then begins to disavow belonging to that place *there*, very much like the experience of my father with respect to California. It is no longer a home *here*, but the place of otherness, *there*. This dislocation of place and othering of the subject is exactly what Judith Butler notes as one of the central qualities of injurious speech:

> To be addressed injuriously is not only to be open to an unknown future, but not to know the time and place of injury, and to suffer the disorientation of one's situation as the effect of such speech. Exposed at the moment of such a shattering is precisely the volatility of one's "place" within the community of speakers; one can be "put in one's place" by such speech, but such a place may be no place.
>
> (Butler, 1997, p. 4)

Hence, it is this loss of place and Self effected by the nun's words that leads Esperanza to look elsewhere. This traumatic encounter is what motivates and leads Esperanza to desire a place, wherein which she can identify: "I knew then," she asserts, "I had to have a house. A real house. One I could point to. But this isn't it. The house on Mango Street isn't it," (Cisneros, 1989, p. 5). Again, we can extend Esperanza's insight to the echoes of many immigrants for whom coming to the United States as the American Dream just isn't it.[11]

I would suggest another reading: in this scene with the nun, Esperanza becomes the Abject. She is not a subject, not an object, but rather qualifies as an Abject (as noun, not adjective). This third identity positionality (abject versus subject or object) challenges us to reconsider how identity comes into being from nothingness. If the Self as subject has authority to speak for her- or himself; and the Self as object is spoken about or defined by others – and only needs to respond or protest to convert that object status to claim subject status; then, the self as Abject presents an impossibility. How does the Abject reinvent herself/himself – with what material, social, or cultural capital does he/she claim access to a subject status? That becomes the most overwhelming challenge. For Esperanza, this reconceptualization of Self as Abject lays the foundation for the re-imagining of a Self.

I would thus conclude by suggesting that it isn't the house itself that Esperanza wishes to possess, but rather she wants to recuperate the stories/narratives of house and home. Near the end of the text, she confirms this desire: "Only a house quiet as snow, a space for myself to go, clean as paper before the poem," (Cisneros, 1989, p. 108). She wants the white house of her parents' ideals. Esperanza's house isn't always already an unreachable material and physical space, but rather it becomes a house of narrative that allows her to create and recreate her identity. It's as if the house on Mango Street was always full of traces and a collection of memories, and the author now wants to clean house and start all over again.

Cleaning house and starting all over again – like "moving a lot" – is a social and cultural strategy to rewrite (or rather to re-writ(h)e) the Self. It also reminds me of my father's muteness. Gloria Anzaldúa inaugurates her *Borderlands/La Frontera* with a powerful insight of survival: "My love of images . . . and words, my passion for the daily struggle to render them concrete in the world and on paper, to render them flesh, keeps me alive"(Anzaldúa, 1999, pp. 1–2). The house that Cisneros wants – "Only a house quiet as snow, a space for myself to go, clean as paper before the poem" (Cisneros, 1989, p. 108) – becomes a blank sheet of paper that sets the scene for her desire. My father's stubborn silence – a clean or blank start – allow his children to speak in a new language, in a new place.

In the final vignette of *Mango Street*, we hear an echo from the beginning:

> We didn't always live on Mango Street. Before that we lived on Loomis on the third floor, and before that we lived on Keeler. Before Keeler it was Paulina, but what I remember most is Mango Street, sad red house, the house I belong but do not belong to.
>
> (Cisneros, 1989, pp. 109–110)

The repetition of the opening lines comes with a difference, no longer is her strongest memory of moving a lot, but of Mango Street and the sad red house. What is also striking here is the reversal of ownership: Esperanza belongs and doesn't belong to the house – and not the other way around as would be expected. She is part of the house's history, rather than the house being part of her history. The house, like Esperanza, has the option of rejecting her presence. In other words, a person may be homeless, but also a house may be bodiless. If we take this idea further: The house as metaphor for the nation may be empty of body and citizens – the house or the nation may reject you in the same ways in which you may reject the place where you belong.

Notes

1 I compare this inability of speaking, of grieving, with Anne A. Cheng's (2000) research in *The melancholy of race: Psychoanalysis, assimilation, and hidden grief*. New York, NY: Oxford University Press.

2 A version of this section appeared in Spanish in a modified form in "Epílogo: Apuntes sobre la identidad y lo latino" *Nueva Sociedad*, Tema: "Cultura Latina en Estados Unidos," *201*(Spring 2006), 146–147.

3 This collapse of identity and/as textuality can be seen most visibly in Maria Elena de Valdés's 1992 article, "In Search of Identity in Cisneros's *The House on Mango Street*." There she proposes that "the most pressing issue is the ideological question of a poetics of identity in the double marginalization of a Chicana" (p. 55). She adds that she is "opposed to any critical strategy which ignored the qualitative perspective of the lyric narrative voice, the referential situation from which she is writing, and the issues she is writing about" (p. 55). My proposed reading, which focuses on *identification* rather than *identity*, circumvents the problem of enumerating marginalizations – since the articulation of marginalizations often collapse or subsume one another, we talk about sexuality *through* race, about color *through* body, about gender *through* economics, and so on. This practice of distinguishing "separate" identities as though they can be marked discretely seems clumsy. But what is really problematic of Valdés's reading is her reification of Cisneros's writing through the figure of the loom (p. 61), thereby the critic is repeating, reducing, the act of women's writing to the very object that "patriarchy" has classically attributed to women and literary production – from Penelope in *The Odyssey* to the present.

4 Emphasis added.

5 This idea of "woman as décor" reminds me of the French pun of "*dé-corps*" (dis-embody), rather than "décor." In effect, the woman who occupies a decorous place in her man's life has already been disembodied, ripped, killed.

6 Of course, I completely disagree with Ellen McCracken's (1989) reading of the novel. She begins her essay by asserting that "[i]ntrospection has achieved a privileged status in bourgeois literary production, corresponding to the ideological emphasis on individualism under capitalism, precisely as the personal and political power of many real individuals has steadily deteriorated" (p. 62). There is a premise here that the practice of introspection cannot and should not be part and parcel of Chicana practices of assuming an identity. It doesn't take much analysis of the novel to realize that Esperanza is incredibly introspective – and what's wrong with that? I find McCracken's dichotomy between "bourgeois individualism" and "community" to be a false one for the articulation of identity. In fact, the text uses both individual and community ideals to forge different identities.

7 In *The Seminar of Jacques Lacan, Book II: The Ego in Freud's Theory and in the Technique of Psychoanalysis, 1954–1955*, Lacan explains that

> Desire is a relation of being to lack. This lack is the lack of being properly speaking. It isn't the lack of this or that, but lack of being whereby the being exists.
> This lack is beyond anything which can represent it. It is only ever represented as a reflection on a veil.

(Lacan, 1988, p. 223)

Desire glues together being and lack. The desiring Self conceives of its being as a response to a lack. The lack cannot be precisely named as such, but rather it emerges as a hint, a suggestion or an insinuation, even. Lacan goes on to elaborate that "[d]esire, a function central to all human experience, is the desire for nothing nameable. And at the same time this desire lies at the origin of every variety of animation. If being were only what it is, there wouldn't even be room to talk about it. Being comes into existence as a function of this lack. Being attains a sense of self in relation to being as a function of this lack" (Lacan, 1988, p. 223). Esperanza's being is shaped by many lacks (here, I venture to consider not only the psychic, but also the social, economic, to name a few) – and by as many desires that follow.

8 For a different reading of how Esperanza's self-naming opens up ways of survival, see Juan Daniel Busch's fine essay "Self-Baptizing the Wicked Esperanza: Chicana Feminism and Cultural Contact in *The House on Mango Street*," esp. pp. 126–129.

9 See essays by Kuribayashi, McCracken, Yarbro-Bejarano, and Gutiérrez-Jones, among others.

10 Freud states that "the complex of melancholia behaves like an open wound, drawing to itself cathectic energies . . . from all directions, and emptying the Ego until it is totally impoverished" (Freud, 1917, p. 253).

11 I am thinking about works that reflect not just the experience of recent immigrants, who can still look nostalgically at their homeland (Gregory Nava's film, *El Norte*, Nicholasa Mohr's short story, "A Very Special Pet," and a host of other Latino/a narratives), but also experiences of citizens of second and later generations who are repeatedly questioned about their place in United States' culture and society.

References

Anzaldúa, G. (1999). *Borderlands/La Frontera*. San Francisco, CA: Aunt Lute Books.

Busch, J. D. (1993). Self-baptizing the wicked Esperanza: Chicana feminism and cultural contact. The house on Mango Street. *Mester, 22*(2), 123–134.

Butler, J. (1997). *Excitable speech: A politics of the performative*. New York, NY: Routledge.

Cheng, A. (2000). *The melancholy of race: Psychoanalysis, assimilation, and hidden grief*. New York, NY: Oxford University Press.

Cisneros, S. (1989). *The house on mango street*. New York, NY: Vintage Contemporaries.

De Valdés, M. E. (1992). In search of identity in Cisneros's The House on Mango Street. *Canadian Review of American Studies, 23*(1), 55–72.

Foucault, M., & Deleuze, G. (1977). Intellectuals and power. In D. Bouchard (Ed.), *Language, counter-memory, practice: Selected essays and interviews by Michel Foucault* (pp. 205–217). Ithaca, NY: Cornell University Press.

Freud, S. (1917 [1915]). Mourning and melancholia. In *The standard edition of the complete psychological works of Sigmund Freud XIV (1914–1916): On the history of the psycho-analytic movement, papers on metapsychology and other works* (pp. 237–258). London, England: The Hogarth Press and the Institute of Psycho-Analysis.

Freud, S. (1920). Beyond the pleasure principle. In *The standard edition of the complete psychological works of Sigmund Freud, Volume XVIII (1920–1922): Beyond the pleasure principle, group psychology and other works* (pp. 1–64). London, England: The Hogarth Press and the Institute of Psycho-Analysis.

Freud, S. (1921). Group psychology and the analysis of the ego. In *The standard edition of the complete psychological works of Sigmund Freud, Volume XVIII (1920–1922): Beyond the pleasure principle, group psychology and other works* (pp. 65–144). London, England: The Hogarth Press and the Institute of Psycho-Analysis.

Fuss, D. (1995). *Identification papers*. New York, NY: Routledge.

Gutierrez-Jones, L. S. (1993). Different voices: The re-building of the Barrio in Sandra Cisneros' *The House on Mango Street*. In C. Singley & S. E. Sweeney (Eds.), *Anxious power: Reading, writing, and ambivalence in narrative by women* (pp. 295–312). Albany, NY: SUNY Press.

Kuribayashi, T. (1998). The Chicana girl writes her way in and out: Space and bilingualism in Sandra Cisneros' *The House on Mango Street*. In T. Kuribayashi & J. A. Tharp (Eds.), *Creating safe space: Violence and women's writing* (pp. 165–177). Albany, NY: SUNY Press.

Lacan, J. (1988). *The seminar of Jacques Lacan. Book II: The ego in Freud's theory and in the technique of psychoanalysis, 1954–1955* (J. A. Miller, Ed. & S. Tomaselli, Trans.). New York, NY: Cambridge University Press.

Levi, P. (1989). *The drowned and the saved* (R. Rosenthal, Trans.). New York, NY: Vintage International.

McCracken, E. (1989). Sandra Cisneros' The House on Mango Street: Community-oriented introspection and the demystification of patriarchal violence. In A. Horno-Delgado et al. (Eds.), *Breaking boundaries: Latina writing and critical readings* (pp. 62–71). Amherst, MA: The University of Massachusetts Press.

Mohr, N. (1975). *El Bronx remembered*. New York, NY: Harper Trophy.

Nava, G. (director). (1983). *El Norte*.

Quintana, A. (2012). *Home girls: Chicana literary voices*. Philadelphia, PA: Temple University Press.

Sifuentes-Jáuregui, B. (2006, Spring). Epílogo: Apuntes sobre la identidad y lo latino. *Nueva Sociedad*, Tema: "Cultura Latina en Estados Unidos", *201*, 146–147.

Stavans, I. (1996). Sandra Cisneros: Form over content. *Academic Questions*, *9*(4), 29–34.

Yarbro-Bejarano, Y. (1987). Chicana literature from a Chicana feminist perspective. *The Americas Review*, *15*(Fall–Winter), 139–145.

Chapter 9

Chencha's gait
Voice and nothing in Myrta Silva

Licia Fiol-Matta

In a 1973 interview, the mercurial Puerto Rican singer, entertainer, and entrepreneur Myrta Silva stated, "*I'm a winner*. I only failed at the beginning of my
career . . . ever since I became a public figure, I have never once failed" (Silva,
1973). Despite the singer's confident declaration, Silva was well aware of the
entanglement between "figure" and "failure." She learned that failure was always
around the corner since she set foot in New York City as a barely teenaged immigrant, circa 1938.[1] She emigrated, she said, to become an artist. Born in Arecibo,
Puerto Rico, in 1923, Silva lived in poverty in the big city along with thousands
of Puerto Rican and Latino immigrants, working an average of 25 revue shows a
week as a means of support and a way to initiate her music career.

In a milieu Ruth Glasser (1997) lucidly describes as dominated by U.S. recording companies and their demand for "ethnic music," Silva advertised her talent
to the RCA Victor as a *guaracha* singer (pp. 129–168).[2] She staked her claim on
her special affinity with the genre by describing herself as matching the genre's
temperament in personality terms:

> On my own initiative, I went to the RCA Victor offices, and asked to speak
> to the head of the Latin department, making it clear that if he did not see me
> they would be lose out on the best guaracha singer there was, of this new
> Latin American genre.
>
> (Silva, 1975a, p. 25)

Approximately three decades after Silva's daring stunt, in 1967, Silva was
awarded the Radio TV Mirror prize as TV's Top Variety Show of New York, and
WNJUC-TV received the award for Outstanding Programming in the Broadcast-
ing Arts for *The Myrta Silva Show*. Silva had become a beloved representative of
the Puerto Rican community in the New York of the 1960s.

While hers was a Spanish-language show, the prize was for all New York–area
television, not just Latino TV. Puerto Rican newspapers ran the news, citing the
magazine's circulation of six million and the prize's standing as the oldest such
prize at the time in the U.S. radio and TV industry. Silva is quoted as saying, "I
accept this prize in the name of all us *hispanos* who live in New York City, so that

it may serve as an incentive, so that you can see that your sacrifices and struggles have not been in vain." She added,

> "Most significant is the fact that this prize has been awarded to me in this city of New York, the greatest city on earth, and where I started my career going hungry and earning a miserable salary of fifteen dollars a month."
>
> (Berenguer, 1967, p. 54)

Silva triumphed in New York City and pioneered Latino television in the United States. Yet, her beloved Puerto Rico had become viciously split about its biggest star. Viewers were quick to question her national allegiances and harbored an uncomfortable-to-repulsed attitude to her unmarried, yet sexual status. Silva's declaration of her greatest love – for her mother, Mamá Yeya – surfaced on occasion as palliative: "*es lesbiana, pero buena hija*" [She's a lesbian, true, but she's a good daughter]. Other viewers simply went into panic mode, ordering their children to "turn off the TV; we don't watch that dyke in our house." The epithet of The Fat Golden One encapsulates the quandary of simultaneous hatred and adoration: Being called fat in Puerto Rico was completely insulting, and certainly desexualizing, but the adjectival phrase "*de oro*" conveyed feelings of appreciation and a statement about sterling character.

What follows sketches the content and trajectory of Silva's music-making, shifting the attention from the gaze to the voice and in so doing paying a little respect to a woman whose supreme object was music and who, until recently, has only been remembered as a repellent image. In *A Voice and Nothing More*, the Lacanian critic, Mladen Dolar (2006), writes,

> apart from those two widespread uses of the voice – the voice as the vehicle of meaning; the voice as a source of aesthetic admiration – there is a third level: an object-voice . . . which functions as a blind spot in the call and as a disturbance to aesthetic appreciation.
>
> (p. 4)

Dolar's "third level" singularly fits Myrta Silva, and when I refer to voice in this chapter, I am specifically tracking the voice as an object-voice, as a part-object in the psychoanalytic sense. Silva consciously worked the "void" into many of her musical interventions, served as a blind spot for the listener, and grew into an aesthetic disturbance to dominant, cultural-nationalist culture. Silva's ability to mobilize desire owed to elements that have everything to do with her musical intelligence and performative power. She was an inherently musical mind who was gifted with a natural harmonic ear and percussive ability. Silva was a certified *timbalera*, a master of the apparently simple yet extraordinarily difficult art of being able to sing and play the maracas simultaneously while fronting a band. (In fact, she was the first woman *timbales* player to be certified by the American Federation of Music, in 1943.) She was a self-taught musician *que tenía la clave* [could follow the beat, usually 3/2]. Silva's percussive approach to voice, particularly in her interpretations of guarachas, constitutes a breakthrough for female singing. She was an extraordinary *sonera* and, adding to her innate musical ear, understood the conceptual density of cadence (known by its various vernacular names, such as *el tumbaíto* and *mi cantao*). Playing the timbales, *soneando*, and bandleading, these musical capabilities inched her toward the masculine position in pop (and let's not forget that this was, decidedly, a man's world). Except for the occasional all-girl band, this positioning of Silva's was simply unheard of. Silva's geniality lay in her uncanny and differently gendered ability to connect with the audience beyond passing entertainment value. She describes it as a capacity for improv:

> I've always worked without a script. I am only great if the audience is. If the audience isn't into it, neither am I . . . As we say in musical jargon, I work *ad lib*. The band . . . can't bend me to its will, because I work *ad lib*.
>
> (Silva, 1973)

Understanding Silva's brilliance and taking stock of her profoundly influential career requires unpacking Silva's astonishing deployment of the signifier. In psychoanalytic terms, her voice came to represent the partial object, the *objet petit a*, that irreducible kernel which causes the subject's desire because it denies the subject its narcissistic illusion of completeness.

When we approach the few authoritative accounts of Silva's career, we find that almost all have naturalized the dominant culture's construction of Silva's voice as perfectly aligned with the guaracha and its lewdness.[3] In this realm, Silva was universally extolled as a brilliant singer. Problematically though, the public came to assume Silva was indeed describing herself when she sang guarachas, even though they also "knew" she was merely punning. The state of disavowal indicates that Silva embodied a complex fantasy world through her performances of voice.

Silva was certainly stung by the public reduction of her musicianship and musicality. Addressing negative comments about her vocal instrument decades after her first hits, Silva retorted, "I've done pretty well with my lousy voice." Referencing her desire to sing the famous *bolero* "Júrame" by the acclaimed Mexican songwriter María Grever, she quoted a conversation between the two. Silva reportedly told Grever, "Since I don't have much of a voice, I can't sing some of your songs," to which Grever responded, "You have what it takes to sing my songs, and that is heart, not a great voice"(Silva, 1981). Throughout her career Silva called attention to voice as an entity that did not have to be only or primarily musically virtuosic in order to command an audience and own a song. Instead, she put into play a virtuosity that José Esteban Muñoz has linked to queer artistry: the brilliant, conceptual staging of negativity and failure (Muñoz, 2009, pp. 169–183).

As a riposte to the over-identification of her person with her work, Silva consciously named herself in her songs and constructed an artistic persona around her given name, Myrta. Subsequently, she found herself inextricably linked to what was at first merely a type in a hit guaracha, "Camina como Chencha la gambá." Beginning in the 1950s, she created a character in a TV skit she developed, the segment "Tira y tápate" [Dodgeball], taking advantage of the built-in publicity generated by her hit song. She named this gossip queen "Chencha." As signifiers, Myrta and Chencha were linked metonymically at first. When they became metaphorically linked, Silva found herself subjected to a signifying chain she could not entirely control.[4]

An early guaracha, "Mis tres novios" [My Three Boyfriends] provides an apt entry point for the analysis of this signifying process. Ramón Rodríguez, the songwriter, was one of the members of Cuarteto Victoria, the group Myrta Silva joined in 1939, whose leader was the famed and esteemed Rafael Hernández, one of the most important and revered musical figures in Puerto Rican and Latin American music. Silva was 16 years old when she recorded this sexually explicit song with the group in 1940. The song brilliantly embodies the deceptive nature of romantic and sexual discourse, as well as the pleasure entailed in this deception. It was written to take full advantage of Silva's performative talents, uncannily present even at this early age.

Silva boasts of her "nice boyfriends" who "please her too much" and the lovers are spoken about in the third person to the song's true addressee, the listener, engaging him in the game of deception. (It is likely that the songwriter had a male listener in mind and that the song was created for live performance in one of New York City's many Latino venues.) Silva's recitative, presumably of her own authorship, makes her intervention sound "just like" sex talk. The speaker addresses a single male lover in the recitative, altering the course of the official lyrics to engage the duped lovers and create a complicity with the audience – who is "in the know" – and to underscore the sexual hook of sound itself, particularly cadence, as the reason for sexual attention. The singer addresses each lover in identical fashion, seeking to make him feel unique, yet it is understood that all the parties involved know what is really going on (that no such fidelity actually exists in desire's register). The lyrics reference "*este cantao*" [this tune], which in turn inaugurates chunks in parlando that are as obscene as censorship of the time would allow. Silva employs slang and double-entendre phrases such as "*mi papi*" [Daddy] and "*me retrato*" [I will open my legs] and plays on the phallic meaning of certain instruments, such as the saxophone that she will "*soplar*" [blow].

Decidedly, the element that makes "Mis tres novios" so successful is Silva herself, affecting a "little girl next door," innocent voice, and cooing and babbling the words so they are blurred or lost until they cede linguistic meaning to another type of meaning: the voice as materiality and call to the other. In this sense, Silva was indeed close to the body, and not in the simplistic and disfiguring sense her detractors reckoned, as dirty and disgusting. In her call to the other, which in "Mis tres novios" is actually the listener and not principally a male lover, the young Silva already intuited the existence of what Dolar terms "the void." While the song's author is not Silva, as with many Silva performances it was written for her, in order to musicalize her specific, non-transferable musical persona. Without Silva's act of self-creation, songs like "Mis tres novios" would simply not have been written. The question of authorship becomes, then, a less than straightforward proposition.

Upon recording "Nada" [Nothing] in New York City in 1942, Silva moved away decisively from the simply playful nature of her songs. It became her lifelong signature song. Notwithstanding that songwriting credits belong to Rafael Hernández, the song does not make any sense without the phenomenological force that was Myrta Silva. In this sense, we can consider that even if not directly penned by her, "Nada" reflects Silva's intentions as she began to inhabit the space of the figure, a singer whose meaning was born in music but who exceeded music's domain to become historically significant as a cultural phenomenon. This distinguishes her from other artists who worked with double-entendre and the obscene.

Silva once again employs the plaintive "girl next door" voice, with its petulant tone and babbling and cooing in the refrain. Although there is no recitative in this song, the entire set of lyrics plays with Silva's persona and the artist's status as an overdetermined signifier (due to her by then highly sexualized, "bombshell" image). The sexual availability of "Mis tres novios" has morphed into a direct and strongly worded complaint: The lyrics employ a first person who does not want to be looked at, talked to, or invited to sing, who goes so far as stating that she no longer wants to be known as Myrta ("*Nada, ya no me llamo Myrta*" [Nothing. I will no longer be called Myrta]). Notice especially her name equated with the abolition of the linguistic signifier: When Silva sings that "my name does not exist" ("*mi nombre ya no existe*") we can consider this the psychoanalytic equivalent to saying "my name from this moment on is a signifier" (as with analysis, the proper name here becomes detached from its ordinary meaning, thus forming new unconscious chains of signification).[5] Rather than the simple, ubiquitous male fantasies of her earliest recordings, the fantasy that Silva embodied for her listeners progressively revolved around the suturing of the treacherous nature of both femininity and masculinity, circling the perpetual state of distress that gender really means as a performance perilously close to failure (to recall Judith Butler's formulations of gender as catachresis, the moment where signification fails because of a figure used improperly; Butler, 1993).

The inclusion of the proper name Myrta in the song "Nada" could have well been Silva's idea, breaching the distance between signifier and signified and between persona and person. Even if she did not directly collaborate with the lyrics, the song was written for her and the signifier can only do its work due to Silva's prior labor and act of self-creation. The signifier of Myrta gained in importance as the years went on thanks to Silva's musical intelligence and artistic development of negativity. "Nada"'s title, "nothing," is what Silva is offering her desiring audience onstage and in records, a negative of everything that the male fantasies of other songs were based on. Structurally, this negative occupies the same position as the "fullness" of the presumptively available woman.

Thanks to her success in New York, the company with which Silva registered her compositions, Peer International, arranged Silva's first trip to Cuba in 1942. Around this time, the child sex object figuration gave way to Silva as a fully developed, autonomous creation, no longer needing the cohort of male musicians behind her. Silva was a frequent return visitor to Cuba until 1959, sometimes for extended stays. She also worked across Latin America and in venues in the United States, always keeping New York as a home base. This period is regarded by most music specialists as Silva's finest, musically speaking. Silva cut dozens of 78-rpm records during this time and had her greatest hits. For the next three decades Silva, literally, circulated, and so did her music, in records and later in radio and TV shows. Silva turned more intensely to self-reference, as first seen in "Nada."

Silva's voice worked the culture's scripts for sexual incitements to arrive at a different end point from Hernández and other male composers who wrote lewd songs, mostly guarachas, for Silva to perform. There was a distinct difference between when Hernández and other Cuarteto Victoria members penned lewd songs as "entertainment" and show attractions, and when Myrta Silva banded about her own sense of humor, which was far from childlike.

Her interpretations sparked the righteous ire of official censors in Cuba of the late 1940s, who banned numerous guarachas, alleging they were immoral and conducive to less than acceptable citizen behavior. Notions of middle-class "normalcy" and morality threatened to derail Silva's career in Cuba when she started running into trouble with that country's censorship board in 1947 (Anonymous, 1947b, July 27). A list of the songs banned by the nascent Radio Ethics Commission features several Myrta Silva performances, among these "Adiós Comay Gata" [Goodbye, Comay Gata], "Camina como Chencha la gambá" [She walks like Chencha, the pigeon-toed woman], "Déjamelo ver" [Let me see it] and "Échale tierra y tápalo" [Toss a little dirt on it and cover it] (Anonymous, 1947a, July 27; Anonymous, 1947c, June 8).

Of these banned songs, "Camina como Chencha la gambá" deserves detailed scrutiny. It birthed the Chencha signifier in Silva's career. The folk Chencha originated earlier, possibly in Spain; it was Silva's idea to create a song based on the folk pun "*camina como Chencha, la gambá*" (she walks like Chencha, the pigeon-toed woman). On more than one occasion, Silva explained that she created characters or situations and presented them to songwriters who created guarachas based on her ideas. Ñico Saquito (Antonio Fernández) had Silva to thank for making several of his songs into hits.[6]

The original recording of 1946 is historically significant, as it was her most successful recording, selling 500,000 copies, an astronomical amount (Silva, 1975a, p. 27).[7] Silva, however, hated it: she thought the arrangement was horrible (Silva, 1975a, p. 27). The fact is that she became indelibly associated with this song, and, as in negation in psychoanalysis, she probably did not own up fully to her resentment. Silva performed Chencha in social spaces as diverse as the Tropicana of Havana, the Escambrón Beach Club in Puerto Rico, and New York's Teatro Hispano. The song capitalized on the meanings the Myrta signifier had by then accrued as an oversexed woman, a simultaneously disgusting and desirable object. The enticement of the song is the subject's over-examination by the listeners, who are visually engaged in "figuring her out" (or more precisely, her gait) as she walks down the street.

This guaracha is somewhat more brooding in tone than others she recorded. The singer feels, decidedly, solitary, distant from the chorus. The song is meant to be funny, but there is an unerring sense that an air of resentment is starting to creep into Silva's musical personality, triggering a process of splitting. It features a slow tempo, and the refrain is repeated twice, not four times, as in the later version of 1956, which Silva produced and preferred. In the original recording, Silva's name does not appear; there is no metonymic operation, only a metaphorical one. The song fades out, and does not have the definitive sound of the later Mexican recording, with its trombones emphasizing the minor chords and its final bars sounding much more ominous.

Spoken asides crucially deviate from the written lyrics; these set into motion a running comment or ironic distancing from the work as it is being performed, one that can be experienced repeatedly, every time we play the song. In certain instances, Silva alters the song's original lyrics. For example, Silva sings of people having changed her name from Myrta Silva to Chencha Silva, that is, coming to define her solely based on gossip about her sexual activity. The song's next-to-last stanza effects a subtle but noticeable transformation in the singer: in a *soneo*, Silva accelerates the tempo of the original: "*camina, camina, camina, camina, camina Chencha*" sounds like an auto-interpellation, a little like a blues lament (as in "carrying on").

The difference between the later version and the first version of 1947 lies in the percussive and rhythmic use of voice. Silva always said that the first arrangement was "horrible," but it is possible that what this expression ultimately meant was that she felt she could not incorporate *her* act of "listening" to the performance, which she achieves in the second version. In *Listen: A History of Our Ears*, Peter Szendy (2007) has written about the arrangement as a very specialized act of listening. By changing the song's arrangement and imprinting her act of listening on the record's grooves, Silva undermined the song's lyrics "from within." Altogether, it's as if Silva had "rewritten" the song to conform to her desire: to embody the empty place which the drive circles, the "nothing," the "void."

Chencha is not equal to Silva herself; the song explicitly refers in a first-person singing voice to a character in the third person. The lyrics had made this evident since the first recording, but the performance, including Silva's improvisations in 1961, amplify the distance between the flesh-and-blood Silva and her character, in the spirit of commentary about such equivocations. The running commentary Silva offers contains a parallel narrative based on negation (in the psychoanalytic sense): An example is, "*que yo nací con mi pata gambá (yo no lo niego)*" (the parenthetical material is Silva's interjection, not part of the lyrics). "*Yo no lo niego*" ("I don't deny it") becomes the rallying cry, but what can be at the heart of an affirmation that is a negation, if not emptiness, a nothing developed further from the original "nothing" of "Nada"? *"Nada, ya no me llamo Myrta"* is eerily echoed in "Chencha's" *"Ya me cambiaron el nombre/ahora me llaman Chencha Silva,"* presenting the monstrous hybrid of Chencha Silva as the place where Myrta once was (Freud famously said, *"Wo Es war, soll Ich werden,"* "Where It was, shall I be") (Freud, 1964, p. 80).

By the beginning of the 1960s, "Chencha la gambá" had become a party staple, part of the collective archive of "ugly feelings" (Ngai, 2005). Silva effected an ironic distancing at the very moment of the 1961 recording, so that every time we listen to the performance inscribed in the record, we can witness Silva practicing an ethics, returning the listener to the problematic societal characterization of Silva and, by extension, any social subject placed in the dangerous position of scapegoat. The pun of "Chencha's Gait" entailed the "knowledge" that Silva herself was queer and that, according to the song's heteronormative logic, she would be hard-pressed to be a "gambá." Silva's reperformance underscores the symbolic violence of the original guaracha. She emphasizes taunts on the street and the societal occlusion inherent in the name change, from the empty set of Myrta (her given name is not included in the song) to Chencha Silva, an entity based on the shared investment in gossip about the actual Silva's sexual activity. Purely sonorous and non-linguistic interjections such as tone, sneers, and scoffs powerfully launch a cynical reaction to the public identification between artist and character, implied in the first version through an abject treatment of voice imposed by the arrangement. In 1961, Silva proffers a "reading" simultaneous with the performance of the song, creating a doubleness that registers as more than simply funny or possibly not that funny. The final verse is a resounding, potentially painful assumption of the persona and name of Chencha: *"¡Que yo camino como Chencha!"* [So I walk like Chencha!], Silva shouts, in a manner quite distinct from the original recording's fadeout, which featured Silva's hushed singing reflecting the "extimate" nature of gossip.

Silva forever remembered her "Cuban" period in an idealized way. Things became more complicated when she relocated to her native Puerto Rico around 1954. She was considered a native of dubious qualifications. The game started to become nasty when her position of social power increased with the beginning of her flush years and her move back home. Once again, the artificial relationship of nativity and national music was illustrated but this time, Silva could no longer stay at a safe remove from the game.

Silva's incursion into business aspects of music began first as a host of a radio program, *Una hora contigo* [An hour with you], and of revue shows in New York City, where she brought with her notable Puerto Rican singers and entertainers to satisfy the hunger for home that the Puerto Rican migrants of the 1950s felt. After a period of difficulty, Silva was hired to create her TV show, which she entitled *Una hora contigo*, like the radio program. It was a variety show, described to me as having various segments. First, Silva would sing the show's theme song, a bolero she wrote, "Una hora contigo [An hour with you]," Segments included a fashion runway hosted by the actress Velda González; interventions by invited singers; Silva herself singing; and a "humor" segment entitled "Tira y tápate," with Silva dressed up as a *comadre* called Chencha, an offshoot of her hit "Camina como Chencha la gambá," but who was no longer an oversexed woman but a homemaker interested most of all in gossip. The humor segment was almost certainly born out of advertising needs. Silva had to procure funds for the show, and she generated revenue by selling products on airtime (González de Modestti, 2007; Monroig, 2007).

Silva became one of the most successful businesspeople in Puerto Rico; to her success on TV she added being an agent, producer of variety spectacles, and author of a column in the magazine *Bohemia libre*. A great deal of her turn to business had to do with the rejection she experienced upon her return, something she clearly did not expect and which she could only partially symbolize. Although unrecorded, it is well known that her contemporaries went so far as to gossip that Silva stole two songs, widely considered her finest, "Qué sabes tú" and "Tengo que acostumbrarme," from her contemporary, Sylvia Rexach. Silva's form of retribution for her ambivalent reception in Puerto Rico happened through her business success. Concomitantly, and in accordance with the birth of the Estado Libre Asociado (Commonwealth of Puerto Rico) and its seemingly inexorable march toward "progress," the desire that Silva had mobilized so brilliantly now became a different desire, that of consumption, catering to tourists in elite hotels, immigrants in working-class venues in New York City, and, most of all, the female consumer on TV.

In 1965, Silva went into what she later called "voluntary exile." She spent a four-year stint in New York City producing, hosting, and performing in the pioneering and critically acclaimed TV show *The Myrta Silva Show*, for which (as we saw in the chapter's opening) she won the prize for Best Variety Show in the New York Area in 1965. Away from Puerto Rico, Silva used humor and specifically the obscene to return to the ethics as well as the *parlando* that had made her a household name. The album *Songs My Mother Never Taught Me, Volume III*, was the third in a series of off-color records produced by Tico Records in 1960s New York. The liner notes portray Silva as "la reina del doble sentido" [the queen of double-entendre], reframing her earliest title, "la reina de la guaracha." In the album cover, Silva looks up to the presumably Catholic sky, clasping her hands in prayer, making the album's transgression both sonic and visual. Almost as a lapidary gesture, Silva returned to obscene music. While the eruption of the obscene in a relatively mainstream way in the Latino recording industry is an important fact, it's not my main interest here. The type of laughter it may elicit in the casual listener is not the type of laughter I'm pursuing in this analysis. Rather, I'm interested in the laughter that some listeners may key into if they tune into Silva's call to thinking.

Silva's record is different from the earlier ones in the series. Aside from being a solo record, it includes, like her earlier classics, a parallel commentary that initially may not be apprehended but is apparent once the listener has decided to look out for it, perhaps after becoming more knowledgeable about what the signifier Myrta stood for – what Silva's persona was – and what her tribulations as an artist under constant examination for deviance had been. Critical listening is now required to understand the comedic ramifications of this record, taken as innocuous because it is "merely" pornographic.

"Dr. Bugalón" is the album's last out of 10 tracks of non-stop, obscene humor. Throughout the record, Silva plays with calling herself "*loca*," as in mentally ill, and also with clear overtones of sexual deviance. In this track, "*loca*" concretely refers to "drag queen." The song's pun is that the doctor who is treating the queens is a "*bugarrón*," a man in the active position who has sex with men while being married or publicly heterosexual. The doctor's last name, the puerile pun of "Bugalón," mixes *bugalú* with *bugarrón*. What Silva does with this *bugalú*, however, can hardly be considered puerile. This song is significant because Silva engages gossip concerning homosexuality and therefore, her own sexuality (a hot topic for Puerto Ricans at the time) by centering attention on the figure of the queen, for whom the closet is not an option and who interacts constantly with a normative male subject because of her desire and economic need. "Dr. John Bugalón" names a psychiatrist, vaguely American, who "specializes in treating queens." In the other tracks, Silva's improvs mentioned psychiatry and taunts about her own mental state, accusations which I'm certain she received as anonymous hate mail, a fact she repeatedly mentions in her *Tira y tápate* columns. An entirely recitative song, the chorus pitches in the doctor's name at precise intervals as the refrain: *El doctor Bugalón . . . El doctor Bugalón . . .*

Silva stages the song as a phone conversation between the receptionist, presumably a feminine woman ("*señorita*") and herself. The receptionist asks Silva if she wants to be treated by the doctor, to which Silva responds, feigning amazement, that she doesn't have that "problem." This response provokes an extreme reaction in the receptionist, to the point that she is cut off "inexplicably" after every *parlando* chunk of Silva's. The suggestion, not so hidden, is that finding out that Silva is not a "*loca*" but instead a "queer woman" has caused such sexual excitement in the receptionist that she has lost the line, amplified by the entrance of the big band in increased tempo and volume. When the receptionist picked up the phone, she could not place Silva as a "woman," mistaking her for a "*loca*." The identification of Silva with the "*loca*" is clear. The other interpretation, of course, is that the receptionist is revolted at the revelation of Silva's gender nonconformity. The revulsion is erotically charged, tinged with sexual fascination: the receptionist keeps "taking the call" that fails after every long chunk sung in *parlando*. In the final recitative, Silva evokes an underground queer scene in New York City. She debunks the phallic dominance of meaning ("we live in a world where everything has to be erect, miss") and establishes her *soneo* (improv) in rhythmic phrases such as "*apunte apunte apunte apunte apunte apunte*" [write it down, write it down, write it down, write it down, write it down, write it down] as the source of sexual excitation. Now, possibly the mainstream listeners who bought these off-color records thought Silva was attacking queers; in my reading, Silva is aligning with queens and all despised subjects.

At song's end, Silva returns to her given name, Myrta (as we have seen, a very powerful name charged with meaning, which she emphasizes sonically by stretching the rolling "r," much like "girrrrl") to identify herself as the caller, and expresses familiarity with a "scene" by listing a string of names belonging to various queens in New York City, with herself as the last name of the list: "please give this message to my friend Evening Dew . . . that all her girlfriends, la Pani, la Michelle, la Miroslava, la Godina, la Roy, Lily of the Valley, la Tina, and la María René, and I, we all are thinking of her." Her alignment happens because queens are in a similar position to hers: objects of ridicule, disparaged as being physically "deformed," presumptively hypersexual and gender non-compliant, yet also feared because of their power to unmask normative subjects and the hypocrisy of society. Silva doesn't make them into martyred exemplars of the "nothing." Instead, she posits them as walking negations. The tone is mocking; what is being mocked is not as clear-cut, however. Is it the queens, or the policemen who beat them up, or hypocritical men who sleep with them and disown their desire ("Big Stick Steve sends her his love . . . and Machete Tato was let go on bail after he was arrested for breaking the Bronx Rat's you-know-what"), or generally the society that diagnoses the queens as abnormal and in need of gender correction? The song, as mentioned, is entirely in *parlando*; it exhibits Silva's intact swing, perfect musical timing, and eerie contemporaneity. It also illustrates her command of *soneo* as the veritable Lacanian letter, paradoxically rigid yet liquid in its mobility.

During her finest musical moments, Silva had embodied the void that Mladen Dolar refers to as the "third level" of the voice, as the "blind spot in the call of the other and a disturbance to aesthetic appreciation" (Dolar, 2006, p. 13). Silva resumed *El Show de Myrta Silva*, with its "Tira y tápate" segment, in Puerto Rico's Channel 11 for two years (1971–73). Her original Chencha creation morphed into a drag queen persona, who sat in front of a crystal ball called Bola [Ball] and supposedly unmasked secrets about celebrity sex lives (in particular tales of marital infidelity, perverse sexuality, and homosexuality). Viewers remember her *"Bola, ¿cómo fue, Bola? Espepítamelo"* [Ball, what? What is it, Ball? Come on, spit it out] and her sneers, chiding, and cynical laughter. Most will swear that every single monologue included outing and queer shaming. This is the only image of Silva that Puerto Ricans remember today. Often they simply confuse the character with the artist, as if they were interchangeable, to the point of occluding Silva's primary identity as an artist, whether singer or composer, forgetting she was also a producer, host, bandleader, and artist agent, among the many roles she took on during her career.

Silva's over the top, highly theatrical brutality is very similar to that of drag queen discourse, which is scathing in its directness. Madame Chencha makes fun of all the characters, not of queer people specifically, and not of anybody as targeted, disgusting subjects. Madame Chencha had her pet peeves, but it was certain behaviors, not entire groups, that set her off. Silva did not mince words as Madame Chencha when she felt people were exploiting a situation for their personal gain. The queer subjects she singles out in her comedy are primarily those who parade around their normative life for all to see, not hesitating to castigate others left and right, to then proceed to engage in so-called illicit behavior out of the public eye while spared from the judgment and punishment they dispense. Without discounting the problematic aspects of Silva's performance as Chencha, Silva always acted with an ethics in mind, what we might call a cynical ethics, fusing Foucault and Lacan.[8]

Slavoj Žižek (1999) has addressed instances of the Lacanian real's eruption into the social fabric. Silva, as master of voice's symbolic power, contained for her listeners and viewers what he calls an "irreducible kernel of jouissance that resists all symbolization" (p. 14). Her extraordinary success as a singer had to do with the "something" akin to the Freudian *Das Ding*, the "thing," which we can playfully link to the *cosa* (thing) that all great *soneros* have. Recall Silva's song, "*Yo tengo una cosa*" [I have a *thing*] which, in its 1960s recording, acquired directly autobiographical qualities relating her to this unsettling, cultural "thing." Recall, also, her memorable recording of "Alcapurria" [Fritter] from *Songs My Mother Never Taught Me*, in which she reminded listeners that "there is a very flavorful *thing* in Puerto Rico, what is it?" [*En Puerto Rico hay una cosa muy sabrosa, ¿qué será?*].

It's not known if her monologues were improvised on the spot or if she created scripts or sketches before going on air. More likely than not, they were not completely extemporaneous. Silva's makeup and gestures clearly owe much to her *loca* figuration as it had been established in *Songs My Mother Never Taught Me*; instead of the working-class comadre that she had visually represented in her first incarnations, Silva's makeup is gaudy, exaggerated, and flamboyant. The final iteration of the Chencha persona borrows heavily from the ritualistic practice known as *espiritismo* [spiritism] and its *mesa blanca* [white table], gesturing to the occult and proscribed religious practices of the same middle and upper classes that condemned Silva for her vulgarity. These subjects, one can surmise, might have felt exposed by Silva's skits in ways that they could not acknowledge to themselves or to the public. There are moments when Silva toes the line between effective sendup and cheap commercial hook, of course, but her positioning is more complex, embedded in what was allowable or possible. Silva had to run her shows through censors for years; a generalized climate of censorship and outright repression abounded. With this in mind, some of the key birthing elements of this new character, Madame Chencha, become clearer.

As she embraced her monstrous figuration Silva embraced her *sinthome*, a late, Lacanian reformulation of the more traditional idea of the symptom, when it's no longer culturally relevant or intellectually sensible to decode any message. There are various manifestations of this *sinthome*: her devotion for her mother, which from being a mask of normalcy to protect her from the accusations encircling her undisclosed (but not closeted) personal life took on an intense life of its own; her creation of a marriage to David Silva, the Mexican actor, which according to testimonies of friends never happened (for what cause we do not know, possibly as a cover, initially at least) and a pregnancy with him, which apparently also never happened;[9] the problematic jouissance of her later years as she became more virulent as Madame Chencha, even endangering her life as she received violent threats in her TV offices (González de Modestti, 2007); and, finally, a more benign jouissance in her portrayal of her bolero songs as her children ("Mis canciones son como mis hijos, y mis hijos no los pongo a pelear" [My songs are like my children, and I don't create quarrels between my children]) (Silva, 1981). In the *sinthome*, Silva returned to the nothing.[10] She had created Myrta at a very early age (practically the very beginning of her career). She resolutely refused to signify anything other than this figure. She created another figure, Chencha, as a secondary character, but it exceeded her control and altered significantly Myrta's artistic trajectory. In part thanks to Chencha's success, collective memory has occluded Myrta. My reconstruction of Silva's brilliant career aims at a reparation for this forgetting. My analysis of voice as a Lacanian part-object aims to restore the performative power Silva commanded as Myrta and Chencha, and demonstrate how both of her memorable creations manifest what I call a thinking voice.

Acknowledgements

This chapter is a revised version of Licia Fiol-Matta (2009), Chencha's gait, *Women & Performance: A Journal of Feminist Theory*, 18:3, 287–301.

Notes

1   Silva's exact date of birth is a bit of a mystery. Accounts vary, from 1922 to 1927. Silva herself gave the date as 1925; she says she arrived in New York City just shy of turning 13, in 1938 (Silva, 1975a, p. 25).
2   On the *guaracha*, see Moore (1997). Díaz-Quiñones, A., (2003), offers a useful discussion in his introduction to Sánchez, *La guaracha del Macho Camacho*.
3   There are no scholarly works on Myrta Silva. All accounts are journalistic. The most comprehensive and less error-ridden is Silva's own, an "as told to" life narrative, "Esta es mi vida", published in *El Nuevo Día* on five consecutive days (February 25, 26, 27, and 28, and March 1, 1975).
4   Lacan elaborated a theory of metonymy and metaphor that is based on Saussurian linguistics, as is well known. He spoke of signifiers that became "quilting points" of a subject's particularity. These signifiers are bound to a subject's own history and are unique for each individual, but depend on the social for their unique meaning. In Lacanian theory, "metonymy," "metaphor," and "quilting point" serve to elucidate the operations of the signifier along the signifying chain. Lacan's classic text on metaphor and metonymy is "The Instance of the Letter in the Unconscious, or Reason since Freud" (Lacan, 2006). In a nutshell, Lacan reformulates Freud's concepts of displacement and condensation via Roman Jakobson. Both represent relations between signifiers. The metonymical structure is a relationship of "word to word," whereas the metaphoric relationship is of "word for word," as he famously states in "The Instance of the Letter." For the "quilting point," "the point at which 'the signifier stops the otherwise endless movement of the signification'" (Lacan, cited in D. Evans, 1996, p. 149), see Lacan's seminar on the psychoses (Lacan, 2003, pp. 258–270). Readers may find useful glosses by Jane Gallop, "Metaphor and Metonymy," *Reading Lacan* (Gallop, 1985,

pp. 114–132) and Yannis Stavrakakis (1999), *Lacan and the Political* (pp. 57–60.) For a definition of the three terms, see Evans (1996, pp. 111–114, 149).

5   With thanks to Patricia Gherovici.

6   "*Yo le daba las inspiraciones, y él componía los números*" [I conceived of the sketch, and he wrote the songs], (Silva, 1975b, p. 50).

7   In an interview, Ñico Saquito stated that "Chencha la gambá" was his most popular guaracha, and that it had broken all sales records. (Galaor, 1949, p. 102.)

8   "The three main types of parrhesiastic practice utilized by the Cynics were: 1) critical preaching; 2) scandalous behavior; 3) what I shall call the 'provocative dialogue'" (Foucault, 2001, p. 119.) In Seminar VII, *The Ethics of Psychoanalysis, 1959–1960*, Lacan (1992) discussed ethics as a subject's relationship to their desire (as "not giving ground on one's desire," in his famous formulation).

9   Miguel Ángel Hernández, personal communication. I also checked issues of the *Cinema Reporter*, Mexico's pre-eminent film journal of the time, corresponding to 1944–46, during which time Myrta Silva recounts that she was in Mexico and married to David Silva (Silva, 1975c, p. 50). This was a weekly publication featuring technical information about films, interviews and articles, and gossip sections, as well as advertisements. David Silva, at the time, was quite famous after starring in the hit movie *Campeón sin corona* [The champ without a crown] and his love life was carefully tracked. I found a reference to a marriage, but to another woman, an American David Silva met when he was trying to make it big in Hollywood.

10 Related to the *sinthome* and queer life, see Edelman, L. (2004), on "sinthomosexuality."

References

Anonymous. (1947a, July 27). Noticias del Director: Suspenden el Programa Coctel Musical. *Diario de la Marina*. Havana, Cuba, 37.

Anonymous. (1947b, July 27) "Chencha" tuvo la culpa. *Bohemia*. Havana, Cuba, 41–42.

Anonymous. (1947c, June 8). Acuerdos adoptados por la Comisión de Ética Radial. *Diario de la Marina*. Havana, Cuba, 37.

Berenguer, J. (1967, July 6). Por labor en TV, Myrta Silva recibe premio de revista. *El Mundo*, San Juan, Puerto Rico, 54.

Butler, J. (1993). *Bodies that matter. On the discursive constructions of "sex."* London: Routledge.

Díaz-Quiñones, A. (2000). Introducción. In L. R. Sánchez, *La guaracha del Macho Camacho* (pp. 9–73). Madrid, Spain: Cátedra.

Dolar, M. (2006). *A voice and nothing more*. Cambridge, MA: MIT Press.

Edelman, L. *No future: Queer theory and the death drive*. Durham, NC: Duke University Press.

Evans, D. (1996). *An introductory dictionary of Lacanian psychoanalysis*. London, England: Routledge.

Foucault, M. (2001). *Fearless speech*. Los Angeles, CA: Semiotext(e).

Freud, S. (1964). *New introductory lectures on psycho-analysis. Standard edition, 22.* London, England: Hogarth Press.

Galaor, D. (1949, April 6). La musa traviesa de Ñico Saquito, *Bohemia*. Havana, Cuba, 102.

Gallop, J. (1985) *Reading lacan*. Ithaca: Cornell University Press.

Glasser, R. (1997). *My music is my flag: Puerto Rican musicians and their New York communities*. Berkeley, CA: University of California Press.

González de Modestti, V. (2007, March 9). *Interview by L. Fiol-Matta*. San Juan, Puerto Rico.

Lacan, J. (1992). *The seminar. Book VII. The ethics of psychoanalysis, 1959–60* (D. Porter, Trans.). London, England: Routledge.

Lacan, J. (2003). *The seminar. Book III. The psychoses, 1955–56* (R. Grigg, Trans.). London, England: Routledge.

Lacan, J. (2006). *Ecrits: The first complete edition in English* (B. Fink, Trans.). New York, NY: W.W. Norton & Company.

Monroig, M. (2007, March 9). *Interview by L. Fiol-Matta*. San Juan, Puerto Rico.

Moore, R. D. (1997). *Nationalizing blackness: Afrocubanismo and artistic revolution in Havana, 1920–1940*. Pittsburgh, PA: University of Pittsburgh Press, pp. 54–56.

Muñoz, J. E. (2009). *Cruising utopia: The then and there of queer futurity*. New York, NY: New York University Press.

Ngai, S. (2005). *Ugly feelings*. Cambridge, MA: Harvard University Press.

Silva, M. (1973, February 10). *Interview by G. Mamery. Mayagüez, Puerto Rico, February 10, 1973*. The Díaz Ayala Collection of Latin American and Cuban Music. Miami, FL: Florida International University.

Silva, M. (1975a, February 25). Gran serie 1: Esta es mi vida, as told to E. Fernández Miralles. *El Nuevo Día*. San Juan, PR.

Silva, M. (1975b, February 26). Gran serie 2: Esta es mi vida, as told to E. Fernández Miralles. *El Nuevo Día*. San Juan, PR.

Silva, M. (1975c, February 27). Gran serie 3: Esta es mi vida, as told to E. Fernández Miralles. *El Nuevo Día*. San Juan, PR.

Silva, M. (1981, exact date unknown). *Myrta Silva, los compositores, su música y anécdotas*. Episode, María Grever. Archives of TuTV, San Juan, Puerto Rico.

Stavrakakis, Y. (1999). *Lacan and the political*. London, England: Routledge.

Szendy, P. (2007). *Listen: A history of our ears*. New York, NY: Fordham UP.

Žižek, S. (1999). *The Žižek reader*. Oxford and Malden, MA: Blackwell Publishers.

Chapter 10

Beside oneself

Queer psychoanalysis and the aesthetics of Latinidad

Joshua Javier Guzmán

Identity categories such as "Hispanic" and "Latino" lack any real specificity despite the fact the former was created by the U.S. Census Bureau and officially first used in the 1970 census, nearly 50 years ago as of this writing, in order to identify and quantify persons with Spanish surnames. By 1980, the term had been widely propagated through Spanish-language media, such as Univision, to get the word out, as it were. While the term "Latino" has recently surfaced in mainstream media and popular culture to identify people of Spanish origin, the sense of discomfort triggered by the seemingly antiquated term "Hispanic" captures the shaky ground one steps on when trying to think through the problem of Latinidad. The term "Hispanic" has always tacitly tickled my curiosity because it holds together two words – *his panic* – that detonate the problem of Latinidad. The question becomes, Whose panic are we talking about and what constitutes this panic? "Panic" as proper to and property of the ambiguous pronoun "his" fails to expose "the Man" behind the curtain if not because "his" can easily connote a nation, a community, Whiteness, the media, Latino, and so on until the only thing guaranteed is a proprietary state of panic. The uncontrollable fear structuring the sense of panic also points to a suddenness or anticipatory glow of pure anxiety. The problem of Latinidad then becomes about chasing this glow, uncovering its source, and assigning it its proper owner. Yet, as we shall see, the glow of anxiety wanes once you approach it. This is not to say we are left with some false sense of mastery having conquered our anxiety, but rather we find ourselves waiting in the dark, lamenting what felt like a desire to know what it was all about. Therefore, can we ever say we know Latinidad?

To answer this question, I begin by sketching something like a poetics of loss, which seems timely since the field of Latino Studies has recently yielded two monographs that either explicitly or implicitly address a politics of loss, both of which I will discuss here. Antonio Viego's (2007) beautiful and slightly gloomy book, *Dead Subjects: Towards a Politics of Loss in Latino Studies*, marks an impassioned plea for Latino Studies scholars to take seriously Lacanian psychoanalysis in their theorization of Latinidad and racialized subjectivity. According to Viego, theories of the racialized subject as completely knowable and whole lend to the management and governing of these bodies in detrimental ways. A

politics of loss enacted by Latino subjectivity resists assimilatory and incorpora-
tive state projects, insofar as it posits the ethnic-racialized subject as unknow-
able. From the psychic scale to the political level, this fundamental loss might
be what causes "the trouble with unity" within Latino politics. Cristina Beltrán's
(2010) recent study of the intersection between Latino Studies and political theory
unpacks the underlying structure of Latino identity and its failure to cohere into
a unified political agenda. Both *The Trouble with Unity* (Beltrán) and *Dead Subjects* (Viego) argue that Latinidad is indeterminate and incoherent. Though these
books are different in method and approach – Beltrán's hopeful democratic theory
(political theory) contrasts with Viego's pessimistic Lacanianism (psychoanalysis) – I begin this essay by setting these unlikely bedfellows side by side in order
to tease out the resonances as a mode of commonality rather than the closeness of
resemblance and identity. In this sense, loss and dissensus articulate what Latinidad *does* to the political landscape and, in effect, embodies in the psychic life of
the Latino subject.

Ubiquitous as the figure of the Latino might be in the political and public imaginary, little work has been done within the field of political philosophy to sustain
a conversation on the impact of Latino politics in the United States. Cristina Beltrán's (2010) *The Trouble with Unity* excites many new possible relations between
Latino studies and political philosophy. Yet the recent turn to Latino politics is
no coincidence considering how Latinos have become the largest minority and
are projected to make up 24% of the nation's total population by 2050 (Beltrán,
2010). I do not offer these statistics as quantifiable evidence of the growing force
of Latinidad in the United States, but instead to outline how this quantifiable measure inevitably produces a qualitative change in the way we come to think about
the temporality of the Latino subject as always having had a political future. As a
result, Latinos are often viewed as "untapped potential," rendering these subjects
as "politically passive and difficult to mobilize" (Beltrán, 2010, p. 4).

Beltrán likens the political reservoir of Latinidad to that of Hobbes's Leviathan
to underscore how the "political logic of Latinidad" implies homogeneity – "the
belief that in some crucial way, Latinos see themselves as part of some larger
whole" (Beltrán, 2010, p. 4). The sheer scale of the Latino Leviathan, if not
already inciting panic, works as a mediating presence predicated on the conflation of "unity with visibility and empowerment and anxiety over internal dissent
and disagreement" (Beltrán, 2010, p. 3). But we should not be alarmed since,
as Beltrán argues, there is no such sleeping giant. Instead, the confederation of
unique singularities explodes the unity of the Latino monster from within, making it vulnerable to fracture and suspension. Surely this troubled unity destabilizes consensus as the primary mode of political mobilization and gives relief to
those who wish nothing more than a passive and inoperative political minority.
However, Latino performativity destabilizes the rigid polarity between unity as
action and disagreement as passivity through the very mechanism of dissensus at
the heart of the binarism. Following Jacques Rancière (1999), Beltrán highlights
how Latinidad performs dissensus not just as a mere conflict of interests over the

limits of nationalism and the disparaging effects of homophobia, racism, and classism. Instead for Beltrán, dissensus "reflect[s] the contradictions and challenges of democracy itself" by contesting the frame in which something is given (Beltrán, 2010, p. 139). In this way, Latinidad is not only incomplete and incoherent; it renders open and incomplete the very political nature of democracy itself.

Like Beltrán, Viego's description of Latinidad allows us to think through the confusing nature of temporality, especially as it relates to both racialized subjectivity and the fracturing force of loss. The political realm opens the descriptive category of Latinidad into "a site of ongoing resignifiability," where the Latino subject is never fully complete but always in process of (re)making itself (Beltrán, 2010, p. 9; Viego, 2007, p. 156). The serial structure of Beltrán's thinking of Latinidad echoes Viego's theorizing of a Latino futurity, a twofold temporality rendering the site of Latino subjugation both ambivalent and unresolvable (Viego, 2007). The Latino scene of interpellation performs a disjuncture in time, existing somewhere between anticipation (I don't know yet) and retroaction (I already knew that). This is evident in the discourse espousing the Latinization of the United States and also in the weird tic of some Latino Studies scholarship to reclaim the past for Latinos. The rhetoric of temporality here registers a temporal lapse between Latinos having already been here and their imminent taking over.

The time lost in this temporal structure does not surprise Viego, because the temporality of the "Latino" resembles the temporality the French psychoanalyst Jacques Lacan attributed to the ongoingness of the signifying chain. The Latino subject operates in a similar fashion to Lacan's future anterior, where he explains,

> What is realized in my history is neither the past definite as what was, since it is no more, nor even the perfect as what has been in what I am, but the future anterior as what I will have been, given what I am in a process of becoming.
> (Lacan, 2007, p. 247)

Like Beltrán, Viego sees the indefinite resignifiability of Latinidad as resisting the impulse to fully know ethnic-racialized subjects; yet unlike the political theorist, Viego emphasizes the future anteriority of Latino subjectivity in order to fully tease out the queer cut in time that tells us something about a fundamental loss inscribed at the site of Latino subjugation (Viego, 2007). According to Lacan, the constitutive loss embedded within the fabric of the subject results from its inevitable inscription in language. Language cuts up the body, and the primordial loss suffered by the subject of language is that of a "hypothesized fullness prior to the impact of language" (Viego, 2007, p. 15), a sense of wholeness that was taken away, blemished, or forgotten. But, as he points out, different languages and social positions cut up the subject in different ways. Attuning to Lacanian psychoanalysis in particular and a politics of loss in general allows Latino Studies to think about the profound and complex ways racialized bodies experience loss, particularly those "losses attributable to the unequal distribution of social and material resources" (Viego, 2007, p. 129).

It is here where Beltrán and Viego converge regarding our discussion on the queer aesthetics of a Latino psychoanalysis. For one, we may think about political theory in tandem with Lacanian psychoanalysis in order to investigate what exactly constitutes the material and symbolic losses inscribed in the Latino subject, and how these losses come to figure in absence of a political community. Following both Viego and Beltrán, it might be time to reintroduce the spatial implications of concepts normally thought of in temporal terms. We may ask: What are the spatial arrangements of historical and psychic displacement for the Latino subject? How can one spatially account for the psychic life of historical and material dispossession undergirding the structure of Latinidad? To help localize the problem of Latinidad, we can look to the aesthetic realm as a place that unfolds the spatial dynamics attributed to Latino temporality and best summed up as the "attraction of rejection" (Islas, 2003, p. 37). I invoke this paradox in order to move to the side of signification and reason (since how can deriving pleasure from betrayal be "reasonable") in order to dwell with the simultaneous push-and-pull dynamic activated by a desire for mastery. What gets rejected here, I argue, is the very fantasy of wholeness – of consensus – that nevertheless lures the Latino political "community" and the psychic life of Latinidad toward Whiteness, understood here as the master signifier of race. In order to expand on this paradoxical formulation, I now turn to a writer whose racialized desire found its limit at the height of the AIDS epidemic, a limit exposing more the shrouds of prohibition lining the fantasy of Whiteness rather than legislating the law of a racialized desire itself.

Arturo Islas, born in 1939, was a gay Chicano professor and novelist from El Paso, Texas. Among his major accomplishments, Islas was one of the first Chicanos in the United States to earn a Ph.D. in English in 1971 and the first Mexican-American granted tenure at Stanford University in 1976. He is best known for his two completed novels, *The Rain God*, which won the best fiction prize by the Border Regional Library Conference in 1985, and *Migrant Souls*, which was the first novel by a Mexican-American writer to be published by a New York publishing house. Both books are now canonical in Chicano/Latino letters. Yet, around his many awards and accomplishments within his short career, Islas struggled to express the contradictory drives at the core of his desire to write. In other words, to know Arturo Islas one must confront the corpus of his texts and appreciate how it reveals as much about queer sexuality and racism as it does the author's own semi-autobiographical experiences of writing as a queer Chicano in the U.S. Southwest.

Over the past decade and a half, we have seen an increase in scholarly attention to Arturo Islas's work, mainly because of two recently released scholarly volumes on the writer: one a critical biography entitled *Dancing with Ghosts* (see Aldama, 2004) and a collection of essays and interviews on Islas's writing entitled *Critical Mappings of Arturo Islas's Fiction* (Aldama, 2008), both following the 2003 release of *Arturo Islas: The Uncollected Works*. These texts were prepared and edited by scholar and Islas's friend, Frederick Luis Aldama (Islas, 2003).

The collections provide intimate insight into the preparation of Islas's later work, for which he is most recognized, including *The Rain God* (1984), *Migrant Souls* (1990), and the unfinished last installment of the Angel family trilogy, *La Mollie and the King of Tears* (1996) published after his untimely death from AIDS complications in 1991. Even more intriguing regarding his earlier drafts, which will later be tamed, polished, and homophobically combed-through, is how Islas was more explicitly exploring his queer sexuality and misgivings about being a gay Chicano from the border who also desired white men, all the while having to deal with a corporal reality that made it difficult to act on these desires in everyday life.

The very shuttering between the biographical and the cultural, between the (queer) author and the (edited) text, is activated by a certain specter of death that haunted Islas since his early childhood. According to the Stanford University press release announcing his death, Islas initially was attracted to the study of medicine, which was "understandable" since he "had polio when he was 8 years old and was in and out of hospitals for long sessions of physical therapy. Polio left him with a permanent limp" (Stanford University, 1991).[1] Islas then suffered from intestinal cancer which resulted in a colostomy procedure in 1969 at the age of 31 where, as Aldama indicates, "he had to learn how to live with a colostomy bag" (Aldama, 2004, p. 237). In 1988, at the age of 50, Islas was diagnosed as HIV-positive, and in 1991 the writer died from AIDS at the age of 52. As Latino literary scholar Ricardo Ortíz states, Aldama's 2003 volume on Islas's uncollected works

> allows readers to see more fully how the unique qualities of Islas' corporeal life inform the shape and functioning of his corpus of texts, in ways that no conventional biographical hermeneutic could ever adequate. [We understand how] the state of his body had come to bear so forcefully on the state of his body of writing.
>
> (Ortíz, 2007, p. 399)

I depart from Ortíz's beautiful textual analysis of Islas's writing and how it mirrors the corporal and material realities of Islas's process of writing, in order to foreground the ways Islas's own psychic life came to bear so heavily on the pieces of writing that never made it to print during his lifetime. As we will see, Islas's desire for white men, often expressed in his personal journals and early fiction, was situated in excess of the well-polished writings that eventually were published and make up the majority of his work. In other words, what gets *lost* is the textual evidence of an internal contradiction constituted by a desire for Whiteness, where Whiteness is understood not as phenotype but as the unconscious fantasy for wholeness.

After his first year at Stanford and a summer vacation at home, Islas returned to Stanford in 1957 with a newfound interest in creative writing and majoring in English. In the fall of 1957, he wrote the short story "The Submarine," which chronicles a young boy's night out with his old friends from high school, some of whom are back from college. The protagonist, "Art," Islas's fictionalized character ostensibly named after the same nickname ordained by the young author's own white friends at the time, joins his old high school peers at the local gay bar "Submarine," where he enjoys his newfound love for drinking. Hesitant at first to drink after seeing his friend and object of desire, J.D., a white "insensitive bastard" who "never really loved anybody . . . not even himself," "plastered" (Islas, 2003, p. 15), Art decides to drink the shots J.D. buys for him and confesses, "After five shots [of tequila], I was feeling pretty damn good. I enjoy drinking now. I acquired a taste for it in my first year away from home after I decided not to be a Catholic anymore" (Islas, 2003, p. 15). By the end of the story, Art and J.D. venture back to J.D.'s parents' house after both falling ill and begin to share a moment on J.D.'s front lawn next to his mother's geraniums. Art quiets J.D. as they approach his house because "[he] wasn't in the *mood* to talk to *his* mother or answer any of *her* goddamn questions" (Islas, 2003, p. 19, emphasis added). The protagonist fantasizes about destroying J.D.'s mother's flowers, and after walking to them nauseated from the liquor, he bends over and "Everything turned loose" (Islas, 2003, p. 19). J.D. reprimands Art and suddenly they sit down "on his mother's geraniums and [cry]." As the sun rises, J.D. reluctantly excuses himself, telling Art to take care of himself if they do not see each other again. Here, Islas ends the story in contradistinction to the whole motive behind Art's initial drive to drink: "All I could say was 'Thanks.' Then I told him to hurry up and go to bed. I must have a way with people. They always do what I say because I take care of them" (Islas, 2003, p. 19).

By the end of the story, the reader infers that the speaker fancies J.D., who either feigns ignorance of Art's desire for him or is himself so emotionally *distant* he cannot imagine *same-sex* desire with his old friend "Fart," a name he personally calls the speaker. The short story ends uneventfully, without climax or satisfactory release. Instead, Islas leaves the reader with an image of an abandoned queer Chicano teenager sitting in a plastered vomit-and-tear-drenched bed of geraniums, themselves a sign of a class distinction, however now blemished, between the two characters (earlier Art mentions J.D. will eventually inherit his parents' "chemical corporation," to Art's disgust). Yet, the speaker's voice and tone drastically shift at the moment of rejection. It is almost as if the speaker takes on the voice and role of the mother in telling J.D. to "hurry up and go to bed." In the speaker's formulation – one can even say fantasy – Art's commands are followed because he takes care of those receiving his commands. The roles switch, whereby the masochistic receiver of J.D.'s indifference – his distance – becomes the sadistic mother, having his "way" with people. However, any feminist will notice that Art's "care" for J.D. comes at the expense of J.D.'s mother and, by extension, her geraniums. And still, the misogyny constituting this story *of* "between men," rather than *about* two men, intensifies an all-too-present signifier, that is, Whiteness, rather than the absence of a signifier as formulated in Lacan's theory of sexual difference. More to the point, the "between" here, staged on the bed of geraniums, perversely acknowledges Lacan's theory of sexual difference, in so far as we are to understand Lacan (1970) when he famously announced, "there is no sexual relation," to mean a non-reciprocity or a non-communicability between the sexes, hence the absence of both mothers in this scene. Instead, we are privy to two subjects who are simultaneously the same yet different. For there to be no sexual relation, Lacan has to move the subject's unconscious structure from the symbolic realm into the Real, the cause of desire as a fundamental void rendering the subject indeterminate. We infer one reason for the subject's calibrated "lack" (as the impetus for desire to arise) stems from the fact that sexual reproduction inevitably makes the One and wholeness impossible and is thus shoddily compensated by the institution of heterosexuality, a couple form propagating a notion of two halves fulfilling one another. Here, Islas ventriloquizes through his literary avatar, Art, a desire to be seen, recognized, and reciprocated if only to experience a provisional sense of Oneness with J.D.

Additionally, the absence of the mother(s) permeates the text as if to promise an overcoming of difference evidenced by the suspension within the story, a generalized wondering whether *anything* sexual might occur between the two male characters. Alas, the mother's absence coagulates into a presence represented as a relation – between two differently racialized men – in the image of vomit-covered geraniums, where the flowers stand in for J.D.'s mother and the vomit induced by the drinking of a lapsed Catholic, in Art's case. Vomit browns the purity of any night garden. And as if to invoke an image of a submarine leaping out of the water, Islas prefaces the geranium scene with Art explaining, "Then all of a sudden, I got sick. I couldn't help it. I just had to throw up. I could barely see the outline of his mother's geranium across the lawn." Why does Art "all of a sudden" get sick and need to "throw up" and walk toward the geraniums? How does Islas use Art to avoid talking to "his mother" or answer any of "her goddamn questions"? Why all the anxiety?

Here I would like to reiterate Kalpana Seshadri-Crooks's (2000) brilliant argument, for which I am indebted for the remainder of this essay, in saying that "the signifier Whiteness tries to fill the constitutive lack of the sexed subject" (Seshadri-Crooks, 2000, p. 6) where the "sexed subject," in Joan Copjec's (1994) terms, is less about the incomplete subject than her "sovereign incalculability" (Seshadri-Crooks, 2000, p. 7). Whiteness operates like Lacan's master signifier, existing outside of any signifying chain, yet highly organizing, because it makes (racial) difference possible. This dual role of Whiteness as master signifier reveals Whiteness as both terrifyingly blinding while making perception possible. The master signifier Whiteness compensates for the subject's lack by producing a lack of lack, which Lacan describes as anxiety. The faint outline of J.D.'s mother's geraniums represents for Art "complete mastery, self-sufficiency, and the *jouissance* of Oneness" with J.D. (Seshadri-Crooks, 2000, p. 7). At the same time, they illegitimate their relation by reminding the reader there is no witness to the event, no visibilizing of their care: "I told J.D. to go to bed before his mom sees us. Now, I wish she had seen us" (Islas, 2003, p. 19). Here, we cannot ignore the writer's use of the past perfect tense with the present "Now," almost as if to invoke Lacan's use of the future anterior, as discussed earlier. In so doing, Art mimics the mother, disguises her care as his, and the result is a position Islas, the writer, will become familiar with for other reasons later in his sexual life. In other words, Art gets to dominate; Art gets to briefly top. The speaker assumes her voice, the object cause of desire, in hopes to initiate desire in J.D., but cannot. Instead and as we continue to see, Islas's protagonists' sexuality will evolve and refine into a tacit relation, one of visible disavowal, though anxiously terrorized by Whiteness. But in 1957, Art's 19-year-old boyish desire for J.D. exposed him as the effeminate brown boy he was, a role that will take some educating in order to know what he will have been, given what he was in the process of becoming.

Islas tarries with the non-reciprocal sexual relation between J.D. and Art in 1957, after rejecting his Catholicism and questioning his belief in God – both attributes his highly pious mother and grandmother would most definitely frown upon. In 1958, he writes the beginning of what was intended to be a theological novel, youthfully entitled "An Existential Documentation" and where the speaker encounters a wealthy classmate who ostensibly may be the cause of his religious renunciation. The boy "believes that ideas are all that matters" and criticizes the speaker, a young Chicano from the border, for being too available, and ridicules what he calls the speaker's "need for people" (p. 31). The speaker then wonders what organizes their different world-views, stumbling on his own faint attraction to his classmate:

> He does not believe anyone wants to give him anything. Perhaps it is because he has everything he wants materially. He wanders about alone in his sports car, swims in the sea, and climbs the cliffs along the shore. He claims that he has never known love or loved anyone. *It is an emptiness in him that begs to be fixed.* I want him to realize that he, too, is running after his *soul.*
>
> (p. 31)

Next, the speaker begins a small diatribe on the sanctity of poverty, then reflects on his hometown on the border and envisions "spending as much time in the Mexican Bordertown as possible," to the disapproval of his Chicano relatives because they "cannot see why [he] bother[s] with 'those people'" on *el otro lado,* the other side of the border (p. 32). Perhaps a better question is why does his white, affluent, athletic, and agnostic classmate trigger a desire in the speaker to travel to Mexico in the first place? One may speculate that the text subtly draws a connection between racial identification and sexual desire. As a result, the pattern of attraction performed by Islas's early protagonists underscores a very reveal-ing tension: that is, their burgeoning racial *identification* conterminously emerges beside their (sexual) *desire* for Whiteness.

For Freud, however, both desire and identification are positioned in a dichoto-mous opposition, where identification is scripted teleologically toward compul-sive heterosexuality. As Diana Fuss (1992) argues, we may think of identification as a form of vampirism whereby "the desire to be the other (identification) draws its very sustenance from the desire to have the other" (Fuss, 1992, p. 730). Fuss reorients Freud's theory of identification and desire queerly, and in efforts to smooth out the homophobic assumptions in the dominant psychoanalytic understanding. Meanwhile, Fuss's reformulation helps us read the speaker's desire to "fix" the emptiness in his white male peer. For one, the speaker circumscribes the lack in the other (who has "everything he wants materially") by gifting him a copy of Georges Bernanos's *The Diary of a Country Priest* (Islas, 2003, p. 31).[2] And like the existential quest of the young priest of Ambricourt in the novel and film, the speaker imagines a trip to the other side of the border to explore an insultingly close poverty "not as an attainment of sanctity" but a geography of poverty "as a denial of the false god of materialism" (Islas, 2003, p. 33). In other words, the classmate attempts to compensate for the speaker's lack of worldliness, his deliberate naiveté about others and the world of ideas. In exchange, the speaker offers a novel in hopes it might explain his "need" for people. Islas ends the gifting scene by trailing off into another topic: "This is why I gave him the *Diary*. Maybe he will realize . . ." (Islas, 2003, p. 31). The ellipses recall the elliptical mood in the previous story and the inconclusive hailing of and by the Latino subject. However, here a slightly older speaker than in "The Submarine" learns that the desire for Whiteness, for wholeness, means a circumscribing of an emptiness or a split that begs to be sutured.

I suspect Islas, the writer, understood how writing was a way of finding a gap and holding its place in order to produce some form of meaning, hence the *Diary*. Later in his work, the experience of living on the border will provide Islas the perfect suture, at least in the literary publishing world. For example, themes of migrancy pepper Islas's later writings and will be more forcefully explored in his second novel *Migrant Souls*, though "An Existential Documentation" provides an early glimpse into the energetics behind Miguel Chico's character, the important protagonist in the Angel Family Trilogy (of which *Migrant Souls* is the second installment). One cannot avoid bringing up one of the most striking passages in the novel, one that responds (some years later) to his Chicano family's disapproving of his visit to the "Mexican bordertowns." In the novel Miguel Chico, a queer Chicano who escapes the barrio on a scholarship to a prestigious university, explains the experience of his family's migrancy as such:

> They were migrant, not immigrant, souls. They simply and naturally went from one bloody side of the river to the other and into a land that just a few decades earlier had been Mexico. They became border Mexicans with American citizenships.
>
> (Islas, 2003, p. 31)

This passage interrogates the notion of the border through an image of a vibrant toggling back and forth over the Rio Grande. José Muñoz also reads this passage as an example of what he terms disidentifications, whereby the minoritarian subject is forced to inhabit two spaces at once, and "doubly true for the queer Latino son" (Muñoz, 1999, p. 32) since the *effect* of the migrant drive is the wearing down of borders and geographic coherency. As a result of the disidentificatory function of the novel, Muñoz ponders, "Can we perhaps think of Miguel, a thinly camouflaged authorial surrogate, as a border Mexican with citizenship in a queer nation or a border queer national claiming citizenship in Aztlán?" (Muñoz, 1999, p. 32). Instead of offering answers to Muñoz's questions, I take his invitation to hold open the "sovereign incalculability" at the heart of Islas's text. Muñoz reads the underlying queerness "thinly camouflaged" in a novel ostensibly about a Bordertown Chicano family and their elusive queer Latino son as evidence of a subject actively negotiating his "fragmentary existences" (Muñoz, 1999, p. 32). And, as if to anticipate Muñoz's queries, the young speaker in "An Existential Documentation" meditates near the end, "There are times when I do not question with my mind or heart; there are times when my entire being is a question mark" (Islas, 2003, p. 30). In other words, Muñoz's questions animate the incommensurable relation between the speaker and the author's own racialized sexuality as it emerges in the U.S. borderlands post Stonewall. But how do we understand the split subject and the geopolitical border together in these texts? If the master signifier Whiteness holds out the promise of unity, how is not the incoherency of borders a white fantasy? For one, Whiteness organizes difference, and makes distinction possible, leaving subjects on an often-violent quest for completion, in search of a superior form of being over difference—arguably the (political) unconscious desire to build a wall, as it were. But the wearing down of the geopolitical border, the *effect* of the migrant drive, is of a different order than the circumscribed lack constitutive of the ethnic-racialized subject of language, where one's "entire being is a question mark."

Whiteness will offer to answer the ontological question, to fill a lack that cannot be filled. For this reason, it comes as no surprise to readers of Islas that when we get to a 1962 fictionalized epistle entitled "Dear Arturo," we see a more mature subject emerge, articulating his sharpened desire for a white man and a slow disavowal of his "ethnic details" (Islas, 2003, p. 36). In the letter, penned from Arturo to Arturo, we first catch a glimpse of a character who will become a moving force behind Islas's later writings, the author's biographical grandmother, later fictionalized as Mama Chona, though not named and only mentioned in the opening of the letter as a "well-educated Mexican aristocratic lady" and who only appears "real" to him when she "would weep because she had to wash the dishes [when] it was the maid's day off" (Islas, 2003, p. 36). He opens the letter, under her specter, explaining his ethnic and familial background only to quickly disavow it: "Whatever there is of the Mexican in me will emerge in subtle ways" (Islas, 2003, p. 36). The text then moves to describe the speaker's failed relationship with a man named Gary who is "so self-protective." Gary, dismissive of others, only uses people to "give him pleasure as he lords it over them with his *superior* intellect and love of opera" (Islas, 2003, p. 37, emphasis added).[3] We learn that Gary rejects Art for another man, Eric, but in the letter, Art cannot help but seem needy, and cruelly attached to Gary, which becomes even more reason for Gary to pull away, leaving Art explaining in the letter presumably to himself: "Gary's soul, just like yours scuttles hastily out of sight whenever another confronts . . . Elusive monsters" (Islas, 2003, p. 38). Gary's elusive character does much to explain the ubiquitous yet uncapturability of Whiteness – its unmarkedness – terrorizing its subjects in its monstrosity. The terror and lure of Whiteness is even evinced in Eric's admission that "he himself [got] caught in the net, 'the attraction of rejection'" (Islas, 2003, p. 37).

The very schema of the elusive sexual encounter becomes more familiar to Arturo Islas, the author, by 1973, after he meets and moves in with his significant lover, Jay Spears, and together they explore the SM and San Francisco bathhouse scene of the mid- to late 1970s. Yet in 1969, Arturo Islas almost dies and undergoes multiple surgeries, including a colostomy procedure leaving him wearing a colostomy bag for the rest of his life. One can easily imagine the terrible timing of the procedure, at the height of the sexual revolution in San Francisco's gay scene, in effect leaving Islas constantly concerned with his own mortality and inhibition to fulfill his partner's desire to penetrate him. So much so, this particular inhibition figures prominently as the colostomy bag in the first installment, *The Rain God* (Islas, 1984), with Miguel Chico lamenting he "will always be a slave to plastic appliances" (p. 7); or gestures to "the appliance at his side" (p. 159); and after waking from a dream, realizes "there is no sleep after changing the bag" (p. 160). In short, what begins as elusive monsters comes to perversely figure as the tethered monster *to his side* at the biographical moment the author himself is able to enter into a (tumultuous) relationship with Jay Spears, who Aldama describes as "the aspiring force behind his fiction writing" (Islas, 2003, p. 241) and the model for the characters Sam Godwin in *Migrant Souls* and Virgil in *La Mollie and the King of Tear*. With his partner by his side, Islas is able to finalize a draft of *The Rain God* by editing out, at the behest of racist and homophobic publishers, the protagonist's sexual desire for white men all the while keeping indeterminate his racial identification as a queer writer from the U.S./Mexico border.

In ending, I turn now to one of the most interesting sketches in his uncollected works, a short story entitled "Reason's Mirror, or the Education of Miguel Angel" dated 1975, which is composed of the beginning drafts of what later would become *The Rain God* and the subsequent inauguration of the Angel family trilogy. The short story is actually really short, only about a page long, and begins with an epigraph by the Mexican writer Octavio Paz, in which he criticizes Western enlightenment and modernity. Paz states, "Modern man likes to pretend that his thinking is wide awake," but this "thinking has [only] led us into the mazes of a nightmare in which the torture chambers are endlessly repeated in the mirrors of reason" (p. 49). It is hard once again to escape, as Ortíz (2007) rightly points out, the "proto-Sadean knot of sexual, anatomical and even textual transgressions" (p. 406) of the epigraph which mirrors the story that follows and which I would like to quote at length:

> The two of them were standing on a bridge, facing the incoming fog. The monster held him close from behind and whispered into his ear in a relentless,

singsong manner. "I am the manipulator and the manipulated." It put its velvet paw in Miguel's hand and forced him to hold it tightly against his gut. "I am the victor and the slayer. I am what you believe and what you don't believe. I am the love and the unloved. I approve and turn away. I am the judge and the advocate." Miguel wanted to escape but could not. The monster's breath smelled of fresh blood and feces. "You are in my caves, and you will do whatever I tell you to do." It moved away from him. Miguel Chico continued to feel its form pressed tightly against him, and the odor of its breath lingered, forcing Miguel to gasp and struggle for air. The fog, he thought, would revive him. He kept his back to the monster and looked down and out at the sea, no longer visible. "Jump!" the monster said in a tone of exhilaration. "Jump!" Miguel felt loathing and disgust for the beast.

(Islas, 2003, pp. 49–50)

Miguel then jumps with the monster in hand and feels relief. Soon after waking, the speaker begins to write about the dream with the "hot Finnish sun on his shoulders" (Islas, 2003, p. 50).

An edited version of this story makes its way into the last chapter of *The Rain God*, where we learn that the monster stands in for Mama Chona, the monstrous matriarch of the family who disapproves of Miguel Chico's sexuality, calling him a *malcriado*, a badly raised child. In the last scene of the novel, the beast-like character of Mama Chona almost bleeds to death in a bathtub, surrounded by her large family, presumably because "her uterus is falling out" (Islas, 2003, p. 177). The absurd magical realism of the final chapter underscores the Gothic tropes Islas the writer admired in works such as Victor Hugo and Marquis de Sade, tropes he adopted and practiced in his sex life. This scene showcases how the "monster" is not only Islas's own dealings with his colostomy bag, but also the grave disappointment of coming of age as a gay Chicano man post Stonewall with a "form pressed tightly against him" that might be filled with what Leo Bersani (1987) calls, "the shifting experience that every human being has of his or her own body's capacity, or failure, to control and to manipulate the world beyond the self" (p. 216).[4] This "form that presses tightly against" us also "lingers," forcing us to gasp and struggle for survival (or sex).

What I am attempting to highlight is how "Reason's Mirror" opens up questions regarding the queer aesthetics of a Latino psychoanalysis by adhering to the ways in which the imminence and immanence of death from AIDS in Islas's writings – since I also think this piece can be read backwards from his death from AIDS – poses an ontological question to Latinidad, where "death" and "Latinidad" are set beside each other forming what can be called a paraesthetic. I borrow this term from literary scholar David Carrol, who defines paraesthetics as "a faulty, irregular, disordered, improper aesthetics" (Carrol, 1987, p. xiv). I feel it is akin to Shoshana Felman's notion of "radical negativity," amounting to an aesthetics that cannot be subsumed under negation, opposition, contradiction, or correction. Rather, it operates "outside of the alternative" as the very "scandal" of nonopposition (Felman, 2002, p. 13). This besideness maps an amoral, noncathartic, and indefinable sense of belonging via a spatial agnosticism that suspends the Latino subject in an ongoing process of longing.

To this point, it is important to underscore that the draft was initially written as the beginning of a manuscript *American Dreams and Fantasies* written in the summer and fall of 1975, on a getaway trip to Finland, and was drastically revised into *The Rain God* some years later. Islas fled to Finland to get away from the sadomasochistic and crumbling relationship with Jay Spears. Islas had begun to obsess over Spears, who became more distant, venturing alone into the S/M scene where he sought to penetrate others as he could not do with Islas. This made Islas even more insecure. According to Aldama (2004), at this time Islas realized that if he did not work on his "psychological baggage – his inherited victim/tyrant patterns – he would simply repeat these dynamics with others" (p. 92). (Readers of Islas may understand "the victim/tyrant patterns" as also describing the fictionalized character of Mama Chona.) The following year, in 1976, Jay moved to San Francisco to pursue a career opportunity, intensifying Islas's insecurities and fear of solitude. Reflecting on his emotional state, Islas confesses in his journal on May 3, 1976: "fear, rage, sense of abandonment – all turned inward" (p. 92). That September, he writes in his journal again: "My preference is for sex. The more and the heavier, the better" (p. 93). Eventually, this leads the writer to frequent the S/M and bathhouse scene even more, confessing in his journal that he knows he is "looking for Jay in those SM bars" (p. 96). Those elusive monsters indeed. We can imagine the proto-Sadean torture chambers reflected in the very sex labyrinths of dirty mirrors, strobing lights, and the smell of "fresh blood and feces" coupled with the sounds of annihilation; or, as the very racial unconscious of Western enlightenment and modernity.

When racial difference and sex come into play for Islas and his characters, something incommensurate emerges. One story may be told about the historicity of race as the symbolic and social *reasons* for this incommensurate relation. The story I have attempted to sketch via Islas's semi-autobiographical texts moves *to the side* of signification in order to explicate how this incommensurate relation exposes the limit of rational thought *within* the social world. We can even say this incommensurate relation paradoxically operates like an excluded interior. Because Whiteness makes difference possible, it also paradoxically threatens the eradication of difference. The desire for Whiteness mirrors a wish to "overcome difference and to plug the lack that sustains the inter-subjective relations of race" (Seshadri-Crooks, 2000, p. 68). So, when setting aside "death" next to Latinidad, we should understand the nomenclature "death" as a synonym for Whiteness.

Conversely, what the aesthetic realm affords us is an opportunity to linger, much like the odor and breath of Miguel Chico's monster, with this impossible unity. What has been called "queer Latinidad" (Rodriguez, 2003, p. 138) might be understood as a method of giving attention to these troubling discontinuities.[5] Reading *across* these differences, not in order to collapse their singularities but as a way to care for the loss of a whole, comes to figure as a longing for something else without recompensing for a whole that never really existed. Whether it is the viewer registering the incompleteness inherent within the subject reflected in reason's mirrors, or perhaps Islas's registering the loss of care in a world that sets up the transmission of love as an impossible project, both of these scenarios demand a recognition that minoritarian intellectual projects, such as Latinidad, are usually set up to fail. However, this failure should be taken seriously and not as an imperative to fill the void, as it were, since any good work of art "is formed around something missing" (Johnson, 2010, jacket). Instead, what I'm talking about is a failure that takes the form of a jump, a jumping with our monsters over the edge of rationality if only to risk a project that begins the way Islas's story ends: that is, with a dream.

The *Rain God* begins with the following beautiful sentence: "A photograph of Mama Chona and her grandson Miguel Angel – Miguel Chico or Mickie to his family – *hovers* above his head on the study wall *beside* the glass doors that open out into the garden" (Islas, 1984, p. 3, emphasis added). At the end of the novel, Miguel Chico wakes up from a version of the dream mentioned above and feeling a "sense of release":

> He looked, once again, at that old photograph of himself and Mama Chona. The *white* daisies in her hat no longer *frightened* him; now that she was gone, the child in the picture held only a ghost by the hand and was free to tell the family secrets.
>
> (p. 160, emphasis added)

The reader gathers in the first instance that Mama Chona and Miguel Chico were crossing the border "captured . . . in flight from this world to the next" (p. 4). In the same photograph, they were holding hands and then were not. A phantom greenlights the telling of the family secrets.

The trouble with unity involves the allure of Whiteness in its terrifying capacity to both initiate difference and equally obliterate it, which is the reason why the daisies (a sign of racial and class disavowal heightened on the border) terrorize young Miguel Chico. Except now, with a sense of release, Miguel Chico no longer feels the anxiety that used to torment him then. As a result, the paraesthetic here draws our attention to the glass doors opening out to the garden – the space of play and fantasy – another world *right here*, beside the photograph. This world comes into the picture when the terrorizing pull of Whiteness abates and the subject's limit emerges with a resounding: "Jump!"

Notes

1 English professor, novelist Arturo Islas dies. *Stanford University News Release*, April 18, 1991. Retrieved March 26, 2018 from https://web.stanford.edu/dept/news/pr/91/910418Arc1431.html.

2 *The Diary of a Country Priest* was also made into a film in 1951 by the French filmmaker Robert Bresson and released in the U.S. in 1954 when Islas was in high school, though perhaps he encountered the film at Stanford.

3 I am reminded of Wayne Koestenbaum's (1993) fabulous meditation on the opera queen (a name he identifies with as well) and the interplay between art and the erotic, opera and sexuality. The opera queen leaves the viewer entranced by the highest form of diva worship. Of course, the class and racial distinctions are also what classifies this form of art as particularly campy, albeit a racially unmarked instantiation of what the diva herself might want.

4 I recycle this quote from Ricardo Ortiz's essay "Arturo Islas and the 'Phantom Rectum'" which can be found in Bersani, L. (1987). Is the rectum a grave? *October, 43*, 216.

5 Here, I am indebted to Juana Maria Rodriguez's (2003) brilliant thinking through queer Latinidad and would like to reiterate R. Ortíz's epigraph of Rodriguez's method: "As an object of study, queer *latinidad* demands a practice that moves across geographic, linguistic, and imaginary borders, not simply because it is more provocative to do so, but because the very disciplines that divide Latin America from North America . . . have been based on paradigms constituted through our marginalization."

References

Aldama, F. L. (2004). *Dancing with ghosts: A critical biography of Arturo Islas*. Berkeley, CA: University of California Press.

Aldama, F. L. (2008). *Critical mappings of Arturo Islas's fictions*. Tempe, AZ: Bilingual Press/Editorial Bilingüe.

Beltrán, C. (2010). *The Trouble with unity: Latino politics and the creation of identity*. New York, NY: Oxford Press.

Bersani, L. (1987). Is the rectum a grave? *October, 43*, 197–222.

Carrol, D. (1987). *Paraesthetics*. London, England: Routledge.

Copjec, J. (1994). *Read my desire: Lacan against the historicists*. Boston, MA: MIT Press.

Felman, S. (2002). *The scandal of the speaking body: Don Juan with J. L. Austin, or seduction in two acts*. Stanford, CA: Stanford University Press.

Fuss, D. (1992). Fashion and the homospectorial look. *Critical Inquiry, 18*(4), 731–732.

Islas, A. (1984). *The rain god*. Palo Alto, CA: Alexandrian Press.

Islas, A. (1991). *Migrant souls*. New York, NY: Avon Press.

Islas, A. (1996). *La Mollie and the king of tears: A novel*. Albuquerque, NM: University of New Mexico Press.

Islas, A. (2003). *Arturo Islas: The uncollected works* (F. L. Aldama, Ed.). Houston, TX: Arte Público.

Johnson, B. (2010). *Persons and things*. Boston, MA: Harvard University Press.

Koestenbaum, W. (1993). *The queen's throat: Opera, homosexuality and the mystery of desire*. Cambridge, MA: Da Capo Press.

Lacan, J. (1970). Encore: Le séminaire, livre XX. In J.-A. Miller (Ed.), *Le Séminaire. Livre XX. Encore, 1972–73*. Paris, France: Seuil.

Lacan, J. (2007). *Ecrits* (B. Fink, Trans.). New York, NY: W.W. Norton & Company.

Muñoz, J. E. (1999). *Disidentifications: Queers of color and the performance of politics*. Minneapolis, MN: University of Minnesota Press.

Ortíz, R. L. (2007). Arturo Islas and the 'phantom rectum'. *Contemporary Literature, 48*(3), 398.

Rancière, J. (1999). *Dis-Agreement: Politics and philosophy* (J. Rose, Trans.). Minneapolis, MN: University of Minnesota Press.

Rodriguez, J. M. (2003). *Queer Latinidad: Identity, practices, discursive spaces.* New York, NY: New York University Press.

Seshadri-Crooks, K. (2000). *Desiring whiteness: A Lacanian analysis of race.* London: Routledge.

Viego, A. (2007). *Dead subjects: Toward a politics of loss in Latino studies.* Durham, NC: Duke University Press.

Section IV

The clinical is political

Chapter 11

The political potentiality of the psychoanalytic process

Carlos Padrón

Prologue

Psychoanalysis has been, since its inception, a deviation from the norm, a discourse and practice on that other that is the unconscious. In its early history, psychoanalysis was referred to in Europe as the "Jewish science" – perhaps symbolic of the position of the Jewish people throughout history as that radical and persecuted other within, or at the core of, the self-sameness of "normal Christian Europe;" or, in other words, as emblematic of the unconscious. Psychoanalytic discourse and practice can thus be thought of as a scene of radical otherness within the entrails of the normal – call this consciousness, the status quo, or ideology.

In this sense, psychoanalysis, by its very nature and history, is on the side of those who have been excluded, persecuted, made invisible, and marginalized. Elisabeth Roudinesco (2001) provocatively claims that "Psychoanalysis must always offer its help in struggles against all forms of discrimination – anti-Semitism, homophobia, racism, and any other kind of persecution. As a discipline, it has always been persecuted with the type of argument used against minorities" (p. 121). Psychoanalysis is on the side of silenced minor histories and struggles and works on inheriting them and the plights of those whom Frantz Fanon (2005) called the "wretched of the earth." From the socio-political and historical Western point of view that places European, Christian, heterosexual, male, and white people as central or normal, these individuals have been erroneously perceived as the "underdeveloped," the "savages," the "infantile," those who are supposedly waiting for "civilization" to "illuminate" them. This is how, for example, the Christian colonizers imagined the "Indians" in the "discovered" so-called Americas. This conceptualization from a position of misogyny, hetero-normativity, and racially/socio-economical privilege continues today to inflict itself upon the poor, the queer, people of color, immigrants, and women.

In contrast, psychoanalysis assumes difference or otherness as an irreducible reality and draws its assumptions and clinical practice from a position that assumes no point of normalcy or primacy. In psychoanalysis, difference is the primary starting point. The unconscious stands as a testament to such difference or otherness, and our work problematizes the categorization of the individual in relation to an "average," seeing this as a derivative and defensive formation against difference. Indeed, the framework of psychoanalysis places us within the scene of a rich but suppressed otherness which is constitutive of the world. It is an otherness or even a darkness through which we can begin to imagine the state-of-things as being otherwise.

Given that this is the case, psychoanalysis is in a unique position to foster political potentiality in a patient's subjectivity, particularly in working with individuals who are excluded, deprived of centrality in their particular cultures and societies, and considered in so many ways the "wretched of the earth."

In this essay I will share my experience in working with Antonio,[1] whose life history and various aspects of identity have placed him in the position of one of the "wretched." Through his story, which I find to be representative of my work with other individuals with similarly complex histories (including childhood, political, and cultural trauma), I will explore how the psychoanalytic process can enhance political potentiality in an individual's subjective sense of self. I hope that Antonio's case will illustrate the ways in which patients, due to their perceived otherness and related abuse, discrimination, and marginalization, can sometimes play out and interpret, within the analytic process, fantasies that unconsciously weave together the heterogeneous intra-psychic and socio-political dimensions of their lives. I will alternate in this essay between presenting some aspects of my treatment of Antonio and theoretical articulations that sprang from my experience in treating him and others. It is my attempt at re-creating, on a small scale, the dynamic interplay between theory and practice in psychoanalysis.

Introducing Antonio

I treated Antonio for three years, beginning five years ago, when he was 36 years old. A Latin American gay man, he was born and raised in a country historically and culturally defined by sharp socioeconomic, cultural, and racial divisions and tensions. He emigrated to the U.S. many years ago, escaping sexual, socio-political, historical, and racial persecution and discrimination. He was applying for asylum when we started treatment.

When Antonio first came to see me, he suffered from complex and debilitating post-traumatic symptoms. He was extremely withdrawn; he had recurrent nightmares in which he re-experienced his multiples traumas; he suffered from medically unexplained loss of hair and rashes on his body; he got terrified whenever anybody approached him from behind; and he was depressed and in a state of constant anxiety and fear.

The youngest in his family, Antonio was born and raised in the capital city in his home country. His father, who was considered white, was raised in the capital, but his mother was indigenous and grew up in the countryside. In the capital, there was considerable bias against poor, uneducated, and "savage Indians." Due to his background, Antonio felt that his very being, his origin, was torn between what in Latin America historically has been called, with racial and socio-political prejudice, the divide between "civilization and barbarism."

With time, he told me that although he lived in the capital where discrimination against indigenous people was rampant, he always identified himself, though in secret, with his mother's indigenous "glorious past," from before the time when the white Spaniards (associated, in his mind, with his father) colonized and destroyed the peaceful and blissful existence (related to his mother) of the original population with their violence. This was his own interpretation, which led, in his interactions with me as his psychoanalyst, to the unconscious fantasy of a wished-for peaceful and blissful co-existence with mother before the violence perpetrated by his colonizing father.

In Latin America, especially in Antonio's home country, his physical appearance typically placed him in the minds of others as indigenous or mixed. As such he often experienced racial discrimination, which over time was dramatically intertwined with discrimination based on his sexual identity. Beginning at home, and especially coming from his much older brothers and his father, he was always called "maricón," a pejorative term with harsher implications than the English language pejoratives to which it may be translated. In addition to his racial and sexual identities, Antonio also experienced discrimination because he was born and raised in an extremely poor "barrio," an inner-city shantytown, living in an almost torn-down house that his neighbors called the "house of horrors."

Both of Antonio's parents were emotionally and materially neglectful of him. His father could hardly hold a steady job because of his alcoholism and psychopathology that Antonio could not label because it was never properly diagnosed (probably psychotic breakdowns). The father was constantly in and out of psychiatric institutions, medicated and drinking. Returning home after being discharged from the hospital, he would have violent fits of rage, sexually assaulting his wife and verbally and physically assaulting the entire family. Antonio reported that several times his father cut his own chest with a knife, exclaiming, "This is all Antonio's fault for being a *maricón*. He brought disgrace to the family. He should not have been born; he was a mistake."

Antonio remembers with intense clarity the blood coming from his father's chest and going onto the floor, mixed up with all the dirt. Needless to say, Antonio was intensely afraid of his father's violence, and early on he began to feel guilty for all the violence at home, especially that between his mother and father: between the colonized and the colonizer. Antonio created within himself a deeply entrenched internalized sense of guilt for being indigenous and gay, with its corresponding punishment, attacks, and hate against his Self. Pause for a moment to imagine how a socio-political and historical violence is felt when it is internalized and directed internally against who you are. Antonio lived with that. As an understandable though inhibiting defensive strategy, Antonio became extremely withdrawn, keeping all his thoughts and feelings to himself (especially his rage), including his conflicts over being gay and indigenous, in order to not bring more pain to the family. He was called "*el muerto*" (the dead) because he rarely spoke. This had, in his fantasy, made him invisible to violence and attacks.

But the attacks continued in ways that Antonio could not anticipate, and his exposure to trauma continued. For a long time, during Antonio's childhood, his mother relocated to a faraway town in the country to find work and fill the income gap left by his father. During this time, when his father was hospitalized or drinking, which was most of the time, Antonio was left in the care of his two older brothers. Although he felt abandoned, at least during this time he felt that there was a truce in the civil war of his family. He had memories of them bathing him and taking care of him while they said, "We have hope in you, you are the only good thing that has come out of this family." He felt an intimacy and closeness with his older brothers. But soon his brothers became involved with drugs and drinking. When drunk and stoned, they would become violent just like his father.

It was during this time, when Antonio was perhaps about five or six years of age, that his older brothers began to rape him while they exclaimed, echoing their father, remarks that only added to his internalized sense of guilt: "This is what you *maricones* want and deserve," and "This is the punishment you get for being an Indian *maricón* who brings disgrace to the family." After the abuse, Antonio would go to a room in his house, the "room of punishment," he called it in analysis with me, a hoarding room where waste and garbage had accumulated, his space for punishing himself by hitting himself, cutting himself, tearing his hair out. All of these punishments were precipitated by unconscious guilt for being gay and indigenous in a racist/homophobic culture.

Antonio and I came to understand this history as being constitutive of the meaning of his present loss of hair and the rashes all over his body: unconscious ways of continuing to punish himself to assuage his guilt, this time within the "room of punishment" of his own psyche-soma. Analyzing his guilt in the space of the analytic process, Antonio slowly stopped suffering from these psychosomatic symptoms.

The psychoanalytic process

In his famous paper "On the Therapeutic Action of Psycho-Analysis," Hans Loewald succinctly defines the psychoanalytic process as "the significant interactions between patient and analyst that ultimately lead to structural changes in the patient's personality" (1980a, p. 221). He adds that "structural changes in the patient's personality" and psychic development in the patient "is contingent on the relationship with a new object, the analyst" (p. 221).

In "Psychoanalysis as an Art and the Fantasy Character of the Psychoanalytic Situation," Loewald specified that what is unique about this process is a "re-enactment, a dramatization of aspects of the patient's psychic life history" (1980b, p. 353) created in interaction with the analyst. In this sense, the psychoanalytic process can be understood as "an emotionally experienced recapitulation of the patient's inner life history in crucial aspects of its unfolding" (p. 353). Quoting

Aristotle, who defined tragedy as "imitation of action in the form of action," Loewald says that the analytic process has the form of a drama created by a fantasy function which weaves together memories and desire-fueled imaginative contents from the patient's past entering in dynamic interaction with the present actuality: the specificities of the relationship developed between the patient and her analyst are intertwined with the socio-political and historical context of the patient and the analyst.

In interaction with the actuality of the patient, the psychoanalytic process slowly brings about for explorating the structure of the unconscious configuration through which the patient weaves together past, present, and future worlds in a way that might be causing psychic pain, suffering, symptoms, and troublesome character traits. This is a configuration constituted by the active functions of fantasy, memory, desire, imagination, defense, conflict, symbolization, and drive activity, among other elements.

Furthering his explication of psychoanalysis as process, Loewald conceptualizes the analytic situation as a play: the "make-believe aspect of the psychoanalytic situation" (1980b, p. 354) he calls it. Both patient and analyst contribute in the creation of it. Loewald says in "Psychoanalysis as an Art and the Fantasy Character of the Psychoanalytic Situation":

> The patient takes the lead in furnishing the material and the action of this fantasy creation, while the analyst takes the lead in coalescing, articulating, and explicating the action and revealing and highlighting it as an illusion (note that the word illusion derives from the Latin *ludere*, to play). The patient experiences and acts without knowing at first that he is creating a play. Gradually he becomes more of an author aware of being an author, by virtue of the analyst's interventions that reflect back to the patient what he does and says, and by transference interpretations that reveal the relations between play and the original action that the play imitates.
>
> (p. 354)

The psychoanalytic process allows for both a recreation of the unconscious framework from which a patient's experience of the world is constructed and an immediate demonstration of their actions within that framework as it is transferred onto the analytic situation. Within it, the patient might be unconsciously inclined to assign the analyst the role of a past or present meaningful character, or just an aspect of a relationship which is organized through imagination, fantasy, and desire. Early experiences in the patient's life will be determinant in this, though these "original experiences" or "original actions" are constantly re-fashioned in interaction with the actuality of the patient, and especially the actuality of the analytic situation. Loewald observes:

> The unconscious organization of the past in repetition undergoes change during the course of treatment. In good part these changes depend on the impact

of current experiences with the analyst that do not fit the anticipatory set the patient brings to his experiencing another.

(1980b, p. 360)

Anticipatory expectations and meaning-making in Antonio's case

I remember with clarity the impression that Antonio had on me the first time I saw him, and the way I reacted and felt. He offered me his handshake, before and after the session, and I could feel the cold sweat and tension in his hands. He sat across from me, literally "on the edge of his seat," vigilant, anxious, but at the same time petrified by what looked like paralyzing pain and fear. Who was I for him, that made him feel so vigilant, and anxious, and petrified? It seemed to me like my mere presence, mediated by his anticipatory expectations of what it meant to be alone in a room with a man, a Latin American man, were already traumatizing to him.

It was as if he were ready to run out of the room at any moment and at the same time unable to move. Both wanting and not wanting to be there with me. He did not take off his jacket and held his bag tightly throughout the session, not seeming comfortable in his own skin and much less with me. He talked in a soft monotone, rocking back and forth, playing with his hands and his bag, and rarely making eye contact. Was he rocking to soothe himself? Was he rocking as play? All of this both made me feel paralyzed (I could feel the tension in my own body, perhaps as a way of mirroring the desires and fears of his body) and provoked a deep need to reach across the real and imaginary border that separated us at the time.

I remember that, during our first session, Antonio would sometimes oscillate, even within the short scope of one sentence, from the formal and informal modes of addressing another person in Spanish (between "*tú*" and "*usted*"). I also found myself enacting such oscillation in addressing him, and feeling strange in doing this. What were we re-enacting without knowing? A certain power dynamic, perhaps that between the colonizer and the colonized, captured by language?

Some time into the treatment, I mentioned this oscillation to Antonio, and he told me that he felt unsure as to how he should address me in therapy. I asked him what he preferred, what he felt most comfortable with. He told me that he was ambivalent about it, not knowing how formal or informal this relationship was. He eventually told me that he would settle with the informal "*tú*" (the way friends or family members address each other), which is what we used going forward. I remember feeling a lowering of my own tension once this had been settled, or perhaps negotiated for the first time (without knowing the full scope of its meaning), having found an incipient potential space where we both felt more comfortable to relate and work together, which came from an attempt at bridging the border that separated us, creating a proximity between us, whose meaning we did not understand at the time. It was a place between trust and treason, I can say in hindsight. I knew before he told me his story that it would be difficult to gain Antonio's trust and build the therapeutic alliance.

Based on Antonio's elaboration of his history and how he constructed his experience of the analytic process with me, I can say that his expectations of any human relationship with a man contained a proviso: "He who is there to care for me will betray and abuse me." Intimate relationships were imaginative re-elaborations of personal and historical trauma, and Antonio constructed his experience of the analytic relationship accordingly.

Early in the treatment, I was also struck by Antonio's capacity, or his genuine effort, to articulate his thoughts and feelings, sometimes coming up with images that were his only ways of communicating his sometimes vague and painful experiences. I noticed that whenever he would find himself stuck in continuing his story he would use imagery and metaphors to carry on and over the difficulty. For example, he used the image of the Conquest to understand the unconscious, intra-psychic fantasy dimension that structures his experience of the world, but also his actual experiences at home, in his racist and homophobic home country, and within the analytic process. This image made clearer the complex connections between his conscious experience and its unconscious dimension, between his past and his present, between his intra-psychic world and his socio-political world. It was a way of interpreting himself, a meaning-making and mental-linking process.

He developed this capacity from an early age. As a young boy, he would use popular songs and their lyrics to interpret his complex feelings and self-states. It is a capacity that I believe has allowed him to use the treatment as a space of play, a transitional or potential space to explore unsuspected experiences and meanings that emerged between us. I have come to believe that this capacity has literally saved his life and has been a powerful ally in helping him make sense of the senseless and violent events that have plagued his life and from which he has managed to escape. They were a life force that gave him a sense of freedom as potentiality to be otherwise.

The potentiality of the psychoanalytic process

Antonio's case helps us understand how the psychoanalytic process activates the past and offers the potential for reflection, the creation of new meanings, and change. It grants a framework for experiencing what is historical in a dynamic way – the intertwinement of how personal and historical past experiences will give shape to present and future ones. The past is always alive in the present and the future as a structuring force. But also, as Loewald observes, "It is not only true that the present is influenced by the past, but also that the past – as a living force within the patient – is influenced by the present" (1980b, p. 360). The always dynamic interactions between past and present will structure the equally dynamic potentiality of the future. Loewald, echoing Winnicott, calls this a space of illusion, of play. In the psychoanalytic process, the future as potentiality comes from the re-enactment and playful exploration of the dynamic relations between past and present.

Psychoanalysis deepens the patient's sense of subjectivity as a locus of activity in the creation of a fixed way of experiencing the world that might, for example, be producing pain and suffering. Patients who are aware of their unconscious authorship in the dramatic framework through which perceptions and relationships are experienced may find themselves liberated, able to be other than what they have been before within the recreated drama of analysis. Loewald says that within the analytic process, the "relative freedom from constraints in play and fantasy life is not only a relief from the exigencies of life, it also allows one to see beyond these exigencies" (1980b, p. 367). Freedom here is not only *freedom from* life's constraints and exigencies. It is also *freedom to* see and experience oneself and one's world in life-enhancing ways that enrich meaning. This is the realm of potentiality.

To further clarify what I mean by potentiality, it is important to consider that what Loewald calls "fantasy" is not opposed to "reality." Fantasy is more akin to what the psychoanalyst Jean-Georges Schimek (2011) calls "unconscious fantasy" – "an early established organizing structure, a kind of repetitive scenario which can manifest itself in action and thought, in symptoms, and in dreams so that conscious fantasy is only one of many partial manifestations of a basic unconscious fantasy" (p. 131). Unconscious fantasy, in this sense, is close to the dramatic framework of experiencing I have been discussing.[2] Loewald writes:

> Fantasy here does not mean that something takes place that is not to be taken seriously or that is unreal. Patients . . . often think so, as they tend to think in regard to dreams. While analysts are more sophisticated about dreams and fantasy life, they all too frequently fall into the error of regarding fantasy as being opposed to reality, as something to be eventually discarded or relegated to a psychic enclave. But fantasy is unreal only insofar as its communication with present actuality is inhibited or severed.
>
> (1980b, p. 362)

It is the lively, interactive communication and mutual constitution between fantasy and actuality that allows for potential change in our interior and exterior realities. Present actuality includes the process with the analyst. But even the analyst might err in taking the fantasy of the patient as something opposed to reality. It thus becomes a "psychic enclave" for both analyst and patient. It becomes something that cannot be subject to change, something which just *is* – a fully actualized, self-subsistent thing. Both internal and external realities are, therefore, taken to be dichotomic actualities with no room for potentiality, for change. But when this is the case, we are faced with defensive operations that disrupt the lively communication between the subjective and objective worlds, making them both lose meaning. The analytic process helps the patient become "aware that play or drama and actual life share reality" (Loewald, 1980a, p. 363).

For psychoanalysis, if there is an opposition to be analyzed, whenever it happens, it is not between fantasy and reality; it is, rather, between fantasy and actuality. The drama or play of the analytic process allows for a lived understanding of how the dynamic interplay between fantasy and actuality unconsciously construes the reality of the patient. The ongoing experiencing and interpretation of this dynamic, unconscious interplay between fantasy and actuality, enacted as play between patient and analyst, is internalized by the patient as a process that fosters potentiality for change. Moreover, this process is the unconscious conceived as potentiality itself, a "transitional state between mere inner fantasy and actuality" (Loewald, 1980b, p. 369). Following Winnicott (2006), Loewald writes that it is a "third area" (1980b, p. 369), an area of experiencing which is neither fantasy nor actuality, one that expands "into creative living and into the whole culture of man" (p. 370). It all depends on the patient recognizing the "play of fantasy – a trial action in the sense in which Freud spoke of thought as trial action – which shares in organizing reality, far from being unreal and therefore to be discarded" (Loewald, 1980b, p. 367). The experience and interpretation of the unconscious as potentiality, as that third area that articulates fantasy and actuality, makes possible nascent, creative ways of acting and being in the world, the trial of a potentially different existence considered as an open, never fully actualized process.

The political potentiality of the psychoanalytic process

What is specifically political about the potentiality of the analytic process? Since Aristotle, potentiality is taken in Western thought to be the opposite of actuality. What is potential is what is not yet actual, such that whenever the potential becomes actualized, its condition as being potential is annulled or canceled. Potentiality is conceptualized as a faculty or a capacity. Think about the eyes' potential to see, their capacity to see, the faculty of seeing. Once our eyes see an actual object, then, during such action, their potentiality to see disappears or is annulled in its actualization. Eyes that are actually seeing cannot be said to have the potential to see.

The philosopher Giorgio Agamben has attempted to go beyond the binary opposition between potentiality and actuality. His highly original interpretation of Aristotle confronts us "with a potentiality that conserves itself and saves itself in actuality" (1999, p. 181). In this sense, potentiality is never annulled in actuality but rather remains in it as "shadow":

> Human beings can . . . see shadows, they can experience darkness: they have the *potential* not to see, the *possibility of privation*. . . . The greatness – and also the abyss – of human potentiality is that it is first of all potential not to act, *potential for darkness*.
>
> (p. 181, emphasis in original)

I believe we can use Agamben's re-interpretation to conceptualize the experiencing of the unconscious as one of potentiality: a structuring process and force which articulates the interplay between fantasy and actuality. Inasmuch as potentiality produces actuality and is conserved in it as its shadow, the unconscious is "potential for darkness." The analytic process fosters the patients' experiencing of this darkness, which is the shadow of potentiality inhering the actuality of our world.

Agamben explores the political implications of this new way of thinking about potentiality/actuality. He writes in "On Potentiality":

> Here it is possible to see how the root of freedom is to be found in the abyss of potentiality. To be free is not simply to have the power to do this or that thing, nor is it simply to have the power to refuse to do this or that thing. To be free is, in the sense we have seen, *to be capable of one's own impotentiality*.
>
> (1999, pp. 182–183, emphasis in original)

Insofar as human beings exist as beings who possess the power to know, produce, and act, they always exist in the mode of potentiality. But every human potentiality exists only in relation to its own privation – potential not to act or think in a given way, the potential to experience our own darkness: the unconscious. Other non-human living beings exist only in relation to their potentiality: they can only do this or that. Human beings, on the contrary, are the "animals who are capable of their own impotentiality" (Agamben, 1999, p. 182).

The unconscious as "potentiality for darkness" (or as the very darkness which is potentiality) produces embryonic new ways of acting and being in the world that escape determinism, automatism, and mechanical causality. We are talking about existence as an always open and never fully actualized process that is not transparent to itself: the realm of freedom. Transparency, both in relation to the internal and external worlds, is the result of defensive operations that makes them fixed, inert, given things, hence not subject to change. It is the space of the primacy of consciousness, the status quo, ideology.

Elisabeth Roudinesco writes:

> It is because Freud put subjectivity at the heart of this structure that he came to conceptualize an (unconscious) determination obliging the subject no longer to regard himself as master of the world but as a consciousness of self, external to the spiral of mechanical causalities. . . . For [his theory] is the only one . . . to install the primacy of a subject inhabited by the consciousness of his own unconscious, or again by the consciousness of his own dispossession. . . . The subject is only free because it agrees to take up the challenge of this constraining liberty and reconstructs it meaning.
>
> (2001, pp. 54–55)

Paradoxical as it may sound, only a subject who becomes aware of their own dispossession ("privation," for Agamben), or of their own lack of self-transparency – all ways of referring to the unconscious as potentiality – can begin the political project of freedom: the challenge of taking up the reconstruction of the meaning of an always constrained liberty, a task put forward by the analytic situation.

The political, as I understand it, refers to a space construed from the dynamic interactions of multiples subjectivities. It is a space of dynamic interplay between the intra-psychic and the inter-psychic constituted by a complex gamut of actions, conflicts, expenditures, emotional investments, and discourses. This dynamic interplay then becomes reified in specific institutions, rules, restrictions, modes of organization and governance, and discourses. The political is a process or flux that creates the conditions of possibility of what we take to be the aforementioned *contents of politics*: its specific incarnations. It is the political conceived as potentiality, or as what I am calling *political potentiality*: the unconscious as *dúnamis*.[3]

Let us see this from a perspective that will further elucidate my understanding of the specifically political dimension of the potentiality fostered by the psychoanalytic process. The analytic situation is not only a representation of the world, it is also part of it. It never occurs in a socio-political, historical, or cultural vacuum. The two actors in this process (patient and analyst), together with its specific localization in time and space, are a thing of the world. In talking of analysis as dramatic process, we are thinking about how the subjectivities of the analyst and the patient unconsciously activate and recreate the complex relations between the intra-psychic and the inter-psychic.

There is a *constitutive knot* that is brought to the fore, as unconscious potentiality, between the socio-political, historical, and cultural dimensions of the world, *and* the intra-psychic dimension of subjectivity. The analytic process fosters a space, a political one, according to my previous understanding of it, where to explore how subjectivity is always a singular recreation and crystallization of the socio-political, the historical, and the cultural; but, on that same token, it is also a space where to examine how the latter are always the result of interpretations stemming from specific subjectivities in interaction with it. The analytic process fosters, and has as its main object of interpretation, the third space that ties and unties the knot of these two realms in the patient.[4]

The analytic process becomes, therefore, the site of the exploration of the constitutive relationality between subjectivity and the world, one which is traversed by conflicts, expenditures, desires, emotional investments, and discourses that are inherent to the political as potentiality. For psychoanalysis, it is a relationality structured by language, the stuff of which the analytic drama is made. It is language conceived as the bearer of the socio-political, cultural, and historical dimension of reality, but also as the bearer of individual subjectivity. Considered in this way, language includes its conscious content-based feature, but also its procedural, unconscious ones – gesture, tone, body, rhythm, patterns of affect, modes of relating, its dimension as an open play of signifiers, the fact of it being an interaction between subjectivities that produces signification, and re-creates action, power dynamics, culture, and history.

As Loewald reminds us:

> The injunction to free-associate rather than give a coherent narrative pro-
> motes the tension towards re-enactment because everything that encourages
> the influence of unconscious currents, including those generated by the actual
> presence of the analyst, is promoting reactivation rather than mere represen-
> tational recollection of past experience.
>
> (1980b, p. 365)

Analysis, as a process that fosters political potentiality, or the understanding of
the political as potentiality, promotes the activation of the unconscious procedural
dimension of language: language considered as a structuring process of the political and not only as a content-based fixed set of representations.

Based on this activation and exploration, the patient may thus begin to explore
non-fixed new modes of political self-understanding and understanding the world
she is part of. I am talking about new modes of being in the world that can potentially go beyond the (too) coherent narratives that constitute the patient's subjectivity and political reality. The political potentiality fostered by the analytic
process, and the experiencing of the unconscious as *that potentiality*, can inter-
rupt, problematize, and re-work the political narratives that are at the base of the
status quo, consciousness, and ideology. These are narratives which in patients
like Antonio are more radically at the core of their suffering, discrimination, marginalization, and the suppression of their political agency; narratives which have
become internalized and *made falsely necessary* in the form of a victimhood that
is fixed, insistent, self-evident.

By exploring in analysis the genealogy of the formation of such false necessity as dramatic play between fantasy and actuality, the patient becomes freer
to think about the structure of her drama as *a set of contingencies made necessary* through defensive strategies of self-preservation and adaptation, and through
complex self-identifications with socio-political ideas of normalcy that structure
her subjective and objective worlds as *what is given*, hence with no (elbow) room
for change. Within the analytic process, the patient begins to inhabit a potential
space where there is a radical questioning of what has become natural to them. It
is a space of re-elaboration and re-signification where necessities are made contingent; and that, for this reason, promotes freedom.

Epilogue: Political potentiality in Antonio's case

With Antonio, I always tried to create a potential space between us, the third
area between fantasy and actuality that "expands into creative living" (Loewald,
1980b, p. 370). A space where he could explore the socio-political, historical,
and cultural elements that constituted his subjectivity in dynamic interplay with
the activity of his own mind. A space where, therefore, he could begin to imagine himself otherwise – not determined to be only a victim, for example. This is

not to deny that he was a real victim of abuse and discrimination, but rather a way of understanding how he unconsciously construed the meaning of his own victimhood.

Recall that Antonio's abuse by his brothers occurred in a context of him being and feeling abandoned by his father and mother. The brothers then cared for him. While they bathed him, as I said, they would express their love. For this reason, he construed rape as intimacy, or intimacy as rape: something desirable but at the same time terrifying and hurtful. This was at the core of the construction of his own sense of victimhood, historically related in his mind with the colonized Indians.

In re-creating his relationship with me in this way, it allowed us to explore it as the form of a drama that had historically shaped the experience of himself and the world. The structure of this drama, which informed a way of seeing himself in relation to others, had become necessary and thus natural to Antonio: this is how things simply have been, are, and have to be in the future. It constituted a determinism, an automatism, or a fatalism which constantly dehumanized him now within the scope of how own subjectivity and his own agency. In helping him see how the form of this drama had become falsely necessary within his own mind and in its collusion, the analytic process fostered in him the political project of freedom, the challenge of taking up the reconstruction of the meaning of an always constrained liberty.

Antonio's life was plagued by real constraints. And it pained me that he had to live in a world where abuse, violence, and discrimination are common currency. But I was his psychoanalyst, not his educator, his political activist, or his savior. Had I assumed these patronizing roles within the analytic situation, I would have put Antonio in a passive position that repeated his multiples abuses. I would have become the colonizer of his mind like his brothers, his father, our culture.[5]

What I could do was help him, within the analytic process, to begin thinking of his constraints and privations as being in relation to his freedom; and not, on the contrary, experienced as producing a deterministic, automatic, and hence fully transparent sense of his own subjectivity: I can only be who I am, what history determined me to be: "ugly Indian, savage, marginal, *maricón*." The analytic process opened up the possibility of him fashioning his subjectivity as a place of activity that, having contributed to produce the meaning of his own victimhood, could also create other socio-political meanings, new ways of imagining himself in relation to others, perhaps even by giving unanticipated political meaning to, and finding political potentiality in, being an "ugly Indian, marginal, savage, *maricón*."

The analytic process was a potential place of play that helped him integrate his experience of being part of the "wretched of the earth," with his new experience of being free to understand this in creative ways that could produce an active resistance against the internalized status quo, against ideology and consciousness. Experiencing and understanding his unconscious as darkness, as an impotentiality at the core of his potentiality to act and think in the world, Antonio began the project of imagining his life beyond the paralyzing, inhibiting post-traumatic effects that brought him to analysis. Antonio started to inhabit the politically potential space where he could claim his own sense of authorship and legitimacy in the world.

Notes

1 "Antonio" is a pseudonym. I have changed aspects of his life history and of the history of his treatment for reasons of confidentiality. I will always be deeply grateful to him.
2 From now on, when I speak about "fantasy" I will always mean "unconscious fantasy."
3 This is the original Ancient Greek word for its Latin translation *potentia*, from which "potential" and "potentiality" stem. In its Latin translation, *dúnamis* loses its sense as movement, process, and action that it still has in its translation into words such as "dynamic."
4 As the psychoanalyst Madelaine Baranger writes, this third space, which she conceptualizes as "field," has been thought of in other ways by psychoanalysts such as André Green ("the tertiary"), Thomas Ogden ("the analytic third"), Cesar and Sara Botella ("the intermediate state between waking and sleep"), and Christopher Bollas ("the transformational object") (2005, pp. 64–68).
5 This does not deny my belief that, outside the analytic situation, political activism is necessary in trying to change the socio-political conditions and structures at the core of Antonio's trauma; or my belief that psychoanalysts have valuable discursive and theoretical tools that should be used in the public arena to criticize such conditions and structures.

References

Agamben, G. (1999). On potentiality. In D. Heller-Roazen (Ed.), *Potentialities: Collected essays in philosophy* (pp. 177–184). Redwood City, CA: Stanford University Press.

Baranger, M. (2005). Field theory. In S. Lewkowicz & S. Flechner (Eds.), *Truth, reality, and the psychoanalyst: Latin American contributions to psychoanalysis* (pp. 49–71). London, England: International Psychoanalytic Association.

Fanon, F. (2005). *The wretched of the earth* (R. Philcox, Trans.). New York, NY: Grove Press.

Loewald, H. (1980a). On the therapeutic action of psychoanalysis. In *Papers on psychoanalysis* (pp. 221–256). New Haven, CT: Yale University Press.

Loewald, H. (1980b). Psychoanalysis as an art and the fantasy character of the psychoanalytic situation. In *Papers on Psychoanalysis* (pp. 352–371). New Haven, CT: Yale University Press.

Roudinesco, E. (2001). *Why psychoanalysis?* (R. Bowlby, Trans.). New York, NY: Columbia University Press.

Schimek, J. G. (2011). Unconscious fantasy: Interpretive construct and developmental phenomena. In D. L. Browning (Ed.), *Memory, myth, and seduction: Unconscious fantasy and the interpretive process* (pp. 129–137). New York, NY: Routledge.

Winnicott, D. (2006). Transitional objects and transitional phenomena. In *Playing and reality* (pp. 1–34). New York, NY: Routledge.

Chapter 12

Treating borderline personality disorder in El Barrio

Integrating race and class into transference-focused psychotherapy

Daniel José Gaztambide

This chapter will outline an integration of cultural difference, race, class, and identity into transference-focused psychotherapy (TFP), a psychoanalytic evidence-based treatment for borderline personality disorder (BPD), using a systemic lens to understand those differences within a context of socioeconomic and political inequality. This inequality – between those psychically and socio-politically configured as "haves" and "have-nots," the richest and the poorest, oppressor and oppressed – will be integrated with the psychoanalytic literature on the impact of race, culture, and inequality on the psyche, with insights from liberation psychology. Liberation psychology, with its emphasis on the dynamics of internalized oppression, will be used to outline a "cultural adaptation" of TFP and discuss how reflection on these dynamics can inform psychoanalytic treatment for Latinos and other people of color with BPD in the inner city. In delineating this outline, I will first discuss the question of multicultural competence in the treatment of BPD and what TFP can contribute to this dialogue, followed by reviewing TFP's object-relational formulation of BPD and its approach to treatment. Then I will review the literature on cultural and racial differences in BPD and make a link between this literature and emergent theorizing on the role of inequality in the prevalence of BPD. It is here that I will introduce liberation psychology and develop a psychodynamic formulation of BPD that integrates questions of race, identity, and culture, and further synthesize this perspective with TFP's theoretical apparatus and clinical interventions. I will end with a clinical illustration of a culturally adapted form of TFP as it has emerged from my practice in a diverse metropolitan clinical setting serving the Harlem and Upper Manhattan communities in New York City.

Ethnic minority populations, especially Latinos in the United States, are less likely to receive psychological services, despite experiencing a higher persistence of mental health disorders (Bender, Skodol, Dyck, Markowitz, & Shea, 2007; Breslau, Kendler, Su, Gaxiola-Aguilar, & Kessler, 2005). Research has also shown higher drop-out rates from psychotherapy for ethnic minority patients who may also be of lower socioeconomic status (Wierzbicki & Pekarik, 1993), with a more recent meta-analysis showing the highest rates of drop-out and therapeutic alliance deterioration for ethnic minorities and patients with co-morbid personality disorders (Cooper & Conklin, 2015). In treating Latino and other ethnic minority patients with personality disorder in *el Barrio*, the integration of traditional treatment models with the attending sociocultural context is crucial (Comas-Diaz & Minrath, 1985).

A number of meta-analyses indicate that psychotherapies that have been tailored to the cultural and linguistic needs of specific ethnic minority communities – so-called culturally adapted treatments – are more clinically effective than psychotherapies that do not explicitly integrate culture and language into their interventions, with medium-to-large effect sizes (see Nagayama Hall, Ibaraki, & Huang, 2016 for a review). Furthermore, multicultural competence has been found to be an independent common factor affecting outcomes in psychotherapy, which interacts with other common factors such as the therapeutic alliance and empathy (Tao, Owen, Pace, & Imel, 2015). TFP, with its exquisite level of attention to the tacit, non-verbal, and unconscious dimensions of the therapeutic relationship, has the potential of being a powerful tool for providers working to meet the needs of clients of color living in marginalized and underprivileged conditions.

TFP is an evidence-based, manualized, psychoanalytically oriented treatment for BPD based on the work of Otto Kernberg and his colleagues. I will focus on TFP, as it distills over 30 years of psychoanalytic thinking and practice into a more structured and readily accessible format, which allows these ideas and interventions to be more easily disseminated, as well as subjected to empirical scrutiny through both process-outcome studies and randomized controlled trials (Yeomans, Clarkin, & Kernberg, 2015). It also emphasizes a strengths-based approach that is much needed in working with people of color with complex mental health needs. In my experience, the treatment of BPD has tended to emphasize "risk management" and the provision of skills for coping with emotional dysregulation. Although these skills are important, they are necessarily limited in scope. Patients may attain some control over impulsive behavior and suicidal urges, maintaining a certain level of basic subsistence, all while being seen as "career patients" by their providers who may not expect further or formative change. Patricia Gherovici (see Christian, Reichbart, Moskowitz, Morillo, & Winograd, 2016) has argued that in the analytic exchange, "you make somebody who is by the given situation of society . . . unemployed, unproductive . . . become somebody who works and produces." To put it somewhat differently, the analytic relationship places the patient in the position of producing a new social link in which they are an agent of change and agency. As will become apparent, this depends on the therapist taking on a different political and clinical position that transforms the roles of patient and therapist.

An object-relational formulation of BPD

From the object-relational view espoused in TFP, *personality* is the integration of temperament (constitutional dispositions), capacities, and values. Ideal, or good-enough, personality development within a facilitating environment results in a coherent, integrated sense of self with a broad spectrum of affective experience and core values. In borderline psychopathology, however, this integration does not fully take place. Through repeated trauma or ongoing misattunement, the child does not learn that frustration can be tolerated, and that the caregiver is neither good nor bad, but in Winnicott's sense, "good-enough" – ultimately responsive and trustworthy despite momentary ruptures. Over time the child develops a "dissociated motivational system" in the form of intra-psychic defenses and interpersonal avoidance strategies aimed at maintaining a split between an archaic "bad" object relation and an idealized "good" object relation – a fragmentary relational landscape with little room for the complex nature of reality (Yeomans et al., 2015, p. 14). A brittle sense of self in relation to a perceived arbitrary and untrustworthy other becomes dependent on external validation, leading in turn to a diffuse, and ever shifting, sense of desire, goals, and moral values.

These fragmented self-states yield what in TFP are referred to as "split-off object-relational dyads." These dyads are internal representations composed of an image of the *self*, an image of the *other*, and the predominant *affect* that binds the two (Yeomans et al., 2015). For example, in one moment the person may have the experience of being a "deprived, abused" self-as-victim to a "sadistic, depriving" perpetrating other, with a predominating affect of fear. Yet suddenly, in reaction to a new perceived slight, the person becomes a "powerful, controlling" self who punishes a "weak, slave-like" other, with wrath or hatred activated in an affective storm. In brief moments of perceived responsiveness by the other, the same person suddenly experiences themselves as a "satisfied, cared for" self in the tender embrace of an ideal "responsive, caring" other, generating a feeling of love or gratitude.

This constant and ever-shifting oscillation between different self-states and their perceived "objects" is characteristic of the "paranoid-schizoid" position, defined by a self-organization which mirrors a fantasized chaotic, unsafe, and dangerous world. Within TFP, the goal of treatment is to enact structural personality change by helping the patient usher in and work through the "depressive position." Shifting from the paranoid-schizoid to the depressive position entails losing and mourning the image of the wished-for idealized other and self, a painful process that "might involve the shift of the quest for the ideal to more symbolic realms such as art or spirituality" (Yeomans et al., 2015, p. 13). It also involves coming to accept one's own aggression, previously deemed too dangerous, then projected and experienced as coming solely from the outside, and making reparation by seeing the other in a more balanced manner. We will return to these ideas in discussing a formulation of BPD among people of color in the inner city. For now, I will describe the treatment structure that proceeds from this formulation in TFP.

TFP treatment strategies, techniques, and tactics

TFP as a structured, manualized treatment for BPD identifies a series of *strategies*, *specific techniques*, and *tactics* used to guide interventions. The treatment is "manualized" in the sense that it spells out the procedural elements of the therapy –

where and when certain types of interventions should be used, how to prioritize therapeutic themes, when and how to address issues of safety and the frame (setting limits) versus engaging in exploration of the transference, etc. For a more detailed description of these components, the reader is directed to the TFP manual itself (Yeomans et al., 2015).

The primary strategy in any one session is to identify the object-relational dyad that is *activated* at any given moment in the session. The therapist tolerates the confusion that arises when engaging patients with BPD, slowly beginning to "name the *actors* and the *action*" and assess the patient's reaction to their reflection, while also observing, clarifying, and interpreting *role reversals* within the active dyad. For example, in one moment the patient experiences herself as a hapless victim before the perceived tyrannical therapist. As this dyad is named and reflected upon by the therapist, suddenly the patient takes on the role of the mighty perpetrator, relentlessly attacking the therapist who now falls victim to the patient's wrath and aggression. In addition to reversals *within* a dyad, dyads also oscillate with *other* dyads. Hence, TFP technique involves tracking how dyads *defensively* reverse polarities within themselves, as well as defend against other, split-off object-relational dyads. For example, an active dyad of a tormented patient-victim fearful of a vicious therapist-perpetrator may be used to defensively dissociate experiencing the therapist as a kind caretaker in relation to a soothed self, due to the perceived (and dangerous) vulnerability that it entails.

Identifying and interpreting the "characters and caricatures" that constitute the patient's fragmented experiential world allow patients to increase their capacity to experience relationships *differently*, starting with the transference. Patients learn to tolerate their disparate positively and negatively toned object-relational dyads at the same time, through the therapist's ability to tolerate, reflect upon, and interpret these states. Paving the road toward the depressive position, patients begin to mourn the primitive idealized object-and-self, accepting that such an object is untenable, little by little forming a more differentiated sense of self and others which carries greater depth and three-dimensionality – starting usually with the therapist, initially experienced as an old object, and who over the course of treatment is experienced as a new object, and who is now seen as carrying both positive and negative traits (see also Cooper & Levit, 1998).

Having described the main strategies employed in TFP, I will for the sake of brevity focus on technical neutrality in my discussion of technique, as this will have bearing on how we address racially or culturally relevant material with our patients. In TFP, technical neutrality is understood in terms of both Anna Freud's classical definition and split-off object-relational dyads. In Freud's sense, technical neutrality refers to the therapist taking an *equidistant position* between the patient's libidinal drives, ego defenses, super-ego injunctions, and the demands and constraints of external reality. In TFP, it also means maintaining "an equidistance between self and object representations in mutual conflict and equidistance between mutually split-off, all-good and all-bad object relations dyads" (Yeomans et al., 2015, p. 168), all while remaining connected with the patient's available or potential observing ego, *without taking sides*.

Phenomenologically speaking, the therapist comes to know the different self-states and part-objects of the patient's inner life quite intimately, and learns to shift between these different perspectives without themselves becoming stuck, rigid, or one-sided. It is this *psychodynamic stance* – literally, the therapist keeping their "mind in motion" – that allows for a reflective space in which the therapist (and later the patient's own observing ego) can operate as an "excluded third party." The technically neutral therapist is characterized by his or her capacity to empathize with all sides of the patient's conflict, understanding the purpose of the different positions she takes in relation to the other, while also being able to reflect on how these different self-states operate in relation to each other and to reality. Technical neutrality, with its free-flowing, evenly hovering attention, keeps the therapist's mind open, in motion, and capable of reflection and interpretation.

Technical neutrality, and the position of the excluded third, also bear an important relationship to the patient's available or *potential* observing ego. A part of any TFP formulation of the patient is the therapist's own capacity to appraise the patient's strengths and hold in mind a vision of the patient's potentialities unburdened by the extremes of borderline pathology, a view of "what the patient is becoming and can become" (Yeomans et al., 2015, p. 223). This is very much in line with Loewald's (1960) position that the therapist "holds in safe keeping" for the patient an image of them that lies beneath all the distortions, an image "to be brought into its own" (p. 18). This potentiality develops in part through the patient's identification with the analytic function of the therapist (Strachey, 1969), becoming more and more able to join the therapist in the position of the third and shift from rigid and rapidly oscillating affective states to increasingly more inclusive and free-flowing perspectival shifts.

Given the importance of this reflective third, TFP safeguards this position for the therapist through the establishment of a treatment contract with the patient, based on the minimum *necessary* requirements for the treatment to be effective. This contract stipulates the respective responsibilities of patient and therapist, how the patient will manage and address crises and suicidal and homicidal urges in between sessions, and if relevant, contract around engagement in meaningful productive activity outside the sessions – whether employed or volunteer work. Once there is an established treatment contract and frame, a space is created for patient and therapist to engage in exploratory work. By attending to threats to the therapy (e.g. suicidal or homicidal ideation, recurring crises), exploring incompatible views, and establishing a shared reality through interpretation, the patient can come to develop a more integrated and stable sense of self and others, become better able to tolerate their affective storms, and begin living a life of greater coherence in accordance with their values. As the patient over time experiences themselves-in-relationships in a new way, achieving greater integration of their disparate self-states, they may begin exploring whole new worlds of vibrancy and aliveness. As the patient's object-relational world is reconfigured through the transference relationship, so too may other transitional spaces of human experiencing, such as racial and cultural identity, the self's place in society, love and work, even religio-spiritual beliefs, be transformed (Yeomans et al., 2015).

We will discuss how change in these areas, specifically racial and cultural identity, may conversely impact the object-relational world. Having given an outline of TFP, we will now review existing research on the impact of race and class on BPD.

Racial and cultural differences in BPD

While research shows cross-cultural stability in terms of a basic genetic and neurobiological structure to BPD – cognitive disturbance, disturbed relatedness, affective dysregulation, and behavioral dysregulation – the expression of certain symptoms, such as impulsivity and suicidal behavior, can vary depending on culture, race, and ethnicity (Selby & Joiner, 2008). The available research literature shows a trend toward higher rates of BPD in non-White populations, with even higher rates for women, and those who belong to a lower socioeconomic class (Chavira et al., 2003; Tomko, Trull, Wood, & Sher, 2014), with some evidence of disproportionately higher rates among Latino populations (Chavira et al., 2003; Swartz, Blazer, George, & Winfield, 1990). In studies comparing BPD symptom profiles, there is evidence of higher levels of aggression, hostile behavior, and risk for exposure to violence among Latinos and African-Americans with BPD, with less evidence of suicidal behavior, compared to White individuals with BPD (De Genna & Feske, 2013; Newhill, Eack, & Conner, 2009; Selby & Joiner, 2008).

These disparate presentations of symptom can be explained in part by socioeconomic class and trauma exposure. Studies also show that socioeconomic status mediates the impact of race on personality disorder symptoms (De Genna & Feske, 2013; Iacovino, Jackson, & Oltmanns, 2014). Neighborhood constitution also plays a role, as living in neighborhoods that are more impoverished and at high risk for community violence is associated with greater BPD symptoms and a greater likelihood of psychosocial impairment, such as unemployment or being on disability (Walsh et al., 2013; see also C'de Baca, Castillo, Mackaronis, & Qualls, 2014; Cort et al., 2012; Westphal et al., 2013). Some authors raise concerns on how women of color with BPD may be more likely to be misdiagnosed, as they may not reflect a "typical" BPD presentation (De Genna & Feske, 2013). People of color with BPD may be at higher risk for involvement with the criminal justice system due to their behavior problems being seen through a law enforcement, as opposed to a psychiatric, lens, placing them at higher risk for incarceration, re-traumatization, and harm to self or others (Newhill et al., 2009). This inequality in diagnosis and access to treatment mirrors race and class inequalities in society as a whole.

Culture, inequality, and BPD

Comas-Diaz and Minrath (1985), in a pioneering paper on the treatment of BPD among people of color, argue that negotiating cultural/racial divides "may exacerbate a trauma occurring during the early phases of separation-individuation, thus compounding a sense of identity diffussion [sic]" (p. 419). Straddling different cultural, political, and ethno-racial worlds can generate strength, resilience, and flexibility in understanding self and other from different perspectives. However, difficulties in resolving these tensions can alternatively lead to confusion and rigidity, resulting in a fixed, fossilized identity dependent on idealizing one side of a cultural difference while devaluing the other. Comas-Diaz and Minrath (1985) further argue that unequal access to resources, lack of opportunities, and discrimination create conditions which lead to maladaptive interpersonal strategies that reinforce a cycle of powerlessness and perpetual victimhood. For example, a person of color who experiences difficulty procuring stable employment – possibly due to discrimination and/or lack of opportunities – may develop feelings of anxiety and frustration that affects their performance on job interviews. This may express itself in a form of passive aggression, which results in less likelihood of being hired or maintaining a job. Desperate conditions then lead to desperate behaviors in a mutually reinforcing cycle.

This victim cycle as described by Comas-Diaz and Minrath (1985) has both socio-systemic and psychodynamic underpinnings. They cite Erik Erikson's work with patients with BPD; he argued that the *development of trust* and the *rebuilding of identity* are central therapeutic goals. Fonagy, Luyten, Allison, and Campbell (2017) have similarly argued that mistrust becomes entrenched as an adaptation to abusive and hostile caregivers, and that BPD can be understood "as a failure of communication arising from a breakdown in the capacity to forge learning relationships" (p. 11). A history of adversity that impairs the capacity for trust results in a stance in which the individual cannot respond to new information from the environment, adopting a rigid cognitive-affective style that is resistant to change (e.g. splitting, projective identification, idealization, and devaluation). Fonagy et al. (2017) make an interesting connection between this self-perpetuating cognitive-affective cycle as manifested in BPD, and broader systemic forces, pointing to the work of Wilkinson and Pickett (2009) on inequality and mental health, as well as other prevalence data (cf. Fonagy & Luyten, 2016), suggesting that Western countries with higher levels of inequality also evidence higher prevalence of BPD, as well as higher levels of mental health problems associated with borderline syndromes, such as substance abuse, aggression, impulsivity, and high-risk unprotected sex.

In a groundbreaking book (Wilkinson & Pickett, 2009) and a follow-up review article (Pickett & Wilkinson, 2015), Wilkinson and Pickett document how as inequality between the richest and the poorest individuals in a society increases, so too does the prevalence of medical, mental health, and social problems such as violence and teenage pregnancy. This relationship between inequality and psychosocial factors has in turn been found to be mediated by social capital – the extent to which people are involved in their communities through social groups – and the level of mutual trust among people in their communities. Wilkinson and Pickett (2009) review research pointing to the impact of inequality on increased levels of social evaluation and anxiety about social status, with greater sensitivity to perceived rejection or inferiority. Furthermore, there is some evidence that low self-perceived social status is associated with more symptoms of borderline and other personality disorders (Wang et al., 2013). Greater inequality heightens one's evaluation anxieties by increasing the importance of status on a social hierarchy, erasing our common humanity. Conversely, "getting the measure of each other becomes more important as status differences widen" (Wilkinson & Pickett, 2009, p. 43).

Egregious inequality produces prejudice across economic and racial lines, weakening communal life and increasing the likelihood of social conflict and violence. Wilkinson and Pickett (2009) write that

> With greater inequality, people are less caring of one another, there is less mutuality in relationships, people have to fend for themselves and get what they can – so, inevitably, there is less trust . . . less [likelihood] to empathize with those not seen as equals; material differences serve to divide us socially.
>
> (p. 56)

Inequality, including racial inequality, yields social divisions of haves and have-nots, often configured in our social imaginary in terms of oppressor and oppressed, rich and poor, White and non-White, etc. These divisions create suspicion of the "other" – the marginalized responding with envy, resentment, and fear to the power of the dominant, whereas the latter fear the former and suspect they would "turn the tables" the first chance they get and steal the riches the privileged have "worked" hard to amass. Inequality, and the social divisions that accompany it, generates paranoid-schizoid defenses, fears, idealizations, and hatreds in order to maintain itself.

Liberation psychology and the psychodynamic formulation of BPD

A growing psychoanalytic literature addresses how these social divisions are internalized and "take up root" in the human psyche (for a sample of this literature, see Altman, 2009; Hollander & Gutwill, 2006; Tummala-Narra, 2016). A subset of this literature draws on the tradition of liberation psychology, a perspective born from the intersection of Latin American psychoanalysis and social psychology (Martin-Baro, 1994; Watkins & Shulman, 2008). Liberation psychology studies how oppression structures the defensive operations used by marginalized individuals and communities and what psychodynamic factors contribute to the capacity to resist and engage in personal and social change. In order to develop a liberation psychology–informed psychodynamic formulation of BPD, I will draw on Alschuler's (2007) *The Psychopolitics of Liberation*, who crafted an integration of Jungian theory with major liberation psychology figures such as Paulo Freire and Albert Memmi. I have decided on this text as his theorizing bears an interesting resemblance to the object-relations theory employed in TFP.

Although a review of Jungian theory as elucidated in Alschuler (2007) is beyond the scope of this chapter, I want to point out that the Jungian concept of bipolar complexes bears a striking similarity to object-relational dyads, as these are images of "roles" or "characters" bound by a predominating affect, in which the self identifies with one side of the complex and projects the opposite pole unto the other (Alschuler, 2007, p. 29). Integration takes place through the ego developing a "transcendent function," taking a third position that can observe, hold, and own split-off complexes (i.e. object-relational dyads).

Alschuler's (2007) integration of Jungian psychoanalysis and liberation psychology draws on the work of Brazilian educator Paulo Freire and the Tunisian writer Albert Memmi. Freire (1972, 1973) wrote on how oppressed communities internalize "contradictions" – such as an image of the self as "passive," "object," "weak," and "dependent" on the desire of the other, the oppressor, who is internalized as a self-determining, "active" "subject" who is independent and holds power over the self. If Freire were to cast these "contradictions" in terms of object-relational dyads, he would argue that the predominant affect in this configuration is "fatalism" or hopelessness. In his theorizing on liberation, Freire (1972, 1973) noted that this self-image of the oppressed as "all-bad" in relation to the "all-good" oppressor, oscillated with another contradiction in which the oppressed perceive they can achieve humanity and self-hood by identifying with the position of the oppressor – to be human is to be *like* the oppressor. The oppressed experience a sense of power by taking on the characteristics of the oppressor either in relation to other oppressed groups or individuals, or against the oppressors themselves. The polarity of the contradiction leads to a reversal of terms characterized by rage and wrath.

In observing revolutionary and social justice movements in Latin America, Freire (1972, 1973) noted that oppressed communities engage in these reversals as a way of achieving power, depending on a pathological link which requires there to be a "do-er" and a "done-to." (Benjamin, 2004). Except in this case, it is the oppressed who are idealized as innocent and "all good," whereas the oppressor is now denigrated as "all bad." In relation to other oppressed individuals who do not hold the same view, they might be seen as "less pure" in their ideology, traitors who are just as bad as the oppressor. The oppressors are an enemy that need to be destroyed, a caricature that lacks depth and humanity. In this way, oppression distorts the humanity of *both* the oppressor and the oppressed. However, he saw it as the task of the oppressed to liberate themselves *and* their oppressors. This cannot be accomplished, he argued, by drawing on the same language of violence and cyclical complementarity. Rather, the oppressor-oppressed dialectic itself needs to be subverted. Freire (1973) argued that this contradiction would be resolved by the appearance of a new subjectivity,

> neither oppressor nor oppressed, but man in the process of liberation. If the goal of the oppressed is to become fully human, they will not achieve their goal by merely reversing the terms of the contradiction, by simply changing poles.
>
> (p. 38)

Writing on how oppressive dynamics can be enacted within the pedagogical relationship, Freire (1972) wrote that liberation in education "must begin with the solution of the teacher-student contradiction, by reconciling the poles of the contradiction so that both are simultaneously teachers *and* students" (p. 59). Hence, the contradiction between the teacher who knows and the student who knows nothing is superseded by the dialogue between teacher-as-student and student-as-teacher. Similarly, he argued that only a dialogue that recognizes the complicity of the oppressed in systems of oppression, and the ways that the oppressors are themselves distorted by their power and privilege, can lead to true liberation. In this sense, the oppressed recognize the "oppressor" within them, and at the same time, how the oppressor is victimized by the system as well. An emancipatory, inter-subjective dialogue between teacher and student, or between oppressor and oppressed, sustains this change by helping each member of the dyad to observe their own minds in dialogue with the other, becoming "*conscious of*, not only as intent on objects but as turned in upon itself in a Jasperian 'split' – consciousness as consciousness of consciousness" (Freire, 1972, pp. 65–66).

In his Jungian analysis of the psychodynamic implications of Freire's thinking, Alschuler (2007) writes, "liberation results from transcending the contradictions of oppressive society" (p. 35). Drawing on Jung's transcendent function – the capacity to cultivate a "third" point of view – he adds that "a new synthesis . . . emerges when a person avoids a one-sided adherence to either of the opposites in conflict" (p. 35). In taking this third point, the oppressed reject the oppressor's ideology and develop a more nuanced and realistic view of themselves *and* the oppressor. Rather than seeing injustice and evil as residing in individual oppressors, they come to apperceive the problem as systemic in nature, becoming empowered to resist that system and effect change.

Memmi's (1965/1991) work parallels that of Freire in theme and content, with some additional (and important) contributions. Like Freire, he also argued against the dangers of idealizing the oppressed or their culture. Memmi added that to achieve greater wholeness, the oppressed must mourn the wound brought upon by a history of inequality and marginalization. This necessarily entails mourning an idealized view of one's culture, traditions, and values and adopting a more nuanced representation that allows for both their positive and negative qualities. In addition, for Memmi, it is important to "develop a personal sense of identity and self-esteem that *does not* depend on belonging to an admirable people, culture, ethnicity, or nation" (Alschuler, 2007, p. 56, emphasis added). This distance from an idealized cultural, ethnic, or racial group creates space for a more coherent identity that has "depth," allowing for a fuller range of emotion and human experience. Freire (1973) writes that as the oppressed person engages in this integration-for-liberation, he "would begin to effect a change in his former attitudes, by discovering himself to be a maker of the world of culture, by discovering that he, as well as the literate person, has a creative and re-creative impulse" (p. 47). Working toward the depressive position allows the oppressed individual to work through loss toward a renewed capacity for creativity and play, liberated from fossilized and restrictive identities imposed from without.

Alschuler (2007) sees this as evidence of the transcendent function, citing Jung's recognition that when one sits with the psychic tension between different polarities or contradictions (object-relational dyads, we might add), and "the conflict is endured to the end . . . a creative solution emerges which . . . possesses that compelling authority not unjustly characterized as the voice of God" (cited in p. 66). This novel third option opens a new path toward freedom in the individual's own voice to challenge the injustices of society. From a liberation psychology perspective, then, "*Liberated consciousness means holding the tension of psychic opposites, where the opposites are images of ethnic groups in conflict*" (p. 80, emphasis original). Holding this tension entails integrating the negative and positive qualities of both oppressor and oppressed, seeing the common humanity of both while also recognizing how these tensions reflect a underlying systemic inequality. It is in sustaining this very tension that Freire (1973) wrote that "the contradiction will be resolved by the appearance of the new man: neither oppressor nor oppressed, but man in the process of liberation" (p. 38).

TFP in el Barrio

Although liberation psychology scholars did not write with BPD in mind, their thinking helps formulate the psychodynamics of identity and BPD among communities of color. The oscillation and fluctuation of positive and negative object-relational dyads can be, as Comas-Diaz and Minrath (1985) write, "catalyzed and even exaggerated by the ethnic and racial factors" (p. 421). The transference of ethnic minority patients with BPD toward their White therapists, or toward ethnic minority therapists seen as having a more privileged position, can be augmented by real or perceived class and racial differences, which like other transferences, if ignored, can lead to impasses in the treatment. In complementary fashion, issues of prejudice, discrimination, and guilt can complicate the therapist's countertransference feelings. Comas-Diaz and Minrath (1985) maintain that being attentive to these shifting ethnic identifications in the therapeutic relationship "is essential for working through a client's diffused sense of identity and for complete understanding of the transference" (p. 420).

Comas-Diaz and Minrath (1985) agree with TFP's emphasis on developing a treatment contract with the patient, drawing our attention to how creating a solid treatment frame can be threatened by the intrusion of the social surround. Patients of color struggling with BPD in the barrios of our inner cities "often represent aspects of our society we wish to overlook or deny" (p. 422). Feelings of hopelessness before the gravity and intensity of wholesale systemic failure and personal pathology may leave therapists feeling overwhelmed and unsure as to whether psychotherapy and change is viable. Like with any treatment contract in TFP, the purpose is to identify *precisely* those minimum necessary parameters that make therapy possible. However, in work with ethnic minority clients with BPD, a number of caveats are in order.

Developing a plan for the patient to address suicidal or homicidal impulses in between sessions is essential to creating a context of safety for psychotherapy. For impoverished patients of color who may have grown up facing community violence, the reality of these circumstances and their tendency to impair basic trust and safety must be openly acknowledged and explored in the therapeutic work – avoiding a discussion of such issues runs the risk of alienating the patient and depriving the therapy of important information in developing the contract (Comas-Diaz & Minrath, 1985). Discovering that the patient carries a weapon out of fear of retaliation by community members who "have beef" with a family member demands careful exploration of the reality of community violence, side by side with discussing appropriate limits for the patient to ensure their safety. The therapist's countertransference and level of comfort with such matters should serve as a guide in such contracting. Depending on the patient (and the therapist!), the meaning of "minimum necessary requirements" may change.

Relatedly, contracting with the patient to engage in some form of productive activity needs to be balanced with recognition of the systemic forces that can impact their ability to work. For example, there is ample evidence of inequality in hiring practices for applicants who are of ethnic minority background, more so if they have a history of involvement in the criminal justice system (see Alexander, 2012, for a review). Talking about this reality conveys an understanding by the therapist that she and the patient share a world still plagued by racism and classism, *while also* discussing resources, services, and activities the patient will be required to engage in as a prerequisite for treatment. It is here that the therapist's ability to hold in mind a different view of the patient – mentalizing their strengths and potentialities – is paramount. Many therapists may waive this component of a treatment contract due to an impoverished view of patients of color with BPD as "career patients," "irredeemably damaged," "broken," not capable of greater functioning or achievement in life.

A question may be raised as to whether acknowledging community violence, systemic racism, and inequality means abandoning technical neutrality. We must remember that technical neutrality does not mean political neutrality or some sort of naïve colorblindness. Technical neutrality, as discussed above, means maintaining a mindful, reflective attitude toward (1) the conflicting object-relational dyads driving the patients' psyche, (2) their more adaptive ego functions, strengths, and potentials, and (3) the limits and constraints of reality. Certainly, if we saw the patient's struggles as simply or predominantly of a social and systemic nature, *without attending to the underlying psychodynamic tensions within the patient*, this would entail an abandonment of the technically neutral stance. I would argue, however, that if we neglect these tensions in our shared social reality and how they impact the patient's life and inner world, *this also constitutes an abandonment of technical neutrality*. Acknowledging this reality, and at the same time setting limits and expectations while also exploring the psychodynamic meaning of this reality and these expectations (treatment contract), is part and parcel of a technically neutral stance.

In what follows I will provide a case example to illustrate how TFP could be delivered in the barrios.

Case illustration

"Felix" (pseudonym) was a 35-year-old, bilingual (Spanish-dominant), Afro-Colombian man who initially presented for treatment complaining of "chronic major depression" in the context of years of unemployment after being fired from his last job. He had been previously treated with psychiatric medication and a combination of short-term counseling and anger management. Upon further assessment, Felix reported an extensive history of difficulty managing anger and hostile behavior, self-harm via putting out cigarettes on his arms, emotional lability, a pattern of unstable relationships characterized by idealization and devaluation, chronic feelings of emptiness, identity diffusion, and stress-induced paranoid ideation, meeting diagnostic criteria for BPD.

Felix reported a history of involvement with the criminal justice system, with multiple arrests for getting into fights with others, including police officers. His aggressive behavior and history of incarceration impaired his efforts to find and maintain steady work, as he often left jobs impulsively or was fired as a result of an angry outburst. Part of what emerged in the assessment phase was Felix's persistent sense of feeling targeted by the police, "stopped and frisked" on a regular basis, due to the color of his skin. As a Puerto Rican man, I resonated with his experience of police harassment. At the same time, I noted how Felix related to others in life *as if* they were persecutory, intrusive others with malignant intent. As we were conducting the sessions in Spanish, he also detected my accent and identified me as a Puerto Rican, commenting on how he's "had good relationships with Puerto Ricans, they are good people." I tracked the emergence of two inter-related object-relational dyads – that of a victimized, powerless self/person of color before an intrusive, persecutory other/police officer, alongside a (split-off) positively toned dyad characterized by identification between two Latino men.

In negotiating the treatment contract, attention was given to Felix's experience of his aggressive and self-harm impulses being wholly outside of his control. The alternative to fighting, for Felix, was to pace while smoking cigarettes, ruminating about the violence he wished he had delivered on someone who wronged him, often ending with putting out his cigarette on his arm to "release the tension." These behaviors were explored, resulting in the stipulation that to engage in treatment, Felix had to agree to physically withdraw from or avoid altercations with others and draw on support resources, including visiting the nearest emergency room, if he felt in danger of acting on his self-harm or aggressive impulses. Felix initially scoffed as this prospect, defiantly responding that he "would punch the first son of a bitch who crossed me." I expressed to him that while his reaction was understandable, and it would certainly be important to discuss his anger in more detail, we would not be able to engage in therapy effectively if he could not agree to these terms, as I could not help him if he were dead or in jail. I added that if Felix chose not to participate in this treatment, he could be referred to another clinician or treatment setting.

Felix verbalized an understanding of my reasoning, and following further discussion, agreed to our safety plan. In addition, given his history of depression and unstable work, I discussed the importance of his engaging in some form of productive activity as a part of his treatment. While acknowledging the barriers he faced as a man of color with a prior criminal record, we discussed a plan for him to participate in a vocational rehabilitation program as part of his care. Upon being connected to a job, the contract was revised to include a requirement that he discuss any aggressive thoughts or impulses to suddenly leave his job in session. Having established our treatment contract, we engaged in twice weekly psychoanalytic therapy informed by TFP's principles.

Felix's fantasies about our "shared" identity became a topic of ongoing exploration. I increasingly pointed out how he alternated between an intense level of closeness or *"confianza"* (trust) with others in life, by whom he would "inevitably" feel betrayed, and then viciously attack them in response before cutting them off, now taking on the role of the persecutory other. I also began to note that he seemed to go to great pains to cast me in the role of an almost omnipotently benign Latino other, whom he trusted without reservation, almost as if any slight or momentary misattunement on my part would be intolerable, requiring him to attack me and cut me off. Felix initially dismissed my interpretation, citing his warmth toward me and our shared cultural background as proof of the strength of our relationship.

Over the next few sessions, however, Felix became increasingly irate with me, discussing how the stipulations of our treatment contract felt like "chains that keep me from fighting back." He now saw the safety plan as my attempt to "declaw" him and render him docile before his oppressors, referring to me as a "traitor" to the Latino community, someone who was "basically White." Felix berated me as "just another part of the system," whose purpose was to control him. Being a Puerto Rican with White skin, this series of attacks triggered my own anxieties as someone who "made it" and achieved a middle-class income, professional/managerial class status through my education, and in no small part benefiting from white privilege. My anxieties centered on the perception, within and without, that I was not "really, authentically" Latino, my own body drawing praise (for "being White") as much as scorn (for not "being brown"). I felt the impulse to defend myself and validate my identity and my sense of goodness. As I reflected on my experience of being attacked, put down, and belittled for my body, I began to disembed from my immediate emotional arousal, working my way through the countertransference back to Felix's own experience.

I struggled to maintain a reflective, neutral stance, non-defensively inviting Felix to tell me more about his experience of me as a traitorous White Latino looking over his shoulder, ready to stab him in the back and send him off to the authorities to be locked up. I clarified with him the "actors and the action" of the dyads which were crystallizing in the transference. I interpreted that in negotiating the treatment contract, to ask Felix to withdraw from a confrontation and go to the emergency room (if he could not restrain the impulse to fight or harm himself) felt to him like I was tying his arms behind his back, leaving him defenseless before a world that attacked his Black body as something "dangerous," suspect, and intrinsically bad. I added that feeling "restrained" with me also meant being vulnerable in a way he was not used to with another person, something he needed to defend against lest he be inevitably hurt and betrayed. Felix's affect shifted, from rage to a mournful sadness, remarking on how he is always "waiting for the other shoe to drop" with others in his life, filled with fear and anxiety at how they would "turn on him." Further clarification of this dyad led to us confronting (pointing out discrepancies between) how he split off his yearnings for safety and care from his fear of vulnerability. It soon surfaced that a part of him experienced our initial treatment contracting, and the establishing of the parameters for safety, as my caring enough about him to set limits on his destructive behavior.

In the months following this series of confrontations and interpretations, Felix reported an incident in which a police officer helped him with directions to a building related to his job. He reflected on this experience in treatment, taken aback by the kindness and professionalism he experienced from this officer, feeling that he "took care of me." He began to make a distinction between individual police officers – who could be "good," or "good and bad" – and a larger system of racial injustice that could "turn" even good officers into problematic cops (e.g. Alexander, 2012). With this more systemic perspective on issues such as police brutality or harassment – not to mention the increasingly visible incidents of police-related deaths of people of color – Felix developed a more integrated perspective on himself and others. He began to see other Latinos and people of color in less idealized terms, while also seeing individual White people in a more nuanced light. He maintained an awareness of White privilege and racial inequality, but no longer defined himself one-sidedly in terms of race and ethnicity, allowing for a fuller range of human experiencing. Felix discovered an affinity for the spoken word, and found himself not only expressing his political and cultural views using poetry and art, but also musing on topics related to love, vulnerability, and creating a home for the heart.

The use of art further allowed Felix to identify the aggression he regularly disowned and projected upon others, by writing his poems from the perspective of the other as well as his own. This helped Felix develop insight into how his intense anger drove others away and impaired his ability to work and function. It was in this stage of the work that Felix was able to observe, in its rawest form, how his behavior reflected his own "inner police officer," participating in his oppression. Exploration of this material further revealed his expression of anger not only as a response to fear or perceived injury, but as a pleasurable affect he wanted to see if I would tolerate, accept in him, and help him regulate (via limit setting).

Conclusion

TFP is an evidence-based psychoanalytic treatment for BPD, with a theoretical apparatus highly relevant to work in the inner city with ethnic minority populations. Thinking about racial and class conflict in terms of split-off object-relational dyads allows us to mentalize about a much-neglected area in the treatment of BPD. These dyads reflect systemic inequalities internalized within the psyche, as well as attachment-related fears and anxieties. Tracking, clarifying, and interpreting role reversals within these dyads, along with their dissociation from other affectively toned object-relational configurations, helps the patient identify with all the various subject-positions that populate their psyche – oppressor, oppressed, Black, White, rich, poor, victim, victimizer, do'er, and done-to – in order to go beyond them. In this way, the tools that TFP offers can help patients of color with BPD begin the process of undoing their internalized oppression, and resist the oppression and inequality that continues to persist. To paraphrase Frieda Fromm-Reichmann, in repairing the self, we repair the world. To mirror Freire, to liberate the other, we liberate ourselves as well.

References

Alexander, M. (2012). *The new Jim Crow: Mass incarceration in the age of colorblindness* (Revised ed.). New York, NY: The New Press.

Alschuler, L. R. (2007). *The psychopolitics of liberation: Political consciousness from a Jungian perspective*. New York, NY: Palgrave Macmillan.

Altman, N. (2009). *The analyst in the inner city: Race, class, and culture from a psychoanalytic lens*. Hillsdale, NY: Analytic Press.

Bender, D. S., Skodol, A. E., Dyck, I. R., Markowitz, J. C., & Shea, M. T. (2007). Ethnicity and mental health treatment utilization by patients with personality disorders. *Journal of Consulting and Clinical Psychology, 75*, 992–999.

Benjamin, J. (2004). Beyond doer and done to: An intersubjective view of thirdness. *The Psychoanalytic Quarterly, 73*, 5–46.

Breslau, J., Kendler, K. S., Su, M., Gaxiola-Aguilar, S., & Kessler, R. C. (2005). Lifetime risk and persistence of psychiatric disorders across ethnic groups in the United States. *Psychological Medicine, 35*, 317–327.

C'de Baca, J., Castillo, D. T., Mackaronis, J. E., & Qualls, C. (2014). Ethnic differences in personality disorder patterns among women veterans diagnosed with PTSD. *Behavioral Sciences, 4*, 72–86.

Chavira, D. A., Grilo, C. M., Shea, M. T., Yen, S., Gunderson, J. G., Morey, L. C., . . . Mcglashan, T. H. (2003). Ethnicity and four personality disorders. *Comprehensive Psychiatry, 44*, 483–491.

Christian, C., Reichbart, R., Moskowitz, M., Morillo, R., & Winograd, B. (2016). Psychoanalysis in El Barrio. *PEP Video Grants, 1*(2), 10.

Comas-Diaz, L., & Minrath, M. (1985). Psychotherapy with ethnic minority borderline clients. *Psychotherapy: Theory, Research, Practice, Training, 22*, 418–426.

Cooper, A. A., & Conklin, L. R. (2015). Dropout from individual psychotherapy for major depression: A meta-analysis of randomized clinical trials. *Clinical Psychology Review, 40*, 57–65.

Cooper, S. H., & Levit, D. B. (1998). Old and new objects in Fairbairnian and American relational theory. *Psychoanalytic Dialogues, 8*, 603–624.

Cort, N. A., Gamble, S. A., Smith, P. N., Chaudron, L. H., Lu, N., He, H., & Talbot, N. L. (2012). Predictors of treatment outcomes among depressed women with childhood sexual abuse histories. *Depression & Anxiety, 29*, 479–486.

De Genna, N. M., & Feske, U. (2013). Phenomenology of borderline personality disorder: The role of race and socioeconomic status. *Journal of Nervous & Mental Disease, 201*, 1027–1034.

Fonagy, P., & Luyten, P. (2016). A multilevel perspective on the development of borderline personality disorder. In D. Cicchetti (Ed.), *Developmental psychopathology* (3rd ed., pp. 726–792). Hoboken, NJ: John Wiley & Sons.

Fonagy P. Luyten, P., Allison, E., & Campbell, C. (2017). What we have changed our minds about: Part 2. Borderline personality disorder, epistemic trust and the developmental significance of social communication. *Borderline Personality Disorder and Emotional Dysregulation, 4*, 9–21.

Freire, P. (1972). *Pedagogy of the oppressed.* New York, NY: Continuum.

Freire, P. (1973). *Education for critical consciousness.* New York, NY: The Seabury Press.

Hollander, N. C., & Gutwill, S. (Eds.). (2006). *Psychoanalysis, class, and politics: Encounters in the clinical setting.* New York, NY: Routledge.

Iacovino, J. M., Jackson, J. J., & Oltmanns, T. F. (2014). The relative impact of socioeconomic status and childhood trauma on Black-White differences in paranoid personality disorder symptoms. *Journal of Abnormal Psychology, 123*, 225–230.

Loewald, H. W. (1960). On the therapeutic action of psycho-analysis. *International Journal of Psychoanalysis, 41*, 16–33.

Martin-Baro, I. (1994). *Writings for a liberation psychology.* Cambridge, MA: Harvard University Press.

Memmi, A. (1965/1991). *The colonizer and the colonized* (Jean-Paul Sartre, Intr., Susan Gilson Miller, Afterword., Howard Greenfeld, Trans.). Boston, MA: Beacon Press.

Nagayama Hall, G. C., Ibaraki, A. Y., & Huang, E. R. (2016). A meta-analysis of cultural adaptations of psychological interventions. *Behavior Therapy, 47*, 993–1014.

Newhill, C. E., Eack, S. M., & Conner, K. O. (2009). Racial differences between African and White Americans in the presentation of borderline personality disorder. *Race & Social Problems, 1*, 87–96.

Pickett, K., & Wilkinson, R. G. (2015). Income inequality and health: A causal review. *Social Science & Medicine, 128*, 316–326.

Selby, E. A., & Joiner Jr., T. E. (2008). Ethnic variations in the structure of borderline personality disorder symptomatology. *Journal of Psychiatric Research, 43*, 115–123.

Strachey, J. (1969). The nature of the therapeutic action of psychoanalysis. *The International Journal of Psycho-analysis, 50*, 275.

Swartz, M., Blazer, D., George, L., & Winfield, I. (1990). Estimating the prevalence of borderline personality disorder in the community. *Journal of Personality Disorders, 4*, 257–272.

Tao, K. W., Owen, J., Pace, B. T., & Imel, Z. E. (2015). A meta-analysis of multicultural competencies and psychotherapy process and outcome. *Journal of Counseling Psychology, 62*, 337–350.

Tomko, R. K., Trull, T. K., Wood, P. K., & Sher, K. J. (2014). Characteristics of borderline personality disorder in a community sample: Comorbidity, treatment, utilization, and general functioning. *Journal of Personality Disorders, 28*, 734–750.

Tummala-Narra, P. (2016). *Psychoanalytic theory and cultural competence in psychotherapy*. Washington, DC: American Psychological Association.

Walsh, Z., Shea, T., Yen, S., Ansell, E. B., Grilo, C. M., McGlashan, T. H., . . . Gunderson, J. G. (2013). Socioeconomic-status and mental health in a personality disorder sample: The importance of neighborhood factors. *Journal of Personality Disorders, 27*, 820–831.

Wang, Y., Zhu, X., Cai, L., et al. (2013). Screening cluster A and cluster B personality disorders in Chinese high school students. *BMC Psychiatry, 13*, 116–122.

Watkins, M., & Shulman, H. (2008). *Toward psychologies of liberation*. New York, NY: Palgrave Macmillan.

Westphal, M., Olfson, M., Bravova, M., Gameroff, M. J., Gross, R., Wickramaratne, P., . . . Neria, Y. (2013). Borderline personality disorder, exposure to interpersonal trauma, and psychiatric comorbidity in urban primary care patients. *Psychiatry, 76*, 365–380.

Wierzbicki, M., & Pekarik, G. (1993). A meta-analysis of psychotherapy dropout. *Professional Psychology: Research and Practice, 24*, 190–195.

Wilkinson, R. G., & Pickett, K. (2009). *The spirit level: Why greater equality makes societies stronger*. New York, NY: Bloomsbury Press.

Yeomans, F. E., Clarkin, J. F., & Kernberg, O. F. (2015). *Transference-focused psychotherapy for borderline personality disorder: A clinical guide*. Washington, DC: American Psychiatric Publishing.

Chapter 13

Psychoanalysis of poverty, poverty of psychoanalysis

Patricia Gherovici

Whenever I talk about my experience of conducting psychoanalytic cures with poor Puerto Ricans and other Latinos, those who listen to me cannot help expressing disbelief. Once, as I explained my work with disenfranchised barrio people, a well-dressed, elderly psychoanalyst asked pointedly, "How do you adapt psychoanalysis to the poor?" This remark was not just a technical question about different organizations of timing and payment, but was generated by the widespread consensus that the very idea of working psychoanalytically with minority people of color is, if not immediately dismissed, at least suspected. It is as if the psychoanalytic community could not believe that poor people can afford to have an unconscious. Conversely, this knee-jerk reaction echoes the old reproach that psychoanalysis is a "bourgeois" technique available to well-off people accustomed to indulging their neuroses. I contend that if this were the case, then psychoanalysis would be an impoverished discipline. One might talk about the psychoanalysis of poverty, but I prefer in this chapter to talk of the poverty of psychoanalysis, by which I allude to Karl Marx's famous essay against Pierre-Joséph Proudhon (Marx, [1847] 2008). By doing so, we may highlight the role of "work" that has to be connected with any subjective empowerment.

In 1847, Marx wrote *The Poverty of Philosophy*, a pamphlet in which he criticized the anarchist Proudhon, who had published *The Philosophy of Poverty* one year earlier. Marx disagreed with the famous French anarchist and asserted that Proudhon did not understand the mechanism of value formation that defined, for Marx, capitalistic economy. Similarly, the psychoanalyst Jacques Lacan posited that the Marxist notion of surplus value offers a key to the mechanism of capitalist accumulation but also to psychic economy. For Lacan, psychoanalysis needed to develop a theory of surplus enjoyment in order to account for what Freud called *Lustgewinn*, the "pleasure gain," or more bluntly, the "pleasure profit" (Freud, 1927, p. 162). Lacan's view is that psychoanalytic theory needs to take into account unconscious enjoyment and that unconscious processes follow the logic of capitalistic accumulation.[1] This awareness politicizes his notion of the subject by introducing at the heart of the unconscious a concept from Marx's critique of political economy. Specifically, this concept is *Mehrwert*, or value added – that is, the value added by workers to goods during production which is in excess of their own labor compensation and which is appropriated by the capitalist as profit.

Thus, Lacan combines the unconscious profit granted by the symptom (he calls "jouissance" this mixture of pain and pleasure, the paradoxical pleasure created by displeasure, the phenomenon of "it hurts so good" that one observes so often in clinical practice) with Marx's concept of capitalistic exploitation deriving from the systemic effects of the accumulation of surplus value. For instance, if we argue that the capitalist appropriates the fruit of the employee's labor, the capitalist plays the role of an Other for whom the subject works. This Other enjoys the surplus or the excess product from which the worker is alienated. Similarly, often people sacrifice their desire in order to satisfy the Other and work only for the Other's enjoyment. Like capitalistic profit, jouissance is seen as circulating outside the subject; it is a capital reinvested in the market, as it were. This type of analysis – bringing together the constitution of the subject, social ties, and economy – is a condition for effective interventions at the level of the clinic, politics, and philosophy.

As Lacan (2016) suggests when he talks about James Joyce as the symptom of literature, the analyst reads the symptom as a knot tying together several realms – race, class, and language. From this perspective, and following the Freudian idea of overdetermination, any symptom has several causes working together to determine its effects and nature, which brings about a new concept of causality. By making symptoms readable, psychoanalysis deciphers their messages, whether at a subjective or societal level. A Lacanian approach will be wary of repressing or eliminating the symptom too quickly; one should explore at some length its function in the psychic economy of a subject. This strategy brokers an integration of the social and psychological realms by paying attention to the unconscious interaction of race, class, ethnicity, and language in the production of symptoms.

Indeed, I have to agree that psychoanalysis cannot appear as the only option for inner-city public clinics, but one must question the exclusion of psychoanalysis from the public inner-city clinics; it presupposes that income determines the needed treatment. To announce my program more precisely, I want to reject two attitudes that I see as misguided and linked: the exclusion of poor people from the reach of psychoanalysis and the consideration of poor people as underdeveloped, only reachable as objects of charitable activities, whose problems can only be remedied by a pedagogical strategy of repetitive cognitive behavioral techniques, a patronizing attitude that has the result of infantilizing them.

In order to resist such infantilization, during my work in the barrio I have evolved a strategy that included a minimal form of payment, which entailed a recognition of agency even with totally destitute people. During my work as director of a barrio clinic, for example, the apparently insignificant implementation of a minimal co-payment per session of a couple of dollars brought about crucial changes in the handling of the transference. Patients regularized their attendance, and therapists reported in supervision that patients were more actively involved in their treatments. This minimal co-payment was enough to reinstate agency on the side of the patients. By paying a symbolic fee for the treatment, they were freed from building both dependence and an unpayable debt – which was in most cases paid back by never being cured. The treatment was no longer seemingly free. This change allowed patients to exercise their freedom. Now, they desired to get help and actively sought treatment.

My clinical experience has confirmed the usefulness, pertinence, and emancipatory potential of psychoanalysis with barrio populations. As I argued, psychoanalysis should address the economic forms and social relations deriving from them so as to read the unconscious differently. With this context in mind, I will move on to several vignettes from my work as a psychoanalytically oriented clinician practicing in Philadelphia's barrio.

Caucho

There it was – the analytic couch. The lush Oriental rug was supported by a wooden plank covered with a thick layer of upholstery sponge evocatively called "memory foam." The contraption rested on four plastic milk crates filled with books for weight and stability and was no sturdier than a theater prop. To my surprise, the makeshift couch was not only functional but successfully emulated Freud's divan, at least from a distance. I had hit upon that solution so as to be able to transform my dining room into a consulting room. Here it was, ready for my first private-practice analysand. The custom-made analytic couch I had ordered took months to arrive, which allowed my patients to use this "transitional" couch in which they freely associated, revealing their fears, fantasies, wishes, and dreams.

Adding to my full-time job, first as a staff psychologist and later on continuing as the clinical director of a bilingual outpatient clinic in Philadelphia's barrio, I started seeing private patients in my home office in the evenings. With the daily transition from a community setting into what has been considered, at least in the U.S. context, to be the more traditional place for psychoanalytic practice, I had the opportunity to test and run up against the limits of psychoanalysis.

My relationship to the couch, this uncontested icon of psychoanalytic practice, was loaded if not overdetermined, above all because I did not have one in my daytime office at the *Centro de Servicios para Hispanos*. However, I had noted that by a curious linguistic metonymy, the clinic and the couch were closely related: the etymology of the word "clinic" derives from the Ancient Greek κλινικός (klinikós, "pertaining to a bed, couch") a combination of κλίνη (klínē, "bed, couch") and κλίνειν (klínein, "to lean, incline"). Despite this proximity, nobody would lie on a couch in the clinic of the Bloque de Oro (Golden Block, as the city block was called). This function was exclusively reserved for the two huge couches one found upon entering the waiting room of this barrio clinic. These hosted plenty of daydreaming and sitting naps. Quite regularly, people would arrive hours before their appointments, and then sit there, waiting patiently. A few of them would even go back to these couches after their sessions were finished, just to spend a few more hours waiting for nothing. There was no television screen but only a few tattered magazines lying on a table that nobody seemed interested in reading.

The fact of sharing the introspective boredom of this room offered a pause and suspension in otherwise dull or at times squalid lives, while also providing a sense of community.

Once in a while, the benign somnolence was disrupted by the arrival of a new patient, generally unaware of the house rules. Upon entering the clinic, prospective patients were asked by one of the two receptionists in a very loud voice, "What are you?" This initial question would be followed by "Drugs and alcohol or mental health?" Those who self-identified as belonging to the "drugs and alcohol" group would be told to go and talk to the receptionist at the table on the right side. The "mental health" people would be instructed to walk to the left side of the room, so as to register with the not-so-secretive secretary, and eventually would end up in my office upstairs.

Even if the motivation for requesting treatment was not kept private inside the clinic, from the exterior it was hard for passersby to guess what happened there from the building's gray façade with its two tiny windows with ornamented iron bars. The small sign read *Centro de Servicios para Hispanos* not specifying what type of services we offered at this Hispanic center. The entrance was framed by a pair of painted stainless-steel palm trees that had been "planted" all along the block's curb in an attempt at imprinting a tropical feeling to the famous Bloque de Oro, the barrio's main street. The hub of the barrio was a busy street full of stores, double-parked cars, and trucks covered in graffiti. There was some pedestrian traffic, a rare occurrence in the barrio, where walking was considered quite dangerous. The sidewalks strewn with crack vials and empty syringes had been painted with yellow swirls to hint at the American dream of gold-paved success. They were now tarnished, seemingly disillusioned by a drab reality. Small and by then decrepit, the building had been a funeral home in better times. My ample consulting room with its incongruously elaborate flower carvings in the wall's wood paneling and its tired, lumpy brownish-orange carpet had been the lounge where caskets were displayed for visitation.

Although this office did not have an analytic couch, there was enough space to recreate a quasi-Freudian stage. I would sit with the enormous beaten-up steel Tanker desk behind me while my "clients," as we were asked to call the people we served – using a term that offered them illusory empowerment as economic agents because healthcare is a business like any other – were provided with battered chairs. They sat looking at the window, facing away from my gaze so as to avoid the face-to-face model of interpersonal relationships. To say that the neighborhood was tough is an understatement; on a daily basis, one of my patients would report a crime-related death. There was once a drive-by shooting in the middle of the day, just under my office windows. From time to time, while watering the plants in the office, I thought of the wooden coffins that had been laid in that room for viewing.

Viewing or not is one of the reasons why Freud asked patients to lie on the couch – he could not stand being stared at all day long. There were other reasons as well. When the analyst is not looking at the analysand, the usual focus of attention is suspended. Speech then takes precedence over the gaze. Listening is enhanced. Recumbence helps with free association on the analysand's side as well. The analyst sits out of sight, making it easier for the analysand to fulfill the psychoanalytic commandment of saying whatever comes to mind without any judgment.

With the invitation to say whatever comes to mind, it was in that Bloque de Oro consulting room that one day a patient said, "*Ay, bendito.* I am so upset today. I fought with my husband; then he spent the night on the caucho." Showing signs of not having had much sleep herself, Dolores began her weekly therapy session. I was confused. *Caucho* in my native Spanish has nothing to do with the mythical Pampas' gaucho – *caucho* is the latex extracted from rubber trees. I felt *estuped*; it took me a few minutes to figure out that she meant, simply – couch. Like many patients in North Philly's barrio, where I worked, Dolores was communicating in Spanglish, an amalgamation of English and Spanish. Spanglish was not the only thing that I discovered in the barrio.

When I left Argentina in the late 1980s, my friends gave me a warning: "Forget about Freud, Lacan, and above all, psychoanalysis. Psychoanalysis is dead in the United States." Of course, this was an exaggeration . . . but as Theodor Adorno once quipped, of psychoanalysis nothing is true but exaggerations (Adorno, 2005, p. 49).[2]

First, let me give you some context for such an ominous prediction. I was leaving behind Buenos Aires, the so-called Paris of South America and also the world capital of psychoanalysis. Argentina leads the world in its ratio of psychoanalysts to general public; with a population of over 44 million, there are about 100,000 psychologists (or 200 per 100,000 inhabitants). This is not far from the number of psychologists in the United States, about 106,500, but for a population that is eight times bigger; therefore, the US ratio of 34 per 100,000 residents is six times lower. What is more, in Argentina to be a psychologist means one thing: to be psychoanalytically oriented.

While the cultural influence of psychoanalysis in the United States has been waning, psychoanalytic practice continues to flourish around the world, particularly in Latin America. Not only is the influence of psychoanalysis in Argentina great, its adoption by patients is never accompanied by a stigma. On the contrary, people include this piece of information in their résumés, even listing with pride the name of their analyst and the number of years they have been in treatment. In Argentina, time spent on the couch increases your respectability – you may suffer but you do something about it.

What is crucial is that everyone does it, rich and poor. Most insurance programs cover numerous sessions a year. For those who are financially struggling, psychoanalysts in private practice offer treatment at fees in sliding scales in accordance with the patients' incomes. With many psychoanalytic clinics in free state-run hospitals serving the working classes, in Argentina, Freud's commitment to the treatment of the poor is alive and well. This development might be hard to imagine in the U.S., where psychoanalysis has developed as a very lucrative medical sub-specialty, which has created the perception that it was a practice reserved for the elites. Thus, whenever I talked about my experience having conducted psychoanalytic cures in the barrio, everyone seemed surprised, as if poor people could not afford to have an unconscious.

Coming from a Latin American nation commonly said to be "in development," I was hoping to find in a big United States' city better lifestyle and health. What I witnessed was a reversed American dream. The Third World was right there, in the middle of the U.S. mainland. Because of my clinical psychology training and the scarcity of Spanish-speaking professionals, I had no problem finding employment in the Puerto Rican community of North Philadelphia. Disenfranchised as a minority (I was an immigrant and a psychoanalyst), I found myself working in the middle of a much more disenfranchised community.

In the United States, most psychoanalysts have sustained the belief that psychoanalysis is a neutral, apolitical practice close to the medical model and supposedly immune to the pressures of history. In Argentina, psychoanalysis has been a politically engaged practice, even a dangerous one. During the 1970s' and 1980s' military dictatorship, psychoanalysts became one of the main targets of the state-terror persecution. In an infamous speech, Admiral Emilio Massera, the orator of the military junta, denounced Sigmund Freud, Karl Marx, and Albert Einstein as the greatest enemies of Western civilization. Military ideologues believed that psychoanalysis could destroy the Christian concept of the family. As a result, a great number of students of psychoanalysis and psychoanalysts were "disappeared" – kidnapped, tortured, and assassinated.

Given this background, it was obvious to me that to work clinically with poor and disenfranchised minority people in a ghetto setting implied taking a political position. This statement has consequences in the praxis. However, the idea of the neutrality of the psychoanalyst persists today. After the 2016 U.S. presidential election results, many psychoanalysts who started expressing political views publicly were severely reprimanded and censored by their institutes in the name of maintaining "scientific" analytic neutrality and not upsetting analysands who might find out that their analyst does not share their political views. They have a point here. But this raises the issue of the limits of the neutrality of the analyst and of the deontology of a political psychoanalysis.

As analysts, we are lucky. The couch is like a window from a train in motion through which we have access to what is happening in society. One needs to remain alert, to listen carefully and let the analysands guide us. To think that lower income sidetracks the unconscious from therapeutic exploration is a grave mistake. A psychoanalyst functions as a host for the analysand's speech. As a practitioner, the analyst has the ethical responsibility of offering unconditional hospitality. To those who in their interactions with the mental health system establishment are treated as objects mostly because of their social position, to be welcomed in a space in which they can be seen as subjects is of extreme therapeutic importance. Once this is granted, a patient does not need to know or even care about Freud or Jung or Lacan to do productive work.

My work in the clinic often included dream interpretation. What helped was that Puerto Rican culture pays attention to the meaning of dreams. Like many of my patients at the barrio clinic, Dolores did not mind keeping a pad on her nightstand in which she dutifully recorded her dreams. Before she even started her treatment, dreams would tell her which numbers to pick when playing the lotto. She welcomed her dreams as messages from the spirits of the dead. During our work together, they acquired new meaning – they opened the door to a new realm, one closer to life.

Dolores's dreams were vivid. She remembered them in detail and had no problem associating freely. Not only was Dolores very depressed, she also had severe back pains with no clear medical cause. The pains vanished suddenly after a dream in which she was carrying a cross. Notwithstanding her inclination for self-sacrifice, she realized that carrying her cross (*cargando mi cruz*) was not just an idiom but also contained the last name of her beloved stepfather. Her back pain expressed and condensed her history, bringing her closer to Mr. Cruz. The pains had started a few months before she came to see me, after her mother died very suddenly. Mr. Cruz, now a widower, expected Dolores to replace her mother in his bed. A severe depression followed. One word carried all those meanings, and she simply needed to hear these herself. In just a few months of therapy, Dolores overcame a crippling depression and her back problems. She was able to negotiate adroitly a safe combination of distance and proximity in her dealings with her stepfather while mourning the loss of her mother.

The Puerto Rican Syndrome and the Korean War

But dreams often betray a close proximity with ancient or recent historical events. My clinical experience as a psychotherapist and clinical director with the so-called Hispanic community of North Philadelphia allowed me to make one discovery: I encountered the Puerto Rican syndrome. This diagnosis, which was a novelty for me, describes a group of striking and inexplicable symptoms: attacks of anger, eccentric seizures with no organic origin, anxiety, and fear in a choleric battle with an imaginary enemy, suicidal gestures, hallucinations, amnesia. Labeled "Puerto Rican syndrome," all these manifestations confirm an uncanny return of the somatic grammar of classic hysteria. The "Puerto Rican" syndrome involves a complex symptom formation that brings together clinical and political issues. This baffling psychiatric label links nationality, cultural phenomena, and mental illness.

I want to add a few features that had escaped me when I wrote my book on the Puerto Rican syndrome.[3] I will highlight a forgotten historical event that took place during the Korean War which saw the coining of the syndrome because it sheds new light on its psychic economy. The Puerto Rican syndrome was initially reported among Puerto Rican soldiers, mostly Korean War veterans. This conflict began on June 25, 1950, when North Korea (the Democratic People's Republic of Korea) invaded territories belonging to South Korea (the Republic of Korea). In the context of the Cold War, the conflict was rapidly international-ized: North Korea was supported by the communist bloc of China and the Soviet Union, while South Korea was defended by the United Nations, which at the time brought together a coalition of 19 countries helping the interests of the United States. Among the first units sent to the Korean front by the United States was a regiment famous for its courage and knowledge of the battlefield. It was the 65th Infantry, the only U.S. Army regiment composed almost exclusively of Puerto Ricans, also known as the "Borinqueños" or "Borinqueneers" regiment, Borin-quen being the pre-Columbian name of the island of Puerto Rico. An estimated 45,000 to 60,000 Puerto Ricans participated in the Korean War.

This war ended with a precarious cease-fire on July 27, 1953, after an armistice signed at Panmunjeom established the 38th parallel as the border separating the two Koreas, a territorial situation identical to that which existed before the war. Because of this inglorious result, the Korean War was often referred to as the forgotten war. Not only was this war forgotten, but the active participation of Puerto Rican soldiers who fought under the American banner disappeared from American memory.

It took the 2017 tragedy of Hurricane Maria to remind most Americans that Puerto Rico was part of the country. Thus when they became American citizens a century eartlier, in 1917 to be precise, Puerto Ricans were called to serve the U.S. Armed Forces. As the historian Silvia Álvarez Curbelo (2008a) observes, the colonial power considered Puerto Ricans second-class citizens, lazy, stupid, and impulsive, a mixed-race group unable to effectively fulfill their duty as sol-diers. Persuaded that their racial constitution would not serve the interests of the fatherland on the battlefield, they were given second-rate tasks. This changed in the 1930s, when a new war seemed imminent. Puerto Rico had been previously administered as a large, dependent sugar plantation. Then an indigenous, cultured, and progressive elite emerged and played a more dynamic role under Luis Muñoz Marín's populist leadership. An accelerated modernization transformed Puerto Rico towards the end of World War II. This process involved "violent spatial and psychological displacements" (Álvarez Curbelo, 2008a, para. 6). Nearly 250,000 Puerto Ricans immigrated to the United States between 1947 and 1953. During this transition, Puerto Rican soldiers represented the promise of parity with the United States.

In fact, the 65th Infantry Regiment distinguished itself during the Korean War with exemplary heroism, legendary feats, professionalism, courage, and self-sacrifice. However, in the fall of 1952, there was a dramatic reversal: a group of almost two hundred soldiers of this regiment, that had previously earned a reputa-tion for its valor, abandoned the battle. About a hundred of these soldiers were tried for mutiny in a court martial trial, in consequence of which the regiment ceased to be exclusively Puerto Rican and then was dissolved. At the present time, the first battalion of the 65th Infantry is part of the Puerto Rico National Guard.

This chapter in the history of the 65th Infantry Regiment took place at the time when the first diagnosis of Puerto Rican syndrome was applied to Korean War veterans of Puerto Rican origin. The analysis of Álvarez Curbelo (2008a, 2008b) allows us to comprehend the radical transformation and paradoxical position of the Puerto Rican soldier during the Korean War who would be diagnosed with the Puerto Rican syndrome. At the time, ethnic segregation was quite exceptional, since a historic executive order issued by President Harry Truman in 1948 had put an end to racial discrimination in the United States military.

The action of the "Borinqueños" in Korea had been extraordinary and, in the summer of 1951, peace talks gave hope for a swift end of the Korean conflict. These were days of glory for the "Borinqueneers," a regiment that, while fighting for the United States, considered Puerto Rico their homeland. When the first troops returned from the Korean front, the Puerto Rican government declared a holiday; the entire island celebrated their soldiers as heroes. However, with the stalemate in the peace talks, the morale of the troops began to falter. In May 1951, the regiment lost its skillful commander, Colonel William Harris, who was relieved of his duties along with most of the elite soldiers who composed this unit. They were replaced by less trained men as part of the military's rotation system. The new soldiers were not volunteers and, unlike their predecessors, hardly spoke English. While at the beginning of the armed conflict in Korea the soldiers sent to the front were bilingual and highly trained career military members, the longer the war lasted, more inexperienced, Spanish speaking–only soldiers joined the regiment, and those newcomers were placed under the orders of less senior officers.

Juan César Cordero Dávila, a Puerto Rican, was appointed head of the regiment. The pessimism of the soldiers was not alleviated. What was known as the Battle for Outpost Kelly, in which dozens of Puerto Rican soldiers died, was an action motivated by Commander Cordero's decision to conquer Kelly as an emblem of the loyalty of Puerto Ricans to the United States, a tribute of blood. This failed operation had the highest cost in human lives of all the military actions carried out during the Korean War. Then Cordero was relieved of his duties and replaced by a new commander, Chester De Gavre, an American from Wisconsin who had only contempt for the Puerto Rican national pride of the regiment (Villahermosa, 2009, pp. 237–241).[4]

De Gavre found himself at the head of a regiment of bearded and badly dressed soldiers, who were moreover accustomed to using handkerchiefs under their helmets. It seemed to him indispensable to review the whole disciplinary policy with a swift and drastic "Americanization." In addition to demanding a military salute, haircut, shoe polish, regular maintenance of the uniform, equipment, and weapons, De Grave forbade soldiers to wear a mustache. He admonished them that they would remain shaved "until they demonstrated that they were men" (Villahermosa, 2009, p. 239). This deeply humiliating measure was tantamount to an emasculation for a Puerto Rican male in the 1950s. The order raised serious objections: De Grave's questioning of a soldier's virility was perceived as deeply insulting. In fact, the order was ignored as long as possible; some soldiers resigned themselves to shaving their mustaches only under threat of court martial. De Gavre also changed the regiment's diet: Puerto Rican rice and beans were replaced by

American dishes like potatoes and hotdogs. There was also an order to erase the name "Borinqueños/Borinqueneers" from the regiment's jeeps. Obviously, the morale of the troops deteriorated even more. The intensive training ordered by De Gavre increased their frustration, made worse by supply problems in Korea that prevented an adequate training – there was not sufficient ammunition.

A month later, faced with intolerable conditions and an incompetent, tyrannical command, indifferent to the regiment's idiosyncrasy, the Puerto Rican troops rebelled on Jackson Heights Hill. In the testimonies collected by the court martial, the soldiers declared that they refused to obey the orders simply because they were inapplicable. Not only was it a suicide mission, but the command itself was unable to define the objectives. Of the almost 200 soldiers arrested for "deliberate inaction in the face of the enemy" and "disobedience to the orders of a superior," 92 soldiers and an officer appeared before the court martial. The Puerto Rican government did not publicly oppose the trial of its nationals and tried to silence the story. At the end of 1952, the incidents were made public in a local newspaper that had been made aware of the events by letters sent by the detained soldiers to their families.

If by the end of the year 1950, the Puerto Rican soldiers were "perfect colonial subjects," both for the military authorities and for the local elites, two years later, while on the battlefield, this project was in a downward spiral with hundreds of soldiers dead to defend a piece of barren land; their otherness exposed in broad daylight with fierce force, and the 65th returning home dishonored (Álvarez Curbelo, 2000a). For the Puerto Rican people, proud of their "Borinqueños," it was a question of dignity because the courage and initiative of its soldiers were perceived as fundamental elements of their cultural idiosyncrasy.These military operations of 1952 caused the dissolution of the 65th Regiment. They are but a footnote in the history of the Korean War showing the complexities and antagonisms inherent in all colonial rapports. In the testimonies and depositions during the court martial, Álvarez Curbelo identifies a recurring tendency: the infantilization of the Puerto Rican soldiers, whose capacity to speak and to understand was put in question, or simply denied. All the defendants were found guilty and sentenced to 5 to 16 years of forced labor. They were dismissed from the Army. Eventually, they were pardoned as a result of secret negotiations between the governments of the United States and Puerto Rico.

The role of Puerto Rican soldiers during the Korean War illustrates the asymmetry caused by more than a hundred years of colonial rule. Álvarez Curbelo (2008a) interprets these incidents in the hills of Korea as a paradoxical collective affirmation of identity in the face of irrationality. I would like to understand the Puerto Rican syndrome as a similarly paradoxical collective affirmation of identity in the face of irrationality. There is a structural homology between the appearance of the symptoms grouped under the diagnosis of "Puerto Rican syndrome" and the events of Korea. These details exemplify how history overdetermines pathological symptoms.

Thus the Puerto Rican syndrome was initially diagnosed among soldiers who participated in the Korean War most likely because the incident described earlier made them appear as different, troublesome, rebellious, or potentially psychotic. The difficulty of reading their behavior required a specific diagnosis. The historical factors explain the specific historical and political overdetermination in a diagnosis tied with one of the last surviving colonies. As we saw, a new psychiatric syndrome suffered exclusively by minority soldiers from Puerto Rico was created at a very complex juncture in the island's political status; it had the effect of creating the paradoxical situation of offering an identity to a military group that was in an ambiguous position facing the colonial power.

Today, when someone in the barrio presents with symptoms of an *ataque de nervios*, an Anglo doctor might still read it as a Puerto Rican syndrome and consider it a medical emergency. If someone in the island has an *ataque*, it seems a normal disturbance that can be treated with a dose of *alcoholado*, a fragrant home remedy, a spiritual cologne. This discrepancy repeats the complex situation of the colonized subject who might use the strategy of the *ataque* to unleash fits of destructive rage. Stigma, discrimination, subjection, and rebellion converge in every *ataque*. A lesson one learns in the barrio is that one cannot look at an individual symptom outside of history.

The fact that the Puerto Rican syndrome was diagnosed by U.S. Army doctors working for the Department of Veterans Affairs during the Korean War should not surprise us: military psychiatry has had a considerable influence on general psychiatric taxonomy, as well as on standardized disease classification systems, such as the International Classification of Diseases (ICD), and especially its successor, the *Diagnostic and Statistical Manual of Mental Disorders* (*DSM*). Many new mental disorders and manifestations caused by the war and its aftermath have expanded these classification systems.

Why a syndrome then? As long as a set of symptoms remains mysterious and no underlying cause can be found, it is referred to as a syndrome. A rapid overview of the existing literature on the Puerto Rican syndrome indicates contradictorily that it is hysteria, schizophrenia, hysterical psychosis (not just psychosis) and even more, cross-cultural hysterical psychosis. The Puerto Rican syndrome is described as resulting from common folk beliefs that could at the same time be part of a delusional system, as a sudden homicidal impulse or "suicidal fit," as a multiple personality disorder, and as a manipulative "reaction" pattern for hysterical personalities. It is also understood as an indication of a higher rate of organic brain disorder among Puerto Ricans.

It looks as if everything and its opposite had been said about the Puerto Rican syndrome, but one exceptional feature stands out: no other diagnosis in the psychiatric nomenclature is attached to a nationality. Indeed, we do not talk about American anxiety or French melancholy. The irony, moreover, is that this syndrome apparently attached to a nation comes from a place that is not an independent country and is still caught up in a colonial situation.

Barrio truth

One feature I wish to highlight in the historical reverberations of the Puerto Rican syndrome is its resemblance to the spectacular behavior of classic hysterics, those who, at the end of the nineteenth century, made possible the invention of psychoanalysis and guided Freud in the discovery of the unconscious. This set of symptoms labeled in the 1950s as uniquely Puerto Rican repeats the most canonical form of hysteria, the one very dear to any psychoanalyst, as I hoped I have demonstrated in *The Puerto Rican Syndrome* (Gherovici, 2003).

Hysteria has a peculiar relationship to history, as Freud noted in his observation that hysterics suffer from reminiscences, that is, suffer from memories. Freud said that the work of the psychoanalyst is to make conscious, the unconscious. Lacan described it as the chapter of someone's history where there is a blank space or a lie. The invisible suffering of the inhabitants of the barrio echoes across several decades with the plight of the anonymous soldiers who encountered a tragic destiny in Korea. In all these cases, their stories have remained forgotten. At times, the symptoms a psychoanalyst hears from a patient work as metaphors for a legacy of social marginalization and colonial oppression.

It may happen that the history of a country will read like a case history. What we learn from its tragic or amusing details is that they make better sense when envisaged from a point of view that integrates an unconscious dimension. Thus, an apparently derisive or absurdly mean command to shave soldiers' mustaches had direct and indirect implications that manifest a psychoanalytic truth. This truth is still active in today's attitudes, neuroses, and sudden deflagrations of anger. A psychoanalyst is well equipped to put together the apparent randomness of subjective acting outs and a larger history defined by colonial subjection. What matters is to recapture the individual desire and the pathos expressed in those symptoms. When someone talks to an analyst, it is not so much like talking to a friend as talking to a friendly mirror that sends back the words that were uttered until they take on a new meaning. Here lies the possibility of agency and liberation.

Even without a *caucho*, psychoanalytical treatments can be brief and successful, perhaps because listening to the unconscious means above all taking an ethical stand. This boils down to simply treating the other as a subject. Language shapes our behavior. Words can hurt, but the right word, spoken at the right time, can cure. No wonder that "couch" in English also means to say or express something, to put an idea into words.

Dolores's use of the word *caucho* for couch happened to bring up uncanny resonances of the horrors of the colonial abuse in the Americas. The brutality of the exploitation in rubber plantations mostly in Brazil (but also in Bolivia, Peru, Ecuador, and Colombia) is another little-known historical footnote. Triggered by the invention of vulcanization, the 1850–1920 Amazon rubber boom unleashed a horrendous and ruthless exploitation that decimated the entire native population of those thinly inhabited tropical lowlands. The rubber trade depended more on control of labor rather than on the land itself. The indigenous population was enslaved and worked to death. Rape, mutilation, torture, and murder were used to discipline and intimidate. Dolores's *caucho* story of insomnia, pains, loss, betrayal, and incestuous wishes was unwittingly retelling a forgotten truth about the atrocities of colonial injustice and violence.

Lacan once stated that "Symptoms speak even to those who do not know how to hear them. Nor do they tell the whole story to those who do" (Fink, 2013, p. 1). In the barrio, I also met María, who stormed through the door one afternoon screaming that her children had been transformed into dogs. After the treatment, she was no longer delusional and was soon able to find and keep a home. She started to interact with relatives, attended church, and began making traditional Puerto Rican paper dolls that she would sell to make money. There was also Socorro, who had barely survived being shot in the head during a hold-up, and who managed to move from an unspeakable devastation to the inscription of psychic trauma. She eventually expressed and accepted the loss that she could articulate.

And there was Consuelo who showed that in the face of despair, the last resource may be an *ataque de nervios*, another form of Puerto Rican syndrome. Such symptoms "speak" volumes even to those who do not know how to hear them. And they do not tell the whole story because the unconscious truth is only half-said in order to bypass the censorship of consciousness. When you speak about yourself to someone who is trained to listen, usually a change occurs. A psychoanalyst is a person trained to hear and provide a place where you may speak and hear yourself differently. Words can hurt, words can make people sick, but words can also save. Talking cures.

Symptoms are not only afflictions, they are garbled messages mixing up past history and present despair so as to speak about desire, conflict, inhibitions, and trauma. They are the traces of an often forgotten or censored chapter of history that remains unconscious. Transformation in psychoanalysis is achieved by interweaving past and present so as to open new vistas and possibilities. I dedicate this chapter to the Marías, Socorros, Consuelos, and Dolores of the barrio, all beautiful hysterics whose symptoms appeared as a demand for social sublimation. Their suffering, like a scrawled letter or graffiti on a wall, was addressed to an elusive Other. I cannot stop thinking of those sidewalks painted yellow to recall the American dream, the golden utopia of a prosperous neighborhood replaced by the sad reality of urban decay. Today, it only survives as beautiful murals hauntingly retracing moments of lost glory.

I hope to have addressed the existing bias against the practice of psychoanalysis with low-income populations; this common prejudice impoverishes psychoanalytic practice and theory. Quoting Marx, as read by Lacan, I highlighted the role of "work" as linked with subjective empowerment. Marx ([1847] 2008) criticized the anarchist strategy of Proudhon as too spontaneous. Marx argues that one needs an organization and a theory of surplus value to understand how capitalist economy works. Poverty creates suffering but it is not an affliction, nor is it an essential feature of some racialized groups. Poverty is the result of certain relations of production that are historical and therefore can be changed.

Lacan (1974) famously proposed that it was Marx, not Freud who had "invented" the notion of symptom, which led him to abandon the traditional Freudian notion of the symptom as message and as metaphor.[5] The reasons were clinical. The language of symptoms may be metaphorical, but those metaphors are also carriers of jouissance. The completion of an analytic cure does not rely solely on decoding symptoms; psychoanalysis implies also transforming the psychic economy of jouissance. Then a psychoanalyst who takes into account unconscious enjoyment can intervene clinically and avoid the narcissistic traps of altruism. This type of intervention is never outside history.

To sum up my argument, there are currently two wrong attitudes being adopted and that I see as linked: one is the exclusion of poor people from the reach of psychoanalysis, the other is the way one considers them as underdeveloped subjects who must be dealt with via and only as the object of charitable activities, infantilizing them. By exploring the dynamics of hysteria and unconscious enjoyment as they are condensed but also illustrated by the Puerto Rican syndrome, I want to demonstrate the pertinence and emancipatory potential of psychoanalysis with barrio populations. This is the only way to address historical, political, and economic forms that in fact are also imprinted in the unconscious.

Acknowledgements

Some passages from this chapter include modified sections from "The Puerto Rican Syndrome and the Eye of Maria/El sindrome puertorriqueño y ojo de María" in UNA PROPOSICIÓN MODESTA: PUERTO RICO A PRUEBA/A MODEST PROPOSAL: PUERTO RICO'S CRUCIBLE, exhibition catalog: Spanish/English, an initiative of Allora & Calzadilla edited by Sara Nadal-Melsió, Barcelona.

Notes

1 See Braunstein, N. (2003). Desire and Jouissance in the teachings of Lacan. In Jean-Michel Rabaté (Ed.), *The Cambridge companion to Lacan* (pp. 102–115). Cambridge, England: Cambridge University Press.
2 Adorno, T. (2005). *Minima Moralia: Reflections on a damaged life*. New York, NY: Verso.
3 See Gherovici, P. (2003). *The Puerto Rican syndrome*. New York, NY: Other Press.
4 See also Harris, W. W. (2001 [1980]). *Puerto Rico's fighting 65th U.S. infantry: From San Juan to Chorwan*. Novato, CA: Presidio Press.
5 Lacan, J. (1974). Le Séminaire XXII RSI, session of December 10, 1974, Unpublished papers, Gaogoa.free.fr. Retrieved May 10, 2018 from http://gaogoa.free.fr/Seminaires_HTML/22-RSI/RSI10121974.htm.

References

Adorno, T. W. (2005). *Minima Moralia: Reflections on a damaged life*. New York, NY: Verso.
Álvarez Curbelo, S. (2008a, Spring). War, modernity and remembrance. *Revista: Harvard Review of Latin America*. Retrieved from https://revista.drclas.harvard.edu/book/war-modernity-and-remembrance.

Álvarez Curbelo, S. (2008b). Sangre colonial: La guerra de Corea y los soldados puertor-riqueños. *Caribbean Studies, 36*(1), 219–223.

Fink, B. (2013). *Death by Analysis: Another adventure from inspector Canal New York's Agency.* London, England: Karnac.

Freud, S. (1927). Humour. *The Standard Edition of the Complete Psychological Works of Sigmund Freud, XXI*(1927–1931), 159–166.

Gherovici, P. (2003). *The Puerto Rican syndrome.* New York, NY: Other Press.

Guarnaccia, P., DeLaCancela, V., & Carrillo, E. (1989). The multiple meanings of Ataques de Nervios in the Latino Community. *Medical Anthropology, 11*(1), 47–62.

Jones, F. (1991), Clinical features of young adult Hispanic psychiatric in-patients: The so-called Puerto Rican syndrome. *Military Medicine, 156*(7), 351–354.

Lacan, J. (1973). *Le Séminaire, livre XXI, Les non-dupes errent,* session of 20 November 1973. Unpublished papers, Gaogoa.free.fr. Retrieved May 10, 2018 from http://gaogoa.free.fr/Seminaires_HTML/21-NDE/NDP20111973.htm.

Lacan, J. (1974). *Le Séminaire XXII RSI,* session of December 10, 1974. Unpublished papers, Gaogoa.free.fr. Retrieved May 10, 2018 from http://gaogoa.free.fr/Seminaires_HTML/22-RSI/RSI10121974.htm.

Lacan, J. (2016). *The sinthome: The seminar of Jacques Lacan, book XXIII.* Cambridge and Malden, MA: Polity.

LaRuffa, A. L. (1971). *San Cipriano: Life in a Puerto Rican community.* New York, NY: Gordon and Breach.

Marx, K. (2008 [1847]). *The poverty of philosophy.* New York, NY: Cosimo.

Villahermosa, G. (2009). *Honor and fidelity: The 65th infantry in Korea, 1950–1953.* Washington, DC: United States Army Center of Military History.

Index